Outright Assassination

Outright Assassination

The Trial and Execution of Antun Sa'adeh, 1949

Adel Beshara

ITHACA
PRESS

OUTRIGHT ASSASSINATION
The Trial and Execution of Antun Sa'adeh, 1949

Published by
Ithaca Press
8 Southern Court
South Street
Reading
RG1 4QS
UK

www.ithacapress.co.uk
www.twitter.com/Garnetpub
www.facebook.com/Garnetpub
thelevant.wordpress.com

Ithaca Press is an imprint of Garnet Publishing Limited.

First Paperback Edition

ISBN: 978-0-86372-418-3

British Library Cataloguing-in-Publication Data
A catalogue record for this book is available from the British Library

Typeset by Samantha Barden
Jacket design by Garnet Publishing
Cover photo reproduced courtesy of Badr el-Hage

Printed and bound in Lebanon by International Press:
interpress@int-press.com

*Dedicated to the cause
of truth and justice*

CONTENTS

✧

PREFACE

This study is a history of the trial and execution of Antun Sa'adeh (1949), the shortest, most secret, and most obscure "event" to take place in independent Lebanon. Its dramatic and political significance stems not only from the acceleration of its procedure, during which the greatest moral and legal values were crushed and violated, but also from its lingering effects on Lebanese politics. Yet if the Sa'adeh event was typical among similar events in history, in two other important respects it was quite unusual. First, unlike all previous and subsequent trials in Lebanon, and indeed the Arab World, the Sa'adeh trial defied human logic and the legal norms that govern proceedings under similar circumstances. Second, although the Sa'adeh trial was a political trial in every sense of the word, widely regarded as a pre-orchestrated political exercise, the Lebanese government refused to treat it as a political event. It decided to schedule a courtroom drama, with at least the embroidery of legality, under the criminal law in order to facilitate the use of the death penalty. This book is thus an examination of how the Lebanese State tried to grapple with a political case by means of ordinary criminal law. How did this effort work in detail? What were its strengths and weaknesses, its limits and boundaries? What were the legal and political ramifications of using the law for political purposes?

This book chooses to address these questions by means of a detailed history of the saga. The mechanism of the case, the stage machinery of its enactment, the parts played by those who serviced that machinery, and the politics that triggered it are carefully reconsidered and examined. In the process, the study will raise a number of fundamental issues relating to the nature of the trial, discuss whether it was a political trial or not, and determine why it was steamrolled with unprecedented speed. A secondary emphasis of this book is to stimulate issues worthy of additional investigation beyond the confines of present official and non-official accounts in the literature.

As for the book's structure, it falls roughly into three main sections. In the first section some background to the saga is given with the main focus being on Sa'adeh's political views, struggles, and conflict with the central authorities. The second section is concerned with the most "private" aspect, the actual Sa'adeh Affair – trial, execution, and procedures – with special emphasis on the political and legal particulars of the case from the perspective of both domestic and international law. The final section deals with the post-execution stage. It presents a critical and historical analysis of the reaction to, and consequences of, the execution, and an outline of the various scenarios that have surfaced to explain why it happened and who may have been involved and their motivations. Although some of these topics have been dealt with before, a comprehensive analytical approach has rarely been attempted.

The main sources are records from various domestic and overseas archives, the Lebanese press and periodicals at the time, past and present studies, and the personal accounts and memoirs that have come out in large numbers in the last two decades or so. Notwithstanding their apologetic nature, these memoirs provide valuable insight into Lebanon's politics and constitute perhaps the liveliest and the most interesting portion of the literature on the Sa'adeh affair.

As with every study there were restrictions. We have no transcripts, no court records. We do not hear the prosecution or the defendant. We know the story only as told later by individuals who were around at the time. The trial transcripts disappeared after the trial in 1949 and have never been found. The author attempted to retrieve them in person from the archives of the Military Court in Beirut, but to no avail: they smoldered during the 1982 Israeli invasion, so said the officer-in-charge. To our knowledge, some fragments of the transcripts were published in *The Case of the National Party*, a manuscript put out by the Lebanese government at the end of 1949, but they are extremely inadequate. The manuscript as a whole conveys the proceedings in a highly condensed and one-sided form. It is an utterly indigestible book.

I am well aware of the great disadvantage caused by my inability to consult the trial transcripts and other source-material directly on the case. I tried my best to minimize the damage by drawing heavily upon memoirs of Lebanese statesmen and the press. I hope that one day this discrepancy will be made good. Until then my conclusions cannot be regarded as final even by myself.

No book is written in a vacuum. I would especially like to thank Dennis Walker and Jabr Abdul-Fattah (Bahrain) for their help in translation, Richard Pennell (Melbourne), John Daye, Riad Khneisser, and Amal Kayyas (Beirut), Badr el-Hage (London), and Michel Hayek (NDU) whose comments and guidance have been invaluable. I also owe a great debt to numerous colleagues and friends in Melbourne and in Lebanon who read parts of the manuscript and gave me the benefit of their experience and insight. Needless to say, the views expressed in this book and any faults or shortcomings are solely my responsibility.

Numerous libraries have assisted, more or less knowingly, in providing me with resources. The work of research would be vastly longer and more trying if it was not for the patience and kindness of librarians. My thanks go to staff at the following libraries: Jafet Library at AUB, the Notre Dame University Louaize Library, and Baillieu Library at Melbourne University.

INTRODUCTION

At ten precisely on the night of 6 July, 1949, Antun Sa'adeh walked into the Presidential Palace in Damascus for a pre-scheduled meeting with Husni al-Zaim. He was alone – no personal bodyguards, no aides, only the Syrian Chief of General Security, Ibrahim al-Husseini, with him. No sooner had Sa'adeh entered the main foyer than twelve armed guards quickly formed a half-circle around him to block his view of the outside world. No one uttered a word. There was no need. The message was loud and clear and the first to understand it was Sa'adeh. "I get it", he uttered, with a gentle smile on his face. The scene could easily have been mistaken for a Hollywood production if the characters hadn't been speaking in Arabic. Mission accomplished, al-Husseini calmly departed and Premier al-Barazzi walked in from another door at the other end of the foyer. Without any formalities al-Barazzi called out to Sa'adeh, "You have a score to settle with Lebanon. Go take care of it."[1] With those words Al-Barazzi inadvertently provided the setting for the most sensational legal case of post-WWII Lebanon: the case of Antun Sa'adeh.

As in all good dramas, the Sa'adeh case abounded with ironies. It was short, swift, and very secretive, the entire procedure lasting only thirty-six hours. It was over before it even started. Just about everything about the case was pre-orchestrated – the charges, the evidence, the tribunal, the sentence, the punishment. As it proceeded to its conclusion, other unusual features about the case hid behind a façade of mythical and legal rituals. These were carefully concealed through various instruments so that no detailed reports of the proceedings would reach the public. No one was to learn about the defiant posture of the defendant or about the charges against the regime. It was simply a trial where the government was reluctant to focus on the question of rightness, only the legal issue surrounding the broken law.

The best that can be said of the trial is that it was a typical drumhead court-martial. Every step in the proceedings was improvised: the judges were either incompetent or non-neutral, the prosecutor was also a judge, the evidence was pre-fabricated, and the accused was presumed guilty from the outset. The outcome of a drumhead court-martial is usually execution by firing squad, and that unerringly was the outcome for Sa'adeh. Yet even the execution process was an administrative nightmare. The state sought to make an example of Sa'adeh as a warning to like-minded individuals that a similar fate could overtake them, but it went about it in the most objectionable way. As it did in his trial, it broke every law in the book to have him executed before daylight.

For this reason, the Sa'adeh case has been given several pointed descriptions: a parody of justice, an accelerating tragedy, a pitiful comedy, a shameful blot. Ghassan Tueini, the editor-in-charge of the popular Lebanese daily *an-Nahar*, called it "murder."[2] With equal profundity and depth, Tueini went on to say:

> The authorities have succeeded in arresting Sa'adah, giving him a speedy trial, sentencing him, and executing him, in such a speed which left most people dumbfounded and bewildered. It was difficult to comprehend the reasons for this most unusual and un-called for action, especially that the rebellion was successfully and swiftly suppressed. Even Sa'adeh's arch-enemies were at a loss of words to justify the Government's action. Those same enemies are now saying, "What a great tragedy". Although the Government wanted to get rid of the man as speedily as possible, fearing he would bring terror to Lebanon, yet, by its rash action it has created a great giant, stronger than Sa'adeh ever was, and has made of him a martyr, not only to his followers but to those who never wished him better than death.[3]

None, however, could match the description of Edmond Rizk, former Lebanese Minister of Justice. He called it "outright assassination" ("Un assassinat pur et simple").[4]

The present study is a critical and historical analysis of the Sa'adeh saga, the most dramatic and politically resonant trial of post-independence Lebanon. It is a detailed account of the events leading to it, its salient issues, its history and outcome, and its repercussions. As it progresses, the study will tackle a number of substantive issues relating to the motives and deeds of the main participants: What were the domestic backgrounds of the saga? What was the role of regional powerbrokers such as Egypt and Saudi Arabia? To what extent did international politics influence the trial? What role did Premier Riad Solh play and did he act alone? Why was the trial held on camera and not as a public show trial? Wherein lay the similarities and the differences with other political trials and where do they interconnect? How was the accused treated and how was the scenario drawn up? How was the outcome received and why did its repercussions become uncontainable? Was it a political affair? It is the purpose of this book to answer these and similar questions, insofar as the facts permit an answer.

Although some of these topics have been dealt with before, a comprehensive analytical approach has rarely been attempted. Current scholarships, including those directly on the Khoury era (1943–1952), at best provide a cursory treatment of the saga as part of a general history rather than the thorough analysis it deserves. This approach allows more focus and the inclusion of specific details, but it loses sight of the larger arena in which it happened and ignores the process by which politics overlap, compete and clash, drown or reinforce each other in legal controversies. Indeed, it is exactly in this dialectical process that the Sa'adeh saga should be examined and can best be understood. Moreover, most analyses rely on crude stereotypes within a chronological approach. To gain a fuller understanding of the saga, however, it is important to examine simultaneously other variables such as regime and individual participant behavior – their minds, motives, morality, deeds, and standing under international and domestic law. A multidisciplinary approach is necessary because legal-political controversies occupy an intermediate position between the spheres of politics, religion, culture and psychology, and understanding the part is impossible before one understands the whole.

If, however, it is necessary to recognize the variability of Sa'adeh's trial across time, as well as to situate the saga in its proper political and legal context, then such detailed individual histories are urgently needed. These works, when taken together, enable us to begin to piece together the political background to the saga and its significance for postwar Lebanese history. What remains necessary above all, however, is to begin to embed these insights into a more comprehensive understanding of the nature of Lebanese law and political system, and of the Lebanese Republic in the 1940s. To understand the Sa'adeh saga properly, one must also understand the tumultuous relationship between Sa'adeh and the Lebanese state more generally.[5]

As one of the most tragic incidents of the period, the Sa'adeh trial and execution enlivens histories of the early independence era, but does it merit serious historical investigation in it own right? We have answered "yes." First, an examination of the saga provides many opportunities to cast light on an obscure and neglected period, to date mostly unexplored, of modern Lebanon. It helps to widen the framework in which the Khoury regime should be considered and to evaluate its significance in several intersecting contexts. There is much to learn from the saga about the Lebanese political system, its workings, and its performance under conditions of strain. Moreover, by reconstructing the saga along with the events leading up to it we can instinctively gain a number of insights into the character of Antun Sa'adeh, a person who achieved a great reputation through his writings and revolutionary activities,[6] and into the much-misunderstood politics of the Syrian Social National Party and other active participants.

Second, as an historical event, the Sa'adeh saga has much to offer those who keenly follow and study political trials. Inquisitors will find themselves in the presence of a case that had all the trappings of a political trial, whose course was dictated by definite political aims, and whose conduct was thoroughly political yet calculatingly staged under a non-political law. Thus, the jurisprudence of the case is useful both for legal and political inquiry, particularly regarding the intractable question of why governments react differently to similar circumstances or would attempt to avoid a political trial if they think that the exercise is too cumbersome. The Sa'adeh saga is also useful for testing several hypotheses about political justice: Is there such a thing as a political trial? What are its main attributes? What is a political crime? Is a political trial better perceived as politics or as law? What is the difference between what is properly politics and what is properly law? What should a court do when confronted with a case that questions the legitimacy of law itself? Is law legitimate only when might does not make right? Is power its own authority in politics? Is a political trial a disease of both politics and law, or can a political trial affirm the rule of law? Can a political trial make a positive contribution to a democratic society?[7] As a case study in political justice, the Sa'adeh saga is especially pertinent to Otto Kirchheimer's theory of how governments use the law for political purposes.[8]

Third, as a subject for appraisal, the Sa'adeh saga is protean. A lawyer will view the trial as the focus of many novel and difficult legal questions, both substantive and procedural; the political scientist will perhaps see it as a fascinating study of a constitutional democracy in reversal; the historian will find chief value in the wealth of information – both official and personal – which the trial brought to light, and in the recollections and commentaries of the participants and politicians and officials and other leading figures in the era of the Khoury regime. All scholars and professional men will find much of interest and value in the politics preceding and following the saga.

The importance of the Sa'adeh saga was immediately recognized by contemporaries. In addition to the massive press coverage that appeared shortly after its conclusion, there has been over the years an outpouring of books and monographs about the event. However, it has been mostly in Arabic and often either rather cursory or polemical. The one exception in this regard is Antoine Butrus' celebrated book *Qissat muhakamat Antun Sa'adeh was i'idamehe* (An Account of Antun Sa'adeh's Trial and Execution).[9] Yet, despite the admirable thoroughness of the book, a great deal of work remains to be done. Butrus' book is the starting point for all future research in the sense that he made available, for the first time, far more material about Sa'adeh than had previously been known. However, a reader of his book may still find it hard, within the welter of factual information, to gain a rounded impression of the saga. All is not lost, however. There is an abundance of information in the Lebanese press and memoirs of the Khoury era. And although press coverage of the saga was often tainted by political prejudice and personal animosity toward Sa'adeh or toward the government, several newspapers were able to provide a fair and generally impartial treatment of events as they happened. The most important was *an-Nahar*, which kept its wide readership continuously informed and published almost daily disclosures and comments about the controversy. Personal memoirs and reports also contain valuable information and offer the reader various perspectives from participants and independent witnesses. Nonetheless, they should be handled with care as they illuminate only part of the picture and, because of their restricted scope, do so in a necessarily subjective manner.

Beyond the Arabic language, the saga is hardly known outside a narrow circle of academic specialists. There is no book in English – or in any other major European language for that matter – that attempts to give a concise, clear and authoritative survey of the controversy. There are chapters on certain aspects of the subject, on individual participants or on specific issues, but there is no one volume that provides a unified treatment of the saga with a view to helping the general intelligent English reader as well as the student to form a clear picture of causes and consequences. Even in the most direct studies on modern Lebanon, the Sa'adeh saga is treated by scholars mostly at a quite general level.

The existing secondary literature is even less helpful. In contrast to the rich literature on the general phenomenon of Lebanese political crashes, there are relatively few comprehensive historical studies of the Khoury era. It was not until recently that the drought was broken with the publication of Eyal Zisser's major study *Lebanon: The Challenge of Independence*.[10] Zisser explains the dearth of literature on the "independence era" (*ahd al-istiqlal*) as follows:

> The voluminous struggle over the valid interpretation of Lebanese history failed to elicit much interest in the events of 1943–52. Researchers inclining to a deterministic view thought of that decade as marginal and as devoid of influence on what was in any case destined to follow. For them, an understanding of Lebanon had to be anchored in an analysis of the emergence of Greater Lebanon, of the National Pact, of the 1958 crisis and, most of all, of the civil war. But their counterparts, too, did not find much to attract them to this particular period, at least not beyond the initial struggle for independence and the formulation of the National Pact. Most scholarly histories of either school therefore devote no more than a few lines to the entire decade.[11]

Zisser's book has a chapter on the Sa'adeh saga but it doesn't go far enough. Other attempts are no better.[12] Most are ill-informed, full of factual errors, narrow in scope, bizarre in their organization and emphasis, and generally lacking in enthusiasm. Some can be followed only by Lebanese specialists, while others are far too general and brief to satisfy the needs of the reader who wishes to acquire an adequate knowledge of the subject.

The task here is to portray and explain the puzzling complexity of a political trial that went very wrong. Critical to this task is an understanding of the confusing and muddy borderland where politics, criminality, and law often overlap. However, the reader must be alerted as to what this volume is and is not. It is a multidisciplinary exploration of the historical and theoretical underpinnings of a political saga involving variables in politics and law and societal responses to it. It is not a comprehensive historical work or a legal treatise; although some events and law matters are examined in depth, most are referred to, if at all, at a quite general level. Generally, this volume is less a history of a trial than it is a dramatic representation of a tragic episode.

Structurally, *Outright Assassination* falls into three general sections. The first section is an exploration of Sa'adeh's political discourse and attitude towards the power structure in Lebanon. It covers his turbulent relationship with the Lebanese State from its origin in 1936 to the period immediately preceding the trial. It would be futile to attempt to explain the controversy without a lucid understanding of Lebanese state politics and Sa'adeh's reaction to it. The controversy was ideological as much as it was political, and not a straight-forward treason case as it has often been made out to be.

The second section is an attempt to unravel without interruption the last threads of the plot against Sa'adeh's life. It is a step by step reconstruction of the trial and execution, with its slow and measured procedure, based largely on press reports, published testimonies, and personal recollections of those who lived in that period. In the absence of court records, it is very difficult to confirm the accuracy of the information, but there does seem to be strong consistency between the various accounts. From this re-enactment, the discussion proceeds to an analytical review of the trial process under national and international law.

The third section provides a round-up of the myriad reactions generated by the case both inside and outside Lebanon. The intention here is not to record every detail of the Sa'adeh affair, but to touch instead on the salient aspects, and thus both pave the way for further studies on these topics and to provide a backdrop for those generally in need of dependable information. After that is an enumeration of the various assumptions and theories that have developed about the case in an effort to determine to what extent they differ from one another and why these differences occur. Generally, we will be concerned with developing an inventory of how far these theories have brought us to an understanding of the saga. The section will conclude with a survey of the fallouts from the saga and its repercussions on the main parties.

The present book originated in the need to discover answers. This attempt is made in the full knowledge that, for the foreseeable future, it will not be possible to explain the "why", "who" and "when" of the Sa'adeh saga more accurately until the secret archives of the Lebanese security services and military court, where Sa'adeh was tried and executed, are opened for public scrutiny. Until then we have to rest content with the available information.

NOTES

1 It is claimed that Husni az-Zaim watched proceedings from behind the door but refused to make an appearance. Another claim is that Sa'adeh threw back at him the pistol that Zaim had earlier presented as a token of friendship. Neither claim can be confirmed. See Adib Kaddoura, *Haqa'iq wa Mawaqif* (Facts and Stances). Beirut: Dar Fikr, 1989.

2 *An-Nahar*, Beirut, 9 June, 1949. See also Nada Raad, "Tueini talks about his turbulent relationship with SSNP: death of party founder Saade seen as turning point." Beirut: *Daily Star*, Saturday, 22 May, 2004.

3 Ibid.

4 *Fikr*. Beirut, No. 73, 1 July, 2000: 76.

5 For an introduction on this relationship see Adel Beshara, *Lebanon, The Politics of Frustration: The Failed Coup of 1961* (History and Society in the Islamic World). London and New York: Routledge and Curzon, 2005.

6 On Sa'adeh's life and thought see Adel Beshara, *Syrian Nationalism: An Inquiry into the Political Thought of Antun Sa'adeh*. Beirut: Bissan Publications, 1995; *Antun Sa'adeh: The Man, His Thought*. London: Ithaca Press, 2007.

7 Ron Christenson, *Political Trials: Gordian Knots in the Law*. 2nd ed. New Brunswick, N.J.: Transaction Press, 1999.

8 Otto Kirchheimer, *Political Justice*. Princeton, N.J.: Princeton University Press, 1961.

9 Antoine Butrus, *Qissat muhakamat Antun Sa'adeh was i'idamehe* (An Account of Antun Sa'adeh's Trial and Execution). Beirut: Chemaly & Chemaly, 2002.

10 Eyal Zisser, *Lebanon: The Challenge of Independence*. London: I. B. Tauris, 2000: 176–192.

11 Ibid., xi.

12 See the chapter on Lebanon in George M. Haddad, *Revolution and Military Rule in the Middle East*. 3 Vols. New York: Robert Speller and Sons, Publishers, 1971; Chapter eight in Patrick Seale, *The Struggle for Syria: A Study of Post-War Diplomacy 1945–1958*. Oxford: Oxford University Press, 1965.

1

Essential Background

✧

Antun Sa'adeh has the dubious distinction of being the first and last political figure to be executed in independent Lebanon. A committed ideologue, Sa'adeh was positioned to the left of mainstream Lebanese politics and the confessional system, which he considered too impractical and slow to forge an independent national life.[1] His life was tinged by a spirit of rebellion, which led him to scorn all half-measures and vacillation and which influenced the intransigence with which he later stuck to his program of national revival. But "rebel" he was, and as rebel, we may be sure he paid the price that always goes with such independence of thought and action.

Admired for the broadness of his intellectual sweep, his single-minded concentration on the national cause, and his commitment to rational principles, Sa'adeh was destined for a personal tragedy. But no one, including his political detractors, envisaged that it would be through the death penalty. Many expected him to die in cold blood or to live the rest of his life on the run or in exile, but not to be executed behind closed doors in Star Chamber style.[2] Many more expected the State, in the longer run, to triumph against him but they never imagined that it would be without any physical or moral restraint. This was an intolerable breach of faith.

In order to understand how Sa'adeh came into circumstances that cost him his life, it is necessary to recreate the "rebel" before our eyes, placing ourselves, as far as possible, in his intellectual environment, and to touch upon the salient features of his relationship with the Lebanese State. During the last half-century this relationship has been normally discussed – or more often simply alluded to – primarily within the context of the political development of Lebanon. Because of this, the existing secondary accounts are strikingly inconsistent in the information they provide. They have given rise to an amazing variety of conflicting theories and evaluations. Here, however, we study the relationship as an internal affair involving complex relations among all the players who participated directly or indirectly in it. We explore its evolution phase by phase, and the central issues at question are taken as a whole and considered within a wider context than that of traditional scholarly interest in modern Lebanon.

Lebanon: The Long March to Statehood

At different periods in its history, Lebanon or Mount Lebanon before 1920, a mighty range which begins northeast of Tripoli and extends approximately to a region east of Sidon and Tyre in the south, has held an important position as a shelter for minority and persecuted groups, including its historic Maronite Christian majority, the monotheistic Druze, and local Shi'a Muslims. Other sects that are known to have settled in the Lebanon region are: Greek Orthodox, Greek Catholics, Jacobites, Syrian Catholics, Chaldean Catholics, Nestorian Assyrians, Latins (Roman Catholics), Protestants, Sunni Muslims and Jews. These sects co-existed, often with antagonistic interests, but could not mold into a unity of any measurable degree. Like "outright castes,"[3] each sect managed its own internal affairs and personal status laws independent of the other sects.

In the mid-1800s, as nationalism penetrated the Syrian environment, this arrangement came under close scrutiny. Functionally, nationalism and sectarianism are opposites: nationalism is a collective spirit in which the relationship of the members of a nation is, theoretically, an equal relationship between citizens; sectarianism, on the other hand, refers (usually pejoratively) to a rigid adherence to a particular sect or party or religious denomination. It often implies discrimination, denunciation, or violence against those outside the sect. Moreover, as exclusive communities, sects "defy the environment in which they grow"[4] and their members tend to possess a strong sense of identity that limits "one's contact with others and the kind of occupation that was open to the individual."[5]

With the advent of nationalism, Mount Lebanon found itself at a new crossroad in history. It became the stage for a major literary revival spearheaded by a small but active intellectual stratum willing to question the existing order of things. And so, amidst the pervasiveness of a sectarian mentality, various nationalist tendencies began to appear with fresh concepts and universal claims about how the region should be organized. Chief among them were:

1. A secular Syrianist tendency, which considered Mount Lebanon an indispensable part of Syria;
2. A pan-Arab tendency, which emphasized a national union on the basis of a singular Arab identity; and
3. A Lebanonist tendency, which portrayed events on and around Mount Lebanon within a distinctly Lebanese context.

By the turn of the twentieth century those tendencies were clashing over whether Lebanon's identity was to be considered from a pan-Arab (or pan-Syrian) or a narrower nationalist Lebanese perspective. Although Lebanese Christians were the first intellectuals to promote a sense of pan-Arab (or Syrian) identity, they grew alienated from the movement after pan-Arabist theoreticians, for whom the very concept of historical Lebanon was increasingly anathema, began holding sway. Many felt that Lebanon's identity could only be understood within the context of greater Syria and eventually a larger pan-Arab framework. The dividing lines eventually coalesced roughly around sectarian groupings, hampered by a rigid and static stratification, and the national identity of Lebanon remained undecided.

On September 1, 1920, against a background of intense national confusion, the French High Commissioner in the Levant, General Henri Gouraud, surrounded by a hand-picked audience of local religious and political leaders, declared the birth of *Grand Liban* (Greater Lebanon). The new entity, in addition to the pre-war *mutassarafiyyah* (governorate), included new areas and towns that were inhabited by a majority of Sunni and Shi'a Muslims. It increased the Sunni Muslim population of the new state by eight times, the Shi'a Muslims by four times, and the Maronite Christians by only one-third of their original number in Mount Lebanon. The inclusion of such significant new population groups was deemed necessary for economic viability, but it brought with it serious problems. First, Greater Lebanon engulfed two areas unequal in their level of capitalist development and their access to services and resources: the more advanced area of Beirut and Mount Lebanon, constituting the center, and the less advanced areas of northern, eastern, and southern Lebanon, constituting the peripherics.[6] Second, the new entity was created against the wishes of a significant number of its population. A large number of the center's residents were Christians, and many of them, particularly Maronites, were advocates of the new state. A good number of the peripheries' residents were Muslims, and many of them, in addition to a good number of Christians, leaned toward reunion with a Syrian/Arab nation. The different concentrations of sectarian communities in the center versus the peripheries also meant that Christians, predominantly of the center, had better access to resources while Muslims, predominantly of the peripheries, had less. This access also varied with class differences, with the upper classes of various religious affiliations in both regions having much better access to resources.[7] Third, the inclusion of a substantial Muslim element undermined the new entity because the overall Maronite community slumped to about thirty per cent of the population. The French may have done that in order to weaken the Syrian Arab national movement in Syria and, simultaneously, to secure long-term Maronite dependency on them.

The initial main challenge for Greater Lebanon was to create a sphere for the two large religious groups and several other religious communities to live and function side by side. In 1926, a Lebanese Constitution was drafted under French supervision to pave the way for the Lebanese republic and its transformation toward a Western parliamentary democracy. Under the Constitution, all Lebanese were guaranteed the freedoms of speech, assembly, and association "within the limits established by law." There were also provisions for freedom of conscience and the free exercise of all forms of worship, as long as the dignity of the several religions and the public order were not affected. A structure for the electoral system, legislative and executive institutions in addition to the juridical and bureaucratic structure, was also provided by the new constitution, but it was based on a confessional political representation that followed a ratio of 60% to 40% between Christians and Muslims.[8] The purpose was to give Lebanon a political framework where the different confessional groups in an already polarized and sectarian society could coexist and follow a "national" consensus. However, many Muslims saw the Constitution as an expression of Lebanese independence and Christian and French colonial domination. In fact, Muslim representatives at the Constitution draft meetings made it clear that they were against the very idea of expanding the limits of mostly Christian Mount Lebanon to create Greater Lebanon incorporating Muslim areas and insisted that the record show their reservations. On another level, the Constitution combined two contradictory facts: the implementation of a Western political system based on equality and universal suffrage was one wanted fact, while a deeply rooted sectarianism in both Lebanese political and social culture was another actual fact that counteracted the former goal.[9]

Another problem was this: By superimposing Lebanon's confessional-style politics on a democratic agenda, the new constitution, with tacit French approval, enabled a limited group of Christian families in Mount Lebanon and Beirut and Shiite and Sunni feudal landowner families in the coastal cities to usurp power for themselves. Cooperation among these families took place only in terms of a common interest that strengthened their own positions and increased their wealth. No space was given in this structure for those politicians or groups who aimed to transform the country into a democratic, pluralistic and fair society. From time to time political parties did appear but they were basically thinly disguised political machines for a particular confession or, more often, a specific *zaim* (political leader). Lacking traits common to parties in most Western democracies, they had no ideology and no programs, and made little effort at transcending sectarian support. Moreover, the absence of real political parties, in the sense of constitutionally legitimate groups seeking office, led to a new form of political clientelism, based upon but by no means identical to the older feudal system. It reduced the political process to one of squabbles over patronage rights.[10]

As a result, Lebanon became again a centre-stage for old divisions and disagreements over national identity. Two distinctly "nationalist" camps formed: a Christian Maronite camp that advocated for an independent Greater Lebanon within its existing "historical and natural boundaries;" and a mainly Muslim pan-Syrian Arab camp calling for "either complete unification with Syria, or some sort of federal system respecting a 'Lebanese particularism'."[11] Both camps put on an "ideological" show – the unionist tendency even organized a campaign of civil disobedience to promote its cause – but the rivalry soon fizzled out into political jockeying for power and prestige. As soon as "Muslim politicians had come to realize that, whereas they might be of first-rate importance in Lebanon, in a Greater Syria they would at best be second-rate next to political leaders from Damascus and Aleppo"[12] they sought a face-saving accommodation within the Lebanese system. Likewise, most Lebanese nationalists began to recognize the need for the nascent state to co-operate with its Muslim hinterland and began a process of national reconciliation that involved greater inclusion of Muslims into the political process. That process was suspended with the outbreak of World War II.

In September 1943, elections for a new chamber were held amidst domestic division over Lebanon's "republican" identity. In the ensuing debate, the Lebanese nationalists portrayed themselves as against any foreign influence, be it French or Arab. While paying lip service to the need for friendly relations with neighboring states, they continued to stress the Phoenician (i.e., non-Arab) origins of the Lebanese. For their part, Lebanon's Arab nationalists were careful not to push too hard for Arab union on the grounds that it could incite violence and thus provide the French with an excuse to perpetuate their occupation. Two months after the elections, a deal was struck between the contending parties to enable Lebanon to gain full independence. This would take the form of what would come to be called the National Pact (*almithaq al-watani*), an agreement between two prominent communal leaders, the Christian Beshara el-Khoury and the Sunni Riad el-Solh.

Under the National Pact, Christian leaders accepted that Lebanon was a "country with an Arab face" while Muslim leaders, who had abandoned the idea of union with Syria, agreed to recognize the existing borders of the newly independent state and relative, though diminished, Christian hegemony within them. The traditional division of labour between Lebanon's various confessional groups was upheld with the presidency being reserved for a Maronite, the prime minister a Sunni Muslim and the speaker of the house a Shia Muslim. The ratio of deputies in parliament was to be six Christians to five Muslims. These arrangements were meant to be provisional and to be discarded once Lebanon moved away from confessionalism. The Pact did not specify how and when this would happen. Matters were made worse by the fact that the agreement was never officially written down and the meeting between the two men was more or less a private affair. What the two sides actually committed to would be the subject of bitter disagreement for years to come. According to el-Khoury, as recounted in his memoirs, the agreement was a push for complete independence. The Maronite community would not appeal to the West for protection while Lebanon's

Arabists would not push for a federation with the East. However, whereas el-Khoury saw independence from France as the end game, el-Solh saw it as a prerequisite step towards a pan-Arab union. For el-Solh, the pact meant that the Arabists would agree to the legitimacy of *Grand Liban* and would pursue their objectives for Arab union through democratic means. Both sides agreed that independence meant self-determination; it was the manner in which that independence would translate into concrete policy that would become problematic.[13]

The Independence Era

Following independence on 23 November, 1943, it seemed that the National Pact had established Lebanon on acceptably stable foundations. The Lebanese political system displayed a modicum of unity and was successful in providing a basis for considerable freedom and prosperity. That it could do so depended upon it being asked to do very little. Whereas other parts of the Near East witnessed an expansion of government activity and, in some case, praetorian intervention, during the same period in Lebanon the government remained modest and civil. The Lebanese economy ran with a minimum of government control and with considerable success. Socially, Lebanon seemed to be heading in the right direction following the religious solidarity displayed during its charge for independence. Back then, in a first for Lebanon, the Maronite Archbishop and the Grand Mufti of Lebanon took a united stand against the French. A dispatch to the *New York Herald Tribune* stated on November 16, in the midst of the crisis: "For the first time in many years Moslems and Christians are united against the French."[14] And further "The most interesting aspect of the present disturbances is that members of all religions and sects are united."[15]

With Beshara el-Khoury and Riad el-Solh at the political helm, the Lebanese had strong reasons to celebrate. Beshara el-Khoury was an exceptionally gifted organizer and orator. He had been in the political game almost from the proclamation of Greater Lebanon in 1920, when he was appointed as secretary-general of the Lebanese government, and was widely respected and supported by Lebanon's economic and cultural circles. Though a self-confessed supporter of Greater Lebanon, el-Khoury displayed remarkable flexibility in politics and understood Lebanon's unique social blend far better than his nearest rival, Emile Edde. He rose to the highest office in the state by forging closer relations with the Muslim community or, more precisely, with the Sunni elite, and by publicly acknowledging Lebanon's Arab character and regional reality. Riad el-Solh, on the other hand, was a prominent Syrian Arab nationalist and one-time member of the short-lived Syrian National Congress under King Feisal. An urban notable from a well-established Sunni family, Solh was twice banished from Lebanon, in 1920 and again in 1925, for resisting French rule. His forceful personality, political astuteness, and outspoken views were the main mark of his personality. Solh was widely respected within the Sunni Muslim community in both Lebanon and in Syria, but it was his involvement in the Lebanese national quest in 1943 that finally turned him into a national *zaim*, at least in the eyes of his followers.

Upon assuming the country's leadership, both Khoury and Solh sought to portray themselves as state-builders. The tone of Solh's first cabinet statement, on 7 October 1943, speaks volumes:

> The Government which I have the honour of heading and which emanates from this Assembly, regards itself as the expression of the people's will. It is answerable before the Lebanese people alone, and its policy will be inspired by the country's higher interests. Emanating from the Lebanese people alone, we are for the people first and foremost. It is for the purpose of making this independence and national sovereignty a real and concrete fact that we have assumed the responsibility of power.[16]

In practical policy terms, the Solh statement contained a number of proposals and ideas aimed at strengthening the "country's laws and public functions:"[17]

1. Revision of the national Constitution "in such a way as to make it harmonious with our conception of true independence."
2. Re-organization of the national administration to strengthen the constitutional regime.
3. Reform of the Electoral Law.
4. Conducting a new population census.
5. Greater regional and Arab cooperation in foreign policy.

However, the statement is best remembered for its reference to the sectarian problem in Lebanon:

One of the essential bases of reform is the suppression of sectarian considerations which are an obstacle to national progress. These have injured Lebanon's reputation and weakened relations among the various elements of the Lebanese population. Furthermore, we realize that the sectarian principle has been exploited to the personal advantage of certain individuals, to the detriment of the nation's interests. We are convinced that once the people are imbued with the national feeling under a regime of independence and popular administration, they will gladly agree to the abolition of the sectarian principle, which is an element of national weakness.

The day which will witness the end of the sectarian regime will be a blessed day of awakening. We shall strive to make that day as near as possible. It is only natural, however, that the realization of this objective should call for a few preparatory measures in every field. These measures will require the close cooperation of everyone, so that the realization of this important national reform may receive the full approval of all the citizens without exception.

What has been said of the sectarian principle applies also to the regional principle which, if carried out, would divide the country into several countries.[18]

This movement, however, never occurred; instead of its purported state-building purpose, the independence regime cemented the sectarian divide in the country and helped to aggravate rather than disentangle issues of conflict regarding the character of Lebanese polity. It also reinforced the sectarian system of government begun under the French Mandate by formalizing the confessional distribution of high-level posts in the government based on the 1932 census' six-to-five ratio favoring Christians over Muslims. Viewed from this perspective,

The National Pact . . . consecrated the traditional 'Lebanese way', and thus incorporated the defects of the old order into the new. This blocked the emergence of an efficient and functional administration; worse, it inhibited the various components of the population in their incipient identification with the new state. In the short term, a fairly stable equilibrium was thus ensured, but this was only made possible by sacrificing the prospects of stability in the long run.[19]

Once the regime turned confessional all the precepts of strong and responsible government went amiss. The state became an arena for competing interests and parochial benefits overtook the national welfare.

Many earlier proposals for securing Christian-Muslim co-operation, based as they had been on the Sarrail model of individual equality in a secular state, were reduced by the regime to a singular approach which endeavored to secure co-operation on a strictly confessional basis. The outcome was unsalutory: sectarianism became even more entrenched; the principle of balancing, which created multiple power centers, frequently inhibited the political process; basic philosophical differences between the sects widened; and bickering among elites, not only between Christians and Muslims but also among sects within each religious group, spread like wildfire.

Also during this period, the political system of *zuama* clientelism was institutionalized and expanded. This impaired the efficiency of the central bureaucracy and fostered widespread communal disenchantment owing to the system's basic discriminatory nature. Like sectarianism, *zuamaism* hindered the emergence of a sense of national as opposed to parochial loyalty and turned the state into an arena for petty squabbles and power contests. As a result, corruption and nepotism reached an intolerable level and a steady gap in access to resources opened up, polarizing Lebanese society even further:

> Although Khoury had professed himself defender of the constitution during the French Mandate, after independence he revised it to secure another term in office. He portrayed himself as the president of all the Lebanese, but under his reign his family, relatives, and friends, and the Maronite community as a whole, strengthened their hold over the administration, the judicial system, the army, and the intelligence services. He perfected what may be defined as a method of "control and share" – integrating the feudal bourgeois elites of the Sunnis, Shi'is, and other communities into the political and economic systems in return for their support of the status quo. This may have provided Lebanon with a more stable political system, as those who benefited from it had a vested interest in maintaining it, but it led to widespread corruption.[20]

Both Khoury and Solh were culpable. The pair swept to power in 1943 with a great deal of public credit and a broad base of popular support but turned out to be anything but state leaders. The people gave them a clear mandate to lead Lebanon into a new age: instead, they exhibited none of the necessary leadership principles and ideals of good governance. They offered the country a clear political agenda, but carried to fruition only what was deemed to be beneficial to their own political survival: the Constitution remained basically unchanged; nothing was done to cleanse the national administration; no population census was undertaken; and the electoral law was reformed to suit their own political ambitions. Only in foreign policy can their regime claim some credit, but that was only because the regional and international challenges to Lebanon in those years were hardly problematical.

Lebanon under the Khoury-Solh regime returned to its old political habits. Old and new wounds remained unhealed and social grievances became more acute than at any time before. Some of those grievances were directed at the regime itself; others at the political system; and others still at the political status as a whole. The Lebanese split yet again on national identity: those who felt uncomfortable with Lebanon's "Christian" character rejuvenated their call for pan-Arab unity; others felt that Lebanon was marching to a political tune which was too Arab and too Islamic for their liking:

> This tradition [of Christian tolerance] – let it be stated very bluntly – is now in mortal danger. There are two movements at work in the Lebanon today. The first is that traditional spirit which we have just described and which is cherished by the great majority of the Lebanese population. The second movement may be quite accurately described as the invasion of the Lebanon by Pan-Arabism, as represented by the present Lebanese Government headed by the Prime Minister, Riad As-Solh, a Sunni Moslem from a minority group in the Lebanon, who for the last twenty-five years has worked – against the will of almost the entire Lebanese people – to include Lebanon in an Arab-Islamic union. As long as France with its traditional support of Lebanese Christianity held the Mandate over Lebanon and Syria, the pro-Moslem forces had no chance: Their opportunity came during the War, when with the active connivance of Major General Sir Edward Spears, representing Britain in the Levant, the French lost their hold over Lebanon and Syria. A pro-Moslem Government was then propelled into office in the first elections held in the unmandated Lebanon, and almost without the awareness of the great majority of the Lebanon, the country was swung into the orbit of Arab League policy.[21]

For clarity, it should be said that internal dissatisfaction under the independence regime was not entirely sectarian. On the contrary, the most serious and most articulate challenge to the State and to the regime came from secular groups and secular individuals from various political persuasions. Chief among them was Antun Sa'adeh. He was, and had been from earlier times, the Knight in shinning armor in the secular crusade not only against the State but also against everything it represented.

Antun Sa'adeh: The National Discourse

Born in 1904 into a middle-class family with an intellectual background, Sa'adeh cast himself as a clear-thinking maverick willing to tell his people harsh truths. In the pursuit of this goal he exhibited great independence in thought and action and was principled and committed to one theoretical line all his life. His intolerance of inconsistency, his passion for scientific facts and his belief in deductive reasoning reflected an absolute faith in the omnipotence of reason.[22] Yet, he is often remembered mostly for his towering personality and charisma:

> To most people who met him, friend and foe alike, the impression which Antun Sa'adeh left was that of a man of unusually strong character and striking personality. He possessed a great deal of will power and was extremely intelligent with a deep insight for politics. Though his formal schooling ended before he completed his high school education, he was widely read and highly cultured. Furthermore, he commanded the respect of many of those who met him and exhibited all the qualities and attributes of leadership.[23]

In addition to these personal and intellectual qualities, Sa'adeh possessed remarkable leadership and fighting qualities that he was to display over and again. Writing many years later about his special relationship with Sa'adeh, Hisham Sharabi noted, "When he said, 'The blood that runs through our veins is owned by the nation and it must be produced whenever the nation demands it,' he meant it, literally."[24]

Sa'adeh belonged to a generation which cultivated the imagination more intensely and deliberately than its predecessors. However widely the majority of its members differed in character, aim, and historical environment, they resembled each other in one fundamental attribute: they criticised and condemned the existing condition of society. The problem is they disagreed about the effectiveness of the proposed means of improving that society, about the extent to which compromise with the existing status quo was morally or practically advisable, about the character and value of specific social institutions, and consequently about the policy to be adopted with regards them.[25] The problem, also, is that their disagreements were nationalistic in tone but sectarian in essence.[26] Sa'adeh, however, came to be wholly out of sympathy with these attitudes. He believed that human history is governed by laws which cannot be altered by the mere intervention of groups actuated by this or that ideal. From this arises the first fundamental difference between Sa'adeh and his contemporaries: national and not sectarian interest should be the benchmark of political action. Yet Sa'adeh could not at any time be classified into any of the existing currents: certainly he was in no sense a Lebanese nationalist or a pan-Arab. He believed that the right framework for national activity was Syrian nationalism based upon but by no means identical with earlier nineteenth-century notions of it.[27]

To prove his point, Sa'adeh studied nationalism.[28] He appealed, at least in his own view, to reason and practical intelligence and insisted that all that the people needed, in order to know how to save themselves from the chaos in which they were involved, was to seek to understand their actual condition. Next, Sa'adeh attempted a powerful critique of established situations during which he took direct aim at the *zuamas*:

> The greatest calamity befalling Syria [he wrote in 1925] is the *zuama* who have none of the qualifications for leadership. They are men who, if the truth is to be said, lack all political, military or economic knowledge . . . and if they happened to discuss a substantial national problem, they do this like children.[29]

With this attitude, common to the vast majority of revolutionaries and reformers at all times, Sa'adeh came to espouse a radical view of change. The term he used for that is *nahda* (renaissance), a notion of change not only in the institutions and power structure of society, but also in its ideological foundation, and the beliefs and myths that stem from it. In other words, the crucial issue for Sa'adeh was not to substitute one government for another, or to speed the forthcoming birth of a new system that society could produce in its present condition. Nor was it a question of giving society an additional impetus to speed up its progression towards the realization of goals to which it was clearly progressing. The issue for him was that of changing the whole life of a nation whose development had stopped long ago, and whose objective potential for movement in new directions had shrunk and dwindled away to almost nothing.[30]

Once again Sa'adeh inveighed against the status quo in his country arguing that its institutions were unsuitable to the task of national revival and that, therefore, an alternative arrangement was required for that purpose. He had in mind a highly disciplined political party operating outside of and, if necessary, in opposition to the existing structure. The Syrian National Party (later the SSNP),[31] which he secretly established in 1932, was consciously designed with that objective in mind. Sa'adeh then raised the political stakes by bravely exposing worrying trends about the state of thinking amongst his political opponents. His tone was furious and often brutal. His critique of religious and sectarian "nationalism" was particularly scathing. Sharp, lucid, mordant, realistic, and astonishingly modern in tone, it poured ridicule on what he considered to be naively personal and communal interpretations of nationalism. Sa'adeh also rejected the class-reductionist interpretation of Marxism by defining nationalism as a state of mind for all social forces in which the nation is a "stake" for the various classes.[32]

Behind his assault on the prevailing political doctrines stood more complex emotions connected with his own self-image as the redeemer of Lebanon. As early as 1921[33] he had posed the question of whether Lebanon's interest would be better served by preserving its independent entity or by absorbing it into a union with Syria. And as far back as then the answer was a foregone conclusion: Lebanon is an invaluable part of Syria, no different, certainly no less important, than the rest of the country. A separate Lebanon thus represented one of those demands that Sa'adeh was either reluctant to accept, or unable to fulfil. After the Syrian National Party was founded, he would again break ranks with the Christian Lebanese by denying the sovereign impenetrability of Lebanon's frontiers. "It is clear," he asserted, "that the Lebanese question can only be sectionally justified. The Lebanese question is not based on the existence of Lebanon as something independent, or on the existence of a separate Lebanese homeland, or even on an independent Lebanese history. Its only basis is religious party partisanship and theocracy."[34]

Such pronouncements aroused feelings of atavistic insecurity among the Lebanonists, who felt that Lebanon had a special mission in life and that in order to fulfil this mission Lebanese political independence must be preserved at all costs. In 1936 a campaign was spearheaded by the Jesuit newspaper *al-Bashir* in coordination with Bkirki, the fortress of Lebanese Christian nationalism, to deter Sa'adeh from pursuing his political objectives. While portraying themselves as the true patriots and creative defenders of Lebanon, its architects sought to project Sa'adeh as a traitor who had not been adequately socialized to comprehend the moral principles and realities of the socio-political order. The campaign was relatively successful but did not in the least shake Sa'adeh's belief in his own views. The SNP leader went into damage control explaining that neither Lebanon's destruction nor its merger with Syria was part of his intention. Emphasizing the difference between Lebanon as a "political question" arising from a religious motive and Syria as a "national cause" he stated:

> Our Social Nationalist ideology is a social thing and the Lebanese entity is a political thing and we do not confuse the two. If utility or political conditions required that the Lebanese entity needed to become an actual, physical entity, the question from this aspect remains a purely political one and there is no justification to turn it into a national issue. Because of this, those who consider the Social Nationalist Party a party that exists solely to demand Syrian unity err or misunderstand its cause. Those who try to panic the ultras among the Lebanese by saying that the party wants to annex Lebanon to Syria are deliberately making false propaganda.[35]

Later, Sa'adeh was able to point to numerous factual errors in the Lebanonist nationalist discourse. "If the [Lebanese] Christians refer back to their scripture, the Bible," he asserted in reference to the Phoenician thesis, "they will find that it is defined as the Phoenicia of Syria, not the Phoenicia of Lebanon."[36] Again, "The Maronites, they being part of the Syrian people that is centred in the interior of Syria, are Syriac rather than Phoenician in their original tongue and in culture and blood."[37] With clever use of their deficient historical knowledge of Maronitism, Sa'adeh was, in fact, able to question the Lebanonist discourse as a whole. In several simply and beautifully written accounts, he laid bare the anxieties of Lebanese particularism in a world where impassioned nationalism had managed to flourish.[38]

Alongside his well-reasoned critiques of Lebanese particularism, on another front in 1936, Sa'adeh opened fire on the political establishment and showed that its world-view would lead to national suicide. His targets, again, were the *zu'ama*,[39] who had worked their way back into the system and were presenting themselves as "national leaders":

> Some people took up the leadership of the popular dissatisfaction and exploited it in order to obtain the positions they sought, and they bolstered up this leadership by the remains of family power derived from the principles of a bygone age – principles which consider the people as herds to be disposed of by certain families, dissipating the interests of the people for the sake of their personal power. And when these so-called leaders found that the family and the home were not sufficient in this age to uphold leadership, they resorted to certain words beloved by the people – the words of liberty, independence, and principles – and they played upon these words, words which are sacred when they indicate an ideal for a living nation, but which are corrupt when they fire a means for assuming leadership and a screen behind which lurk ambition and private aims.[40]

Sa'adeh then opened merciless war on the ruling elite and the "opportunists" in the state who were endangering the whole future of the national movement and who aimed to produce only servile *entitism*. As soon as he was finished with the Christian Lebanonists, he began a series of articles which took the struggle right up to the political establishment with all the explosive power of original and genuinely revolutionary thought:

> There is a limit that every government has to stop at as regards the determination of general and ultimate destiny, which is the destiny of the people and not the government. Any government that attempts to bind the destiny of the people to its own destiny is a government in breach of state interests . . . the Lebanese government has developed into an intelligence bureau and ordinary Lebanese can no longer feel safe in his home, or work, or community.[41]

This conception meant, in fact, that the entire edifice of the Lebanese political establishment was corrupt; it meant, as well, that those who were in charge of it were corrupt and thus lacked credibility. Sa'adeh was able to analyse the Lebanese political establishment, its theoretical foundations and system of clientele and patronage politics, no longer as an irrational jumble of accidents, nor as the fulfilment of definite ideas and notions, but as a systematic politically explicable development sustained by leaders soaked in opportunism and self-interest. Ultimately, this fight on two fronts, the clear demarcation of the line of nationalist activism from opposing tendencies, and at the same time concrete explanations of practical tasks, would earn Sa'adeh many enemies. He was derided and denounced on all sides, not merely by direct opponents, but also by the majority of the politically inexperienced masses that he aimed to educate. That would include the pan-Arabists of Lebanon and the francophone Lebanese nationalists, who saw him as a threat to the integrity of Lebanon and to the basic political and ideological foundations of the state.[42] The real charge against Sa'adeh, however, was left to the state, which reacted with indignant rage.

The Political Establishment vs. Sa'adeh

Sa'adeh's political debut in November 1935 presented an instant problem to the political establishment in Lebanon. His vision of a Syrian nation, independent and sovereign, clashed directly with its effort to solidify the Lebanese entity within the French-created 1920 demarcation lines and as a separate state from Syria. It could not have come at a worse time for the central authorities, who were on the verge of a crucial victory brought on by the readiness of the Lebanese Syrian unionists[43] to join the political system after years of boycott and intransigence. There had been the occasional attempts to exclude these "unionists" from the political process but in general, these attempts, which the French initiated after the Great Syrian Revolt of 1925, "did not neutralize the apparatus of the state in relation to [them], but instead tried to neutralize and marginalize them in relation to the state."[44] With Sa'adeh the converse was applied: the French-Lebanese political leadership did not attempt to neutralize and marginalize Sa'adeh in relation to the state, but instead attempted to neutralize the apparatus of the state in relation to him. They did this by utilizing the legal system to frighten Sa'adeh into submission, thus illustrating to the general public the presumptive willingness of authorities to play by the legal rules. However, it soon transpired that the challenge he posed to them was not a mere spontaneous idiosyncratic deviation by a resentful individual, but a calculated act that was both organized and part of a program of resistance.

In 1936, a public statement entitled the "Blue Declaration," issued even as a Syrian delegation was in Paris negotiating with the French

Government for the conclusion of a Franco-Syrian Treaty, raised the stakes between Sa'adeh and the authorities even higher. In the "Blue Declaration" Sa'adeh re-affirmed his faith in Syrian nationalism and again questioned the integrity of Lebanese separatism:

> The Lebanese question is a complimentary part of the broad Syrian cause. It is therefore impermissible to treat it as an independent issue. Just as the Syrian delegation in Paris has no right to represent the Syrian cause in its broad sense and, conversely, the right to represent the Lebanese question, likewise sectarian desires in Lebanon are not entitled to that right.[45]

The authorities responded by encouraging the growth of confessional parties, notably the Phalanges Libanais[46] and the Najjadah.[47] Sa'adeh became the object of a character assassination and was smeared as a treasonous tool of European Fascism. One newspaper, *al-Masa'*, continued to publish slanderous reports about Sa'adeh based on unconfirmed reports about his activity until incensed SNP members gave its owner "a good lesson."[48] The French were not amused and charged Sa'adeh with inciting rebellion. In the last week of February 1937, government security forces clashed with his followers at a political rally in the Lebanese mountain town of Bekfeyya. In retaliation, the government arrested Sa'adeh for a third time on a charge of inciting the people against public order.[49] But with parliamentary elections looming, the Lebanese Prime minister freed Sa'adeh after obtaining from him an agreement to respect and uphold the existence of the Lebanese state. Actually, Sa'adeh gave that agreement on the condition that Lebanon's statehood would remain a matter for the will of the people to determine. The French accepted this condition to pacify him while dealing with more urgent problems brought on by Alexandretta's transfer to Turkey.

In the ensuing period of "peaceful coexistence"[50] between Sa'adeh and the authorities, the SNP leader was allowed, for the first time, to issue a newspaper and to speak more openly about his political views. The authorities allowed this to happen because they thought that compromise might work better with him than confrontation: they were wrong again. Sa'adeh turned his newspaper, *an-Nahda*, into a forum against the French Mandate and its "stooges" in Lebanon and Syria and forced open a long-delayed and still unfinished debate about Lebanon's future. Though not instantly anti-France, the paper moved quickly in that direction.

Early in 1938, the French again swung the cleaver in Sa'adeh's direction. With war in Europe fast approaching, the general suspicion that Sa'adeh was on the Nazi payroll picked up again. The evidence was clearly lacking but Sa'adeh's anti-liberal and anti-parliamentary tendencies, his focus on discipline, youth and nationalism, the cult of leadership and the swastika-like emblem of his party provided enough material to condemn him as a Nazi agent. The well-rehearsed accusation was trotted out, but only as an overture to a deadlier assault on him.

The intensity and sometimes ferocity of the conflict had a telling effect on Sa'adeh. He continued to work steadily and unobtrusively among the young intellectuals and the few groups in the country that shared his concern for the national interest, but his hold over public opinion remained marginal and indecisive. At some point in 1938 Sa'adeh caught wind of a government conspiracy against him and planned his escape. Some in Lebanon alleged that Sa'adeh's physical extermination was intended, but the Lebanese authorities denied that. Nonetheless, as a precaution, the Supreme Council in the party advised Sa'adeh to leave the country, which he did clandestinely in 1938.[51] Two days later, government security forces raided the headquarters of his party, confirming what the party had suspected all along.

The Calm Before the Storm
The outbreak of the Second World War brought immediate changes in every sphere of life, in Lebanon as well as Syria. Various measures were taken to ensure the safety of the two states and bring them under tight control. In Lebanon the French High Commissioner, General Weygand, dissolved the Chamber, dismissed the ministry, suspended the Constitution and delegated the administration to a Secretary of State directly responsible to the President of the Republic.[52] Moreover, suspect organizations were dissolved and some of their leading members were arrested: some were sentenced by military tribunals to exceedingly long terms of imprisonment on charges of subversion and conspiracy. Sa'adeh's supporters and top aides were among the arrested. They were exonerated of the charge of subversion but indicted on the lesser charges of operating without a permit and causing public disorder. Sa'adeh was sentenced in absentia to ten years imprisonment and a further ten years of exile. The sentence was upheld in 1940 by the Vichy-appointed High Commissioner in Beirut.

After the Allied takeover of Lebanon and Syria was completed in 1942, the new Free French administrator brought new persecution against Sa'adeh's followers as part of a general drive against independence-seeking movements. As a result, in the 1943 presidential campaign the SNP broke away from its original policy of neutrality in Lebanese electoral politics and sided with Beshara Khoury: Emile Edde was seen as a symbol of French influence.[53] In exchange Khoury promised to release all SNP detainees if elected to the Lebanese presidency. Khoury did become President in 1943 but before attending to that promise, he was arrested by the French High Commissioner, along with Premier Solh and government ministers, for attempting to annul France's special privileges in Lebanon. In the ensuing struggle, Sa'adeh, who was now domiciled in Argentina serving out an imposed exile, instructed his followers from abroad to support the Lebanese government.[54] For its part, the government, on its reinstatement some days later, released all political prisoners and allowed the SNP, along with other parties, to resume political activity: the issue of Sa'adeh's return was deferred, though.

The new direction freed the government from an important responsibility and reinforced its reputation as democratic and forward-thinking. This is not to suggest that goodwill was exclusively or even mainly the reason behind the government's action: (1) the government lacked both the strength and the adaptability of the French to engage the SNP; and (2) its army, which was still officially tied to the *Troupes Speciales du Levant,*[55] was small and ill-equipped to deal with political disturbances. Moreover, using repression as a domestic policy tool after the SNP had given formal expression to its attachment to Lebanese independence would have undermined the government's image and furnished the French with an excuse to stay longer in Lebanon.

With these objectives clearly in mind, the Lebanese leadership in 1945 reached a formal compromise with the SNP whereby they agreed to legalize the party in exchange for a pledge from the latter to work within the framework of the National Pact.[56] As a complementary condition, the SNP leadership was required to tone down the party's pan-Syrian rhetoric and turn the party into a "Lebanese" organization. The deal advanced in great strides so much so that by 1946 the SNP looked almost indistinguishable from other Lebanese parties and nothing like the SNP of the previous decade. Outwardly:

The word 'Syrian' was removed from the party's name. It was now called the National Party.

The flag of the party was modified and its colours changed.

The party's head office in Beirut began to exercise greater autonomy from its branches in Palestine and the Syrian Republic.

The party's manner of salute was toned-down.

Inwardly, the party was "directed more toward the domestic problems of independent Lebanon than to the national problem as defined by Sa'adeh."[57] It capped off its transformation with a direct attack on the Greater Syria Scheme:

> The Greater Syria scheme is a threat to the independence of the two states in the region it seeks to unite [namely Syria and Lebanon]. It relinquishes the territories of Cilicia and Alexendretta, consecrates sectarianism in Lebanon and seeks to turn the country into a religious safe haven for a particular group. Conversely, it endeavours to establish a Jewish home in the heart of a dear sector, which has struggled hard to defend itself from the alien Jews. In addition to all of this, the scheme calls for a system of government that it is inimical with the foundations of modern civilization and its concepts, as well as with all the values that every open-minded person cherishes.[58]

For a political party that had so signally struggled for Syrian unification, the declaration was a clear ideological reversal: it showed how far it had been Lebanonized within a period of a mere two or three years. Sa'adeh's initial reaction to this development was surprisingly mild and cautious – the proverbial calm before the storm. He tried in vain to dissuade the perpetrators from going further down that path and constantly affirmed his position that no circumstances should deflect the party from its national objectives. His appeals fell on deaf ears. Though still officially the party's undisputed leader, Sa'adeh refrained from taking disciplinary action against the deviationists so as not to give the government an excuse to extend his banishment. The strategy did not proceed entirely smoothly, but it spared the party the pain of an internal split.

NOTES

1 It is customary to associate Sa'adeh with right-wing politics on account of his commitment to nationalism and extreme dislike of traditional electoral politics. That much is true. But Sa'adeh was also a strong advocate of Leftist reforms, the kind that promotes intervention in favor of egalitarianism, and gives little or no authority to tradition. Most Lebanese regard him as neither left nor right but definitively anti-Establishment.

2 In modern usage, the Star Chamber is used, metaphorically or poetically, in reference to legal or administrative bodies that exercise strict, arbitrary rulings and secretive proceedings. It is a pejorative term and intended to cast doubt on the legitimacy of the proceedings. On Star Chamber see William Hargrave, *A Treatise on the Court of Star Chamber.* Legal Classics Library, 1986; and Samuel Rawson, *Reports of Cases in the Courts of Star Chamber and High Commission.* London: Camden Society, 1886.

3 Sofia Antun Sa'adeh, *The Social Structure of Lebanon: Democracy or Servitude?* Beirut: Dar An-Nahar, 1993: 10.

4 Manochehr Dorraj, "The Political Sociology of Sect and Sectarianism in Iranian Politics: 1960–1979." *Journal of Third World Studies.* Volume 23, No. 2 (Fall 2006): 95–117.

5 Simon Haddad, "Christian-Muslim Relations and Attitudes towards the Lebanese State." *Journal of Muslim Minority Affairs*, Vol. 21, No. 1 (April 2001): 131.

6 See Sami A. Ofeish, "Lebanon's Second Republic: Secular Talk, Sectarian Application." *Arab Studies Quarterly*, Vol. 21 (Winter, 1999): 97–117.

7 Ibid.

8 Even though Articles 7 and 12 provide for equality of civil and political rights and equal access to public posts based on merit, Article 95 affirms the state's commitment to confessionalism, but without setting forth how it is to be applied.

9 Ladan Madeleine Moghaddas, *Civil Society and Political Democracy in Lebanon*, MA Thesis, Jönköping (January 2006): 42.

10 See S. Khalaf, "Changing forms of political patronage in Lebanon" in Gellner, E. and Waterbury, J. (eds.), *Patrons and Clients in Mediterranean Societies.* London: Gerard Duckworth and Co. Ltd., 1977: 185–205.

11 David Grafton, *The Christians of Lebanon: Political Rights in Islamic Law*, London: I.B. Tauris, 2004: 104.

12 Philip Khoury, *Syria and the French Mandate: The Politics of Arab Nationalism 1920–1945.* Princeton University Press, 1987: 58.

13 Some Lebanese dispute the existence of the National Pact and have labelled it as "a created legend." See Hala Kilani, "National Pact: myth or reality?" *Daily Star*, Beirut, 21 November, 2002.

14 *New York Herald Tribune,* New York: 16 November, 1943.

15 Ibid.

16 Eugenie Elie Abouchdid, *Thirty Years of Lebanon and Syria (1917–1947).* Beirut: The Sader-Rihani Printing Co., 1948: 81.

17 Ibid.

18 Ibid., 83.

19 Eyal Zisser, *Lebanon: The Challenge of Independence*. London: I. B. Tauris, 2000: 103.

20 Meir Zamir, "From Hegemony to Marginalism: The Maronites of Lebanon" in Bengio, Ofra and Ben-Dor, Gabriel (eds.), *Minorities and the State in the Arab World*. Boulder, CO: Lynne Rienner Publishers, Inc., 1999.

21 G. Akl, A. Ouadat, E. Hunein (eds.), *The Black Book of the Lebanese Elections of May 25, 1947*. New York: Phoenicia Press, 1947: 3–4.

22 On Sa'adeh's distinctiveness see Mustapha Abdul Satir, *Shu'un Qawmiyyah* (National Issues). Beirut: Dar Fikr, 1990: 29–45.

23 Nadim Makdisi, *The Syrian National Party: A Case Study of the First Inroads of National Socialism in the Arab World*, unpub. PhD. Dissertation, American University of Beirut, 1959: 15.

24 Hisham Sharabi, *Images from the Past: An Autobiography*. Beirut: Dar Nelson, 1989: 121.

25 See Philip S. Khoury, *Syria and the French Mandate: The Politics of Arab Nationalism 1920–1945*. New Jersey: Princeton University Press, 1987.

26 An interesting depiction of that era can be found in Edward Selim Atiyah, *An Arab Tells his Story: A Study in Loyalties*. London: J. Murray, 1946.

27 Sa'adeh recalled this phase in his life as follows: "When I began to give serious thought to the resuscitation of our nation against the background of the irresponsible political movements rampant in its midst, it became forthwith certain to me that our most urgent problem was the determination of our national identity and our social reality. Although there was no consensus of opinion concerning this problem, I became convinced that the starting point of every correct national endeavor must be the raising of this fundamental philosophical question: Who are we? After extensive research, I arrived at the following conclusion: We are Syrians and we constitute a distinct national entity." A. Sa'adeh, *al-Muhadarat al-Ashr* (The Ten Lectures). Beirut: SSNP Publications, 1978.

28 Ibid.

29 Sa'adeh, *al-Athar al-Kamilah* (Complete Works). Vol. 1. Beirut: SSNP Cultural Bureau, n.d.: 124.

30 Adel Beshara, *Syrian Nationalism: An Inquiry into the Political Philosophy of Antun Sa'adeh*. Beirut: Dar Bissan, 1995.

31 Sa'adeh renamed the party to the Syrian Social National Party to underpin its philosophical outlook as 'social' or 'societal' oriented. It is not to be confused with 'socialism' or 'national socialism' which, in Arabic, translate into *ishtiraqqiyah* as opposed to *ijtima'iyah*. See Aboud Aboud, *The S.N.S.P.* Sydney: An-Nahda, 1982: 31.

32 Nicos Ponlantzas, *State, Power, Socialism*. London: New Left Books, 1978: 115.

33 Antun Sa'adeh, "al-wihda al-Suriyya" (Syrian Unity), *al-Athar al-Kamilah* (Complete Works). Vol. 1. Beirut: SSNP Cultural Bureau, n.d.: 4–16.

34 Antun Sa'adeh, *al-Muhadarat al-Ashr* (The Ten Lectures): 183.

35 Antun Sa'adeh, *Marahil al-Mas'alla al-Lubnaniyah* (The Stages of the Lebanese Question), 2nd ed. Beirut: Fikr Publications, 1991: 40.

36 Quoted in Inam Raad, *Antun Sa'adeh wa al-In'izaliyun* (Antun Sa'adeh and the Isolationists). Beirut: Fikr Publications, 1980: 54. The Phoenician thesis postulated the existence of a distinctive Lebanese national essence persisting from the Phoenician era to the present.

37 A. Sa'adeh, "The Maronites are Syriac Syrians," *al-Athar al-Kamilah* (Complete Works). Vol. 16. Beirut: SSNP Cultural Bureau, n.d.: 164.

38 See volume 3 of his *Complete Works*.

39 On Lebanese *zuama* politics see Arnold Hottinger, "Zu'ama and Parties in the Lebanese Crisis of 1958." *Middle East Journal* (1961): 85–103.

40 A. Sa'adeh, *al-Muhadarat al-Ashr* (The Ten Lectures): 38.

41 A. Sa'adeh, *Mukhtarat fi al-Mas'allah al-Lubnaniyyah* (Selected Works on the Lebanese Question). Beirut: Dar Fikr, 1978: 44.

42 Inam Raad, *Antun Sa'adeh wa al-In'izaliyun* (Antun Sa'adeh and the Isolationists). Beirut: Dar Fikr, 1980.

43 Raghid Solh, "The attitude of the Arab nationalists towards Greater Lebanon during the 1930s," in Nadim Shehadi and Dana Haffar Mills (eds.), *Lebanon: A History of Conflict and Consensus*. London: I. B. Tauris and Co Ltd, 1988: 152.

44 Ibid., 152.

45 Antun Sa'adeh, *al-Athar al-Kamilah* (Complete Works). Vol. 2. Beirut: SSNP Cultural Bureau, n.d.: 214.

46 A Lebanese nationalist party which endeavoured to establish a degree of organization and cohesion which older groups of Lebanese nationalism had not for the most part possessed. The party described itself as "a patriotic youth organization" and defined its aim as "the establishment of a Lebanese nation, conscious of its duties and rights in an independent and sovereign state." In practice, however, the majority of its adherents, like its leader, Pierre Jumayyel, were Maronites educated by the Jesuits. See The Phalanges Libanaise, *Statutes*, 1 July, 1938, Article 1. See also I. Rababi, "The Phalanges Libanaise: Its Aim and Organization," a speech delivered on 5 February, 1939.

47 A predominantly Moslem organization with Pan-Arab doctrines. Although in principle open to members of all religious communities and purporting to be a "national" organization operating above daily party politics (Articles 6 and 7 of the *Najjadah Basic Principles* (1937) forbid members of the organization from participating in national elections even in their personal capacities before resigning from it), in practice the Najjadah became the anti-thesis of the 'Phalanges Libanaise' among the Lebanese Muslims. Politically, the Najjadah did not oppose the existence of Lebanon as a separate national entity but, convinced that "Lebanon has the same duties and rights as all the other Arab countries," it tried to link it in the general movement for Arab union.

48 *The Syrian Bulletin*, no. 215.

49 *Oriente Moderno*, Vol. XVII, 1937: 231.

50 Labib Z. Yamak, *The Syrian Social Nationalist Party: An Ideological Analysis*. Harvard: Center for Middle Eastern Studies, 1969: 58.

51 Sa'adeh travelled overland to Jordan during which he met King Abdullah. The meeting was brief and fruitless apparently due to a personality conflict between the two men. Sa'adeh then crossed to Palestine and from there to Cyprus in the first leg of a long journey that would take him to Europe and South America. See John Daye, *Sa'adeh wa Hisham Sharabi* (Sa'adeh and Hisham Sharabi). Beirut: Dar Nelson, 2004: 31–32.

52 Albert Hourani, *Syria and Lebanon: A Political Essay*. Beirut: Librairie Du Liban, 1968: 230.

53 Gibran Jreige, *Haqa'iq Ain al-Istiqlal: Ayyam Rashayya*, 4th edition. Beirut: Dar Amwaj, 2000: 22. It is claimed that the party played a decisive role in getting el-Khoury elected to parliament for the Maronite seat in Mount Lebanon in view of its popularity in that constituency.

54 In fact, the only fatality in Lebanon's independence campaign was one Said Fakhr ad-Din, a partisan of Sa'adeh. In 1946, the Lebanese President, Beshara el-Khoury, issued a decree (K/9377) in which he recognized the SNP member Said Fakhr ad-Din as a martyr and awarded him the Medal of National Struggle (*Midaliyat al-Jihad al-Watani*). Ibid.: 33

55 See N. E. Bou Nakhlie, "Les Troupes Speciales: Religious and Ethnic Recruitment, 1916–1946." *International Journal of Middle East Studies*, Vol. 25, No. 4 (Nov. 1993): 645–660.

56 An unwritten agreement between el-Khoury and el-Solh, the National Pact aimed principally at consolidating Lebanon as an independent state within a power-sharing arrangement between the various sectarian groups. The main principles of the Pact were: (1) Lebanon was to be a completely independent state; (2) the Christian communities were to cease identifying with the West and, in return, the Muslim communities were to protect the independence of Lebanon and prevent its merger with any Arab state; (3) that Lebanon, though an Arab country, can still maintain its spiritual and intellectual ties with the West; (4) Lebanon, as a member of the family of Arab states, should cooperate with the other Arab states and remain neutral in conflicts among them; and (5) public offices should be distributed proportionally among the recognized religious groups. See Farid El-Khazen, *The Communal Pact of National Identities: The Making and Politics of the 1943 National Pact*. Oxford: Centre for Lebanese Studies, 1991.

57 Labib Z. Yamak, *The Syrian Social Nationalist Party: An Ideological Analysis*. Harvard: Center for Middle Eastern Studies, 1969: 61.

58 Fayez Sayegh, *The Greater Syria Scheme*. Beirut: The Syrian National Party Information Bureau, 6 December, 1946: 26.

2

CONFRONTATION

The Confrontation Reignites

In March 1947, after extensive lobbying at home and abroad, Sa'adeh was finally re-admitted into Lebanon. It is claimed that in giving assent to Sa'adeh's return, President Khoury expected to draw political capital from the SNP in the general elections which were scheduled in May of the same year.[1] However, upon his arrival, Sa'adeh foiled this plan by declaring all previous agreements between the SNP and the Lebanese government null and void. In a clean break with the political atmosphere of the day, he again questioned the meaning of Lebanon as an entity and its recently-acquired independence:

> The Lebanese entity! What is the real meaning of the Lebanese entity? Is it an iron mould in which thought in Lebanon can be placed to implode into itself? Or is it a sphere of safety, a point from which thought can proceed to diffuse brotherhood throughout the whole nation, to spread unity and unify ranks, and to unite the whole nation on a single future from which we refuse to deviate even by one hairbreadth.
>
> What is it that the Lebanese desire from their entity? Is it to have light all for themselves while the surrounding region can remain enshrouded in darkness? If there is light in Lebanon, it is only to be expected that this light should spread itself out throughout the whole of natural Syria. Could we accept that we Lebanon could have a light without all compatriots in our nation having a share in it? That can never be. [Pointing to the masses] This is the Lebanese entity and this is the authentic expression of the sublime feelings and the grand aims embodied in the Lebanese soul. Anything other than this is baseless. It does not represent Lebanon or the will of the Lebanese people at all.
>
> The Lebanese entity depends for its legitimization on the will of the Lebanese people. In all its positions, the party has demonstrated that, on this issue, it places the will of the people above every other

consideration. The fact that the party was ready to cooperate with the Lebanese Administrations in everything touching on issue of sovereignty, even in times when it disagreed with their internal policy, clearly shows that the party does not want to impose anything on the Lebanese people.[2]

Contrary to the assumption sometimes made about him, Sa'adeh did not consider the Lebanese State, even after its independence in 1943, as an enemy. It is clear from the aforesaid that he was concerned about post-independence rather than the destruction of the state. Those who had the opportunity to work closely with him deny that his attitude toward Lebanon was one of simple denunciation.[3] Rather, they describe him as a person who detested Lebanese confessional (or consensual) politics, but not Lebanon. He was against the system, not against the country. He saw the interests of Lebanon better served in union rather than separation and foresaw great tribulations for Lebanon under sectarian separatism.[4] Despite that, he supported the independence movement in Lebanon in so far as independence served larger national aims. He preferred an independent Lebanon to the mandate but not a separate Lebanon to a unified Syria.

Meantime, Sa'adeh's diatribes against the state of independence in Lebanon were judged both by the government and Lebanese nationalists as distasteful. He was summoned to appear before the *Sûreté Générale* to answer "a few questions," although the real objective was to denigrate him. For the next two months Sa'adeh was to stand at the very centre of one of the longest disputes with the central state. Acting on the advice of his aides, he fled to the mountains above Beirut and skillfully turned his indictment against the government. From his "hideout" within walking distance of security forces tracking his movement, he issued a public statement clarifying the substance of his speech:

> I declared in my speech that I regard the independence that this entity has obtained as a preliminary step that must be built upon to make it an effective force, not an isolated weakling. But the provocateurs turned my views around to make it sound as though I meant that your entity is the preliminary step. There is a world of difference between what I said and what these provocateurs have claimed.[5]

Consequently, Sa'adeh found himself sucked into a whirlpool of activity and involved in endless meetings and writing editorials, appeals, manifestos, and giving press interviews. The officer-in-charge of the manhunt, Farid Chehab, staked Sa'adeh's office from "a house on the opposite side"[6] but refrained from arresting him "because I was convinced that it was in Lebanon's best interest not to arrest him at that stage. His arrest, according to my assessment of the situation, would have created problems of which Lebanon stood in no need."[7] The political leadership in Lebanon had other ideas, but it was not very daring. A statement issued by Sa'adeh to the French News Agency in Beirut on 6 March was suppressed, but little else was done to ensnare him. Sensitive to voters' response, the government must have become increasingly aware that pursuing Sa'adeh any further could irritate the general public. Yet it did not want to be seen as losing ground or defeated.

The tit-for-tat game between the authorities and Sa'adeh lasted until the May elections. Putting the dispute with the government on hold, Sa'adeh spared no effort to participate, devoting most of his time and resources to the election campaign. He did not run for election himself but his supporters took part in most constituencies. In issuing the Policy Platform for the elections, Sa'adeh chose to widen the usual debate on reforms to focus on policy objectives that looked more broadly to issues concerned with independence and state building. He re-affirmed his commitment to Lebanon "as a sphere of safety for the strugglers and battlers"[8] but refused to put local issues ahead of Syria's national concerns. The door on compromise slammed even tighter.

Far from showmanship, the elections turned into one of the most fraudulent elections in Lebanon's history.[9] The SNP under Sa'adeh failed to win any seats but was consoled by the wide public denunciation of the results. In the light of the rigging, Sa'adeh declared the next day that the elections were "a mere exercise to maintain a group of irresponsible and totally individualistic politicians in power."[10] The comment was not taken lightly by the government, which renewed the search for him with a large reward for his delivery "dead or alive." Not many Lebanese were enthused by the offer and took it as a mere public relations exercise to deflect attention away from the rigging controversy.

Undeterred, Sa'adeh hit back in characteristic fashion with a public proclamation that amounted almost to a declaration of war:

In this difficult hour and amidst this great chaos, salvation is still possible. But it depends on your willingness to partake in it. Don't be deceived by falsehood! Salvation will not come about by voting out a group of selfish politicians and voting in another group of selfish and reactionary politicians. Salvation comes when the self-seekers and reactionaries in power step down and, equally, when the self-seekers and reactionaries who covet power for themselves are defeated.[11]

Tough and frank, the rhetoric stirred the curiosity of many sophisticated listeners and erudite cynics, but it didn't give Sa'adeh any more than valuable coverage in the local press. The government responded with a barrage of propaganda reminiscent of French days. Its newspapers in Beirut began to smear Sa'adeh as a British agent and to publish false reports about his location, claiming at one point that he had secretly slipped away to Jordan.[12] Rumors also circulated that his grip over the SNP was waning. Others claimed that Sa'adeh was planning an armed attack on the government. Still calm and politic, Sa'adeh coped with the renewed attack on his person not too differently from the way he had dealt with earlier clashes with the French.[13]

The psychological war between the two sides persisted for several more months. Neither scored any stunning victories but within the wider spectrum of opinions, including those of loyalists, Sa'adeh clearly edged ahead for standing firm on what he believed in. There is no record that he ever lost his temper and he seldom refused invitations to speak. The government, too, refused to buckle and kept the pressure up. It was left to independent mediators to work out a solution acceptable to both sides. A breakthrough was finally achieved in October whereby the government agreed to withdraw the warrant of arrest against Sa'adeh in exchange for a formal pledge from the SNP leader to uphold the sanctity of the Lebanese entity within its existing borders. Although the pledge failed to meet the President's demand for "unconditional loyalty," it served its purpose, and the bickering subsided.[14]

A New Dimension: Zaim's Rise to Power

Early in November 1947 a confrontation with the government was averted at the last minute after Sa'adeh agreed to cancel a planned demonstration against the partition of Palestine. Unable to resist the temptation, the following day he issued a carefully conceived statement against the government:

> We never thought that the Lebanese government would stand as a stumbling bloc between the nation and its cause on this day. However, it appears that private considerations were more important and more precious than the nation's cause. The government, it seems, has preferred to gamble with the nation's cause than give up its exclusive stance and witness in the flesh the masses rallying behind the social national renaissance. We declare right here that this stance [of the government] will not in any way influence the ongoing struggle between us and reaction, which wants to keep the nation steeped in its feudal decadence.[15]

Following the UN partition resolution of 29 November 1947, Sa'adeh stepped up his oratory against the "selfish reactionary regimes" of the Arabs. He shaped his rhetoric according to the exacting requirements of the situation and, matching words with deeds, placed his followers in a "state of war" for Palestine. Conscription started promptly and weapons were sought from various quarters to arm the fledging militia. This caused grave apprehension in Beirut and raised the prospect of having to deal with a combative SNP in the event of defeat. Under the banner "No Arms to the Social Nationalists," the government blocked the flow of military weapons to his followers and tried to silence him by banning his newspaper *al-Jil al-Jadid*. However, Sa'adeh continued to repeat, rephrase, adapt, and supplement his political articles using sympathetic newspapers like *Kul Shay* to get his message across. He met repeated thrusts from the government, but he refused to budge from his ideological position vis-à-vis the Lebanese state. In October 1948 he harked back to his homecoming speech likening the independence of the country to life "behind the great wall that surrounds the complex of the prison erected by foreigners."[16] He added sarcastically, "The foreigner has never left us. He has merely backed away just like when a cat backs away from a mouse to entertain itself: as long as the mouse is within sight of the cat it remains under its control."[17] Soon afterwards, intelligence reports of an SNP plan to overthrow the regime by force began to reach the Premier's desk. The so-called plan clearly did not imply operative or concrete ideas, but Sa'adeh's warlike oratory created grave concerns.

Believing in the reality of the plot, the government tried to shut out the SNP.[18] Its effort was frustrated by Husni az-Zaim's rise to power in Syria on 30 March, 1949[19] which caused an immediate schism between Sa'adeh and the Khoury regime. False news reports that the Syrian coup was masterminded by SNP officers in the Syrian Army sent cold shivers throughout the Lebanese Establishment. The suspicion deepened after Zaim announced a reform program for Syria based upon but by no means identical to Sa'adeh's reform doctrines.[20] No doubt the ex-SNP Akram Hourani had a strong hand in the way it was devised but few knew that. The timing of the coup was also crucial. It came hot on the heels of rumors that Fawzi al-Qawakji, the field commander of the Arab Liberation Army during the 1948 Arab-Israeli War, had plotted to link up with SNP army officers in Lebanon and Syria as part of a wider assault on Arab regimes.[21] "In this way," explained Taha Hashimi, "Qawuqji believed that the movement will result in the unification of the Arab countries and the establishment of a republic. Then he will attack the Jews and push them out of Palestine."[22] Suddenly, the prospect of an SNP takeover in Lebanon seemed very real.

The temperature of the Lebanese regime would have shot higher if it had known what Sa'adeh was planning. On April 10, following the announcement of Zaim's reform program, Sa'adeh secretly instructed the party's Damascus Chapter (*mounafadhiyyah*) to contact Zaim and offer him "all the material and moral potentials at [the party's] disposal."[23] Despite concentrated intelligence monitoring of Sa'adeh, the overture was not picked up by the Lebanese government or by the press in either Lebanon or Syria. A week or so later, a two-man SNP delegation turned up at the Presidential palace with a memorandum but it was not allowed to meet Zaim in person.[24] The memorandum was carelessly, or perhaps deviously, bundled away by the staff and the matter ended there. Three weeks later another opportunity arose. On 9 May, a Syrian army intelligence officer entered southern Lebanon in broad daylight and killed a Lebanese civilian suspected of spying for Israel. His subsequent capture and imprisonment by the Lebanese sparked a crisis and led to the closure of borders between the two countries.[25] While the local Syrian and Lebanese press traded accusations, Sa'adeh set up a legal taskforce inside the party to review the incident. Its key findings and recommendations, published in *al-Jil al-Jadid* on 22 May, came out strongly in favour of the Syrians because, at the time of the incident:

1. There was no formal treaty between Syria and Lebanon on cross-border disputes;
2. The "artificial foreign-designed" borders between the two countries were imprecise and had no clear demarcation lines or points. Therefore, there was no way for the assailants to distinguish between Syrian and Lebanese territories;
3. Lebanon and Syria were still, technically, in a state of war with Israel;
4. Kamal Hussein's treachery was detrimental to both countries;
5. Treason falls under military and not civilian jurisdiction;
6. Neighbourly wellbeing and security should prevail over local considerations in such circumstances.

At other times, that might have gone unnoticed, but now the situation had become too critical. On reading the report, Zaim's senior adviser Sabri Qubbani sent him a copy of *al-Jil al-Jadid* in hopes of catching his attention. A self-confessed Arab nationalist, Qubbani was a moderate, pragmatic bureaucrat who admired the discipline and dedication of the SNP and its leader. Although he monitored his duties and assumed, as much as was possible, an impersonal role, the pressures of increasing responsibilities, burdensome decisions, and Zaim's disrupting behaviour motivated his sensitive reserve. When he realized that the SNP legal document had failed to strike a responsive chord with Zaim, he proceeded physically to set up a meeting between Sa'adeh and his leader:

> I walked in on Zaim in his office in the General Staff. He was agitated, fuming with rage. He said, "Riad, that son of a . . ., is stalling the release of Tabarah. I swear I will turn his life into hell. I will seize every Lebanese vehicle and turn Lebanon upside down. Pack your things right away. I am sending you over to Beirut with a letter to so-and-so." I said, "Excuse me, but I don't see how these measures can be practical. No one will benefit from this rupture and conflict with Lebanon except the Jews. What's more, negotiations with the Lebanese are still in progress.[26]

In his recollections, Qubbani mentioned the event with a tremendous sense of pride and gratification. Speaking for the most part from the third-person point of view and casting his questions in a nonpersonal vein, he proceeded to ask Zaim: "Did you read the party's legal memorandum that I sent to you? Were you to ask our leading legal experts to explain our point of view, we would not be able to come up with a memorandum nearly as good as theirs."[27] Then he dropped a sweetener: "Had you taken any interest in the SNP," he told Zaim, "we wouldn't have this Tabarah crisis today."[28] Appearing surprised by this demonstration, Zaim responded with a counter-offer, "Is it possible for meet to see Sa'adeh in person tomorrow?" Qubbani retorted "Let it be the day after tomorrow, Friday, for it will be a holiday and you will have ample time to discuss matters with him at length. You can meet him in your private home away from prying eyes."[29] And so it was. Sa'adeh arrived in the Syrian capital on Friday morning after secretly crossing the Syrian-Lebanese borders. He was flanked by party officials. But Zaim's impulsiveness got the better of him and the meeting had to be rescheduled:

> At exactly seven and a half in the morning, on Friday 27 May, I was climbing the stairs of Zaim's house. I was alone . . . When he opened the door for me I found him standing upright and dressed in full military uniform, holding his gloves and cane, as if he was ready to leave. I greeted him with astonishment on my face, "Where to? We have a meeting with Mr . . . He looked at his watch and said, "Right, true. I have half an hour left; hurry and come back along with him. I am leaving to the front with the ministers at exactly eight." I said, "Allow me to remind you, sir, that Sa'adeh is not like other men, and that this historical meeting may have an impact on the policies of Syria, if not the entire Middle East. It would be inappropriate to meet with him in a rush. Let's hold the meeting tonight at eight in the evening after you have completed the tour at the front.[30]

Qubbani was decidedly embarrassed, but his crusading momentum was too great for him to stop without first accomplishing at least one meeting between Sa'adeh and Zaim. With Syria on the brink, he opined that a meeting between the two men was essential not only to their own survival but also to the vital interest of Syria. At Sa'adeh's temporary residence, Qubbani launched into a tirade against Zaim and spoke at length about his obnoxious and dubious character. Describing Zaim as "a man not like other men"[31] he cautioned Sa'adeh about Zaim's polemical excesses and his inclination to leap hastily to foolish conclusions: "I do not think you have met anyone like the coup leader; he is one of a kind, peculiar and impulsive. Words such as nationalism, patriotism, doctrines and principles have never found their way to his heart or carved out a space in his mind."[32] Then he dropped an important piece of advice: "To succeed in your mission, I hope you will listen to his nonsense and bragging no matter how long it takes . . . From the start parade your strength and the strength of your party, for he believes in power only, and respects only those with forceful appearances."[33] The oration was quite dramatic but Sa'adeh remained "calm and cheery".[34] Like others now and then, he found it difficult to imagine that such a man could be so obnoxious. Zaim, with his dash and reform mind, fit his image of a statesman much more readily, despite his long-time ill-concealed pattern of misconduct. Sa'adeh, therefore, chose to remain more broadly focused on the positive side of the regime.

That evening the meeting between Sa'adeh and Zaim went ahead, oddly enough, without a hitch. After a brief stint, Sa'adah launched himself with an oration on the coup but the immediate focal point of his address was the apparent corruption and ineffectuality of the traditional regimes. For the moment, the pressing objective for Sa'adeh was to try to win Zaim's favour and to build a rapport of some sort with him. According to Qubbani, who met both men separately after the meeting, the discussion was concise, constructive and free of ceremonial niceties.[35] Zaim did not attempt to emotionalize the issues or claim too much for himself (probably because the Front tour that day had tired him out) and Sa'adeh walked away satisfied by the positive and unusually conciliatory tone of the Syrian leader. Contrary to press reports, which appeared several days later, the question of armed revolution was not raised during the meeting. Nor was there mention of a coup d'état in Lebanon, as was widely rumoured. The two men agreed to combine their resources against the Lebanese government, but no definite program for accomplishing this objective was laid:

> Sa'adah pledged to prepare the people and to stir up public opinion against the Lebanese government, enlisting for this purpose the power of his party and its potentials. In return, the coup leader vowed to support the party at the international and the Arab League levels and across natural Syria. Furthermore, the two parties agreed that Lebanon should remain a republic until such time the vital foundations of the two countries – single foreign representation, a unified military defense system, and the consideration of both

countries as a single economic cycle – have developed sufficiently [for a union].[36]

The meeting was secret and discreet, as intended. All three, Qubbani, Sa'adeh, and Zaim understood its essential value and, indeed, vowed to respect its secrecy. However, Zaim's egocentricity shot up quickly and he began to boast about the meeting to his foreign minister, Adel Arslan.[37] The following day, Arslan turned up in Beirut to give Solh the lowdown. The Lebanese Premier reacted aggressively to the point of hysteria and quickly sought to contain the situation. That took two forms: internally, he moved rapidly to reconcile his *de facto* party, an-Najjadah, with its antithesis, the Phalange, in a bid to create a common front against the SNP; and, externally, he appealed for help to Egypt and Saudi Arabia and started, for the first time, to send positive signals to Zaim to draw the Syrian leader away from Sa'adeh. By his own admission, Solh also convened an emergency session of the Security Council (*majlis al-amen*) in Lebanon to debate the future of the SNP and the kind of punitive action to take against its adherents.[38]

The Jummaizeh Incident

The mounting distrust between Sa'adeh and the Lebanese government exploded at Jummaizeh on 9 June, 1949. The details are not altogether clear. It started when Sa'adeh turned up at a building in the Jummaizeh district of Beirut, to which the editorial offices of the SNP newspaper *Al-Jil Al-Jadid* had recently moved, just as a Phalange meeting was getting underway in a café situated on the opposite side. Yussef Salameh, who was at Sa'adeh's side, recalls:

> We climbed the short stairway to the first level, taking everyone by surprise. Sa'adeh then walked into a vacant office after asking everyone there for a short intermission in order to write an article for the forthcoming issue of the newspaper. Hisham [Sharabi] and I waited with the others in the sitting area, which was spacious. About half an hour later we heard a loud roar from the café on the other side of the street. A party member, who was waiting in the room with us, was quick to point out that the café was owned by a Phalange sympathizer and that pictures of Pierre Jummayel adorned its front-windows on all sides. A few minutes later the clamor increased and with it the level of defiance and abuse.[39]

No sooner had Sa'adeh finished his weekly article than an SNP military officer pulled up in front of the building accompanied by five armed men. They lined up in military fashion and gave him the party salute as he walked back to his car. Intimidated, the throng of armed Phalange sympathizers gathered in front of the café and on the main street opened fire and stormed the building. In the confusion that followed, several members of the SNP were injured, but Sa'adeh escaped unharmed. According to Hisham Sharabi, the Lebanese Gendarmerie arrived belatedly on the scene and arrested the SNP members instead of the attackers![40] The printing press owner, Michel Faddoul, recalls that his brother "called the fire brigade, the police, the local gendarmerie office for help, but in vain because the lines were down on orders from the Prime Minister, Riad Bey."[41]

As news of the incident spread, SNP adherents gathered at Sa'adeh's house "I remember Sa'adeh walking down the stairway of his house calmly, deliberately, and with a wrinkle on his forehead. I remember him making his way through the large crowd in the front garden and around his house with the smile of a confident man."[42] The incident confirmed the existence of a government plot against Sa'adeh and the SNP, but the government denied the allegation despite massive press criticism. Soon afterwards, the Lebanese Premier inadvertently announced to the press that "the government had made all the preparations to dissolve this party [SNP] and had fixed the deadline for the previous Saturday. But the Jummaizeh incident which took place the previous Thursday, that is 48 hours before the deadline, forced us to bring the dissolution order forward and to promptly begin the process of purging."[43]

There are still many questions that have never been fully answered regarding the incident at Jummaizeh, particularly the question *was it premeditated*? One view is that it was a spontaneous clash but the government capitalized on it for its own good:

> . . . the government may well have wanted to exploit the tension between the Phalanges and the PPS [SNP] in order to work for the elimination of the latter. But it must be remembered that the Phalanges, though generally cooperating with Khuri, were opponents of Sulh. So were the leaders of the PPS who, ever since the advent of Za'im, had blamed Sulh for conspiring against them. At that particular time, the Phalanges were also critical of Khuri, accusing

him of having used the government to throw its weight against their candidates in Beirut in the 1947 elections (and even once before, in the 1945 by-elections in the Biqa). Moreover, in the wake of the June incident, the government had some fifty Phalanges men arrested. The regime's relations with the Phalanges became even more tense after a second major incident, which occurred on 18 July 1949, this time involving the Phalanges and a group of communist port workers in Beirut.[44]

The alternative view is that the government had foreknowledge of the incident and possibly direct involvement in its planning and execution. It rejects any overtly political interpretation of the incident as highly speculative, particularly where unconscious motivations may have played a larger than usual role. Pointing to the government's disproportionate response to the belligerent parties, proponents of this view see the incident more as a sequence in an unfolding cycle of violence and suspicion rather than as an isolated event. It was part of a general pattern in which the conspiracy was orchestrated by the government "which withdrew its security forces from the place at the zero hour, according to information leaked out by concerned parties."[45] Naturally, a panicking government that has already decided the fate of its adversary is not one that would wait around patiently for a pretext to emerge to make its move: it creates the pretext.

Following the incident at Jummaizeh orders went out to security forces to track down Sa'adeh. The government justified its action on the ground that Sa'adeh was preparing a massive armed coup against the regime. It gave no further details about the plot except to say that the SNP leader had "a systematic plan" to stir up internal riots as preparatory to a military takeover. Recently acquired documents reveal a more somber view of the so-called plan.[46] At any rate, Sa'adeh escaped before the Lebanese Gendarmerie arrived at his house and arrested whoever was there. He spent the next few days moving about the Lebanese capital until he made his way to Alley in the Shouf. At some point in this escapade he received a signal from Zaim to come back to Syria. The details are unclear. The message was conveyed to him through Major Toufiq Bashur, a senior officer in the Syrian army and a personal friend of Sa'adeh, who in turn enlisted the help of a party member, Najib Bulus, to reach the SNP leader. Bulus later recounted:

As I drove to Beirut I noticed a Lebanese Security vehicle following me from a distance. In Beirut I contacted comrade Elias Saad, a relative, and asked him to meet me at once . . . the meeting took place at Café Mansour. Again I noticed a Lebanese Security Patrol near my car. I asked Saad to find out for me Sa'adeh's whereabouts. A short time later he returned with an answer but forgot to bring with him the password that I would require to state to see Sa'adeh. I said to him "stay put to deceive the security patrol outside. I will leave from the Café's backdoor."[47]

Bulus goes on to say:

I took the first taxi to al-Hadath and got out at mid point in the street where the building was situated. When I approached the entrance the guards called out "stop, stop." I said "Long live Syria. I am comrade Najib Bulus. I am here to see Sa'adeh." When the guards asked for the password I replied, "I don't know it." But Sa'adeh, who knew me, heard my voice and instructed the guards to let me in. I found him sitting in a small and shabby room. He asked me "What news do you bring me?" I conveyed to him the message that I had been asked to deliver by Major Bashur. He said "Are you certain it was Major Bashur who gave you this message?" "Yes," I replied. He then said: "Inform the Major that I agree to the meeting and to start making arrangements." He thanked me and implored me to take care on the way back.[48]

Sa'adeh arrived in Damascus on 14 June. Several conjectures have been offered as to how he crossed into Syria but the most widely accepted one is that when he arrived at the Lebanese border checkpoint the driver occupied the attending officers with the necessary paperwork while Sa'adeh slipped across on foot over a side hill. Once the car crossed into the vacant stretch that separates the Lebanese checkpoint from the Syrian checkpoint, Sa'adeh strolled down to the main highway and climbed back. The attending officer at the Syrian checkpoint turned out to be an SNP member and instantly passed the vehicle through.[49]

Sabri Qubbani was among the first to welcome Sa'adeh. "He was sitting in a private section of the room with two army officers. The three of them, dressed in khaki shirts and khaki pants and with hair unkempt, appeared to be in a state of emergency. They were sitting around a large table covered with pieces of paper and letters."[50] Although outwardly calm, Sa'adeh was akin to a volcano waiting to erupt. Two days later,

Zaim scheduled an evening meeting at his private residence but later changed it to the General Staff Office. Qubbani attributed the eleventh-hour venue change to Zaim's desire "to parade his power and supremacy at work before Sa'adeh. He wanted to lure Sa'adeh into his den where the military police, armed with Tommy Guns, cram the place, on the stairs and behind doors so that if he hollers the walls would shudder at his thunderous voice."[51] Qubbani knew Zaim like the back of his hand and keenly shared his thoughts with Sa'adeh. While waiting their turn to see Zaim, he made several crucial observations to Sa'adeh which the latter took with him to the meeting.

Predictably, Zaim put on a remarkable act to impress his guest. "Welcome. Thank God you are safe"[52] he said before launching into a tirade against the Khoury regime. Sa'adeh was more cautious. He assured the Syrian leader that all earlier reports of an SNP plot to overthrow the regime in Lebanon were idle talk and that the weapons confiscated by the Lebanese army in the previous days "were ordinary weapons of the kind you would expect to find in Lebanese villages."[53] Describing the occasion as a "historic meeting," Qubbani also confirmed that the two men discussed security arrangements, including the flow of arms and ammunitions, but insisted that it was strictly for deterrent purposes:

> Sa'adah did not want to raise weapons in the face of the Lebanese regime. The idea never even occurred to him, and so he never prepared for that day . . . Five hundred guns with their ammunition were enough to stop [the Lebanese regime] from pursuing its virulent campaign against the party without even needing to use them.[54]

Contrary to the impression sometimes given in the press and other publications, Sa'adeh's primary concern was to break the cordon around his supporters in Lebanon, not to topple the regime. The thought of party members made homeless, jailed and atrociously tortured in Lebanon troubled him every step along the way. His words to Qubbani are revealing:

> My only concern right now is for the party members who have been banished or arrested and the torture they are enduring. Some have their lost their businesses and had to close down for the sake of their beliefs; others have fallen while trying to escape with

party documents containing members names and other matters. I hope to God we succeed and triumph after all the enormous sacrifices we have made.[55]

Already an independent report published by *an-Nahar* immediately after the Jummaizeh clash had adjudged his party's ammunition and weapons cache as hardly regime-threatening.[56] Yet, the Lebanese government continued to insist that this one shortcoming did not diminish the value of the remaining evidence, which was ample to prove Sa'adeh guilty.

Meanwhile, Zaim responded to his guest with outlandish offers of "weapons and ammunition on a large scale as soon as a truce with the Jews is signed."[57] He vowed to remain a loyal friend "to the very end"[58] and indeed presented Sa'adeh with his own personal pistol as a token of their friendship. As the two men rose to their feet, Zaim offered his guest the protection of his security guards but the SNP leader politely declined the offer. Instructions then went out to Qubbani to act as a liaison officer with Sa'adeh and to Colonel Ibrahim al-Husseini, Zaim's Chief of Security, to look after the logistics.

On the surface, the meeting was both constructive and businesslike. It was much more relaxed and well-intended than the first meeting and provided a promise for further progress. Sa'adeh got his wish and the promise of Syrian support against the Lebanese regime and Zaim gained an ally and relative bargaining strength vis-à-vis his Lebanese foes. The outlook for Sa'adeh looked even rosier as the deal concretized:

> I bid [Sa'adeh] goodbye and headed straight to Lieutenant Colonel al-Husseini. He was a very hard man to catch . . . The moment I phoned him, he dropped everything and the two of us headed in his car to Sa'adeh's headquarters. Every now and then I would point the driver in the right direction . . . It turned out, by sheer coincidence, that Sa'adeh's headquarters was situated not far from the Colonel's own house. On the way, I briefly explained to al-Husseini the gravity of the mission and the importance of the party and the scope of its movement as well as its impact on the future of Arab unity and national duty, which is an incentive for us to extend help as far as we possibly can . . . I left, confident that things were moving steadily toward the target we all held in common.[59]

While the SNP looked hopefully for new revelations which it supposed would finally yield decisive proof of its innocence, Sa'adeh took the offensive yet again, with a sensational new expose that poured more fuel on the raging fire.[60] More than that, Sa'adeh now sought to re-draw the battle lines with the Khoury regime: "At this stage in the war that the Lebanese Government has declared, trampling over the most sacred principles of national life, I dare the government to accept the following challenge: to pick out a time and place for a single decisive battle between the power of the [Syrian] National Party and that of the government and its sectarian allies using all the weapons kept with its army but allowing the officers and regular soldiers to choose between fighting or not fighting the [Syrian] National Party."[61]

The expose was widely circulated among party members in Syria and Lebanon. Smuggling it into Lebanon wasn't difficult[62] and brought with it swift retaliation from the Lebanese government. The government took the statement "as evidence that the party's strength was intact and that its campaign against it had failed to undermine the party or sap its power."[63] Predictably, the security forces of the state were unleashed on suspected SNP pockets resulting in the arrest of many more. In the process one party member was reported killed and the house of another was burned to the ground after it was ransacked.

Critics were not amused. They adjudged the renewed drive against the Syrian nationalists as a potent ingredient of the government's failure to contain Sa'adeh and questioned the utility of using strong-arm tactics while Zaim was courting Sa'adeh. The press was equally disappointed and ruthlessly disparaged the government. *Al-Sayyad* wrote:

> The plan was supposed to be carried out with precision, and Antun Sa'adeh was supposedly heading the list of those to be arrested, especially given that he had been under close surveillance from the moment the Security Council had decided [to dissolve the SNP]. Yet what took place was, in every sense, inexplicable. Antun Sa'adeh, George Abdul Massih, and other party cadres have managed to escape, despite the secrecy that was maintained and Sa'adeh's presence in Beirut, and at Al-Jumaizzah in particular, the night he fled.[64]

An-Nahar dropped a bigger bombshell by reporting in bold print that the government had been unable to find a single pertinent document implicating Sa'adeh in a plot to overthrow the regime.[65] The so-called plot apparently amounted to little more than consultations with Lebanese army officers in broad daylight, hardly a plan to overthrow the regime.

To a large extent, it consisted simply of encouraging public discontent to force the regime to step down.[66] Less helpful was the booty seized from SNP offices: a short instructional manual "on what course of action party members should follow in the event of a military coup or a revolution."[67] No weapons of significant value or quantity were discovered.

The Charge of Treason

Suddenly, it seemed necessary to do something if the pretense of central authority and that of government righteousness were to be maintained. Official and private investigations went on fitfully, but neither turned up much.[68] Incredibly, no effort was made to consider alternative solutions even as both sides traded invectives. The persistence and passion with which each side maintained its arguments now mattered just as much as the arguments themselves. With Sa'adeh on the offensive and local critics not far off, the government came up with a novel idea reminiscent of the famous *bordereau* in the Dreyfus Affair in France almost fifty years before. It made the incredible claim that Sa'adeh was an Israeli collaborator and that, in exchange for Jewish support, he had passed very important and sensitive military information about the Arab campaign in Palestine. In the political context of the day, it was a most sensational allegation. The government made the denunciation public with all the fanfare of an espionage scandal claiming that it had crushing proof. On June 20, it published the text of a letter containing specific instructions from Sa'adeh to his aide-de-camp in Haifa, Muhammad Jamil Yunis, to contact the Israelis and ask for financial and military assistance. The next day the Public Prosecutor gave the claim a cloak of judicial legality by formally charging Sa'adeh with subversion. The indictment against Sa'adeh contained three astonishing claims:

1. That Sa'adeh had sought help from a foreign state and that this state now was Israel.
2. That "the purpose was not merely to stage a military coup in Lebanon and seize the reins of power in it, but also to undermine the Syrian state and Husni Zaim in particular on account of his firm stand against the Zionists."
3. That "the contact [between Sa'adeh and the Israelis] reached the point of an actual treaty whereby Israel agreed to supply

[43]

the party with weapons and funds to carry out a military coup
in Lebanon and destabilize the Zaim regime in Syria."[69]

Now the Sa'adeh case created an enormous uproar, with the many
anti-SNP newspapers and politicians screaming about treason. Even
those who did not scream much about the SNP were generally still
strident about the treason and its irresolute prosecution. They knew
little about the charges and the evidence, but this did not matter: loyalist
newspapers daily published further details of supposed evidence, retelling
as factual the rumours then current. When rumours did not suffice,
fresh stories were invented by the ever imaginative press. Outside
government circles, the publication of the letter caused a stir and led to
speculation about its authenticity. Making the most of so sensational a
story, the popular daily *an-Nahar* published an elaborate review of the
indictment. It found no single item of substantial evidential value in it
and doubted if the relevant documents, especially the supposed treaty
between Sa'adeh and the Israelis, could be produced.[70] The paper stopped
short of dismissing the letter as a hoax, if only for the sake of circulation.
Other newspapers and public forums then entered the fray and the issue
became an occasion for attention-getting for the government.

Meanwhile, Sa'adeh considered the matter so urgent that he drafted
a reply and dispatched it to the Arab News Agency, which in turn cabled
it to its Cairo office for broadcasting on Arab radio stations and for
circulation to affiliated newspapers.[71] The dispatch was not published,
most likely at the behest of the Egyptian government.[72] Eventually,
the Damascene daily *al-Alam* published a shorter version of it with a
supplementary foreword from Qubbani "to divert attention away from
Sa'adeh's location."[73] Its content was robust, declaring in the most
categorical terms the letter as a gross forgery.[74]

As the Lebanese debated the treason charge against Sa'adeh, directed
towards confirming or refuting the authenticity of the purported letter,
Solh actively sought ways to clear the air with Damascus. He enlisted the
help of Saudi Arabia and Egypt and began to make positive overtures to
the Syrian leader.[75] With their suspicions already aroused by the presence
of Sa'adeh in Damascus, the Saudi and Egyptian governments reciprocated
by bringing their own pressure to bear on Zaim.[76] The man entrusted
with the task of swaying Zaim was Muhsin al-Barrazi, the then Syrian
ambassador in Cairo. He returned to Syria at the behest of King Faruq

to coordinate the talks. Barrazi was Solh's brother-in-law. A gullible dupe and a facile manipulator of words, he was close to the ruling families in both Egypt and Saudi Arabia. Mohammad Fadhel Jamali in his *Experiences in Arab Affairs* describes him as "the one who feeds the Egyptian papers with the help of Saudi money."[77] Barrazi was prolific in his new role. Within days of his arrival he managed to draw Zaim away from the Greater Syria concept and into the Egyptian-Saudi bloc. The Damascene newspaper, *an-Nasr*, in its issue of 22 June, quoted the Syrian leader as saying:

> I want to make it clear that the Greater Syria project has become out of date for two reasons. First, the rapid progress and the industrial and agricultural improvement which Syria will enjoy shortly will open a deep gap between Syria and the Hashimite governments. Secondly, I have decided to join the Saudi-Egyptian camp because those two kingdoms have demonstrated extreme friendship, assistance, and nobility toward new Syria. It is my opinion that this strong unity between Syria, Egypt and Saudi Arabia will be a strong front against the Greater Syria project.[78]

This was no doubt a crucial setback for Sa'adeh. Again he solicited Qabbani's help to "get some explanation for things that no longer seemed to make sense to him"[79] but to no avail. Zaim procrastinated in order to avoid any more meetings with him: "No sooner than I would broach Sa'adah's request [for a meeting] he would change the topic and ask me to put off the whole thing until after the referendum."[80] The resulting break in communication with the regime created all sorts of problems for Sa'adeh, which Lieutenant al-Husseini further exacerbated by breaking off all contacts with the SNP. Al-Husseini's silence added ominous undertones to the situation. The crisis really hit home when Zaim issued his orders to dissolve all political parties in Syria ahead of the plebiscite on 25 June. Despite repeated requests to spare the SNP from the dissolution order, in acknowledgement of previous commitments, its offices across Syria were shut down and its members were subjected to serious transgressions: "News arrived from some provinces that local authorities there have gone to extremes in pursuing party members and bearing down heavily on them. Even members' private houses were raided and shut down."[81] Zaim "had turned into a totally different man."[82]

Unbeknown to Sa'adeh, Zaim was all that time in the Lebanese town of Shtura trying to thrash out a secret deal with his Lebanese counterparts, Khoury and Solh. According to *an-Nahar*, Sa'adeh was an item on the meeting's agenda, but the paper gave no further details.[83] However, "it has been variously suggested that the Lebanese Premier, Riyad al-Sulh, 'bought' him from Za'im and that Egypt was induced to put pressure on the Syrian dictator to hand him over."[84] Andrew Rathmell, in his *Secret War in the Middle East*, posits the issue in a somewhat inverted manner:

> The SSNP has always claimed that Egypt's King Faruq first encouraged Sulh to move against the SSNP and then pressured Za'im to hand him over. The reason, the party argues, was Sa'adah's opposition to the armistice accords with Israel. In this view, Sa'adah 'paid . . . the price of the Israeli-Arab armistice accords'. Although Sa'adah's opposition to the armistice talks may not have been the motive, it does appear that the SSNP's accusations are accurate. The Egyptian establishment's hostility to Sa'adah is shown by the fact that even two years after Sa'adah's execution, the Egyptian commentator Muhammad Heikal sought to blacken the party's name by claiming that Sa'adah had agreed with Israel in 1948 to mount a coup in Lebanon.[85]

Curiously, after the plebiscite, Zaim asked Qubbani never to "bring [Sa'adeh] here. He should never appear in public. The Lebanese are seriously demanding him. I deny that he is in Syria, but they have spies planted everywhere. I hate to create a crisis now that they have agreed to release Tabarah and reluctantly to recognize me and my government."[86] It was an oblique admission that the deal with the Lebanese had included Sa'adeh, but it proves that Zaim was disinclined at that stage to give him up. Perhaps he was buying time to force Sa'adeh out of Syria.

While Zaim procrastinated, his newly-appointed Prime Minister, Muhsin al-Barrazi, struck hard. Al-Barrazi cancelled all previous commitments to Sa'adeh "due to delays in Syrian-Israeli truce talks"[87] and issued a ministerial directive to Syrian newspapers via the publications department to launch into the SNP.[88] Sa'adeh was placed under tight surveillance and al-Barrazi's private security unit started to collect background information and intelligence data about the SNP. This information, according to Qubbani, was passed on to the Lebanese government without Zaim's knowledge.[89] Al-Barrazi also aroused questions in Zaim's mind about the danger that Sa'adeh represented and the risk he ran to his own regime by arming the SNP.

The situation took another turn for the worse when the local security forces rounded up SNP members in the northern Latakia district ahead of a planned party assault on Lebanon. Sa'adeh was in the Syrian capital at the time working on a plan of action against the Lebanese regime and grappling with recent developments. By all accounts he was privy to everything around him but resisted all appeals, from inside and outside the party, to change trajectory. Finally, on Saturday, 2 July, he broke his silence to Qubbani:

> The situation we have reached is appalling because your friend [Zaim] has broken his promises to us. We are fighting a life-or-death battle here. For us to remain hand-tied toward the extermination measures taken against us in Lebanon would only mean the end for us. Let us die honourably if death is our only way out of this crisis.[90]

Words like these infuriated and frustrated Qubbani more than invective and lies possibly could. But he was not able any longer to assist because he had resigned in protest against al-Barrazi. A plea for help formed Sa'adeh's last words to him:

> For the last time I plea with you to call your man, Husni, to discuss the situation and make him understand that if it were not for his promises to us, we would have taken a different course in our war with the [Lebanese] government. I am asking you this even though I know you have resigned from your job and no longer associate with him. But human lives are being spent and any help could make a difference.[91]

Qubbani's only recourse was the *Deuxième Bureau*. "Don't bother," he was told. "It is useless. Yesterday, the Premier issued orders to the police to keep tabs on all party members in Damascus and to locate Sa'adeh. The plan to help Sa'adeh is now history."[92] Qubbani quickly passed the information on to the party secretariat in Damascus and pleaded with him to relocate Sa'adeh to another part of the city "just in case".[93]

In retrospect it does not seem difficult to perceive, when one is familiar with the details in question, that the logical course for Sa'adeh was really to flee the Syrian capital. Why he did not change tack or hold back remains a mystery to this day. The silence is curious but it has not prevented many analysts (including those far removed from his outlook) from assuming without warrant that Sa'adeh was overcome by his altruistic nature. The theme of self-sacrifice does indeed resound through his writings: "life is but an honourable stand;" "the blood that flows through our veins is not our property but the property of the nation and therefore must be produced at any point it demands it;" "we all must die, but few will die for the sake of a belief." However, altruism only dogmatizes the matter and sheds hardly any light on objective factors. Even if the explanation is only partially true, it does not mesh well with Sa'adeh's strong beliefs in human struggle. Therefore, the answer lies somewhere else and more directly in the mixed signals that Sa'adeh continued to receive from the Syrian regime. To illustrate: while the cleansing of his supporters in Latakia was taking place, at the other end the Syrian military was providing his supporters with logistic and hardware equipment: "On one occasion . . . [Syrian] gendarmerie and army vehicles [of the Syrian army] even took part in helping the nationalists transport weapons from the mountains to the borders."[94] The fact that Zaim did not personally attempt to intimidate Sa'adeh is also crucial: it may possibly have given Sa'adeh the impression that, in spite of everything, Zaim was merely procrastinating because he was under pressure.

The Final Showdown

Despite the explosive nature of the situation and Zaim's impulsiveness, in early July 1949, Sa'adeh proclaimed a revolution against the regime in Lebanon. The revolution was planned by two junior army officers, neither of whom had any experience in revolutionary warfare. A large map of Lebanon was produced by the officers to evaluate the surrounding topography and to determine the appropriate targets and other details of the attack including troop strength, armament, etc. After deliberating with Sa'adeh, who shared their sense of urgency and devotion to military affairs, they came up with a plan that proved well beyond the party's capabilities.[95]

On the same day, at a session of the party's top cadres, a military revolutionary committee headed by Sa'adeh was formed to oversee the revolution. Sa'adeh, though, had relatively little to do with the actual mechanics of the insurrection. That was left entirely to the military officers who quickly surrounded themselves with a core of reliable nationalists. Logistically, the plan consisted of specific practical targets: the Rashayya Fortress in the Lebanese South; gendarmerie precincts on the outskirts of Beirut; and the seizure of key highways to isolate the country's provinces from each other. Abdullah Qubarsi records in his autobiography that Sa'adeh's optimism was aroused by the expectation of widespread support for the revolution inside Lebanon once it got underway:

> Under no circumstances could I envisage that Saadeh foresaw victory by taking over some police precincts or cutting roads off here and there. He most probably thought that these actions would inspire his allies . . . [and] the forces opposing Beshara al-Khuri and Riyad al-Sulh to rally around the uprising. Saadeh was banking on the chance that the anger of the people will erupt with the mere declaration of the revolution.[96]

By now Sa'adeh was borne aloft by a force greater than himself. As a first step, on 4 July, 1949, he issued a communiqué reflecting the urgency of the situation. It contained a chronology of events and a statement of objectives. Comparatively little is known about how Sa'adeh worked on this communiqué, but it is known that he used the occasion to deliver a few appropriate remarks. He emphasized that the revolution was purely an act of self-defense directed not against the people of Lebanon but against the ruling clique: "Those who currently exercise power over the Lebanese people through methods of terror, rigging of elections, and violent intimidation of the emerging political forces that embody the principles of a new social life . . ."[97] Sa'adeh also made it clear that the revolution did not aim to affect the status of Lebanon as an independent entity but only the system of government and its confessional underpinning. He thus carefully avoided any mention of unity with Syria.

In preparing the document Sa'adeh followed his usual habit in such matters using great deliberation in arranging his thoughts and molding his phrases mentally. He scolded the government for the Jummaizeh incident and other acts of foolhardiness, defended himself against the various charges, and warned the people of harsher conditions if they failed to rise up. The objectives of the revolution were most clearly formulated in seventeen points:

1. To bring down the government and dissolve the parliament.
2. To form a [new] government.
3. To draw up a modern constitution emanating from the will of the people that would replace the present constitution, which lacks sound constitutional character, guarantee full equality of civil and political rights for the people, and base political representation on the national interest instead of the confessional or narrow clannish interests.
4. To let the previous political circumstances pass.
5. To consolidate the Lebanese independence on the basis of the free will of the people.
6. To uphold all international treaties and agreements concluded until now.
7. To protect public security and private property.
8. To counter communism.
9. To secularize state and society.
10. To purge the Administration of bribery, corruption and despotism.
11. To set up a national economic policy based on the economic unity of [geographical] Syria and the necessity of a stable industrial-agricultural development.
12. To erase immediately the injustice inflicted on the workers and farmers.
13. To put an end to capitalist monopoly and tyranny.
14. To release and compensate the prisoners who were unjustly detained [during the reprisal campaign].
15. To reinstate every Social Nationalist and anyone else who lost his job during the campaign of detention and persecution.
16. To reinstate and compensate every Social Nationalist who was discharged from the public service on account of his membership to the [Syrian] Social Nationalist Party.
17. To suspend all regulations that nullify civil and political rights.[98]

On the day of the uprising, armed units of the SSNP attacked a number of gendarmerie posts near the Syrian-Lebanese frontiers, in southern Biqa' (Rachaya and Mashghara) and in the mountains over Beirut. Their mission was to seize weapons before the main contingent, led by

Lieutenant Assaf Karam, moved in to occupy those areas. Hisham Sharabi, who was at Sa'adeh's side, described the mood as follows:

> Although Sa'adeh was speaking about the revolution as though it was certain to succeed, still in the statement which he issued just before the proclamation of the revolution he indicated that it was the "first social nationalist revolution". Was he expecting that the uprising might fail and that it would be followed by a second revolution in the future? Was he discreetly grasping that the revolution was a mere adventure set off by despair and that it was very unlikely to succeed? I believe that he did indeed understand all of that. But, nonetheless, he did not reveal any worry. He kept on speaking in a very confident way and laughing merrily, as though he did not have a worry in the world.[99]

Only hours into the uprising, things went horribly wrong. The SSNP units that engaged Gendarmerie posts seized only a few weapons and were outnumbered by a larger and better-equipped force. In view of the large number of SSNP members thought to be hiding in the Lebanese village of Bshamoun, a special task force was sent there to prevent them from linking up with other rebels. In the ensuing engagement, the officer commanding the force, Captain Tufic Chamoun, was killed. Several members of the SSNP were injured and considerable numbers arrested.

The collapse of the uprising was imminent. There was a clear lack of planning and a grave deficiency in personnel: the participants were small in number, ill-equipped and inexperienced in military warfare. With the exception of one or two field officers, the insurgents were mostly irregular recruits and civilians who probably had never been in a military situation all their life. It soon became apparent that the Lebanese Government was being alerted in advance of their plans through Muhsin al-Barazzi, who passed the information to his brother-in-law Riad Solh in Lebanon. Rightly or wrongly, some blamed the collapse of the revolution on faulty weapons. In reality, the fundamental problem lay in Sa'adeh's tenacity and in his exaggerated optimism that the uprising would destroy the inertia of the local population. On balance, he had neither the resources nor the time to communicate and coordinate with the general population in Lebanon, so much so that most Lebanese remained oblivious to the uprising.[100]

Treachery at the Palace

The collapse of the uprising placed Sa'adeh at the crossroads of life. He had several options, but each option was as problematical as the next one. Surrender was one option but it went against his character. Fleeing was another, but that would amount to dereliction of duty: "I confronted Sa'adeh with the [travel] documents in my hands and suggested that he should leave ash-Sham [Syria] at once because his life was in danger. I stretched my hand out expecting him take them from me but he refused to even look at them. Instead he looked at me and said: "Do you really expect a leader who has called a revolution and whose supporters have answered his call and are staring death in the face in search of martyrdom, to abandon them for the sake of his own personal safety?"[101] Persons close to Sa'adeh later claimed that he didn't think that the Syrian President would dare double-cross him in the presence of his Chief of General Security, Major Adib Shishakli, who was a Syrian nationalist at heart.[102] The third option for Sa'adeh was to seek political asylum in Syria or to confide in Zaim. Sa'adeh decided to have one last crack at Zaim.

As late as 3 July, Muhammad Baalbaki of the Beirut daily *Kul Shay*, overheard Sa'adeh saying "Zaim is different [from Muhsin al-Barrazi]. He has expressed to me his readiness to adopt the views of the party . . . and he is helping us."[103] It was scarcely a good reason for optimism. With Egypt and Saudi Arabia breathing heavily down his neck, Zaim was in fact under more pressure than at any time before to rein in Sa'adeh. He was battling on two fronts, Husni al-Barrazi and now King Farouk's private emissary, Brigadier General Muhammad Yusuf, who arrived in Damascus at the beginning of July with instructions to twist Zaim's arm.[104] The Brigadier's mission was to convince the Syrian leader that Sa'adeh was a British mole stirring problems to facilitate Hashemite and British expansion over the Eastern Mediterranean and that, if Zaim didn't comply, the Lebanese government would seek foreign military assistance to stop his rebellion.[105]

There also are, or there seem to be, good grounds for believing that Zaim was under a different kind of pressure from his personal friends and staff:

> One day Captain Ibrahim al-Husseini turned up at my house and said: "We are in a morass and I have fears about its consequences."

Husseini was Zaim's right hand man and Chief of the *Deuxième Bureau* in the Army and the Head of the Military Police. Husseini added: "Antun Sa'adeh is in Zaim's protection, but I think that Zaim intends to hand him over to the Lebanese authorities." I was truly astonished. How on earth could Zaim think of this after he had assured Sa'adeh, gave him a house in Damascus to live in, and regarded him as a political refugee! I replied: "This is just not possible."[106]

The author here is Nadhih Fansah, Zaim's brother-in-law and private secretary. When Fansah turned up for work the next morning, Zaim was there to listen and to reply to his queries. "Deport him. Give him travel clearance to another country of his choice," Fansah supposedly told him. "Great idea", responded Zaim. "I will ask him to go to Argentina where he has a substantial family and a strong party base."[107] Elatedly, Fansah dashed over and kissed Zaim: "I repeated to him not to cause a shameful blot to be recorded against his administration by handing Sa'adeh over to the Lebanese State."[108] Both Fansah and Colonel al-Husseini repeated the waning to Zaim that day: "Husni, do you swear by your military honour that you will not hand Antun Sa'adeh over to the Lebanese authorities?" "By military honour," he replied.[109] The belief today is that al-Husseini also pressed Zaim to dump Sa'adeh in advance of a 25,000 pound reward that the Lebanese government had set aside for Sa'adeh's capture.[110]

On the morning of 6 July, al-Husseini turned up at Sa'adeh's command centre to convey a message from Zaim. It was a request for an evening meeting at the presidential palace. Projecting a relaxed attitude, Sa'adeh responded in a conciliatory spirit but did not give his guest a definite yes or no answer. Sensing a problem, al-Husseini quickly responded with a trumped-up story about how Zaim had finally agreed to bolster the insurgency with an additional three hundred soldiers from the Syrian Army. That sent Sa'adeh's mind into a spin.

Earlier that day, and possibly even before, confidential reports had reached the SNP of a plot to surrender Sa'adeh to the Lebanese authorities. They came from three principal directions: (1) Sabri Qubbani; (2) the Syrian diplomat and poet Omar Abu Riche;[111] and (3) Major Tufic Bashur, Commander of the Fourth Battalion in the Syrian Army. Bashur twice met Sa'adeh to dissuade him from meeting with Zaim, but was unsuccessful. After the first attempt the Major pleaded with the SNP to "persuade Sa'adeh to leave the country at once because treason is about to unleash its venom"[112] but Sa'adeh ignored the plea. The second meeting was more melodramatic:

> When we (Sa'adeh, Sobhi Farhat, Bashir Moussali and I) got there Sa'adeh and the Major went into the main lounge room alone while the rest of us stayed outside. They emerged from the meeting Sa'adeh first followed by the Major with tears in his eyes. Then, in a trembling voice, the Major cried out: "Please, persuade him to flee. You mustn't leave him to die like this. Muhsin al-Barrazi, Riad Solh and King Farouk are conspiring against him."[113]

Sa'adeh annoyingly ignored the warning. At once he let it be known to everyone that the meeting would go ahead as long as he could see a "one in a million"[114] chance of regaining the Syrian leader.

At twilight, Sa'adeh asked his chauffeur to refuel the car for a relaxing drive. Contradictory assertions have been made about his intentions, one account alleging that he was planning to abscond to Jordan after realizing the hopelessness of the situation. But the opposite assertion has been made, from a very different point of view, that he was merely using up the time to reflect before the meeting with Zaim.[115] We believe that the latter suggestion carries more weight than the former[116] but even if it is accepted it is not easy to prove. According to his chauffeur, Sa'adeh did not utter a single word during the one-hour drive. When they reached the outskirts of Damascus Sa'adeh stopped the car and asked the driver to turn back.

At ten sharp, an army jeep with al-Husseini at the wheels rolled up to collect Sa'adeh. As he made his way to the waiting vehicle, Sa'adeh removed his pistol, the very same one given him by Zaim during their second meeting, and handed it over to one of his aides, saying: "It is not proper to meet the President armed and whilst I am under his protection."[117] His private secretary, Mustafa Suleiman, offered to come along with him, but al-Husseini shoved him aside. "You, my son, stay here," and then he took off.[118] Stunned and confused, Sa'adeh's chauffeur quickly jumped into his car and followed them with a party officer at his side.

The Presidential Palace was only a short distance away. It was a warm summer evening and everyone was going about their business as on any other day. Apart from the troops bivouacked in and around the Presidential palace, no unusual activities were reported. During the day Lebanese security vehicles had whizzed in and out of the Syrian capital, but by nightfall they had all but disappeared from public view.[119] Al-Husseini entered the Presidential Palace in the normal way and walked Sa'adeh to the main chamber. The moment Sa'adeh stepped inside he was surrounded by the presidential guards from all sides. Minutes later, Muhsin al-Barrazi walked in from the other end of the chamber to utter his infamous words: "You have a score to settle with Lebanon, go take care of it."[120] Outside the Palace, Sa'adeh's chauffeur and his companion were overpowered and arrested on Al-Husseini's orders.

Sa'adeh was handed over to two Lebanese emissaries, the Chief of General Security Farid Chehab and a senior officer in the Lebanese army whose identity is still unknown.[121] The pair asked the Syrian authorities for a two-hour intermission to organize the extradition from the other end. Then they left to Lebanon to deploy extra security forces along the Beirut-Damascus highway in anticipation of the handover. Sa'adeh spent those hours at a gendarmerie post on the Syrian side of the borders with Lebanon. At two in the morning, he was whisked across the border by Syrian intelligence officers, some fifteen of them, and handed over to Farid Chehab who in turn handed him over to the Lebanese army.

The Plot to Kill Sa'adeh
The small convoy made its way through the still of the night without visible security or military measures. The operation was carried out in complete secrecy from the point of view of the Lebanese government. At a certain point in the Bekaa valley, near Anjar, the convoy confronted "a pile of rocks in the middle of the road which was not there on our way to collect Sa'adeh."[122] It was a false alarm. Farid Chehab's recollections of the incident are telling: "I thought the party may have caught wind of the mission and had set up a deadly trap for us. There were only two cars on the road, mine and the jeep. I checked my pistol and then got out to investigate. There was no movement. So we steered the cars toward one side of the road and drove on."[123]

When the convoy got closer to Anjar, the driver of the army jeep signaled to Chehab to stop. He got out and walked toward Chehab and said "I have orders to liquidate him. What do you think?" Chehab curtly answered him: "I strongly disapprove. We are not killers. This is not proper behaviour towards the State." He instantly replied: "I agree." It later transpired that the Lebanese army officers in the convoy had been instructed to kill Sa'adeh on the route on the familiar pretext of attempting to escape.

President Khoury tacitly conceded to the existence of the plot, but placed the onus of responsibility squarely with the Syrians. He claimed that President Zaim had agreed to hand over Sa'adeh on the condition that he (i.e., Sa'adeh) would be liquidated on the way to Lebanon.[124] Yet Khoury conceded that the Syrian President did not raise a single objection when he broke to him the news that Sa'adeh was still alive: "Finally, at six Husni Zaim picked up the phone. I said 'I am grateful for your assistance to Lebanon on this night. The man [i.e., Sa'adeh] is under arrest and will be tried in a military court in accordance with the law.' He replied: 'Fine. Fine. There is really no need for you to thank me for anything.' "[125]

What do the Syrians say? The Syrian historian and diplomat Walid al-Mouallim has stated that when Riad Solh came to Damascus to seek Sa'adeh's repatriation he brought with him a letter from the Lebanese president asking Zaim to "hand over Sa'adeh to the Lebanese authorities or organize his murder in Damascus."[126] This view is strongly confirmed in Nadhir Fansah's revealing recollections of that era:

> Without delay I went to see Zaim to enquire about Sa'adeh's status. He said 'I am under considerable pressure from the Lebanese President, Sheikh Beshara Khoury, and from Riad Solh.' I replied 'Is it not shameful to surrender a person you know for certain that he will be executed after you have granted him protection?' He replied 'They are demanding of me even to organize the details of his murder right here in Damascus, but of course I will not do anything of the sort. Therefore, I will hand him over to them.'[127]

Since then, more evidence implicating the Khoury regime has emerged. In 1991, the Lebanese ex-president, Charles Helou, told *al-Dayar* newspaper that "Lebanese fingers" were definitely involved in a plot to kill Sa'adeh before his trial but refrained from openly naming the perpetrators. He literally said:

> Husni Zaim answered the request of the Lebanese government and turned Antun Sa'adeh in. At this point, I am not sure how

important this issue is, since one of the people in charge, whom I am not going to name, suggested to the government that Sa'adah should not make it to trial. He proposed that Sa'adah be killed by one of the guards in a police station who would thus supposedly be taking vengeance for the death of one of his family members killed by [Sa'adeh's supporters]. Sheikh Beshara, however, rejected the idea.[128]

Conclusion

The confrontation between Sa'adeh and the Lebanese State remains to this day one of Lebanon's longest and most dramatic events. Its passion and intensity surprised almost everyone but not as much as the intrigue, revolution, and betrayals that marked its history. Out of it, two different and conflicting perspectives have emerged: To the defenders of the established order, Sa'adeh seemed a degenerate outcast. They recognized his potential but continued to treat him with primitive tolerance. To erudite Lebanese and the politically observant he was the first dissident of Lebanon who spoke with the soft anger and naked courage of a non-conformist. Neither could prove conclusively if Sa'adeh was anti-establishment or anti-Lebanon, even though his words and deeds clearly implied no treachery.

For a while the confrontation for both sides seemed like an eternal process destined to end either in slow death or in a showdown. It ended with a showdown. From the standpoint of the Lebanese state, it was purely self-defense against a citizen who had deviated from the norm and was bent on destroying its entity and absorbing it into a larger unit. For Sa'adeh, it seemed more like a phase in a long and drawn-out battle between a reactionary regime lacking true national legitimacy and the principles of modern life. His method might have been unconventional but the aim was familiar. Like a "father of the nation", he sought to reshape the very character of the Lebanese state by challenging its ideological underpinnings and foundations of power.

On 7 July, 1949, the long arm of the law finally caught up with the rebel Sa'adeh and now all that was left for the "winner", the State, to do was to put him on trial for the public to judge for itself. This was the "moment of truth" that most Lebanese had been anxiously waiting for – public scrutiny of the simple facts from the independent perspective of the law. What they got did not remotely come close to that. It is revealed in the next chapter.

NOTES

1 Walter L. Brown (ed.), *Lebanon's Struggle for Independence*, Part II, 1944–1947. North Carolina: Documentary Publications, 1980: 142.
2 A. Sa'adeh, *al-Athar al-Kamilah* (Complete Works). Vol. 14. Beirut: SSNP Cultural Bureau, n.d.: 15.
3 See Nadim Makdisi, "The Syrian National Party: A Case Study of the First Inroads of National Socialism in the Arab World." PhD, American University of Beirut, 1960.
4 Abdullah Qubarsi, *Nahnu wa Lubnan* (Lebanon and US). Beirut: Dar al-Turath al-Arabi, 1988.
5 Antun Sa'adeh, *al-Athar al-Kamilah* (Complete Works). Vol. 14. Beirut: SSNP Cultural Bureau, n.d.: 63.
6 *Sabah el-Kheir*, Beirut, 12 July, 1988.
7 Ibid.
8 Antun Sa'adeh, *al-Athar al-Kamilah* (Complete Works). Vol. 14. Beirut: SSNP Cultural Bureau, n.d.: 110.
9 George Akl, Abdo Ouadat, and Idwār Ḥunayn, *The Black Book of the Lebanese Elections of May 25, 1947*. New York, N.Y.: Phoenicia Press, 1947.
10 Ibid., 112.
11 Ibid., 96.
12 Ibid., 115.
13 The campaign against Sa'adeh was not free of humor. A reporter for the widely-read *al-Hayat* alleged that a Lebanese security force assigned to the task of capturing Sa'adeh directed him to Sa'adeh's hideout after he wandered off on his way to interview the SNP leader. Ibid.
14 On the course of negotiations between Sa'adeh and the government, with Emir Farouq Abi Lama' as the intermediary, see Nawwaf Hardan, *Ala Durub an-Nahda* (On the Pathways of the Renaissance). Beirut: Dar Bissan Publishing, 1997: 193–196.
15 Antun Sa'adeh, *al-Athar al-Kamilah* (Complete Works). Vol. 14. Beirut: SSNP Cultural Bureau, n.d.: 156–157.
16 Antun Sa'adeh, *al-Athar al-Kamilah* (Complete Works). Vol. 15. Beirut: SSNP Cultural Bureau, n.d.: 214.
17 Ibid.
18 An example was the time when it tried to disperse a modest gathering organized by the Beirut Executive branch of the Party on February 28, 1949, on the eve of Sa'adeh's birthday anniversary, although the meeting was being held in a private garden. That attempt nearly ended in a clash with a throng of young men attending the celebrations. Having failed in its bid, the government then proceeded to ban the official ceremony which the Party was planning to hold in the Normandy Hotel on the day of Sa'adeh's birthday. Consequently, the Party was forced to celebrate in a private house in an atmosphere of intimidation by the secret police which spoiled the social nature of the occasion.
19 Alford Carelton, "The Syrian Coups d'Etat of 1949," *Middle East Journal*, Vol. 4 (1950): 4.
20 Zaim stated that the number of deputies in the new parliament would be decreased, that suffrage would be extended to educated women, and that the civil

service would be purged, while the lower echelons would be given better working conditions. He proposed a widespread distribution of abandoned state lands to the peasants and the imposition of a limitation upon the size of landholdings. Zaim also promised to re-arm the army with the most modern weapons. See Gordon H. Torrey, *Syrian Politics and the Military: 1945–1958*. Columbus: Ohio State University Press, 1964: 125.

21 For further confirmation that Qawuqji was planning a coup see Hani al-Hindi, *Jaysh al Inqadh* (The Salvation Army). Beirut: Dar al-Quds, 1974: 112.

22 Taha al-Hashimi, *Mudhakkirat* (Memoirs). Beirut: Dar al-Tali'a, 1967: 234. Taha al-Hashimi, a former prime minister then in exile in Syria for opposing the Iraqi royal family during the 1941 Rashid Ali coup, was appointed by Mardam as the Inspector General to supervise the new army. It was named the *Jaysh al-Inqadh* or Rescue Army.

23 *Al-Jil al-Jadid*, 25 May, 1949.

24 Ibid.

25 Eyal Zisser, *Lebanon: The Challenge of Independence*. London: I. B. Tauris, 2000: 169.

26 See Qabbani's recollections in the Syrian *al-Dunia* newsmagazine in the second half of 1949. The entire series can be found in Abdul Ghani al-Atari, *Sa'adeh wa al-Hizb al-Qawmi* (Sa'adeh and the National Party). Damascus: Al-Dunia Printers, 1950: 158–205. Hereafter cited as "Qubbani's recollections."

27 Ibid.

28 Ibid.

29 Ibid.

30 Ibid. On Zaim's military ego see Alford Carelton, "The Syrian Coups d'Etat of 1949," *Middle East Journal*, Vol. 4 (1950): 9.

31 Ibid.

32 Ibid.

33 Ibid.

34 Ibid.

35 Ibid.

36 Ibid.

37 Ibid.

38 *Al-Hayat*, Beirut, 11 June, 1949.

39 Yusuf Salamah, *Haddathanii Y. S. Qala* (Memoirs). Beirut: Dar Nelson, 1988.

40 Hisham Sharabi, *al-Jamr wa al-Rimad* (Embers and Ashes). Beirut: Dar al-Tali'a, 1978: 208.

41 Michel Faddoul memoirs of the Jummaizzeh incident (unpublished).

42 Yusuf Salamah, *op. cit.*, 78.

43 *Al-Hayat*, Beirut, 11 June, 1949.

44 Eyal Zisser, *Lebanon: The Challenge of Independence*: 184. Zisser's interpretation is factually inaccurate: (1) at the time of the clash, the Phalanges and Premier Solh were not 'opponents' but allies united with an-Najjadah by a common enmity towards Sa'adeh; (2) the Phalanges was not the only victim of the 1947 rigged elections. Even if it was, the issue is not directly relevant here; (3) the government did not arrest 'some fifty Phalanges' after the clash, but twenty-one of them none of whom was charged or jailed; (4) the July 18 incident between the government and the Phalanges falls outside the scope of Jummaizeh and thus is immaterial.

45 In *Istijwab Jumblatt al tarikhi lil hukuma hawla istishhad Sa'adeh ome 1949* (Jumblatt's Historical Interpolation to the [Lebanese] Government in Regard to Sa'adeh's Martyrdom in 1949). Beirut: SSNP Information Bureau, 1987.

46 Ahmad Asfahani (ed.), *Antun Sa'adeh wa al-Hizb al-Suri al-Qawmi al-Ijtimae' fi Awarq al-Amir Farid Chehab, al-Mudir al-Ome lil al-Amn al-Ome al-Lubnani* (Antun Sa'adeh and the Syrian Social Nationalist Party in the Private Papers of Emir Farid Chehab, the General Director of the Lebanese General Security). Beirut: Dar Kutub, 2006: 40–41.

47 Hanna Toufiq Bashur, *Min Dhakirat Abi, Major Toufiq Bashur* (From My Father's Recollections). Damascus: Maktabat al-Sharq al-Jadid, 1998: 101.

48 Ibid.

49 Antoine Butrus, *Qissat muhakamat Antun Sa'adeh was i'damehe* (An Account of Antun Sa'adeh's Trial and Execution): 51–53.

50 "Qubbani's recollections."

51 Ibid.

52 Ibid.

53 Ibid.

54 Ibid. Sa'adeh also asked for freedom of movement for the party, especially at the border-points with Lebanon.

55 "Qubbani's recollections."

56 *An-Nahar*, Beirut 16 June, 1949.

57 Ibid.

58 Ibid.

59 "Qubbani's recollections."

60 Sa'adeh, *al-Athar al-Kamilah* (Complete Works). Vol. 16. Beirut: SSNP Cultural Bureau, n.d.: 159–163.

61 Ibid., 159.

62 The countryside between Lebanon and Syria is fairly open. Both countries lacked, and still lack, the right measures to monitor and control their borders. Back then and even today people from both countries are able to traverse the borders on foot and with considerable ease.

63 "Qubbani's recollections."

64 *Al-Sayyad*, Beirut, 16 June, 1949.

65 *An-Nahar*, Beirut, 16 June, 1949.

66 Ahmad Asfahani, *op. cit.*, 40–41.

67 *An-Nahar*, Beirut, 16 June, 1949.

68 See Asfahani, *op. cit.*, 40–45.

69 *An-Nahar*, Beirut, 21 June, 1949.

70 *An-Nahar*, Beirut, 22 June, 1949.

71 "Qubbani's recollections."

72 Ibid.

73 Ibid.

74 A. Sa'adeh, *al-Athar al-Kamilah* (Complete Works). Vol. 16. Beirut: SSNP Cultural Bureau, n.d.: 161–163.

75 See Nadhir Fansahh, *Ayyam Husni Zaim: 137 Yawman Hazzat Suria* (Days of Husni Zaim: 137 Days that Shook Syria). Beirut: Dar al-Afaq al-Jadidah, 1983.

76 "Qubbani's recollections."

77 Mohammad Fadhel Jamali, *Experiences in Arab Affairs: 1943–1958* (Located in Widener Library, Harvard University under the title: *Arab Struggle; Experiences*

of Mohammed Fadhel Jamali). Also at http://www.physics.harvard.edu/~wilson/Fadhel.html

78 *An-Nasr*. Damascus, 22 June, 1949.
79 "Qubbani's recollections."
80 Ibid.
81 Ibid.
82 Ibid.
83 *An-Nahar*, Beirut, 25 June, 1949.
84 Patrick Seale, *The Struggle for Syria: A Study of Post-War Diplomacy 1945–1958*. Oxford University Press, 1965: 71.
85 Andrew Rathmell, *Secret War in the Middle East: The Covert Struggle for Syria, 1949–1961*. London: I. B. Tauris, 1995: 49.
86 "Qubbani's recollections."
87 Ibid.
88 Ibid.
89 Ibid.
90 Ibid.
91 Ibid.
92 Ibid.
93 Ibid.
94 Ibid.
95 Details of the two plans are discussed in Nawaf Hardan, *Ala Durub an-Nahda* (On the Pathways of the Renaissance). Beirut: Dar Bissan, 1997: 245–255.
96 Abdullah Qubarsi, *Autobiography*. Vol. 4. Beirut: Dar Al-Furat, 2004: 51.
97 An English-language version of the communiqué can be found in Adel Beshara, *Syrian Nationalism: An Inquiry into the Political Philosophy of Antun Sa'adeh*. Beirut: Dar Bissan, 1995.
98 A. Sa'adeh, *al-Athar al-Kamilah* (Complete Works). Vol. 16. Beirut: SSNP Cultural Bureau, n.d.: 169–171.
99 Hisham Sharabi, *al-Jamr wa al-Rimad* (Embers and Ashes): 227.
100 The first and only communiqué of the uprising reached comparatively few people in Lebanon because the local authorities were alerted to it by the Syrians and, thus, were able to confiscate most of it.
101 Elias Jurgi Qneizeh, *Ma'ather min Sa'adeh*. Beirut: Dar Bissan, 1989: 207.
102 Antoine Butrus, *Qissat muhakamat Antun Sa'adeh was i'damehe* (An Account of Antun Sa'adeh's Trial and Execution). Beirut: Chemaly & Chemaly, 2002: 83.
103 Ibid., 76.
104 "Qubbani's recollections."
105 Ibid.
106 Nadhir Fansah, *op. cit.*, 129.
107 Ibid.
108 Ibid.
109 Ibid.
110 Muti'e as-Samman, *Watan wa Askar* (Homeland and Soldiers). Beirut: Dar Bissan, 1995: 322–327.
111 Abu-Riche was born in Acre, Palestine to a Palestinian mother and Syrian father. He received his educational upbringing in Syria and continued his tertiary studies at the University of Damascus. He also studied at the American University in Beirut in 1931, and later read chemistry at the University of Manchester. Returning to

Syria, he produced literary works and attended to his duties as Librarian of Aleppo, Syria. In 1949, the Syrian government appointed him ambassador to Brazil. As a diplomat until 1964, he would also serve as ambassador to Argentina, Chile, India, Austria and finally the United States. See Sabry Hafez, "Obituary: Omar Abu-Riche". *The Independent*, London, 19 July, 1990: 31.

112 Hanna Toufiq Bashur, *Min Dhakirat Abi, Major Toufiq Bashur* (From my Father's Recollections) (Damascus: Maktabat al-Sharq al-Jadid, 1998): 102.

113 Ibid.

114 Antoine Butrus, *Qissat muhakamat Antun Sa'adeh was i'damehe* (An Account of Antun Sa'adeh's Trial and Execution). Beirut: Chemaly & Chemaly, 2002: 82.

115 Ibid., 84–85.

116 First, Sa'adeh did not mention to anyone that he was going to Jordan, not even to his chauffeur, or leave behind any instructions to indicate that he was escaping to the Kingdom. Second, it would not have been like Sa'adeh to leave in this manner without first ensuring the safety of his wife and three children who were cooped up in the northern Syrian city of Latakia.

117 Antoine Butrus, *Qissat muhakamat Antun Sa'adeh was i'damehe* (An Account of Antun Sa'adeh's Trial and Execution). Beirut: Chemaly & Chemaly, 2002: 86.

118 Ibid.

119 A Syrian bystander has related that that day Damascus "teemed with officers of the Lebanese General Security . . . we counted more than two hundred taxicabs and private cars zigzagging various parts of the city including designated areas where taxicabs were barred."

120 President Zaim was not present but, according to Adib Qaddura, he was listening to everything from a concealed corner in the Chamber.

121 Antoine Butrus, *Qissat muhakamat Antun Sa'adeh was i'damehe* (An Account of Antun Sa'adeh's Trial and Execution). Beirut: Chemaly & Chemaly, 2002: 88.

122 Interview with Farid Chehab, former Chief of Lebanese General Security, *Sabah el-Kheir*, 7 July, 1980.

123 Ibid.

124 In Khoury's words: When the meeting [between Sa'adeh and Zaim] ended and the guest bid farewell to his host, Sa'adeh walked out only to find the Presidential Palace encircled by a unit from the [Syrian] General Security account. The head of the unit then walked across and arrested him. Immediately after that the [Syrian] Chief of General Security called his Lebanese counterpart and asked him to bring along with him an armed unit to collect the detainee at midnight on the borders between the two countries, on the condition that Sa'adeh would be killed before he arrived in Beirut. The Damascene Chief of General Security was deadly serious about this condition. See his *Haqa'iq Lubnaniyyah* (Lebanese Truths), Vol. 3, Beirut: Awraq Labnaniyah, 1961: 240–241.

125 Ibid.

126 Walid al-Mouallim, *Souria 1918–1958: al-Tahdi wa al-Muwajaha*. Damascus: Babel Publications, 1985: 113.

127 Nadhir Fansah, *Ayyam Husni Zaim: 137 Yawman Hazzat Suria* (Days of Husni Zaim: 137 Days that Shook Syria). Beirut: Dar al-Afaq al-Jadidah, 1983: 85.

128 *al-Dayar*, Beirut, 1 March, 1991.

3

THE TRIAL

The Khoury regime decided to railroad Sa'adeh to trial with indecent haste and in total secrecy. Despite the lack of preparation and the complete exhaustion of the accused, who had had an average of no more than a few hours' sleep over the previous two days and none the previous night, the government seemed under some fixation to wind up the case as quickly as possible. The investigation and prosecution team worked around the clock to have the case ready in just one day. In order for this to happen, several rules were relaxed, and though this was not exactly unprecedented, the rapidity of the relaxation was rather unusual. Thus, any semblance of judicial impartiality ended before the trial had even started.

The trial itself fell outside the bounds of formal judicial fairness. It was rather unusual in that it happened at a time when large sectors of Lebanese society thoroughly disapproved of Sa'adeh's desperate course and hoped that he would suffer the fullest penalty of the law. In another respect it defied the logic of the situation. With the regime's legitimacy on a knife-edge and public concern for the country's democratic institutions mounting following wide-scale allegations of corruption,[1] a messy trial was hardly appropriate. The case offered the Khoury regime the chance to re-affirm its commitment to government transparency but, to Lebanon's misfortune, it didn't take it up.

This chapter deals with the trial in both its procedural and substantive aspects. It addresses a number of fundamental questions relating to the political nature of the charges, the reasons for secrecy and speed, why the trial was held in a military tribunal, and several other aspects relating to the character of the evidence and motives of participants. A final evaluation of the trial's overall fairness in light of domestic and international standards appears in the last section of the chapter.

Preparations for Sa'adeh's Trial

The Khoury regime initiated legal proceedings against Sa'adeh without delay. In the early hours of July 7, Sa'adeh was removed to the Gendarme Barracks in Beirut where he was personally guarded by al-Rufae' in the traditional manner of "placing his chair against the door."[2] At the same time the President and Prime Minister Solh, accompanied by his adviser Nazim Akkary, converged on the presidential palace and held a "full one hour" closed troika meeting.[3] It was followed, at three in the morning, by a general assembly of the government and again by an extraordinary session of the Council of Ministers, attended by representatives from the Lebanese judiciary.

The government made three crucial decisions during those meetings. First, it decided to try Sa'adeh under the Emergency Law introduced during the 1948 Palestine War. Originally drafted during the French mandate over Lebanon, the Emergency Law was intended for situations of grave public insecurity or disorder, whether by the threat or actuality of war, internal disturbances or by natural disasters. It provided for wide powers of arrest, detention and search, regardless of the protective provisions in the Criminal Procedures Code, and empowered the Lebanese military to detain and try *in camera* suspects considered a "danger to security and public order."[4] Arms smugglers and spies on the Israeli payroll were the primary targets when the law was invoked in 1948.

Further, the Emergency Law authorized the creation of exceptional courts to hear matters arising during times of emergency.[5] These were essentially military courts which were given wide jurisdictions: the accused had no right of appeal; the prosecutor had greater powers than in ordinary circumstances; and the Executive power played an important role in ratifying judgments and in the composition of the courts. The Law also gave the President the authority to delegate cases covered by general laws to the exceptional military courts. As elsewhere, it provided a list of guarantees required to satisfy fair trial standards in all cases tried in military courts. Thus, defendants were entitled to:

- be informed promptly and in a language he/she understands the nature of the charge against him/her;
- the necessary time and facilities required for preparing a defense and contacting a lawyer;

- be tried without undue delay;
- be present during the trial, and to be given the right to make a defense to the charges and to be provided with legal assistance;
- have a translator, if the trial is in a language that he/she does not understand;
- not be forced to testify against one's self or to confess guilt.

The Emergency Law remained active for the whole duration of the Palestine war. For incomprehensible reasons, it was not repealed at the end of hostilities or after the signing of the armistice with Israel on 23 March, 1949.[6] In contrast, the state of emergency in both Syria and Egypt was lifted at war's end and Jordan followed suit upon signing an armistice with Israel on 3 April, 1949.

The second decision taken by the government that night resolved that Sa'adeh should be tried *in camera* and as quickly as possible. The government even reserved for itself the right not to broadcast this decision until after the trial. Both the place and time of the trial were to be kept confidential and the press was not to be allowed into the courtroom during proceedings. Speed meant the conduct of the trial in the shortest possible time and should not be confused with the standard right to a speedy trial. The decision to steamroll the trial was subsequently justified on the rather predictable ground of national security:

> We saved the country from plunging into a sea of blood. Had the Social Nationalists [i.e., Sa'adeh's supporters] and their friends caught wind of the trial, sentence and implementation they would have re-grouped and stormed the jail or court to save Sa'adeh. Imagine how many people would have suffered in the process and who knows what would have happened to the country after that.[7]

This explanation, however, does not comport with the facts: (1) the government had total control over the security situation in the country on the day of the trial; and (2) the SNP remnants that were at large had neither the resources nor the energy to challenge the regime. Therefore, one cannot look exclusively or even mainly inside the government excuse for an explanation. Even if the government explanation is partially true, there are other more cogent reasons for its behaviour. First was the concern of the Khoury regime about the potentially disruptive threat that a public trial could inflict on the brand of politics which it had carefully cultivated since 1943. An open trial could leave the government vulnerable to having the tables turned on it by an astute defense or by Sa'adeh himself. This occurred, for example, in 1936, when Sa'adeh was able to slice through the maze of court rules and turn the trial into a forum for his political views. As a non-lawyer, he could repeat the process and get his message across, whether or not it was relevant or admissible under normal court criteria, and without the *legal* constraints that lawyers are subject to. Moreover, such trials have a habit of revealing themselves as oppressive, even in circles that are not sympathetic to the views of the defendant. At Sa'adeh's first trial in 1936, the French sought to discredit Sa'adeh as a potential threat to the Lebanese State, but the trial generated a great deal of publicity and public sympathy for the accused for the contradictory and oppressive nature of the conspiracy charges he faced.[8] Another example: in 1882, the Egyptian leader Arabi Pasha became the object of increasing sympathy outside Egypt after reports of maltreatment surfaced in the press and at his trial. At one point, "the special correspondent of the *New York Herald* conceived a plan to purchase Arabi from Egypt with money supplied by Gordon Bennett and P. T. Barnum."[9]

Second was the need to circumvent judicial constraints under existing international and domestic laws. A year earlier, in 1948, Lebanon had been directly involved in the creation and adoption of the Universal Declaration of Human Rights. The Declaration, proclaimed in a resolution of the General Assembly on 10 December, 1948, listed numerous civil, political, economic, legal, social and cultural rights to which people everywhere were entitled. Although originally conceived as a statement of objectives to be pursued by governments, and therefore not part of binding international law, nonetheless, the Universal Declaration was a potent instrument used to apply moral and diplomatic pressure on states that violated its principles. The domestic law was equally problematical in that like its French counterpart it was based on modern laws, including the rules governing judicial procedure[10] and universal notions of individual rights and universal equality under the law. Under both conventions the conduct of a trial behind closed doors for the sake of "public security" or "national interest" was not entirely inadmissible, but the procedure was complex and subject to powerful prohibitions. Haste was also subject to certain restrictions and procedural requirements that could not be discarded without damage to a fair trial.

Third was to prevent the case from flaring up into a political affair. A public trial could have loosed a flood of events which the government was ill-equipped to deal with. As the Dreyfus affair in France had earlier demonstrated,[11] the passion, intensity and moral fervour that surface during such trials can be too powerful for any government to control. In the courtroom the case could easily develop into a legal tussle over Sa'adeh's character and opinions and thus bring the government's own loyalty into question. It was also risky because "to try a man's character or his opinions flies in the face of due process itself. Neither good procedure nor unbiased judges can give sanctity to a character trial. Nothing deteriorates so rapidly as the quality of character trials once they are started."[12] Character trials almost always boomerang on those who attempt to use them. From Nuremberg, to the Soviet show trials of the 1930s to the Nazi mock tribunals of the same period, governments have done irreparable harm to themselves when they attempted to impose the penalty of disgrace by trial of a man's opinions, beliefs, or associations and, ultimately, they become the object of wide indignation.

The third crucial decision made that night revolved around the political character of the case. Sa'adeh was to be tried not as a political criminal but as a common criminal. The reason is fundamentally that since the defendant had breached the Criminal Code, particularly the articles relating to public safety concerns, the designation of the case as a capital rather than political offense was within the bounds of the law. President Khoury paraphrased the issue as follows:

> The accused will not be tried on the basis of his political ideology despite its full negation of the Lebanese entity, in itself dangerous, but on the basis of actual deeds. He is accused of sedition and of taking direct part in it, of the murder of gendarmeries, and of other unlawful actions arising from his unruly behaviour. As to whether he is entitled to a secret or open trial, it is a matter reserved to the military tribunal to decide.[13]

The government probably weighed its chances of success and concluded that a political trial or a public criminal trial involved significant risks. In any case, a public trial would require it to relinquish control of an explosive situation and to place it in the hands of a judiciary, who might be disposed to exercise their independence to the full. There was also the strong chance that the accused would use the courtroom as a stage to dramatize his views and in the process gain "attention, care, an immediate physical audience . . . notoriety, perhaps fame, perhaps immortality."[14] In court, wrote Father Philip Berrigan, "one does not look for justice; one hopes for a forum from which to communicate ideals, convictions, and anguish."[15] From this perspective, depriving Sa'adeh of the opportunity to repeat his early success in the courtroom was an astute tactical move by the government. However, it perverted the regular course of justice.

Criminalizing the case was also crucial for the overall unity of the government's legal strategy. Without a criminal tag the right to conduct the trial in a military tribunal and, conversely, to invoke the right of secrecy and speed would be annulled. Under the Lebanese penal code, the military tribunal does not have the right to deal with cases of a political or non-criminal character. Those are reserved strictly for the civil system, which precludes secrecy in any case that comes before it.[16]

The Permanent Military Tribunal

The case against Sa'adeh was heard at the Permanent Military Tribunal. Members detailed to such tribunals are generally persons who in the opinion of the convening authority are best qualified for the duty by reason of their age, education, training, experience, length of service and judicial temperament. In Sa'adeh's case, these criteria were annulled and the judging panel was hastily assembled to avoid delays. It was composed of a civilian judge (Justice Gabrail Bassil), a senior army officer (Lieutenant Colonel Anwar Karam, President), and three junior officers from the Lebanese Army: Captain Tanios Samarrani, Captain Aziz al-Ahdab, First Lieutenant Ahmad Arab.

The trial's opening was attended by key figures from the ministries of Defense and Internal Affairs, the Lebanese Army, the Gendarmerie, the judiciary, the first secretary of the Prime Minister Office, and several "independent" observers including President Khoury's sons, Khalil and Michel. It is not clear how the audience was selected, who informed them, or what criteria were used for admission. What is certain is that it was a small audience hand-picked from among loyalist and inner government circles. None of the names that became known in the course of time either knew Sa'adeh at the personal level or sympathised with his ideas, which indicates that the audience was carefully scanned.[17]

[68]

Sa'adeh was brought into the courtroom at noon flanked by soldiers armed with machine guns and other light weapons. He was unshaven, with hair tousled, and wearing a light brown suit. After the courtroom cleared of the rumbling noise of soldiers walking in and out and everyone had been seated, the presiding judge opened the hearing with the customary questions to Sa'adeh about his full name and date and place of birth. He then asked Sa'adeh to nominate another defense lawyer because John Tian, his first selection, had declined the offer to represent him. Why Tian had forsaken Sa'adeh at such a critical moment has never been satisfactorily explained. The official explanation that he "snubbed Sa'adeh for ideological reasons" is not overwhelmingly convincing since Tian and Sa'adeh were close personal friends and the lawyer was strongly indebted to Sa'adeh for his recent election as Chairperson of the Lawyers Syndicate in Lebanon. A snapshot taken in March 1949, only four months before the trial, shows Sa'adeh and Tian sharing a drink at a party function!

Sa'adeh then nominated an able local lawyer named Emil Lahhoud. Short, quick, and imperious, he was one of the most seasoned trial lawyers in the country. Lahhoud was whisked into the court within minutes and agreed to take on the case on the condition that the trial be adjourned for 72 hours so he could study the evidence. The judges quickly conferred amongst themselves and rejected his request. Lahhoud then asked for 48 hours, but his request was again overruled. He went down to 24 hours: the motion was blocked yet again. This last objection made the task of the defense a formidable one and served to confirm certain prevailing suspicions about the trial. In protest, Lahhoud withdrew from the case and the left the courtroom.[18]

Recognizing that the trial was a mockery, Sa'adeh interceded with Lahhoud: "Stick around, Emil. I don't need you to defend me, just to stay and keep note of what I say so that you can repeat them to the comrades."[19] But Lahhoud brushed the suggestion aside and, in a perfectly calm voice, said "Antun, this smells fishy to me."[20] In a recent seminar on Sa'adah's trial, Attorney August Bakhos recounted how he and several other colleagues vainly tried to dissuade Lahhoud from leaving. He allegedly answered them, "They brought him here to kill him, not to try him."[21] He subsequently explained his departure in philosophical terms: "It is better for the sentence to be passed so oppressively than to be issued the way it was previously prepared . . . so that it would be said that we defended him but were not successful."[22]

The feeling inside the courtroom favoured the selection of another lawyer, but the court would brook no delays and appointed first lieutenant Elias Rizkallah as Sa'adeh legal counsel. Sa'adeh strongly objected to this "on the ground that he did not know the officer and did not know if he was competent enough to take on the case or whether he was learned in the law."[23] However, the presiding judge dismissed the objection and told Sa'adeh "to speak out in his own defense within what is humanly possible."[24] Apart from the judges and attending military officers no one else in the courtroom had previously heard of Rizkallah. Until recently, it was commonly believed that he was appointed on the spur of the moment to get proceedings underway. This was not the case, however. Rizkallah was in fact appointed before the trial opening and his selection was made on purely political grounds. Apparently, during a top level meeting between President Khoury and his military chiefs a few hours earlier, the President floated to the Army Commander General Chehab the idea that Sa'adeh's legal representative at the trial should be an army officer commissioned on behalf of the Military Court. But Chehab politely declined the idea on the ground that he knew of no officer with the right qualifications for the job. The President then leaned toward Al-Rifa'i for someone under his command and Al-Rifa'i proposed Rizkallah.

Rizkallah's own recollections, brief as they may be, are revealing:

> One morning as I was heading to my office in the gendarme headquarters, two non-commissioned officers under my charge and fully armed blocked my passage to the office saying that they have orders to do so. At this point, one of Brigadier General Al-Rifa'i's guards approached us and asked me to go up to Al-Rifa'i's office, which I did. Instead of receiving me inside his office as usual, Al-Rifa'i stepped out himself and asked me to accompany him to the officers' room. His eyes sparked as he said to me, 'This bastard is here.' I returned, 'Who is this bastard?' He said, 'It's Antun Sa'adeh himself.' I replied, 'What have I to do with that?' He answered me outright with an edge in his voice that Sa'adeh is due to be taken shortly to the military court, where he will be immediately tried, sentenced to death and executed within a few hours, and that I have been personally appointed to defend him in my capacity as a trial attorney for the court.[25]

Rizkallah "initially refused to obey the orders,"[26] but al-Rifa'i snapped back, "These are orders of the authority. To refuse to obey them is insubordination."[27] Rizkallah acceded.

After Rizkallah's appointment the presiding judge invoked article 68 of the Military Penal Code, or the secrecy clause as it is known in Lebanon to this day, and ordered the journalists and members of the public to leave the courtroom at once.

The Opening Session

With the legal preliminaries over, the trial finally got underway "in an atmosphere of tension and fear."[28] The presiding judge began by asking the state attorney to read the charges, which were the basis for the trial. Three main charges were read out:

1. Inciting and participating in an armed rebellion against the status quo in Lebanon with the intention of seizing power.
2. Engaging in hostile action against military barracks and the Army, its officers and troops.
3. Causing death to Captain Toufiq Chamoun and attempting to cause death to other members of the Security Forces and attacking police stations and similar installations.

When the state attorney had finished reading the charges, "the questions began to rain down on [Sa'adeh] like a torrent; all of them pointing to death and execution. Sa'adeh answered every question calmly and with exemplary courage. Every question invited more questions."[29] The prosecuting attorney produced scores of documents to substantiate the charges against the SNP leader. Had Sa'adeh nurtured any hope of receiving charitable treatment at the hands of the judges, it must have quickly dissipated when six of his own sympathizers were brought into the court and put on the stand to tell the facts of the raid. The presiding judge, assuming the dual role of judge and prosecutor, asked them in order "Do you identify this man behind the steel bars?" All of them answered in the affirmative except one, a disabled young man who apparently had lost some of his bodily movements under torture: he snapped back at the judge, "Be quiet. Call him by his proper title."[30] The gendarmerie beside gave him a strong blow which sent the man crashing hard to the floor.

Only fragments of two testimonies were published by the Khoury regime. They are reproduced here *in extenso* because they shed some light on the proceedings and also because the answers reveal certain absurdities bordering either on stupidity or ingenuity, depending on how they are read.[31]

The first testimony is from one Mohammad Ibrahim al-Shalabi:

> To a question he answered: I don't have any knowledge of the incidents at Birj al-Barajina and Sarhamoul. I did not travel with him from Syria. I was at An-Nadwa Café in First Avenue in Damascus and the time was ten-thirty. We boarded a mini-bus belonging to a person by the name of Bashir, all fifteen of us, but Antun Sa'adeh was not among us. We met up with two cars at the intersection with Dawoud Street. I saw the leader Antun Sa'adeh in one of them. The buses then took off but I did not know where we were going. I slept on the way and was awakened when we got there. I did not know where I was. It was there that I met the accused. We gave him the salute and he then addressed us and handed out the weapons. My share was a rifle and twenty bullets. From what I could gather from the accused's speech is that we were on a mission to fight Zionism. He told us to use force if force is used against us and might if might is used. I don't know where Antun Sa'adeh went after that.

The second testimony is from one Abdul Sattar Mustafa Maatouk, also a Syrian:

> To a question he answered: This indeed is Antun Sa'adeh. I saw him behind Syria's borders ten kilometres from Lebanon. I don't know what the place where we got to is called. I am from Tell Bneen below Saydnaya. I saw this man Antun Sa'adeh handing out weapons to those who were in the car and delivering a speech and inciting them. He was telling them you must take this place and that place, and I remember Rashayya which has a fortress as one of the places he mentioned. There were three guys in the car from Rashayya, but I don't know their names. They mentioned the Rashayya fortress and said that it had two entrances. They gave a detailed description of it.
>
> Q: Can you remember the type of weapons that Antun Sa'adeh, who is presently with us, handed out?
> A. There was an assortment of weapons.

Q. Who else was with him?

A. The people who were with him were many. They came in two cars. I don't know what type they were. All I know is that their registration was Lebanese.

Q. How many people approximately were in the cars?

A. The large vehicles were three buses. They brought us from Damascus to Zahle after they said to us that there was a wedding in that city. There were twenty-two in the bus that I was riding in and twenty-five in each of the remaining two.

Q. Where were you when you were picked up and who picked you up?

A. We were picked up by the operator of the Beirut Garage for a fee of sixty liras for each car. A group of passengers climbed in with us at a hotel in Damascus called Hotel Lebanon in the district of al-Hreiki. They were not armed then, but shortly after we left the city, we stopped in Beirut Street, which is at the end side of Damascus in Lebanon's direction, and waited there for the groom for a full two hours. Then they said that the groom might have already passed. Shortly after we crossed Maysaloun, to the left, they took us to a spot somewhere there and then to Lebanese territories. We parked at a place until dawn when the leader (pointing to Antun Sa'adeh) turned up and asked everyone to get out. He then gave a speech and they rejoined with "long live the leader," and "long live the National Party."

Q. Repeat the words that the leader was uttering.

A. We, the drivers, remained inside the cars near the meeting. Of the words that I heard from him I remember: "You must be on full alert", "attacks" and other inflammatory speeches.

The evidence produced at that session showed that the SNP and its mass organization were involved in the organization, preparation and execution of the rebellion. As leader of the rebellion, Sa'adeh was held responsible for the attacks on government installations and the slaying of a military officer at Sarhamoul. The SNP leader expressed regret for the Sarhamoul incident, pointing out that casualties are inevitable in armed conflicts, but the court rejected his explanation. It placed the culpability for the single fatality squarely on him on the grounds that he was the leader and instigator of the rebellion.

The Public Prosecutor Address

The presiding judge then granted leave to the Public Prosecutor, Youssef Charbel, to address the Court. By all accounts, Charbel delivered a masterly and comprehensive speech during which Sa'adeh was compelled to stand for two hours. All we can do, in the absence of the original text, is to attempt to give some notion of its scope and effect from a revised version penned after the trial. First, Charbel took all of twenty minutes to catalogue the criminal violations perpetrated by the SNP. He placed the onus of responsibility entirely on Sa'adeh for three reasons:

1. Because he was outright leader of the SNP and supreme commander of its armed forces at the time of the rebellion.
2. Because he personally issued the order for the rebellion.
3. Because he was personally involved in the preparation for and execution of the rebellion, including the distribution of arms and incitement to killing.[32]

Unable to control himself, Charbel proceeded to attack the character of Sa'adeh, seriously endangering the right of the defendant to an impartial trial. Fairness allows the prosecution to attack the character of the defendant only after the latter has attempted to show his good character in his own aid.[33] Against this principle, Charbel addressed himself to a vital question: Was Sa'adeh a man of principle or a mere opportunist? "I believe," he observed, "that Sa'adeh was not an advocate of a genuine and credible ideology, but of an opportunistic and power-hungry idea. In the depth of his heart he assumed it was genuine, but really it is flawed historically, scientifically and practically, and history attests to that."[34] The strategy of the prosecution was to concentrate its fire on Sa'adeh's "dictatorial" personality and the SNP's "terrorist" proclivity. A composite picture of Sa'adeh as a cold-blooded murderer and an agent of foreign endeavours was pieced together on the basis of inconclusive evidence and recollections of alleged conversations. Mustering every ounce of his strength, Charbel stigmatized Sa'adeh as an eccentric and egotistical man: "A man of Antun Sa'adeh's character is easily tempted to parade his powers before the masses, or to be driven by a grudge or a target that really doesn't help him and blights the general good."[35]

The stinging attack on Sa'adeh's character was followed by a savage attack on his national program. With icy logic Charbel portrayed

Sa'adeh as a self-deceived utopianist who never really understood the moving forces of society and history: "Antun Sa'adah built this [Syrian] homeland of his on historical and scientifically deductive principles that he repeatedly mentioned in his speeches and addresses. Sa'adah, however, was not aware of the fact that science is not yet capable of accounting for the facts of this universe tangibly enough in terms of time, the principle of evolution, human races, origins of nations, and how countries form."[36] Charbel went on to ridicule Sa'adeh's pan-Syrian ideology as out of touch with the intrinsic reality of Lebanon:

> If we consult so-called history from the beginning until the present, we will realize this glaring fact. Yet, amidst the realm of claims and assumptions, there are tangible facts that time has produced, and on which homelands, combining diverse factors, were built; homelands including Lebanon, that upheld the banners of fraternity and tolerance until it became an example to follow and a guiding beacon. This is the homeland that Antun Sa'adeh and his party have sought to destroy and to subsume with another weaved in his vivid imagination. This is indeed contradictory not just to the people of Lebanon who, despite their diverse sects, collaborated in building this homeland, but also contradictory to the idea of Arabism which, in itself, is consistent with the presence of several separate states independent from one another, but which, nonetheless, share the bonds of fraternity and neighbourliness.[37]

He added "Gentlemen, those who adhered to these sound principles lived and let others live as well. Those, however, who tried to turn their fantasies into a reality and their nonsensicality into scientific or social bases, ruined their lives and those of many others."[38]

Charbel now reached that point in his speech for which he was to be sharply criticized later. Sa'adeh, he callously argued, was a national traitor who, in his obsession with power, sold his soul and his country to the Zionist Jews. Coming hot on the heels of the recent debacle in Palestine, it was perhaps the single most stirring issue of the day. Charbel began by declaring his satisfaction with the conduct of Arab governments in Palestine and with the "sects and groups" who, although lacking the resources and energy of governments, did not "obstruct in principle or organized form the endeavour" in Palestine and "did what they could" to help save it.[39] With the same icy aplomb he had exhibited throughout his address, Charbel then suggested three ways the SNP "betrayed" the Palestine cause:

1. by passing invaluable information to the Jews about the state of the Arabs;
2. by contributing to the handover of a section of Palestine to the Jews; and
3. by secretly communicating with them for a treaty.[40]

This was the climatic point toward which Charbel had been skilfully manoeuvring the court. For his evidence he reproduced a testimony by one Mohammad Arakah and a copy of a short letter from Sa'adeh to one of his aides in Palestine instructing him to establish contacts with the Zionists. He also presented the court with randomly selected pieces of evidence plucked out from internal SNP memos confiscated by the security forces. Charbel's prosecution strategy now rested on proving that not only was Sa'adeh a traitor but also an opportunist. He declared:

> The attitude of the leader of the national party, Antun Sa'adeh, as regards the cause that he worked for many years, and as regards the dreams that filled his vivid imagination with hope, enthused us to go back to legendary incidents recorded in history such as that of Imru' Al Qays.[41] We said:

> > *My friend sobbed as our fate became clear*
> > *He was sure that our end was similar to that of Caesar*
> > *I said to him don't let a tear fall off your eye for*
> > *No one would blame us when we die seeking the summit*

When we saw that Sa'adeh was not moved by those words out of pride and arrogance, we said: At least say, out of pretence,

> *It is written that we take these steps*
> *And he whose fate is to take a step, shall walk*

With cutting sarcasm, Charbel chose to conclude (some say open) his speech with the following prose:[42]

> *Once the starlings could fly around a bit*
> *They began to suppose themselves soaring eagles*

On the only occasion he uttered during the prosecution phase, a perfectly nonchalant Sa'adeh evened the score quickly with some prose of his own:

> *A starling cowers even when flying,*
> *But an eagle stays lofty when dying*[43]

The prosecution's speech stands as a classic example of how the legal process can be prejudiced by misstatements of issues, abuse, and inflammatory appeals. In the course of his circus marathon, "Sa'adeh took momentary looks at [Charbel] and shook his head"[44] when the Prosecutor bandied out negative epithets. However, if the public prosecutor thought he could unbalance Sa'adeh with his vindictive and bullying tactics he was wrong: the SNP leader displayed superabundant physical and psychological energy and managed to preserve his manner and his temper the whole time. He listened to the speech with intense interest, occasionally taking notes, and allowed the speaker to deliver his address uninterrupted.

A Short Adjournment

At half past three in the afternoon, the presiding judge adjourned the trial for five minutes. Waiting journalists were re-admitted into the court to take commemorative snap-shots of the trial and to report on proceedings. In his recollections of the trial, Berri recorded: "During the photo session all cameras aimed at Sa'adeh standing behind the steel bars with a carefree smile as if someone else was on trial, or as if he was an independent observer from another planet witnessing a process of justice in a trial that exhibited everything but justice."[45] In the pictures that appeared in the Lebanese press the following day, Sa'adeh looked exhausted and worn out. *Al-Hayat* described his personal condition as follows:

> He was dressed in a white jacket, a grey pair of trousers, and an American brightly-colored tie. He obviously had not shaved in days, his hair was uncombed. He was visibly disturbed, sometimes casting wandering glances, sometimes smiling. Yet, he was generally calm turning his eyes around the place.[46]

Another description can be found in *al-Qubs*:

His eyes were blood-red on account of the sleepless tiring nights he spent. They could not rest on one thing. Sometimes he would gaze at you, or be fixated on the floor. His face was red having been touched by the rays of the sun. His mouth tried to give way to a smile that only momentarily lightened up his face, then immediately vanished in resignation and despair.[47]

The court was ready to proceed when Sa'adeh abruptly stopped the trial and demanded some food. The judges, in total disbelief, "gave him a dirty look and were rather surprised at the ease with which he turned proceedings around."[48] The presiding judge had a gendarmerie run over to his house, which was situated near the court, to fetch some food. He returned minutes later with a bowl of spaghetti and a cup of traditional yogurt. Sa'adeh devoured only "two spoons of spaghetti and three of yogurt"[49] and went back to finish his answer.

The Defense's Speech

The next order of business was Rizkallah's speech for the defense. The court-appointed counsel had had no previous legal experience and had never been in a situation where he had to defend someone in a trial. He made up in courage what he lacked in trial experience. Rizkallah's speech, prepared on the spot, lasted "a few minutes" and pleaded for leniency on the ground of insanity:

Gentlemen,

The defense regrets that the matter at issue includes current events that it cannot discuss nor can it defend the person who carried them out. Nonetheless, we would like to cite the following facts:

Rebellion against the government and the rulers;
Armed deviation from the homeland state and the higher interests of the country;
Riots, disorder and offenses against public security, and acts of aggression;
Gunfire and the gleaming metal of bayonets and the shedding of blood

But I want you to look deeper through all of these facts to the psychology of this man from whom all these things preceded and so forth.

[78]

We have here a man who imagined that he carried a mission to build and construct. Yet suddenly he in an almost unconscious way turns into a dangerous instrument of wide ranging destruction. I have to stress my point that he changed in a subconscious way since he found himself standing at a point in his life when his judgment could get impaired on the crossroads of those two possible futures, the future of construction and its opposite, the choice of becoming a destroyer.

His intention was to soar up towards the first horizon yet at just that point he found himself drawn by a deviation in thought towards that second horizon so that he became – without properly understanding this – in a setting that he himself had not chosen as there gathered around him elements made up of malcontents and violent and destructive people so that he with them rolled up his sleeves for direct action.

Thus, gentlemen, you have before you a man in the depth of whose personality a tornado raged that snatched away from him his clarity of mind and rational understanding so that what he had considered evil at his way of looking at things now seemed to him to be good and acts of terrorism to bring long desired redemption.

Given this confused psychological condition pressing in upon the man, I request that you think seriously not about a complete exoneration of the accused given that his record is centered with the smell of gunpowder and caked with blood but that you do exonerate him of the deeds that he committed. That would be on the grounds that the things he committed only stemmed from a chronic confusion in his psychological context that dense clouds were more and more shrouding.[50]

Rizkallah's then read out article 233 of the Penal Code, which set out the grounds for leniency.[51] He made no attempt to cross-examine witnesses. Nor did he ask Sa'adeh to take the stand. His speech was short and sharp designed to satisfy a predetermined role and to save Sa'adeh from death. Even if he had been allowed to spend more time at the tribunal it is most unlikely that he would have been able to mount an effective defense given that he was given almost no time to study the case. Rizkallah's approach to the case was also self-defeating because in any trial where the government has a political reason for prosecution and is determined to obtain a conviction, normal tactics (for example, using influence to get the charges dropped or pleading guilty to a lesser charge to get a reduced sentence) will not work.

At any rate, Sa'adeh disdained the plea of insanity. He made his feelings known to Rizkallah: "When I finished my address Sa'adeh looked askance at me and scolded me saying, 'Insane am I?' I answered him confusedly, 'Let God be the judge between you and me, Sir.'"[52]

Sa'adeh's Address

It was Sa'adeh's turn next to address the court. Despite the deadly seriousness of the charges and the controversial nature of the evidence, he was not allowed to plan his defense and was instead compelled to deliver an extemporaneous speech. He rose to the challenge. His two-hour address, though rudely interrupted by the prosecution "to break up the rhythm of his defense . . . mesmerised the whole courtroom, including the Guards, who were now being rotated every ten minutes."[53] Sa'adeh delved into philosophical issues "as though he was making an address to history and the nation."[54] This was less problematic than legal technicalities, but he ran the risk of slipping into the quicksand of Lebanese politics. To be sure, Sa'adeh had several options to choose from had he chosen to contest the prosecution case on legal grounds. For example, he was in a position to raise a cloud of legal and ethical issues associated with the evidence presented by the Public Prosecutor. He could also have argued, as Lahhoud subsequently did in the trial of his sympathizers, that since his revolution communiqué did not call for murder and intimidation of public institutions he was innocent of any capital offenses. Contesting the case on legal premises would have given Sa'adeh the ammunition to expose the trial for what it really was, a travesty, but he had neither the legal competence nor the time to consider this option.

Although Sa'adeh's speech has vanished with the other records of his trial[55] it is possible to surmise its main points from newspaper reports (inaccurate as they may be) and individual accounts and recollections of the trial. Speaking fluently and with occasional fire, Sa'adeh ridiculed the charge of the prosecution that he was a national traitor. He reminded the court that he was "Lebanese from father to son. I don't really think that there is anyone out there who can claim to be more Lebanese than me . . . I never denied the Lebanese State or the Lebanese entity, but my desire was to convert Lebanon into a base from which to launch the party's ideology to neighbouring entities."[56] He continued in a historical résumé to explain the difference between Lebanon as a "political question" arising from a religious motive and Syria as a "national cause" in its own right. With enormous patience he reminded the court that he had never attempted to force the issue of Lebanon's reincorporation into Syria on the Lebanese people:

> He said that Lebanon is part of geographical Syria. The task of convincing the Lebanese people of this fact required the eradication of a major obstacle, namely, sectarianism. He was at pains to emphasize that the Party's commitment to a sectarian-free life for the Lebanese was not motivated by the desire to protect its image as a Non-Sectarian Party but because it was an integral part of its National Program . . . When sectarianism had been eliminated, Sa'adeh went on to tell the court, the national association between Lebanon and the rest of Syria will revert back to its natural character and all negative feelings and suspicion will vanish.[57]

Sa'adeh's egalitarian approach to the union question had been one of his stronger points, but he was often either misunderstood or misconstrued. At the core of his ideology lay the belief that reunification depended on the will of the people, not governments. Sa'adeh was explicit about this. He believed that reunification, as a national principle, had to be preceded by a program of intense national education in order to overcome the existing psychological barriers [and to point] out the kind of problems and contradictions that prevailed in Lebanon. It had to consist of making the Lebanese more aware of the national question and their stake in it. Inevitably, this would lead to Lebanon's dissolution as a separate political entity but its re-incorporation into Syria would not be a question of merger or annexation, but one of genuine unity.[58]

At some point in the speech, the presiding judge interrupted Sa'adeh to ask him specific questions about the rebellion:

> *The presiding judge*: Why then did you rebel against the Government?
> *Sa'adeh*: The Party had been insulted. The revolution was a mere response to correct this situation.
> *The presiding judge*: How can that be? Just because the Party had been insulted you declare revolution on the State and murder its men?
> *Sa'adeh*: As I said, the Party had been insulted and revolution was the only practical response. During any revolution there are bound to be victims on both sides.

Sa'adeh: I take full responsibility for the revolution. I gave the orders for it.[59]

To scuttle the charge of collaboration with the Jewish state, Sa'adeh went into a long explication of Zionism: "The focus of Sa'adeh's address was on the national factor as the principal determinant of the Party's policy and on the vital issues sweeping the Nation, like the Zionist menace and Sectarianism, which he regarded as just as dangerous as Zionism."[60] Sa'adeh did not enter into a tangled debate with the prosecution over the authenticity of his evidence. Instead, he used the courtroom as a forum to explain his views on Zionism. His exact words are not available, but if his earlier writings are any indication to go by, the speech would probably have been about the danger that Zionism posed not only to Palestine but to geographical Syria as a whole. Sa'adeh would have almost certainly repeated the warning, which all his writings continued, that Zionism would succeed unless it was confronted by a systematic counter-plan. What we are not certain of, though, is whether he dared to repeat his savage condemnations of Arab regimes for their pitiable handling of the conflict in Palestine.

Sa'adeh concluded his speech with the words: "As I finalize my defense, I leave it to the conscience of the judges and their integrity to determine my fate."[61] A "deathlike stillness" then came over the court. Everyone, it seemed, was stunned by the speech. One witness described it as the most memorable moment of the trial.[62] The Government-appointed Trial Commissioner, Michel Talhama, later recalled, "It would have taken ten attorneys to come up with the arguments that Sa'adeh produced and still they wouldn't have been as articulate and far-sighted as he was."[63]

The Prosecution was equally amazed: "I assure you that [Sa'adeh] strongly and freely delivered a lengthy defense of himself that took quite a long time. No attorney could have covered the case so comprehensively like the defendant, Antun Sa'adeh, who discussed the matter through from A to Z."[64] On concluding his address, which lasted about two hours, Sa'adeh was taken back to prison and the judging panel retired to deliberate on its verdict.

The Verdict

Approximately two hours later, the five judges returned to the courtroom to pronounce the verdict. Inside and outside the courthouse the guard had been reinforced substantially that evening in anticipation of any last minute mishap. The opinion of the court was delivered by the presiding judge, Aziz Ahdab. He claimed that the verdict was unanimous, but at least one Lebanese newspaper said it was a majority ruling.[65] Sa'adeh was sentenced to execution before a firing squad in accordance with Articles 308, 309, 314, and 315 of the general penal code, which penalized the membership of any organization that incited public disorder through violence or carried arms against the state with the intent of bringing about its overthrow, and Article 119 of the military penal code on the execution of the death penalty. The sentence was irrevocable. The decree governing the trial did not provide for any judicial appeal against the decisions of the special tribunals and prohibited the courts from reviewing any aspect of the operation of the tribunal. Invariably, when a person is convicted of a capital crime on circumstantial evidence alone, a substantial segment of the courtroom can be counted on to cry out against the verdict. At the pronouncement of the sentence by the presiding judge, "the courtroom was filled with commotion, voices cried out loudly with strong condemnation . . . Some left outraged, cursing and grudging."[66]

Sa'adeh was not present in the courtroom when the verdict was pronounced. He was brought back to the court later that evening and advised of the judgment by the clerk of the court in the presence of the state attorney and troops of the Lebanese army, in accordance with Article 84 of the Military penal code. Sa'adeh received the verdict with a self-possession that was remarkable under the circumstances. "Thank you," was all he said in reply. He was then taken away in a waiting army jeep, accompanied by an exceptionally strong guard of mounted and motorized soldiers who had their weapons at the ready. A detachment of the Lebanese army guarded all approaches to the two-kilometer distance between the courthouse and the prison and snipers took up positions on rooftops to foil any last-minute rescue attempts. On arrival, Sa'adeh underwent a routine medical check-up, in keeping with prison rules, and sipped a cup of tea with the medical officer. He then took his jacket off, folded it around his shoes to create a pillow, and slept.[67]

Evaluation of the Proceedings

The trial of Antun Sa'adeh has posed a range of questions that retain their urgency to this day. Why did the Lebanese Government conduct the trial in such a secret and hasty manner? Was the trial political and, if so, why did the Government refuse to treat it as such? Did Sa'adeh receive a fair trial? The following is an evaluation of proceedings in Sa'adeh's trial from various angles.

1. The Administration of Justice

Under Lebanese law, Sa'adeh's trial seemed fair in the sense that the accused was permitted to make a full defense of his actions and explain his position with virtually no interference from either the prosecution or the court. He was also able to have the services of an appointed counsel in support of his position, and his counsel was permitted to comment on the charges. A number of other features of the trial, however, suggest that certain factors were at work which undermined both the substantive and procedural fairness of the proceedings.

At the substantive level, the trial disclosed glaring shortcomings from beginning to end. It was railroaded with unprecedented speed and without respect to the defendant's basic legal and human rights. Everyone, it seemed, was involved in the mockery: the regime, the army, the security apparatus, even the judges. The tribunal was more concerned with securing a conviction than uncovering the truth and every step in the trial was timed so that the defendant could not have an opportunity to defend himself. But on still other grounds Antun Sa'adeh's trial was flagrantly unfair. The right of the accused to a reasonable time to prepare for trial was shockingly violated. Although the court did not deny him the right to engage a lawyer of his own choice, it went to great pains to thwart this right. When a competent trial counsel was found, he was allowed no time to familiarize himself with the case or to prepare his defense. He resigned in disgust.

It is also quite obvious, both from the speed and secrecy which enshrouded the case, that transparency was lacking. The Khoury regime tempered the force of the law and violated in so many words all the legal norms that apply in a constitutional state. Yet in the eyes of the world it wanted to be seen to use them to some extent. As far as we can tell, the government regarded the time over which the trial happened as sufficient for the mechanism of justice. However, one cannot help but wonder why it went to such extreme lengths if the case was so straightforward and the outcome was certain. Again, a rationale seems to be more of a rationalization. And again, upon piercing the veil of reason, the acceleration of procedures is a strong indication that the decision was largely resolved in the individual minds of the several justices of the court before it was heard.

A striking irregularity is the decision to court-martial Sa'adeh under the Emergency Law of 1948. Despite its inappropriateness to the case, the Emergency Law was invoked to enable the government to conduct the trial in secret "since the two justifications for secrecy, namely the threat to the security situation and public morals, were absent."[68] Kamal Jumblatt, in his 1949 interpellation to the Lebanese Chamber, called it the "first violation" of the law because "it is illegal to declare a state of emergency across Lebanon except on the basis of a law passed by the Lebanese Parliament."[69] Jumblatt added an interesting sidelight to the issue:

> It is noteworthy that the emergency law that the Lebanese government relied on in pursuing the SNP is decree no. 34 L.R., issued in February 1936, during De Martel's era. It aimed to ensure the safety of the French armies occupying Syria and Lebanon, and, in turn, to maintain the state of the mandate. It appears, therefore, that the Lebanese government had resorted to a decree issued specifically to protect the colonial armies.[70]

The application of the Emergency Law outside the rubric of the Palestine War was unjustified and morally wicked. No one who is conversant with the 1948 State of Emergency can legitimately consign the Sa'adeh case to the law governing it. Besides, the military tribunals established under that Law did not possess the adequate means or experience to deal with such complex issues as those arising from the case. The procedures in these tribunals were deeply flawed and fell seriously short of international standards for fair trial. A recent report by the Centre for Democracy and the Rule of Law has noted, "The military justice system in Lebanon is intrinsically unfair and does not comply with normal legal standards internationally recognized."[71]

At the procedural level, many limits were breached which affected not only the credibility of the trial but also its legality. First, the trial violated Sa'adeh's right to a legal counsel and to communicate freely and privately with him. Since Sa'adeh was forced to accept an assigned counsel not of his own choosing, after his own lawyer withdrew in disgust, it could be safely argued that at no stage of the trial was the accused represented by counsel except nominally. Elias Rizkallah, Sa'adeh's assigned counsel, did not possess the legal qualifications or the competence to deal with the case. He was not even a registered legal practitioner. Judging from his performance at the trial he seemed to be familiar with only the rough edges of Sa'adeh's case. Moreover, as a member of the security apparatus and married into the Gemayel family, one of the traditional arch-enemies of Antun Sa'adeh and his party, Rizkallah's appointment to the case was a clear breach of the principle of impartiality.

There was a breach of the principle of equality of arms in relation to the right of the defense to call and examine witnesses. Questioning of witnesses by both the prosecution and the defense is vital to procedural fairness and provides the court with an opportunity to hear evidence and challenges to that evidence. Cross-examination, noted John Wigmore, is "the greatest legal engine ever invented for the discovery of truth."[72] Moreover, under constitutional law, to which Lebanon subscribes, the right of the accused to adequate time and facilities to prepare a defense includes the right to prepare the examination of prosecution witnesses. There is therefore an implied obligation on the prosecution to give the defense adequate advance notification of the witnesses that the prosecution intends to call at trial. This did not happen. The identities of the six witnesses who took the stand in Sa'adeh's trial were not disclosed to the defendant until the trial. This confronted Sa'adeh (and his legal counsel) with an almost insurmountable handicap and deprived him of the necessary information permitting him to test the witnesses' reliability or cast doubt on their credibility.

A fundamental principle and prerequisite of a fair trial is that the tribunal charged with the responsibility of making decisions in a case must be established by law, and must be competent, independent and impartial.[73] This right may not be suspended even in states of emergency.[74] Despite the serious nature of the case against Sa'adeh, these criteria were not observed at his trial. The judging panel in the trial did not have the appropriate legal training or qualifications needed to deal with the case. Regardless of the character of its individual members, its composition alone created the appearance, if not actual lack, of impartiality. Independence was absent because the tribunal came under the Ministry of Defense, making it a special court subordinated to an organ of the executive. Impartiality, which requires that judges have no interest or stake in the case and do not have pre-formed opinions about it, was also missing: the panel condoned as well as participated in the violations of the defendant's legal rights. In doing so, its members demonstrated a judicial incapacity for the proper administration of justice.

Fair trial demands the respect of the rules of evidence. This principle was violated at least twice with Sa'adeh: (1) some evidence was elicited under duress in violation of standard practice which stipulates that trial evidence, including confessions by the accused, elicited as a result of torture or other cruel, inhuman or degrading treatment, must not be used in any proceedings except those brought against the suspected perpetrators; (2) some crucial evidence was based on anonymous testimonies and a forged photocopy of original documents – a breach of evidential authenticity, which requires that evidence as diverse as documents, physical evidence, telephone calls, and scientific processes must all be authenticated, unless it belongs to a class of evidence where the evidence is self-authenticating. When the facts at issue are withheld or distorted, a fair trial cannot be held.

Finally, the prosecution's refusal to disclose the evidence he intended to use against Sa'adeh until after the trial had started rendered the trial as a whole unfair. In proper trials, all evidence must normally be produced at a public hearing, in the presence of the accused with a view to adversarial argument. There are exceptions to this principle, but they must not infringe on the rights of the defense. It is also a standard legal norm that

> When prosecutors come into possession of evidence against suspects that they know or believe on reasonable grounds was obtained through recourse to unlawful methods, which constitute a grave violation of the suspect's human rights, especially involving torture or cruel, inhuman or degrading treatment or punishment, or other abuses of human rights, they shall refuse to use such evidence against anyone other than those who used such methods, or inform the Court accordingly, and shall take all necessary steps to ensure that those responsible for using such methods are brought to justice.

The overzealous prosecutor at Sa'adeh's trial did the exact opposite of that. He fed the court fake evidence and inflammatory outpourings to conceal his bad logic. His address to the court represented one of the most blatant attempts at legal manipulation. It is the prosecutor who decides whether or not to formally charge a defendant with a crime. It is the prosecutor who decides which particular charge or charges to file against the defendant. Once these decisions are made, the prosecutor will file the charges with the appropriate court. Many weeks, if not months, of pre-trial preparations then begin. The prosecutor must interview the witnesses and ensure that any appropriate analysis of the physical evidence is performed. These preparations are much more intense in a death penalty case than in any other because of the stakes involved. They must be approached with the same degree of diligence afforded the trial itself. Fair trial demands it. In Sa'adeh's case, the state prosecution violated every elementary judicial norm in organizing the trial. What should have taken weeks to prepare was completed in several hours, even though the trial was much more than a simple case of proving the guilt or innocence of the defendant: the charges carried a possible death sentence.

2. Secrecy and speed

That the trial took place in secret and swiftly was irregular in itself. Secrecy and haste appertain to totalitarian regimes where the administration of justice, like almost everything else, is degraded to an instrument of social oppression and intimidation. History shows that secrecy and haste in the trial of public figures has traditionally taken place on two grounds: (1) because the State lacked the evidence needed to justify conviction before the public; and (2) because the State's case was so weak or vulnerable that a secret trial became the only practical avenue for conviction. Had Sa'adeh received a proper trial, the Khoury regime might not have been able to secure a conviction with the death penalty. There was sufficient and potentially dangerous evidence to incriminate key regime officials on charges of a very serious nature. Revelations of the government's plot to dispose of Sa'adeh before the start of proceedings had the potential to turn the trial in favour of the accused and embarrass the regime.

The matter is also intriguing because it goes against the norm of historical behaviour. Traditionally, governments in similar situations have used the courts to make a political point rather than simply to settle disputes or to try persons accused of breaking the law. The result often was a public trial in constitutional democracies or a show trial in totalitarian regimes giving the government an opportunity to show that it has the power and control to root out and punish unacceptable behaviour.

A public trial, moreover, can make a positive contribution to a democratic society. The state, as the main litigant, stands to obtain a number of benefits from prosecuting dissidents with the aid of a public trial. First, public trials serve as a tool to intimidate radical movements and provide a pretext to control political dissidence. They "can have a *symbolic value* in enabling the state to signal to opponents that it is upping the stakes of political struggle"[75] particularly where the state is subject to democratic or constitutional constraints. Public trials can also serve to discredit political opponents or damage their credibility in the eyes of the public. Even if they are not fully successful in the sense of securing a conviction, negative epithets bandied about at such trials can be damaging. Secondly, public trials can exhaust dissident groups and drain them of their vitality especially if the charges are serious and large resources and levels of organizational energy are needed to wage them. Thirdly, public trials can be used to indoctrinate the people or to mobilize social support for the state by implanting in the minds of the masses "a few stereotyped, simplified accusations."[76] Finally, public trials "force political energy to be *diverted* on to a particular *legal* battle rather than the original *political* target."[77]

Unless it has a legally weak case to present, the government and the wider polity have much to gain from a public trial:

> The state may use a trial to confront a resister with his doctrinal folly, to enmesh him in leeching formalities, to extort that most conclusive of tributes to power-abnegation. If the resister does submit, obviating the need for extirpative punishment, the state may claim to have acted with merciful forbearance. If the resister does not submit, his obstinacy is further proof of his guilt and the state may claim the sanction of justice. In either event the process of trial, by providing a ritual for obscuring the crude application of power, sustains the moral equilibrium of political authority.[78]

Besides, the community has an interest in seeing that proceedings are kept public. It likes to know how the judicial system functions and to see that the accused is given a fair and impartial trial and that the prosecution is accorded a proper opportunity to present its case.[79] From the standpoint of justice, public exposure of proceedings "constitutes an ever present check on the judge, stimulating his sense of responsibility and curbing his prejudices."[80] The conduct of the trial in secret circumstances, on the other hand, serves to distort the truth-finding process:

> A fully public trial . . . has been considered to have certain other advantages not to be found in restricted trials. Among these beneficial attributes are the increased testimonial trustworthiness resulting from the reluctance of witnesses to testify falsely before a public audience; the possibility of the attendance of those who may provide evidence yet who are unknown to the parties; and the affording to the public an education in legal processes with the consequent creation of increased confidence in judicial remedies.[81]

Open processes of justice also serve an important prophylactic purpose and provide an outlet for community concern, hostility, and emotions. Secrecy, on the other hand, does little more than cloak potential corruption, foment distrust and prevent the community from seeing justice done. It breeds cynicism, paranoia, and distrust in the society because closed-door proceedings understandably make people apprehensive.

Sa'adeh symbolized everything the regime opposed. A public trial on the charge of threatening the national security of Lebanon would have seemed a valuable propaganda opportunity to a regime that characterized itself as the defender of the regime and Lebanese statehood. It would have acted as an indicator of the government's commitment to the rule of law, especially since its credibility was on the line. Even if politically explosive, an open trial with such a well-known defendant would have directed public attention to the legal system and the principles of justice they represented. That can be a sign of a healthy political system, especially in an emerging state:

> Though apparently limited to the peculiarities of the case at hand, [political trials] are at bottom a form of collective negotiation and exchange among individuals and groups affected by the different possible outcomes. They are institutionalized procedures for deciding not just the ostensible conflicts among participants but certain issues about the regulation, circulation, distribution, and operation of power as well.[82]

There are also direct gains for society from public trials, particularly if they are about "an offense of a political character:"[83]

> Political trials within the rule of law provide society with the
> occasion to examine, and perhaps redefine, itself. Such trials do
> not, perhaps cannot, resolve the tensions forever . . . Political trials
> confront tangled issues, tied in tight knots. While a trial might not
> untie the knot, but only cut it, our reflection on the knot in front
> of us will help us to understand the next one much better. Hard
> cases, the adage has it, make bad law. Nevertheless, hard political
> cases make a better understood society.[84]

By opting for secrecy and speed in trying Sa'adeh, the Khoury regime
committed a grave moral mistake. It had an opportunity to vent its
frustration and all the while maintain its commitment to due process
and the values of modern democracy: instead, it chose to put the reason
of state above the rule of law. The preservation of the right to a public
trial is important both to the individual defendant and to the community
at large.

3. Political vs. Capital

Another shortcoming of the trial lay in the decision to try Sa'adeh as a
"common" rather than as a "political" criminal. Lebanese judicatories
now argue that the "official" interpretation of the law was flawed because
it overlooked Article 196 of the Code of Political Crimes, which defines
as "political" any crime committed with "political intent" but not for
selfish or vile reasons. They pose two questions: (1) was "political intent"
visible in Sa'adeh case, and answer in the affirmative; (2) was the offense
committed for selfish or vile reasons and answer in the negative.

A basic incompatibility did in fact exist between the Lebanese
Criminal Code and the way in which the government interpreted
the law. For unlike criminal codes that juxtapose political crimes with
common crimes, the Lebanese Criminal Code, in harmony with its
French counterpart, is based on a clear distinction between the two.
It defines the common crime in the European sense as "such acts as
offend the sentiment of humanity or violate the rules of conduct exacted
by the common or average probity of present day civilized people . . .
which show a deficiency of probity in the author of them, and lascivious
acts."[85] Also, in harmony with the French code, Lebanese Law identifies
political crimes "in the nature of the right violated, by the motives by
which the action is impelled and by the end the authors pursue."[86]
Article 196 of the Lebanese Penal Code states:

> Political crimes are deliberate crimes committed by the author with a political intent. They are also crimes that impinge on individual and public political rights as long as the author had not been impelled by selfish and vile purpose.[87]

As defined in the above passage, political crimes include "those felonies and misdemeanours which violated only the political order of the state, be that order exterior, as in attacking the independence of the nation, the integrity of its territory, the relations of the state to other states; or interior, as in attacking the form of government, the organization and functioning of the political powers and the political rights of citizens."[88]

Moreover, Lebanese Law accepted the concept of a "political intent" as something which can be logically imputed to an accused, once again an offshoot of the French penal code, which identifies the political offender as one who operates on a higher evolutionary level than a common criminal. A French treatise on criminal law stated, "The political offender is not like other offenders; he violates the criminal law because he combats the particular political regime that applies the law."[89]

This goes a long way toward explaining why the French were indulgent towards political offenders during their mandate over Syria and Lebanon and why they preferred exile or imprisonment to the death penalty. Given that the offending act in 1949 was directed toward the authority of the regime and the elaborate system of privileges and restraints on which the political institutions were based, and not towards private life or property, its designation as a "capital crime" constituted an unreasonable breach of the Lebanese Criminal Code.

Since the target of Sa'adeh's revolt was the government and not the bases of social existence, the offending act could not have crossed the cut-off point between a "pure" political crime and a common crime committed with political motivation. It remains a political crime *par excellence* as it did not involve acts of odious barbarity and vandalism prohibited by international law or the laws of insurrection. The death of one person in the confusion is not, in itself, a sufficient ground for criminality: killing or incitement to kill was never an intended part of the revolution.

Two other factors rendered the offending act as a political rather than a capital crime. First, the offender did not fit the character of a common criminal since his act was not "designed for the sole end of benefiting or avenging himself"[90] but for purposes that are clearly more elevated than those manifested by common criminals. The true political criminal, says Ferri:

> . . . is a pseudo-criminal and ought not to be considered in the same breath as the ordinary criminal. The latter is atavistic, harks back to a primitive and savage time; he is anti-social, antihuman, and is not to be confused with the political criminal since the latter is not anti-human, does not attack the bases of our human life, our life as social beings, but attacks only the bases of our political or governmental order which is transitory. The ordinary crimes, and particularly the *mala in se* or the natural crimes are regressive, whereas the political crimes are progressive. The natural crimes are involutive or involutionary; and the political crimes are evolutive or evolutionary.[91]

The second factor is the "public" nature of the offense, which again is directly related to the mind of the author of the act, his motives and end or goals:

> Political criminals are characterized as being quite different from conventional criminals: they often announce their intentions *publicly*, challenge the very legitimacy of laws and/or their applications in specific situations, attempt to change the norms they are denying, lack personal gain as a goal and appeal to a higher morality, pointing out the void between professed beliefs and actual practices.[92]

The 1949 offending act revealed a political concern "that is in striking contrast to the self-serving goals of those guilty of ordinary offenses against persons and property."[93] The conscious purpose or the subconscious urge of the offender was "to indulge in the prohibited conduct as a means to some larger and more social ends"[94] and he even gave notice to the public of his intentions. If from this point of view, the political criminal is blameworthy and ought to be punished in the interest of the established order, his criminality cannot be punished under the name of natural or common crimes or compared with that of the ordinary malefactor.[95] To do otherwise would throw the concept of morality into chaos. For example, is it right to place a habitual criminal on a par with a man who commits a crime for the first time because of exceptional circumstances which are not likely to occur again?

4. The Political Character

Sa'adeh's trial much more closely resembled a typical secret political trial conducted behind the iron curtain than the sort of judicial proceedings we now have a right to expect. Yet one of the glaring ironies of the trial was that the government continually insisted on labeling it as a non-political trial even though it had all the trappings of a political trial. Otto Kirchheimer, whose pioneering work *Political Justice* remains unexcelled for its erudition and analyses of political trials, argues that a political trial aims to affect in one way or another power relationships within society. It is one in which government or people seek through litigation to strengthen their own position and to weaken that of their opponents.[96] A political trial, then, is

> . . . any trial or impeachment that immediately affects or is intended to affect the structure, personnel, or policies of government, that is the product of or has its outcome determined by political controversy, or that results from the efforts of a group within society having control of the machinery of government to use the courts to disadvantage its rivals in a power struggle which is not itself immediately political or to preserve its own economic or social position.[97]

Scholars will disagree on the order of things – "motivation" for Theodore Becker,[98] "defendant" for Reginald Major,[99] and "procedure and impact" for Leon Friedman[100] – but will concur, at least in principle, that a political trial is the result of efforts by either the defendants or those who control the government to use the courts for political purposes. It may be for the purpose of degrading a political adversary or simply to silence critics. Either way, it involves either challenges or abuses of the authority of government.

Contrary to the government view, the trial of Antun Sa'adeh was a political trial *par excellence*. Throughout the trial the stakes were political as much as they were legal. The case clearly falls in that category "in which the defendant is tried for an offense which is itself political in nature and represents a direct challenge to governmental authority."[101] At least two components of the indictment against Sa'adeh supported this: (1) inciting and participating in an armed rebellion against the status quo in Lebanon with the intention of seizing power; and (2) treason, expressed in the allegation that Sa'adeh collaborated with the

enemy (Israel) in time of war. Needless to say, revolution and treason
rank among the most serious possible offenses against the state.

The political attributes of Sa'adeh's case were also manifested by
the political background and standing of the defendants. As a product
of a specific and identifiable set of political events, the case had a political
agenda all its own and transcended in significance the boundaries of
personal grievances. Its motives and objectives were thus political.
The accused was a "political person," to use a typology of Reginald
Major, and his views were at sharp variance with political orthodoxy.
All or part of the evidence against him was drawn from observations of
the accused's political conduct and political leitmotifs. The prosecution
address, for example, was more of a political speech than a legal
document and its character was frequently more of an accusation against
Sa'adeh's political ideology as a whole than of one against the individual
accused. A demonstrable connection between the defendant's ideology
or organizational activities and the trial process can also be gauged from
the charges leveled against the defendant.

Government interference in proceedings, whether to speed up
the trial or to influence its outcome, also rendered the trial political.
This interference seemed to have occurred throughout proceedings and
aimed at bringing disrepute to Sa'adeh and to the political orientation
he represented. The government enlisted the services of the tribunal to
strengthen its own position and weaken that of its political foes. It is
by directly involving the courts in the struggle for political power that
the trial becomes political.

Therefore, the government's reluctance to treat the case as political
is tenuous. It was made in bad faith to ensure "the imposition of the
fullest penalty of the law against [Sa'adeh]" – the death penalty. Under
Lebanese law, only capital offenses are punishable by death: political
crimes are also punishable, but involve lesser penalties and may give rise
to temporary imprisonment, hard labour or fines. As Antoine El-Gemayel
has observed:

> Such crimes are defined as intentional acts prompted by a political
> motive directed against the political rights of an individual or com-
> munity. The Lebanese criminal system differentiates between political
> crimes and political offenses in terms of punishment imposed for
> each. Punishment for political crimes includes incarceration, exile,
> house arrest or civil degradation, while punishment for political

offenses includes imprisonment, house arrest or fines. Civil degradation imposed for political crimes is generally accessory and automatic. When it is imposed as original punishment, it must be judicially declared.[102]

The government's reluctance may have also stemmed from an inherent fear of a political trial. Political trials can be problematic for any government especially if the evidence is flawed or if the accused is able to mount a strong case. Even with strong evidence, a political trial might not always end on a good note for the government. A political defendant has at his or her disposal a number of tactics that can potentially turn the case against him around. For example, he can try to create a political climate in which the people see that prosecution is unjust, and the government is made to realize that there could be serious consequences if there is a conviction:

> Whereas formerly the political criminal was treated as a public enemy, he is today considered as a friend of the public good, as a man of progress, desirous of bettering the political institutions of his country, having laudable intentions, hastening the onward march of humanity, his only fault being that he wishes to go too fast, and that he employs, in attempting to realize the progress which he desires, means irregular, illegal and violent.[103]

The government cannot, in those circumstances, keep the trial centred on technical legal issues, where it might be most impervious, or prevent the accused from building wide public support and adapting the legal strategy to that purpose. Criminalization, on the other hand, offered the government greater control over the case. For one thing, "when protest assumes a 'criminal' rather than a 'political' form . . . the issues become confused, with a political cause being given a criminal label. Dissidence can then be presented as being 'against the law' with the grievances or issues that gave rise to it being submerged or pushed into the background."[104] The "criminalization" of political disputes, as in the present case, is thus "a central aspect of the exercise of social control."[105]

To this catalogue of political motives must be added a last one: the impulsiveness of a political trial. Capital cases naturally raise difficult questions of law, but "they do not involve the dual legal and political agenda that political trials simultaneously address."[106] In contrast, political trials which operate within the rule of law often present entanglements of facts, political issues, and ethical judgments. "They might have far-reaching political consequences, often knocking powerful figures out of the arena."[107] Such trials "up the ante and involve . . . tensions and much more. Its agenda (often more latent than manifest) includes, in addition to those inherent in the criminal law, the tensions of our public identity, our myth of history, and our sense of destiny."[108]

As Kirchheimer has so aptly noted, political trials in democratic societies pose risks and uncertainties for all sides in the proceedings. Obviously the Lebanese government felt that a full-blown trial might not have been to its advantage but might have increased the morale of its adversary. As many political defendants and their supporters would attest, success in politicizing the proceedings, securing favorable press attention, avoiding convictions, or in changing the beliefs of some of the jurors or other trial participants produces a sense of heady optimism and encourages renewed hopes and efforts for change. Obviously the converse is also true; a trial that succeeds in none of these goals may be the occasion for much frustration.

Conclusion

When the political regime and the judiciary behave in a manner unbecoming of the law, no one should expect a fair outcome. Sa'adeh's trial was a total shamble amounting to judicial lynching. Throughout the trial the government exhibited scant regard for the niceties of jurisprudence and little more for the letter of the law. It was really nothing more than an open-and-shut exercise in accusation and punishment, a trial more appropriate in the cruel days of the Middle Ages than in the supposedly civilized world of the 20th century.

As for Sa'adeh, the horror of the trial would be exceeded only by the shocking treatment that was subsequently meted out to him. What started out as a mockery on 7 July would turn into a greater mockery before the next daybreak.

NOTES

1   On the state of the Khoury regime in 1949 see Michael C. Hudson, *The Precarious Republic: Political Modernization in Lebanon*. London: Westview Press, 1985: 87–105 and 264–272.

2   *Beirut*, Beirut, 8 July, 1949.

3   Ibid.

4   See Beshara Haykal Khoury, *al-Mahkmah al-Askriah wa khususyatuha* (The Military Court and its Particularities). Beirut: Dar Sadr, 2005.

5   Ibid.

6   See Matthew Hughes, "Collusion across the Litani? Lebanon and the 1948 War" in Eugene L. Rogan and Avi Shlaim. (ed.), *The War for Palestine: Rewriting the History of 1948*, 2nd ed. (Series: Cambridge Middle East Studies No. 15). Cambridge: Cambridge University Press, 2001.

7   Abdullah Qubarsi, *Abdullah Qubarsi yatadhakar* (Autobiography), Vol. 4. Beirut: Dar al-Furat, 2004: 68. The resort to 'national security' excuses in the conduct of secret trials has come under close scrutiny in law literature. A recent study opens: "Executive secrecy, especially in the realm of national security, poses grave problems for the legal process. This is because of the need to reconcile procedural fairness to individuals affected by contested decisions with the safeguarding of secret material on which such decisions are based. Governmental decisions are normally considered legitimate within liberal democracies if they are demonstrably within the law and are rational, principled, and proportionate. In the security realm, the difficulty is in devising appropriate political and legal mechanisms by which these criteria can be shown to be satisfied while also protecting secret material. The normal constitutional processes of adversarial legal proceedings and ministerial accountability to Parliament may seem to the executive to be insufficiently protective of secrecy. On the other hand, to give the executive free rein to determine the boundaries of its actions without any independent review or control is to invite political abuse and pays no regard to the rights of the individual." Ian Leigh, "Secret Proceedings in Canada," http://www.ohlj.ca/archive/articles/34_1_leigh.pdf.

8   See John Daye, *Muhakamat Antun Sa'adeh* (The Trial of Antun Sa'adeh). Beirut: Fajr an-Nahda, 2002.

9   John Semple Galbraith, "The Trial of Arabi Pasha," *Journal of Imperial and Commonwealth History*, 7:3 (1979): 274–292.

10 The early preparation of these laws and procedures took place during the French mandate, but its antecedents lay in past historical and religious codes: the Code of Hammurabi; the Canon Laws of oriental churches; the Syrian-Roman Custom Book; Islamic Law, and the Ottoman *Khat Kol Khan*, which proclaimed legal principles of freedom, personal property and equality among citizens, in keeping with European codes of the time.

11 The Dreyfus case underscored and intensified bitter divisions within French politics and society. The fact that it followed other scandals – the Boulanger affair, the Wilson case, and the bribery of government officials and journalists that was associated with the financing of the Suez Canal – suggested that the young French Republic was in danger of collapse. The controversy involved critical

institutions and issues, including monarchists and republicans, the political parties, the Catholic Church, the army, and strong anti-Semitic sentiment.

12 Thurman Arnold, "Due Process in Trials," *Annals of the American Academy of Political and Social Science*, Vol. 300 (July 1955): 126.

13 Beshara Khoury, *Haqa'iq Lubnaniyyah* (Lebanese Truths), Vol. 3: 242.

14 Ronal O. Sokol, "The Political Trial: Courtroom as Stage, History as Critic," *New Literary History*, Vol. 2, No. 3 (Spring 1971): 502.

15 Philip Berrigan, *Prison Journals of a Priest Revolutionary*. New York: Holt, Rinehart and Winston, 1970: 111.

16 See Antoine Elias El-Gemayel, *The Lebanese Legal System*, Two Volume Set. Rowman & Littlefield Publishers, 1985.

17 At least one known person at the trial, Saeed Taki Deen, subsequently joined the SNP and became its propaganda dean. See Suleiman Taki Deen, *Sirat al-Adib Saeed Taki Deen* (The Life of the Literati Saeed Taki Deen). Beirut: Druze Heritage Foundation, 2004.

18 There have been many instances in history in which defense counsels were harassed and intimidated to such an extent they were forced to withdraw from proceedings. The trial of Zamani Lakwot and six others in Nigeria is a glaring example. The African Commission, in its evaluation of the trial, found that the accused were denied their right to defense, in violation of Article 7(1)(c) of the African Charter, and called on the Nigerian Government to free the complainants. [The Constitutional Rights Project (in respect of Zamani Lakwot and six others) v. Nigeria, (87/93), 8th Annual Activity Report of the African Commission on Human and Peoples' Rights, 1994–1995, ACHPR/RPT/8th/Rev.I].

19 George Abdul Massih, *Muhadarat al-Mukhayyam al-Sayfi* (Summer Camps Lecture Series). Beirut: n.p., 1971: 29.

20 From the private papers of Rizkallah published in Antoine Butrus, *Qissat muhakamat Antun Sa'adeh was i'damehe* (An Account of Antun Sa'adeh's Trial and Execution). Beirut: Chemaly & Chemaly, 2002: 102.

21 Gibran Jreige, *Ma' Antun Sa'adeh* (In the Company of Antun Sa'adeh). Beirut: n.p., n.d.: 186–187.

22 Ibid. Former army Captain, Esam Karam, expressed his opinion that the authority succeeded in driving Attorney Lahhoud to walk out in order to arrive at the previously-decided sentence. See Butrus, *Qissat muhakamat Antun Sa'adeh was i'damehe* (An Account of Antun Sa'adeh's Trial and Execution). Beirut: Chemaly & Chemaly, 2002: 104.

23 Butrus, *Qissat muhakamat Antun Sa'adeh was i'damehe* (An Account of Antun Sa'adeh's Trial and Execution). Beirut: Chemaly & Chemaly, 2002: 105.

24 Ibid.

25 Ibid., 101.

26 Ibid.

27 Ibid.

28 Ibid., 102.

29 From an interview with the court clerk, Ibrahim Berri, *Sabah el-Kheir*. Beirut: 12 July, 1980.

30 Ibid.

31 Lebanon. Ministry of Information, *Qadiyat al-Hizb al-Qawmi* (The Case of the [Syrian] National Party). Beirut: Ministry of Information, 1949.

32 See the introduction to *Qadiyat al-Hizb al-Qawmi*.

33 See Jerome F. Goldberg, "Right of the Prosecution to Attack the Character of the Defendant (A Limited Recognition of a New Exception)," *Journal of Criminal Law and Criminology* (1931–1951), Vol. 41, No. 4 (Nov. – Dec., 1950): 456–462.

34 Ibid.

35 Najam al-Hashim, *A'khir Ayyam Sa'adeh* (Sa'adeh's Last Days). Beirut: n.p., 1999: 87.

36 Ibid., 87–88.

37 Ibid., 88.

38 Ibid.

39 See the introduction to *Qadiyat al-Hizb al-Qawmi*.

40 Ibid.

41 Imru' al-Qays was an Arabian poet of the 6th century, the author of one of the Muallaqat, an anthology of pre-Islamic Arabic literature. He is the son of Hujr, the last king of Kindah which is part of the present Republic of Yemen. He was born around 501 and died around 544. His mother was Fatmah bint Rabi'ah the sister of Kulib and Al-Muhalhl, two of the well-known Arabic tribe leaders. Imru' al-Qays was named after Imru' al-Qays Ibn Aban, a close friend to his uncle al-Muhalhl. Even though he was raised in luxury as a result of being the son of the king, he suffered because he was deprived from ruling after his father's assassination. That is why Arabs called him al-Malek-al-Delleel or the Shadow King. See Abu a-Fadl Ibrahim (ed.), *Diwan Imr' al-Qays*. Cairo: Dar al-Ma'arif, 1984.

42 The Public Prosecutor's address was incorporated into the *The Case of the National Party* in 1949 but, curiously enough, without Sa'adeh's reply. It is interesting to observe also that the Information Ministry in Lebanon published the speech without the epitaph with which the Public Prosecutor closed his speech. However, Captain Aziz al-Ahdab, who was on the judging panel, has confirmed that the Public Prosecutor did in fact utter this prose. It is also cited in the private notes of Elias Rizkallah.

43 Although a firm reason for its omission is lacking, it is a reasonable conjecture that the Government intentionally left it out to discredit the claim that Sa'adeh hit back with his own stinging prose when he addressed the court.

44 Ibrahim Berri, *Sabah el-Kheir*. Beirut, 12 July, 1980.

45 Ibid.

46 *Al-Hayat*. Beirut, 8 July, 1949.

47 *Al-Qubs*. Beirut, 10 July, 1949.

48 Ibrahim Berri, *Sabah el-Kheir*. Beirut, 12 July, 1980.

49 Ibid.

50 Butrus, *Qissat muhakamat Antun Sa'adeh was i'damehe* (An Account of Antun Sa'adeh's Trial and Execution). Beirut: Chemaly & Chemaly, 2002: 111.

51 Under that article a defendant is entitled for leniency if at the time of the criminal conduct he or she, as a result of mental disease or defect, either lacked substantial capacity to conform his conduct to the requirements of the law or lacked substantial capacity to appreciate the wrongfulness of his conduct.

52 Ibid.

53 Ibrahim Berri, *Sabah el-Kheir*. Beirut, 12 July, 1980.

54 Ibid.

55 Elias Rizkallah, the one person who was in the ideal position to jot down the speech, recorded only three lines. When asked why he did not document the speech, he

replied: "I was taken by the meticulousness of his defense and clarity of his intellect." *Muhadarat al-Mukhayyam al-Sayfi* (Summer Camps Lecture Series): 30.

56 *Al-Hayat*. Beirut, 9 July, 1949.
57 Ibrahim Berri, *Sabah el-Kheir*. Beirut, 12 July, 1980.
58 Adel Beshara, *Syrian Nationalism: An Inquiry into the Political Philosophy of Antun Sa'adeh*. Beirut: Dar Bissan, 1995, p. 167.
59 *Al-Hayat*. Beirut, 9 July, 1949.
60 Ibrahim Berri, *Sabah el-Kheir*. Beirut, 12 July, 1980.
61 Ibid.
62 Butrus, *Qissat muhakamat Antun Sa'adeh was i'damehe* (An Account of Antun Sa'adeh's Trial and Execution). Beirut: Chemaly & Chemaly, 2002: 115.
63 Najam al-Hashim, *A'khir Ayyam Sa'adeh* (Sa'adeh's Last Days). Beirut: n. p, 1999: 85.
64 Ibid.
65 *Beirut*. Beirut, 9 July, 1949.
66 Butrus, *Qissat muhakamat Antun Sa'adeh was i'damehe* (An Account of Antun Sa'adeh's Trial and Execution). Beirut: Chemaly & Chemaly, 2002: 114.
67 Ibid.
68 See *as-Sayyad*. Beirut, 18 July, 1949.
69 *Istijwab Jumblatt al tarikhi lil hukuma hawla istishhad Sa'adeh ome 1949* (Jumblatt's Historical Interpolation to the [Lebanese] Government In Regard to Sa'adeh's Martyrdom in 1949). Beirut: SSNP Information Bureau, 1987: 34.
70 Ibid.
71 http://www.cggl.org/scripts/index.asp (26 October, 2007).
72 John H. Wigmore, *Evidence in Trials at Common Law*, vol. 5, sec. 1367, Chadbourn rev., 1974: 32. Also Robert Burns, *A Theory of the Trial*. Princeton: Princeton University Press, 1999: 98.
73 The key question in assessing the independence of military judges is whether they are subordinate to military authority in their role in administering justice. Military judges have been deemed to be independent if they are autonomous of their superiors in their judicial capacity, notwithstanding the fact that they have been appointed by their superiors and remain subject to the hierarchical authority of their superiors in all but the administration of justice.
74 The Human Rights Committee called on Lebanon to transfer the competence of military courts in all trials concerning civilians to the ordinary courts. UN Doc. CCPR/C/79/Add.77, April 1997.
75 Ibid., 282.
76 Marc Hensen, *A Show Trial Under Lenin: The Trial of the Socialist Revolutionaries. Moscow 1922*. London: Maetinus Nijhoff Publishers, 1982: 188.
77 Peter Hain, *Political Trials in Britain*. London: A. Lane, 1984: 281.
78 Ann Fairfax Withington and Jack Schwartz, "The Political Trial of Anne Hutchinson," *The New England Quarterly*, Vol. 51, No. 2 (June 1978): 231. See also Charles F. Abel & Frank H. Marsh, *In Defense of Political Trials*. Westport: Greenwood Press, 1994: 51–77.
79 Carl S. Krueger, "Constitutional Law: Public Trial in Criminal Cases," *Michigan Law Review*, Vol. 52, No. 1 (Nov., 1952): 52.
80 Ibid.
81 "The Accused's Right to a Public Trial," *Columbia Law Review*, Vol. 49, No. 1 (Jan., 1949): 116.

82   Charles F. Abel & Frank Marsh, *In Defense of Political Trials*. Westport: Greenwood Press, 1994: 67.

83   On the use and misuse of this cliché see Theodore Schroeder, "Political Crimes Defined," *Michigan Law Review*, Vol. 18, No. 1 (Nov., 1919): 30–44.

84   Ronald Christenson, "A Political Theory of Political Trials," *The Journal of Criminal Law and Criminology*, Vol. 74, No. 2 (Summer, 1983): 557.

85   Quoted in Robert Ferrari, "Political Crime," *Columbia Law Review*, Vol. 20, No. 3 (Mar., 1920): 308.

86   G. Vidal, *Cours de droit criminel et de science penitentiare* (cinquieme edition, 1916): 112.

87   A distinction between common and political crimes was introduced to the Ottoman Penal Code in 1860 as part of the Tanzimat reforms. See Dick Douwes and Norman N. Lewis, "The Trials of Syrian Ismailis in the First Decade of the 20th Century," *International Journal of Middle East Studies*, Vol. 21, No. 2 (May, 1989): 215–232; and J. Bucknill and H. Utidjian, *The Imperial Ottoman Penal Code*. Oxford, 1913.

88   Ibid.

89   Robert Vouin and Jacques Léauté, *Droit penal et procedure pénale*. Paris: Presses Universitaires, 1969: 34.

90   Theodore Schroeder, "Political Crimes Defined," *Michigan Law Review*, Vol. 18, No. 1 (Nov., 1919): 35.

91   Robert Ferrari, "Political Crime," *Columbia Law Review*, Vol. 20, No. 3 (Mar., 1920): 311. Also Ferri, *Criminal Sociology*. New York: D. Appleton and Company, 1916: 335.

92   Charles E. Reasons, "The Politicizing of Crime, the Criminal and the Criminologist," *The Journal of Criminal Law and Criminology*, Vol. 64, No. 4 (Dec., 1973): 474 (italics added).

93   Francis A. Allen, *The Crimes of Politics: Political Dimensions of Criminal Justice*. Cambridge: Harvard University Press, 1974: 29.

94   Theodore Schroeder, *op. cit.*, 35.

95   Vidal, *op. cit.*, 112.

96   Otto Kirchheimer, *Political Justice: The Use of Political Procedure for Political Ends*. Princeton: Princeton University Press, 1961: 46.

97   Michal R. Belknap (ed.), *American Political Trials*. Westport: Greenwood Press, 1994: xvi. Belknap identifies six distinct varieties of political trials: (1) Treason; (2) seditious libel; (3) espionage and sabotage; (4) political assassination; (5) cases determined by political considerations; and (6) cases that are deliberately politicized.

98   Theodore L. Becker (ed.), *Political Trials*. New York, 1971: xv–xvi. Becker identifies four subtypes of political trials: (1) the political trial, in which the nature of the crime is clearly political and the impartiality of the judge applying the law is not called into serious question; (2) the political "trial," in which the indictment is clearly political and the impartiality and independence of the court is questionable at the beginning of the proceedings; (3) the "political" trial, in which the charge is quite unpolitical in nature but is only a subterfuge, and the real political aspects of the case are disguised or hidden; and (4) the "political trial," which combines "hooked up" charges with a simultaneous implosion of judiciousness in the legal proceeding.

99 Reginald Major, *Justice in the Round: The Trial of Angela Davis*. New York: The Third Press, 1973. In Major's view, no matter what the charge, if the accused is a "political person," whose views are at sharp variance with what is considered political orthodoxy, or if all or part of the evidence against him is drawn from observations of his political conduct, then the trial is probably political.

100 Leon Friedman, "Political Power and Legal Legitimacy: A Short History of Political Trials," *Antioch Review*, 30 (Summer 1970): 158.

101 Michal R. Belknap (ed.), *American Political Trials*: xvi.

102 Antoine El-Gemayel (ed.), *The Lebanese Legal System* – Volume II, Washington, DC: International Law Institute, 1985: 396.

103 Vidal, *op. cit.*, 111.

104 Peter Hain, *op. cit.*, 285.

105 Ibid. R. Quinney in his *The Social Reality of Crime* (1970) argues that criminal law is made, enforced and administered by interest groups largely for their own gains.

106 Ronald Christenson, "A Political Theory of Political Trials," *The Journal of Criminal Law and Criminology*, Vol. 74, No. 2 (Summer, 1983): 554.

107 Ibid., 558.

108 Ibid., 556.

4

EXECUTION

O rdinarily, the pre-execution period is a fairly involved process that may take weeks and months on end to finalise. The condemned often has to go through an exhaustive appeal process, including appeals to the highest court in the country or to a court of higher jurisdiction. A hearing before the Board of Pardons is then held as a last attempt to have the death sentence commuted. When all these things fail, the condemned should have the right to apply to the President of the Republic for amnesty, pardon, or commutation of sentence, which may be granted in all cases. The death penalty may not be carried out until all rights to appeal have been exhausted, or the time limits for filing such appeals have run their full course, and recourse proceedings, including applications to the President, have been completed and requests for pardon and commutation have been exhausted.

With Sa'adeh, the pre-execution process was a hypocritical farce. The entire process took less than five hours to complete ending in a last-minute frenzy of activity. Despite the irreversibility of the death sentence, the right of the condemned to adequate time to prepare and complete all appeals and petitions for clemency was compromised by the relevant authorities. If that was not enough, Sa'adeh's last hours on earth were marked by procedural lapses during which the condemned was treated in a very undignified manner.

Board of Pardons

Because Sa'adeh was tried in a military court and because his death sentence was irrevocable, his case was not subject to review by a higher court of appeal. His only avenue of relief was clemency from either the Board of Pardons or the executive branch which, in Lebanon's case, is vested in the President of the Republic. It is entirely up to the defendant to decide whether or not to use these procedures. It is also the avenue that the state has to pursue to carry out a death sentence. The administration of these procedures is necessary under Lebanese Law and may possibly require a re-study of the case to ferret out factual errors.[1]

Sa'adeh was aware of his *appellate* rights but deferred them. Judging from subsequent remarks he made, he did not expect the death sentence against him to be carried out expeditiously. By law, the state had to allow adequate time between sentence and execution for the preparation and completion of appeals and, in cases of well-known personalities, for the preparation of petitions for clemency. It did not cross Sa'adeh's mind that the State might tinker with the law again, as it did during the trial. Having endured a marathon hearing without sleep the previous night and having had little to eat during the day, he was too exhausted to even think about it, let alone to contemplate his next move. An exhausted person almost always develops a passive outlook, thereby losing the will to act.

The death sentence against Sa'adeh was referred to the Board of Pardons for review immediately after the trial. The Board was composed of the five judges Emil Tian (Chairperson), George Suefi, Badri al-Ma'oushi, Rida Tamer and Zahdi Yakn. Theoretically, the Board's duty is to review the conviction and other records of the case, including:

(1)   the evidence submitted during the trial;
(2)   the information submitted during the sentencing hearing;
(3)   the procedures employed in the sentencing hearing.

The Board addresses all substantive and procedural issues raised on the appeal of a sentence of death, and considers whether the sentence of death was imposed under the influence of passion, prejudice, or any other arbitrary factor. If the Board finds that (A) the sentence of death was imposed under the influence of passion, prejudice, or any other arbitrary factor; (B) the admissible evidence and information adduced does not support the conviction; or (C) the proceedings involved legal errors requiring reversal of the sentence, it remands the case for reconsideration or imposition of a sentence other than death. The Board cannot reverse or vacate a sentence of death on account of any error which can be harmless. Also, in order to award the death sentence, it requires a unanimous verdict by all judges. In the case of a non-unanimous verdict, it can recommend commutation of the death sentence to life.

According to President Khoury the Board "unanimously" ratified the death sentence. However, the *Beirut* newspaper claimed that the ratification, which lasted three hours, was a majority one. The evidence is inconclusive either way, but there are better reasons to believe the newspaper's claim. The Lebanese government's publication *The Case of the National Party*, for example, does not use the term "unanimous" when alluding to the Board's decision. It simply states "The Board agreed that no other sentence was more appropriate than death." More decisive is Kamal Jumblatt's interpellation to the Lebanese Parliament in which the young parliamentarian expressed his gratitude to "the judges" who refused to ratify the death sentence.[2]

To complicate an already complex situation, the highly-reliable Lebanese *an-Nahar* newspaper reported that only three of the Board's original members (George Suefi, Rida Tamer and Zahdi Yakn) were present at the ratification and that three other members had to be added to the Board that evening in order to obtain a majority ruling. By *an-Nahar's* account, the three additional members were not judges but men of uniform: Lieutenant Gendarmerie Fayez Abdul Baqi, and Captains Na'oum al-Bitar and Abdul Majid al-Zain. If true, then the government must have faced formidable opposition from the original Board, whose members were brought to the Tribunal in military vehicles "as they do under dictatorial regimes,"[3] in obtaining even a majority ratification. What is certain now is that, in addition to the two absent members, one of the three remaining members, George Suefi, refused to ratify, apparently for the lack of substantial evidence and discrepancies in trial procedure. The Board's Chairperson, Emil Tian, also did not ratify but requested the matter be referred to the President. Shortly after Sa'adeh's execution, Tian resigned from the Board citing "external interference in the justice system" as the reason for it. In 1991, President Charles Helou revealed that Tian's resignation was actually prompted by Sa'adah's case. He recalled:

> What is not known is that the Chairman of the Board of Pardons and Court of Appeal, Emil Tian shortly afterwards submitted his resignation, giving no reason for it, and never withdrew it. At that time, I became minister of justice, and tried to dissuade him from resigning. After lengthy discussions, he disclosed his secret, namely that the reason behind his resignation was the sectarian balance in carrying out the decision [to] execute Antun Sa'adeh along with the others [i.e., his supporters].[4]

The final position of the original Board of Pardon was thus:

Emil Tian (Chairman): neutral
George Suefi: refused to ratify
Badri al-Ma'oushi: absent
Rida Tamer: ratified
Zahdi Yakn: neutral

The Sa'adeh case, therefore, remains one of many where death sentences have been awarded despite dissenting opinions on either guilt or punishment. When judges disagree on the guilt of the accused, the dissent may be sufficient to constitute reasonable doubt. Furthermore, dissent on a death penalty raises serious concerns about the fairness of the trial itself. That aside, with the ratification of the death sentence, Sa'adeh's case was all but over: the trial, sentence, and ratification of his conviction were finalised before 7 July was over. All that now remained was the approval of the President.

The Appeal for Clemency

Actually, even as the Board of Pardons was meeting to consider the legality of the death sentence against Sa'adeh, Elias Rizkallah was at the presidential palace presenting his case for clemency. He was whisked away to the President's office right after the trial to coincide with the Board of Pardons' decision. According to the existing law in Lebanon, the President has the unfettered discretion to deny clemency at any time, for any reason. But he also has the unfettered discretion to grant, at any time, for any reason, the following forms of clemency:

(1) Amnesty, a pardon extended by the state to a group or class or persons, usually for a political offense. Unlike an ordinary pardon, amnesty is usually addressed to crimes against state sovereignty, that is, to political offenses with respect to which forgiveness is deemed more expedient for the public welfare than prosecution and punishment.
(2) Commutation: the executive's substitution in a particular case of a less severe punishment for a more severe one that has already been judicially imposed on the defendant.

(3) Pardon: the act or instance of officially nullifying punishment or other legal consequences of a crime. There are a number of pardons that the President could consider:

1. *Absolute pardon*, which releases the wrongdoer from punishment and restores the offender's civil rights without qualification.
2. *Conditional pardon*, which does not become effective until the wrongdoer satisfies a prerequisite.
3. *General pardon*, which is identical to amnesty.
4. *Partial pardon*, which exonerates the offender from some but not all of the punishment or legal consequences of a crime.

By Rizkallah's own account, President Khoury was waiting for his arrival with the endorsement of the death sentence already in his hands. He wrote:

> I walked in on the President in his office. Minister Gabriel Al-Mur was next to him. He was not courteous and received me rather indifferently. I was enraged by this, which drove me to declare boldly, "I was coming not as an officer with a limited capacity, but as an attorney in a weighty case to implore you to have mercy on he who had been sentenced to death and is on his way to death." This caused the president to grow even more arrogant, and me to grow more furious. However, I insisted on pleading for mercy, but my request was turned down.[5]

He added:

> I later learned that the president was told of what I had accused Sa'adeh of [i.e., insanity] in order to help him avoid his tragic end. This threw the military court into confusion; it could not proceed with the trial before setting up a medical committee to check the leader's mental capacity. However, it could not postpone the session since there was an agreement concluded between the Lebanese and the Syrian authorities to carry out the death sentence as soon as possible, i.e., within 24 hours. A rush of phone calls was both made and received by the two authorities to hasten the execution. In the meantime, there were attempts to stop the execution made by Kamal Jumblatt and Sami Solh.[6]

Jumblatt and Sami Solh, a cousin of Premier Riad, implored Khoury to think twice about executing Sa'adeh for different reasons. The unfathomable Jumblatt tried to stop the execution by appealing to the President for wisdom and fairness in the light of previous inaction against similar insubordinates. He was one of the very few Lebanese politicians who seemed to have cared about Sa'adeh's life. As for Sami Solh, he seemed more concerned about the longer-term repercussions of Sa'adeh's execution on the Solh family. Upon hearing of the court's verdict he went straight to the Presidential Palace to see Khoury, but the latter tactlessly snubbed him with the words "go convince your cousin [Riad Solh] first."[7] But Riad retained his hard-nose stance and kept invoking the law at every turn. A frustrated Sami then burst out, "You must not go through with that and embroil yourself. This man is dangerous and his followers are also dangerous." He added, "From a humanitarian point of view it is unacceptable . . . besides the crime is political and therefore deserves a lesser penalty."[8] The Prime Minister was unmoved.

Another person whose name has been mentioned in this regard is the Lebanese literati Amin Nakhle. A personal friend of Riad Solh, Nakhle was stunned by the sentence. He visited the Prime Minister at his residence in Beirut to persuade him to commute the sentence to life imprisonment with hard labour. Legally, of course, only the President of the Republic can commute a death sentence. Nakhle later related that on entering Solh's house he found the prime minister's wife "on her knees begging her husband not to execute Antun Sa'adah. 'If you execute him, our life will be ruined.'"[9]

Astonishingly, the strongest opposition to the death penalty came from the President's son, Khalil. Apparently, Khalil burst into tears when he learned that his father had approved the death order, but the ever-present Habib Abu Shahla, one of Khoury's henchmen, advised him to butt out, telling him "you are still a young lad to understand these matters."[10] Khalil did not know Sa'adeh personally but was among the select few who attended his trial. His opposition to the sentence may very well have been triggered by that lone encounter with Sa'adeh, who often impressed all who had contact with him with his strong moral fervor.

The President's signature on the death order effectively removed the last "legal" barrier for the implementation of the court's sentence. It was countersigned by Prime Minister Riad Solh, who was also the Minister of Justice, and Defense Minister Majid Irslan. The order now became a government decree subject to Article 150 of the Military Code, which stated that the death penalty shall be carried out before a firing squad at a time and place designated by the Minister of Defense.

Procedural Arrangements

Initially, the Minister of Defense chose the courtyard facing the Military Tribunal building as the site for the execution. At the last minute, however, "the site was deemed technically inappropriate and unsafe for the firing squad because there is a wall behind it that overlooks the Race Course and an area with condensed pine trees."[11] The site then switched to a remote section of the old shooting field and a security unit was dispatched to prepare the site and to dig a grave at a nearby cemetery. The choice fell on a small open field with sandy mounds that enclosed the area from the seafront. A wooden post chopped off from an old electricity pole was quickly erected into the ground and reinforced by steel and soil for uprightness.

Whilst these preparations were taking place, a small military unit was dispatched to a nearby church to locate an Orthodox priest for the last rites. The unit headed for the nearby Saint George Orthodox Diocese of Beirut. What happened next is best left for the priest who attended the execution, Iliya Barbari, to describe:

> When I opened the door at the sound of the bell, around midnight, I found myself before officers of the Army who asked me to quickly get dressed and bring along my cross and clerical particulars. I said: "What is going on?" and they replied "we are to execute the traitor Antun Sa'adeh tonight and we want you to confess him and offer him the last rites before his execution." I said "I cannot do something of that kind until you bring permission from the archbishop as our church laws require." They said "We do not have the time. We will take the responsibility for it." Once more I excused myself, but they continued to insist, repeating that an infraction against church laws is less harmful than sending a Christian to his death without having completed his religious obligations. I finally gave in and reluctantly rode in their jeep through streets crowded with security forces both military and police patrolmen and with weapons held ready to fire. We saw Prison al-Ramel appear. It was brightly lit up both from without and within. We got down at a place where other officers were waiting for us.[12]

The priest was escorted by the officers to the office of the prison director and the following conversation transpired:

> *The prison director*: ". . . I have been in the army for about thirty years and this would be the 13th execution I will witness."
>
> *Father Barbari*: "I have spent thirteen years in clerical garb and this is the first time that I am to view an execution."
>
> *Captain Najjar*: "I am the army's doctor and this is the first time I would be examining a person sentenced to execution by firing squad."
>
> *The prison director*: "Man should show courage in these sorts of circumstances."
>
> *Father Barbari*: "I am not afraid but I don't know the person."
>
> *The prison director*: "This condemned traitor Antun Sa'adeh has committed treason. He is an unbeliever atheist who actively propagates his atheism. Do you think such a man would pay any heed to you, Father – that atheist anti-religious traitor?"[13]

It was now about one-thirty on the morning of July 8. Suddenly, a company of judges and military officers, commissioned to attend the execution, showed up: Michel Talhama, the Government-appointed Trial Commissioner, followed by Justice Gabrail Bassil on behalf of the Military Tribunal, Magistrate Fouad Boulus of the Court of First Instance, Court-clerk Michel Abu Shakra, Lieutenant Jamil Lahhoud of the Beirut Garrison, and officers Mohammad Jawwad and Habib Braydi. Also present was a Justice of the Peace (*Mukhtar*). Everyone then rose to their feet and walked across to Sa'adeh, who was lying in "a small cell that didn't deserve the title of a room."[14]

Sa'adeh was still asleep with his legs propped against the wall when the party arrived. They looked at each other in total bewilderment and began to speak loudly to wake him up. When he woke up, Sa'adeh rose to his feet and gave the party a gracious welcome. The Government-appointed Trial Commissioner, Michel Talhama, then informed him that his death sentence had been approved by the Board of Pardons and the President and began reading out the death order. "Enough. Enough," interrupted Sa'adeh. "Thank you. I am ready."

Talhama then informed Sa'adeh that a priest was at hand to conduct the last rites. "Welcome, Reverend," he said at once. He thanked the party with a composed smile and asked for permission to put on his jacket, which was bunched up under his feet. They let him do so and he thanked them again and put it on. The Reverend moved closer and asked him about his faith and Sa'adeh replied "I was born an Orthodox and an Orthodox I shall die."[15] Barbari got down to work. "I asked him if he wanted to carry out his religious obligations and he answered why not. I asked him to confess, and he replied, "I have no sin for which I want forgiveness. I have not stolen, I have not been a charlatan, I have not borne false witness, I have not killed, I have not deceived, and I have not caused misery to anyone."[16] The Reverend then placed the stole over Sa'adeh's head and read the prayers of forgiveness. Sa'adeh listened to him with humility and piousness and at the end of it crossed himself three times, in accordance with the Orthodox faith. He then took the holy bread and thanked the priest.[17]

After the conclusion of the religious rites, Sa'adeh was handcuffed and led out to the prison office. There he asked to see his wife and daughters but was told that was out of the question. They offered him a breakfast which he refused with thanks, although he did accept a cup of coffee which he drank with his right hand and supported with his left. "The handcuffs would glint and cling every time they knocked against the cup."[18] In keeping with Lebanese tradition, he was offered a cigarette with the coffee, but declined it explaining that he didn't fancy smoking all that much. As he drank his coffee, Sa'adeh "ran his eyes from face to face as though he was fare-welling us without getting anyone uptight."[19] Here, the Reverend burst into tears as did some of the officers, "one of whom sobbed violently."[20] After he drank the coffee, he once more insisted on meeting his wife and daughters, but his request was again refused. At this point tears ran down his face. He shook his head and gave a bitter smile. He lifted his head and, speaking in colloquial Arabic as always, said: "Give me one country in the world that doesn't allow at the very least forty-eight hours between sentence and execution."[21] There was a deathly pause.

The silence was broken by Justice Fouad Bulus. With little time left for the execution, he implored Sa'adeh to draw up his last will so that the other present judges could witness it in writing. If the assemblage was expecting to hear about massive fortunes or last-minute undisclosed wealth, it was disappointed:

At 2.00 o'clock on July 8, 1949, we, Justice Fouad Boulus of the Beirut Court of First Instance, in accordance with instructions issued on 7/7/1949 by the President of the same Court to represent him at the execution of the Military Tribunal verdict of 7/7/1949 sentencing Antun Khalil Sa'adeh to death. Next, in accordance with Article 457 of the Law of Summary Trials, and with the assistance of clerk Michel Abu Shakra, the convicted criminal was brought before us and asked whether he had anything to declare before the sentence against him is carried out. He replied: "I own several patches of land in Dhur Shweir I would like to leave to my wife, Juliet al-Mir, and daughters, Sofia, Alissar and Raghida, in four equal quarters. I also have on me four hundred Syrian pounds, which have been deposited in the prison's vault. I would like to leave the whole amount to my wife along with all my other effects and, furthermore, appoint her as legal guardian over my three under-age daughters.

The will was then drawn up accordingly after the testator Antun Sa'adeh declared that he had nothing else to add to it or to bequeath. The will was then undersigned by myself, the clerk, and the testator at the same time and day, on 8/7/1949.

Testator	Clerk	Magistrate
Antun Sa'adeh	Michel Abu Shakra	Fouad Boulus

However, there is, or there seem to be, good grounds for believing that the will was tampered with after the execution. Elias Rizkallah, Sa'adeh's counsel, who was present at that moment, revealed a slightly different account with a touch of sarcasm:

[Sa'adeh] stated in his will that the family was to inherit the 'enormous booty' that he received from foreign authorities according to the accusations that were recklessly hurled at him. The will comprised 13 liras, a watch, a pen and a foundation for a cottage that he had started in Dhur Shweir, but could not afford to complete. We were all stunned when he disclosed to us what he possessed.[22]

A war of words then broke out between Sa'adeh and the State Commissioner after the latter bluntly refused Sa'adeh a meeting with the press or a paper and pen to write down "a word for history."[23] Reverend Barbari describes the scene as follows:

He asked to address journalists but they told him that was impossible. He asked them for a paper and a pen but they refused. He said I have something that I want to put down for history. One of the officers shouted out to him in warning, "Beware not to attack anybody lest we harm your dignity." Sa'adeh smiled once more saying, "You cannot do that because no one has the power to degrade somebody else, though a person can degrade himself." He repeated, "I have something to say which I want history to record." We all fell into a dense silence that was itself almost audible.[24]

The row was settled after Rizkallah personally stepped in and "insisted that [Sa'adeh] should be given the opportunity and that was it." So what did Sa'adeh say? There is no formal transcript of his words. According to local press reports he made a short but emphatic appeal in which he accused the Lebanese Government of instigating a massive conspiracy against him and his party. Hisham Sharabi has related the following words: "I consider that the Lebanese government has implemented a major plot against me and my Party. But I regard those who plotted against me, those who passed the death sentence against me and those who will execute the judgment, with contempt."[25] In contrast, Rizkallah's account speaks of an elaborate statement covering recent events in Syria and Lebanon and mentioning foreign intervention as a vital factor in the conspiracy against him. A report published in the Lebanese *Al-Sayyad* claimed that Sa'adeh made "startling revelations before his execution, but the authorities cautioned those who were there against making any public disclosures."[26]

As for Reverend Barbari, he said:

Speaking honestly, I was in a vortex of emotions and I don't think I can remember every single word he said. But I vaguely heard him saying: "I am not concerned how I die but rather about what I die for. I do not count the years I lived but rather the works I carried through to achievements. This night they will execute me, but those dedicated to my ideology will triumph and will then avenge my death. All of us die but few among us have the honor of dying for a belief. The shame of this night for our descendants, our communities abroad, and the foreigners. It seems that the independence that we watered with our own blood on the day we planted it must now draw new blood from our veins."[27]

[115]

On another occasion, the Reverend recalled Sa'adeh describing his crime as political and his principle as honest:

> . . . one I would live and die for . . . if we glance through the pages of history, we will not find a sentence like the one passed against me. If we probe the history of the barbaric Middle Ages that were known for their savageness, we will not find measures as twisted as this one. History has no records of a conspiracy like the one concocted against me and my party . . . If we consult the laws of all the countries of the world, we will find not a single article that would allow a man to be tried, sentenced to death and executed, all at this amazing speed. My arrest, trial and execution are only hours away from one another. It is something that contravenes all laws. Future generations will not remain silent about it. [The conspirators] may have won the battle against me, but the party will win the war against them. If they have been unjust to me, my supporters and those who believe in my ideas will even the score.[28]

Sa'adeh then leaned toward the Reverend and whispered in his ears these exact words: "Swear to me, revered Father, by all that you hold dear to announce everything you saw and everything you heard from me to everyone."[29] According to Said Taki ad-Din, Sa'adeh told Barbari, "I don't care if I die; it's what I die for that matters. I don't count the years that I lived; I count the deeds I did. They will execute me tonight, but believers in my creed will be victorious and their victory will be vengeance for my death."[30] It is noteworthy that *Az-Zaman* similarly quoted Sa'adeh at those moments, saying "Antun Sa'adeh has now died, but his name will be immortalized and his party will live on."[31]

The Execution

At 2.30 in the morning, Sa'adeh was handcuffed and led out to the prison's courtyard and then to a waiting military jeep. As he marched out, the night wardens locked up the peepholes on the cells, a custom practiced when a prisoner is about to be condemned to death, to conceal Sa'adeh's identity from his imprisoned sympathizers. One of them, however, got up to investigate and fainted when he realized that the person at the centre of the commotion was Sa'adeh himself:

I heard his footsteps . . . these are surely his footsteps, I could never mistake them. It was exactly their pace as if he was coming to the social function in my house . . . or parading the members at a party occasion, not as if he is walking to his execution. Fearful silence subdued the place. I visualized him before me, and mumbled, 'Long live Syria, long live Sa'adeh.' I fainted as teardrops inflamed in my eyes.[32]

Sa'adeh walked to his death "with strong quiet steps and smiling unperturbed as though an execution was something that he had undergone many times before. He did not burst out into hatred or vengefulness or bluster like somebody hiding fear."[33] As he approached the jeep he saw a white coffin on his right. For a third time he asked to see his wife and three children, but was again denied. "His features sharpened and in that brief instant of that night, alone, the lightning of emotions appeared through the storm of his manhood."[34] He climbed into the waiting jeep, flanked by six soldiers and an army officer. A combined detachment of the Lebanese Army and gendarmerie guarded the five-minute route while the convoy, consisting of mounted police and several military vehicles, as well as a separate jeep for the coffin, made its way to the execution site. No journalists or members of the public were allowed in the vicinity of the route and soldiers were ordered to shoot at any movement.

When Sa'adeh saw the execution post he uttered, "I was anticipating this fate from the very first moment I was arrested."[35] He again protested against the swiftness of the trial and execution, but all to no avail. He then walked to the death post "calmly, showing no anxieties or irritability and wore the white gown."[36] Captain Najjar, the military physician, stepped forward to examine Sa'adeh's heart and pulse. Sa'adeh gave him a friendly smile and sarcastically said, "Is my pulse beating faster out of fear?" When Captain Najjar had finished his medical examination, Lieutenant Braydi moved closer to blindfold Sa'adeh with a scarf and the following exchange took place:[37]

Sa'adeh: "Why are you covering my eyes? Seconds and it will be all over. I told you I don't have a fear of death."

Lieutenant Braydi: "It is the law."

Sa'adeh: "I respect the law."

Lieutenant Braydi then asked Sa'adeh to kneel down.

Sa'adeh: "I have no fear of bullets. Can't we do away with these formalities?"

Lieutenant Braydi: "It is the law." He then tied Sa'adeh to the post.

Sa'adeh: "Thank you."

After the court-clerk read the death sentence, Sa'adeh gave him an otherworldly smile and thanked him.

The death squad of twelve men chosen from the elite corps lined up. Sa'adeh was heard complaining that the gravel under his knees was paining them and asked the attending officers if it was possible to remove it and they did. He thanked them twice. Lieutenant Braydi then shouted, "Fire." According to one eye-witness, the order was given in French (*feu*) and Sa'adeh was heard saying loudly "say *nar*," its equivalent in Arabic. As they fired, he cried out "*Tahya Suria*" (long live Syria). It was a perfect last line for Sa'adeh, typical in its combination of ideological fervor and the cause of his life-struggle.

Seconds later, Sa'adeh was dead, "his head hanging down and his right lung splattered out and his left arm shattered: it was now only held to his shoulder by some skin so that it hung down."[38] In keeping with execution customs, Lieutenant Braydi then stepped forward, placed his pistol against Sa'adeh's head, and fired one shot. Five minutes later, after Captain Najjar had examined the body and declared Sa'adeh dead, the corpse was untied and placed in the coffin.

The convoy headed directly to the cemetery to bury Sa'adeh without a funeral. "They were about to bury [him] without any prayer had I not shouted out."[39] The State Commissioner for these matters, Hassan al-Zein, who had the arduous task of arranging a speedy burial, reluctantly concurred. "Pray but make it snappy," he told the Reverend.[40] A short funeral was administered by Reverend Barbari, assisted by a second priest. The only other person allowed into the church was the Justice of the Peace. During the funeral service, "blood dribbled from coffin which, by all accounts, was poorly-built from . . . timber."[41]

Sa'adeh was laid to rest in a remote part of the cemetery. A wooden cross, assembled on the spot, was placed on top of his grave and security guards were placed around it to prevent any person from approaching the site. Four days after the execution, Sa'adeh's next of kin, Nayfi Mujais, attempted to have the corpse exhumed for reburial in the family grave, but the Minister for Interior Affairs rejected her request: she was told that the corpse could not be exhumed before a lapse of one year. On 13 January, 1950, five months after the execution, Sa'adeh's supporters secretly moved the corpse to a more decent section of the cemetery. Shortly afterwards, George Abdul Massih, who became the first Chairman of the SSNP after Sa'adeh's execution, allegedly removed the corpse and placed it in his house in Beit Meri.[42] Meanwhile, a proper grave was erected in the cemetery where Sa'adeh was originally buried by party members who contest Abdul Massih's account: the grave has become a rallying-point for his supporters and on 8 July of every year, at the precise time of Sa'adeh's execution, they roll up in droves to pay their respect to him.

The Litigation Continues

After executing Sa'adeh, the government decided to administer heavy doses of coercion against his followers. With an additional force of one hundred and fifty new recruits to the gendarmerie[43] it launched a nation-wide campaign arresting anyone suspected of aiding the rebellion or demonstrating any empathy for Sa'adeh. Hundreds were rounded-up and tried in tribunals set up specifically to deal with the suspects.[44] Lebanese General Security Forces even crossed to Syria to collect twenty Lebanese nationals who had recently been detained by the Syrian police for taking part in pro-SSNP activities.[45]

The litigation against the suspects began in earnest on 16 July. First up were those who took part in the rebellion. Over two days, sixty-eight of them were tried in a military tribunal on charges varying from public disorder to taking part in an armed rebellion to attempting to overthrow the government forcibly.[46] Since martial law was still in force, the tribunal operated under accelerated procedures and without right of appeal. The trial was public but attendance was restricted. As before, the case for the prosecution was presented by Youssef Charbel, who delivered an accusatory political speech about Sa'adeh and his national ideology, and described the accused as victims of Sa'adeh's political opportunism. The prosecutor thus sought to put the defendants' political views on trial, but refused to consider the case political. Treated as ordinary criminals, the defendants were handicapped by the court's denial of most of their arguments. In other ways, too, the defendants were at a disadvantage. The courtroom was overcrowded and its atmosphere was not conducive to a sober analysis of evidence.

The trial lasted a mere fifteen hours. Twelve of the accused were sentenced to death and fifty-three to imprisonment with hard labour varying from life to three years. Of the twelve who received the death sentence, six had their sentence commuted to life imprisonment and the other six were executed at approximately the same morning hour and precise spot where Sa'adeh was executed.[47] A press release issued by the Bureau for Propaganda, Publication and Information in Beirut, described how President Khoury evaluated the execution files:

> The Board of Pardon spent two full days studying the cases of the twelve condemned to death. Likewise, His Excellency the President also spent a fairly long time going through the files and examining the sentences one by one and the result was condemnation of six to death and commutation to life imprisonment with hard labour for the other six. These are: Mustafa Said Mula'ib, Youssef Hussein Qa'id Bey, Khalil Yaacoub al-Tawil, Said Abdul Raouf Hammad, Nseir Saleh Raya, Fayez Fahd Zein. It was learnt further that the reasons that caused His Excellency to commute the sentence of the six are due to the fact that Mustafa Said Mula'ib had lost his cousin during the rebellion and so the government, out of mercy, does not want to cause the family any further hardship; that Youssef Hussein Qa'id Bey had been cooperative in the investigation which helped to clarify the case; that Khalil Yaacoub al-Tawil benefited from his slender age of few months past his eighteenth; that Said Abdul Raouf Hammad was under-age and his brother is among the six to be executed and so it wouldn't be fair to execute two brothers for the same incident; and that Nseir Saleh Raya and Fayez Fahd Zein did not play a vital role in the rebellion.[48]

While President Khoury was considering the fate of the accused twelve, a large demonstration was taking place in front of the Defense Ministry and the presidential palace calling for commutation of all death sentences.[49] It probably explains why Khoury was mildly compassionate towards the accused six and why this time he was more observant of the rules of the appellate process. Nonetheless, it should not deflect from the cruelty that was subsequently administered against the condemned six: denied the right to see their immediate relatives, despite repeated pleas from outside the prison walls, they were each pierced with twelve bullets in the body and a single one to the head and left to rot where they were executed.[50] According to *an-Nahar*, the six faced the firing squad with "exceptional courage."[51]

A week later a second group of rebels was brought to trial over attacks on gendarmerie stations. And again the defense counsels for the accused attempted to argue the case on political grounds, pointing out that the defendants were members of a recognized political party: they were unsuccessful.[52] To make its case more serious, the prosecution tried to link the defendants with "terrorism" which, under Lebanese Law, are criminal, not political acts. The tribunal voted in favour of prosecution and sentenced most defendants to long prison terms with hard labour. Two rebels tried in absentia were given the death penalty.[53] Three defendants, arrested for collecting two hundred Lebanese pounds in aid of the families and children of their comrades[54] were adjudged not guilty.[55]

Next up was the trial of those adherents of the Syrian National Party who were detained after the Jummaizeh incident. Nineteen in total, they were tried under Article 119 of the Lebanese military law, which stipulated the imprisonment of anyone caught with illegal weapons or explosions. The central issue was a basket of broken down hand-grenades found in the printing building at the time of the incident. The accused denied any knowledge of the basket and were rather bewildered by the charge. Their defense attorney,[56] a man with a reputation for republican reliability, raised fundamental legal questions about the admissibility of the evidence. He furthermore told the tribunal that the basket may have been the work of police agents in a classic "Reichstag Fire"[57] mould to show that government propaganda about an SNP revolution being imminent was actually true.[58] The tribunal refused to accept his logic, but returned light sentences: almost half of the accused nineteen, including future scholars Labib Zuwiyya Yamak and George Atiyah, were adjudged not guilty, and the rest were jailed for two months and banned from carrying firearms for five years.[59] Ironically, the accused were re-detained upon their release, "after the authorities were alerted by the Bureau of General Security that the offenders were active functionaries in the [Syrian National] Party and therefore should be incarcerated for the time being."[60]

But the end was not yet in sight. The Lebanese government had one other opportunity to vent its anger. On 30 August, the functionary corps of the party was brought to trial *en masse* for acts unrelated to the planned uprising. In fact, none of them had taken part in the actual rebellion. The trial itself, though, was a sensation in that the weight of some of the evidence presented in earlier trials was carefully evaluated and shown to have been completely mishandled through tampering or falsification. If this evidence of the prosecution had been offered at Sa'adeh's trial before a learned court, the great bulk of it would have been excluded either on the grounds of incompetence or irrelevance. First of all, it was revealed that Sa'adeh was not an enemy of the Lebanese State and that his party never intended to use force against the established system. This fact emerged during proceedings not from the actual testimonies of the defendants, whose opinions on this issue mattered but a little, but from the testimony of Ni'met Thabet, the ex-president of the Syrian National Party, who Sa'adeh had expelled from the party in 1948 for propagating a Lebanese-accommodating policy. Thabet bluntly told the tribunal that Sa'adeh never devised a plan for the destruction of the Lebanese state but was merely appalled by the government's duplicity:

> The late Antun Sa'adeh always insisted on an unequivocal propagation of the party's ideology defending this stance on the ground that if some Lebanese are allowed to speak openly about an Arab nationalism why they can't be allowed to speak of a Syrian nationalism. I tried to convince him that the political situation in the country allowed one but not the other, but he was not convinced.[61]

The prosecution tried to capitalize on Thabet's disagreement with Sa'adeh to extort an unsympathetic testimony on the SNP, but to no effect. Thabet told the tribunal that his dispute with Sa'adeh was never over Lebanon's right of existence but over strategies and priority options.[62] He well noted that the French mandatory authorities found no evidence to indict Sa'adeh on subversion or treason against the Lebanese state. To the profound displeasure of the prosecution, Thabet then gave a flattering opinion of Sa'adeh's attitude towards Palestine, thus contradicting the allegation of a Sa'adeh-Zionist pact.

Secondly, we learned that the evidence on the basis of which Sa'adeh was convicted for high treason, namely his collaboration with the Jewish State, was completely baseless. This was the highlight of proceedings. It began when one of the two primary suspects in the saga, Mohammad Jamil Yunis, took the stand to answer for his part in the conspiracy:

The Court's Chairman: "Did you act as an intermediary between Sa'adeh and the Jews?"

Yunis: "I have no knowledge of this at all."

Chairman: "It can be inferred from the investigation and testimonies of witnesses that you made contact in Tarshiha through [one] Jabar al-Dahesh with the Jewish leadership to plot jointly against the Lebanese entity and to destroy the status quo in it, and this is confirmed in documents and testimonies."

Yunis: "I demand that you read out the document in full."

The Chairman here produced a testimony by one Muhammad Araka and read out several paragraphs from it. He then told Yunis that Araka's testimonial file contains a letter written by him. At Yunis's insistence, the Chairman holds out a copy of the letter and reads it out loud.

Defense counsel Mughabghab: "There are two primary witnesses involved here, Muhammad Araka and Ni'mat Thabet. I demand they be brought to the court for questioning."

The Prosecution: "There is no need for another testimony from Muhammad Araka as he has already provided one to the police investigator."

Yunis: "Araka testified under political pressure."

Defense counsel Mughabghab: "I insist on having Araka brought to the court."

Defense Counsel Taki ad-Deen: "I am rather bewildered that the prosecution has not charged Araka for making contacts and negotiating with the Zionists."

Prosecution: "The answer is in Araka's testimony itself."

Defense Counsel Lahhoud: "Yunis requested that the document be read out in full and I second his request."[63]

A letter, ostensibly written by Yunis to Sa'adeh about his [Yunis'] trip to Palestine, was produced on the spot and read out by the Chairman.

Yunis: "This is only one part of the letter. I implore you to read the other part."

The Prosecution: "There is no need for that. It suffices that the defendant has confessed to having made contact with the Jews."

Defense Counsel Lahhoud: "Meeting with Jews is not a sufficient ground for conviction as many people meet Jews and are not deemed criminal.

How do we know whether or not Muhammad Yunis met the Jews to spy on them or for them? I therefore insist once again on a full reading of the document because it would be sacrilege if we say "There is no God" and omit the second part of the holy verse."

The Prosecution: "I believe that the allegation as stated in Araka's testimony stands. At any rate, we are here to prosecute him on the charge of plotting against the Lebanese State. As for the Jewish issue, it is merely to inform the public opinion who Muhammad Yunis really is."

Defense Counsel Lahhoud: "I insist on a full reading of the document."

Defense Counsel Mughabghab: "I second the notion and call on Araka and members of the High Arab Committee to come forward to testify about this person."

The Chairman: "Yunis is accused of many things, and this charge is only one of them."

Defense counsel Mughabghab: "Either the document is withdrawn or read in full."

The Chairman: "Is there any reason preventing the prosecution from reading the whole document?"

The Prosecution: "Fine. Fine. I will read it."[64]

> My dear Leader
> A Syrian Social Nationalist salutation
>
> I am in Yarka today. Nothing significant to report from my side, except that on the 8th of May I met with the officer-in-charge of intelligence in the Galilee Battalion. I have unearthed detailed secrets on the area in which he is stationed and will submit my report on my return.
>
> The Lebanese Phalange organization and Archbishop Ignatius Mubarak are communicating and negotiating with Israel to topple the regime [in Lebanon] in order to establish a Christian state and suppress the other sects.
>
> A number of our local citizens have shown me recommendation papers given them by Archbishop Mubarak to use in Israel. I will attempt to obtain copies of these documents.
>
> Should you need to send special instructions regarding this issue, please do so through Muhammad Araka when he contacts the [party's] Headquarters.
>
> My sincere social nationalist regards
> Muhammad Yunis
> 13 May, 1949.

Apparently, the letter was forged to appear as though Sa'adeh had been soliciting an Israeli passport when in fact he was attempting to obtain copies of the authorization papers issued by Archbishop Mubarak to his (Mubarak's) emissaries. Sa'adeh had hoped to use these permits to expose the ruse between Israel and its Maronite allies in Lebanon, but the government beat him to it through Muhammad Araka, who was apparently a double agent.[65] Instead of investigating Mubarak and the Phalange about the plot, the government forged the letter in a moment of panic to "turn Lebanese and Arab public opinion against [Sa'adeh], including first and foremost Husni az-Zaim."[66] Since then, abundant evidence has emerged about Israeli-Maronite contacts during this period and about the plot itself.[67] After the prosecution read the original letter "there was thunderous applause in the court. The document was declared null and void and the charge was dropped in an official court of law."[68]

The trial lasted two days. Almost all of the defendants received prison terms varying from one to four years. They were also charged collectively twenty-five thousand Lebanese pounds to pay for the trial's expenses. Absent party functionaries were sentenced in absentia to various prison terms and deprived of all their civil rights. Their properties and belongings were also confiscated and placed in government trust. Muhammad Yunis received the harshest penalty: he was sentenced to four years imprisonment and deportation to another country upon his release.[69]

Alongside these trials, the Khoury regime conducted a systematic and institutionalized repression of Sa'adeh's followers. On 13 July, a memento was issued to the State's public service warning members affiliated to any political party or organization of "severe penalties."[70] The warning was enforced almost immediately against Sa'adeh's sympathizers at all levels of the government, the armed forces, the various ministerial departments, the educational institutions, and the judicial system.[71] The accused individuals were detained in army barracks to meet the overflow in state jails.[72] *The Times* estimated the number at 800.[73] Special administrative tribunals were set up to try them, but the procedure was mostly inefficient. Some prisoners were released after preliminary investigations, others were detained without charges. Tribunals were kept busy, however, trying the huge backlog of cases which included some fifty suspects who were still on the loose.[74] Ironically, many were convicted for acts unrelated to the planned uprising, including three sergeants and one staff sergeant, who were tried in camera by the military tribunal and given various prison terms on flimsy evidence.[75] To make this possible, the tribunal interpreted the law to include any member of the Syrian National Party caught with weapons, legal or not, even when there were no specific plans to use force. In most cases, the procedure was as pedantic as the other trials of this period and really nothing more than an open-and-shut exercise in accusation and punishment.

The defendants suffered untold personal loss of prosperity and reputation. Some lost everything they had. Others were discredited over quite innocent events or connections they may have had with Sa'adeh or his party. We know in retrospect that the cleansing operation pitted friends and staff against each other and created an atmosphere of mutual distrust between colleagues. It caused tremendous hardship to those involved and lingering fear and uncertainty to individuals and their families. To add to the insecurity, the government used odious measures to ensure that subversives were swiftly rounded up: anyone caught trying to raise money to help affected families was arrested;[76] a ban was imposed on foreign newspapers that published regular reports on Sa'adeh;[77] a midnight raid was made on a hospital to capture suspected SNP patients "causing fear in the hearts of staff and patients;"[78] a memorandum was circulated to Lebanese embassies and consulates all over the world asking diplomats to pressure host governments to extradite suspected SNP affiliates;[79] pressure was brought upon the Hannawi regime in Syria to expel Sa'adeh's wife from the country;[80] an author was arrested for attempting to publish a book on Sa'adeh, etc. These measures pale by comparison with other great political purges of the twentieth century. Still, they were monstrously out of proportion to the presumed misdeeds of the accused. Eventually, as outrageous evidence emerged about the injustices perpetrated against Sa'adeh, the government was forced to abandon most of these measures causing another major dent to its reputation.

Execution: The Irrational Choice

The ideal that every man is entitled to a fair and impartial trial is the cornerstone of civilized government. If a government destroys or damages that ideal it does irreparable harm to the structure of society. Unfair trials harm the moral leadership of the authorities who permit them and scrape out the cement which binds the legal institutions together. As one observer has justly noted, the degradation of the ideal of a fair trial "is the first step on the road to a police state."[81] The stage of appellate review is, in this respect, one of the essential elements of a fair trial. It is a link in the judicial process that controls the timing, the standards, and the scope of review of trial court decisions. It is also a fairly involved and time-consuming process that requires of the decision-making authorities (1) correction of error (or declaration that no correction is required) in particular litigation; and (2) declaration of legal principle, by creation, clarification, extension, or overruling.[82] In the discharge of these basic functions several others of subsidiary but significant importance are also served:

* ensuring principled decision-making in the trial courts;
* diffusing accountability within the legal system;
* ensuring uniformity of principles; and
* making justice "visible through the reasoned opinion." [83]

Moreover, the proper exercise of these functions requires that the decision-maker have full and accurate information about the offender, the offense, and the needs of society, in order to determine whether to spare the condemned prisoner. This is often done with the view that the public interest would be better served by sparing the life of the condemned rather than taking it, particularly in cases where executive clemency may facilitate the healing of political wounds.

Despite the irreversible nature of the death penalty, the Lebanese government failed to observe the legal safeguards afforded to the condemned during the review stage. First, the right of the condemned to adequate time and facilities to prepare his submission to the Reprieve Committee and the President was clearly violated. There was never a submission in the first place. The entire process was steamrolled. Sa'adeh was not even consulted about whether he wanted to make a submission for pardon or for the commutation of his sentence.

The execution order was rushed to deny Sa'adeh fair access to the clemency authorities and the opportunity to present his case or to contest the legality of the trial. He was left without an attorney, without knowledge of the information held against him, without an opportunity to appear personally before the clemency authorities, and without a proper hearing at all. It converted the clemency proceedings into an opportunity for the reprieve authorities to exert, without checks, all their powers of suppression against him. What is even more perplexing was President Khoury's refusal to give reconciliation through clemency any serious consideration. Khoury, a lawyer by profession, would surely have known that proceedings leading to the imposition of capital punishment must conform to the highest standards of independence, competence, objectivity and impartiality; that all safeguards and due process guarantees for the condemned must be scrupulously observed. Yet he authorized the death sentence without delay, contravening the most elementary principles of the clemency review.

The government did try to defend itself on the ground of "national security," but its argument is highly dubious. First, there were no clear national security implications to speak of since the revolt was well and truly defeated and the dangerous elements in Sa'adeh's party were behind bars. Second, there are many instances like Sa'adeh's case where the rule of law was maintained under more difficult circumstances. The Nuremburg Trials is one example. In spite of the problematic situation under which they were held, justice was administered according to law and the accused were given a full and proper trial. Those condemned to death were granted sufficient time to contest their sentences:

> Upon the completion of every trial the record of the case is sent to the Military Governor for review. He has power to mitigate, reduce, or otherwise alter the sentence imposed, but he may not increase its severity. No death sentence may be carried into execution unless and until confirmed in writing by the Military Governor. The defendants have been given the privilege of sending petitions for review to the U.S. Supreme Court and other high governmental offices.[84]

Another example is Robert Brasillach. The French author and fascist journalist was tried by the High Court and sentenced to death for collaboration on 19 January, 1945. At first, Brasillach's attorney, Jacques Isorni tried to have the sentence overturned on procedural grounds and when that failed he made a direct request for pardon to General de Gaulle. In spite of political insecurity in France and public anger with fascist collaborationists, the General refused to sign the decree to carry out the death sentence until after all rights to appeal and the time limits for filing such appeals had been exhausted: it took eighteen days, not long enough in some opinions.[85]

Sa'adeh's execution was exceptionally degrading. Few political executions in history would match the brutality and inhumanity shown during his speedy execution. When, on 20 January, 1793, the National Convention condemned Louis XVI, King of France, to death, it scheduled his execution for the next day. Louis spent that evening saying goodbye to his wife and children;[86] Lieutenant Nathan Hale who was executed by the British in 1776 was granted his last wish for writing materials and wrote two letters, one to his mother and one to a brother officer;[87] Charles I, on the day of his execution, was allowed to go for a last walk in St James's Park with his pet dog. His last meal was bread and wine;[88] John Brown, the American abolitionist who planned to liberate the slaves through armed intervention, was allowed to spend a few hours with his wife before his execution during which they talked about God and John Brown's will and the education of their children;[89] the Greek philosopher, Socrates, who was executed for his beliefs,[90] was entitled to have visitors. On the day of his execution, all of his friends gathered to be with him one last time; Captain Beall, who was sentenced to death on the trumped up charge of being "a spy and guerrilla," was given the chance to see his mother, who remained with him for a considerable time. In the course of the morning of his execution Beall expressed a desire to have a photographic picture of himself made, and his wish was complied with;[91] Thomas More's execution was scheduled for at least one week after judgment during which time he received a visit from his wife Alice and on the day of his execution was allowed to speak briefly from the execution block to the large crowd that had gathered to watch the event;[92] Julius and Ethel Rosenberg, who were sentenced to death in the electric chair allegedly for espionage, were executed after no less than two years from the trial's end, despite the designation of their crime as "worse than murder."[93] One execution in history that comes close to Sa'adeh's cruel and degrading ending is that of the Duc d'Enghien, who was tried secretly and sent to his death at once "by torchlight between three and four o'clock in the morning,"[94] which was also roughly the morning hour when Sa'adeh was executed.

Perhaps no execution in Lebanese judicial history has been the subject of as much criticism as the Sa'adeh case. It was, and still is, widely seen as the most striking instance of a state overstepping its legitimate boundaries. Ghassan Tueini put the matter in the following context:

> Antun Sa'adeh was indicted on the charges of stirring up sedition and riots and assaulting public forces, in addition to perpetrating acts of sabotage and killings. These are charges that befit a gang leader . . . or some chieftains that the government is fully aware of, or anyone who may contemplate the possibility of triggering a squabble that involves misery, crime and irresponsibility. Antun Sa'adeh, however, did not stir up sedition for its own sake. He did not revolt, attack and kill just for the sake of revolting, attacking and killing. Antun Sa'adeh was a man of principles with a mission to accomplish.[95]

Whether independent Lebanese are supportive of Sa'adeh's innocence or guilt, almost all agree that his execution was unwarranted. To most, the punishment was extremely severe and did not fit the crime. Sa'adeh was not a criminal and his criminalization by the government was carried out under the wrong law in order to facilitate the use of the death penalty. What is more, his execution does not measure up to historical precedents. Political dissenters in the Arab World, including the most rebellious among them, traditionally received much lighter sentences for their actions. They were either imprisoned or banished, but rarely executed. Even under stringent colonial rule, the penalty that was most often meted out to rebels was fairly lenient in comparison with Sa'adeh's. It was designed to frighten would-be rebels into obedience rather than to spur them on to bolder action. Arabi Pasha, Suleiman al-Murshid, Abdul Kadir al-Jazairi, Sultan al-Atrash, Ibrahim Hananu, Abdul Rahman al-Shahbandar and many others were rebel leaders who inflicted far greater damage on the established authorities than Sa'adeh's diminutive rebellion; yet they were not executed or degraded like Sa'adeh.

If there is any one lesson above all others to be drawn from the Sa'adeh execution, it is its pointlessness. Killing an opponent, by execution or other means, may and does perhaps bring momentary relief and satisfaction to those in power, but it does not solve the underlying conflict: it merely delays it. Physical extermination has the potential to transform a foe into a hero, which can seriously undermine the state or erode its legitimacy. It can also foster new divisions within society and a strong sense of resentment toward the authorities, particularly from those in society who do not in the first place support violence as a means of settling political disputes. Most important of all, physical extermination of dissenters, even within the proper framework of the law, leaves the government open to dangerous criticism and exposes those in power to retaliation and vengeance.

In countries like Lebanon, where the state depends on a tender balance between diverse social groups, compromise rather than vengeance is the apposite policy to pursue in times of political conflict and social schisms. Compromise was the fundamental principle on which the Lebanese state was founded in 1920, and the 1943 National Pact, authored by Khoury and Solh a mere six years before they sent Sa'adeh to his death, was essentially built on compromise. By executing Sa'adeh, the Khoury regime robbed itself of a golden opportunity to solidify internal compromise as an enduring and living principle in the political life of Lebanon.

Occasionally, exceptional circumstances may arise when a society has to resort to capital punishment to protect itself or to protect the innocent, but it does itself a great disservice when it does so for political expediency or to cut down a political adversary who is not a criminal in the ordinary sense of the word. Executions, in such instances, serve only to perpetuate impunity and negate the concept of justice: they are yet another example of violations of the right to life.

Conclusion

Few people in history have faced their trials and deaths as squarely, calmly and with as much integrity as did Sa'adeh. The only thing that overwhelmed this enduring feature was the brutality and inhumanity meted out to the accused during his final hours. But what really makes Sa'adeh's execution a unique event in Lebanese (and indeed Arab) politico-judicial history is that it was the first and last political execution of its kind carried out outside the realm of proper judicial procedures. Virtually nothing was allowed to disturb the smooth façade of this pre-orchestrated event.

The case was, inescapably, an accelerating tragedy. The government had from the first formed the irrevocable decision to put Sa'adeh to death, and the speed of the execution is indicative of how absolutely determined it was. It undoubtedly considered the execution as the best means of ridding itself of an irreconcilable citizen. Whether it had considered carefully the implications of its action, however, is another matter. The government probably hoped that the execution would be startling at first, but it would live in the imagination of men for a long time as a warning. It also probably hoped that it would go away quickly and with little political fuss: it miscalculated. An execution in which the greatest judicial and moral values had been crushed and violated could be blotted out from the consciousness of the people with ease. Indeed, doubts surfaced as soon as the execution was over and the government came increasingly under fire.

In certain cases the trial is not over when the verdict is reached. The dialog on the issues may continue for many years, particularly if the death penalty is involved or if the accused had been put to death in suspicious circumstances. Only complete clarity and the full truth can help people recover from the wound inflicted upon their consciousness.

NOTES

1 Before and after Sa'adeh, when the death penalty was involved, almost all capital sentences resulted in a presidential review for a possible pardon. Sentenced criminals were routinely given a sufficient delay before execution so that their requests for pardons could be examined. If granted, clemency would usually entail a commutation to a life sentence.

2 *Istijwab Jumblatt al tarikhi lil hukuma hawla istishhad Sa'adeh ome 1949* (Jumblatt's historical interpolation to the [Lebanese] Government In Regard to Sa'adeh's Martyrdom in 1949). Beirut: SSNP Information Bureau, 1987.

3 Antoine Butrus, *Qissat muhakamat Antun Sa'adeh was i'damehe* (An Account of Antun Sa'adeh's Trial and Execution). Beirut: Chemaly & Chemaly, 2002: 120–121.

4 *Al-Dayar*. Beirut, 1 March, 1991.

5 Antoine Butrus, *Qissat muhakamat Antun Sa'adeh was i'damehe* (An Account of Antun Sa'adeh's Trial and Execution). Beirut: Chemaly & Chemaly, 2002: 123.

6 Ibid., 124.

7 Sami Solh, *Ahtakim ila al-Tarikh* (I Leave it to History to Judge Me). Beirut: Dar an-Nahar, 1970: 94.

8 Ibid.

9 Antoine Butrus, *Qissat muhakamat Antun Sa'adeh was i'damehe* (An Account of Antun Sa'adeh's Trial and Execution). Beirut: Chemaly & Chemaly, 2002: 93.

10 Ibid., 94.

11 *Beirut*, 9 July, 1949.

12 According to the priest's brother, Georges Barbari, the security forces called on the priest twice not once – at dusk on 7 July, while the trial was still in session, when they were repelled by the priest's request for consent from the archbishop, and at midnight between 7 and 8 July. Though overlooked by Father Barbari, the first incident has been cited by at least one vital source on Sa'adeh's execution. See George Abdul Massih, *Muhadarat al-Mukhayyam al-Sayfi* (Summer Camps Lecture Series): 30.

13 Najam al-Hashim, *A'khir Ayyam Sa'adeh* (Sa'adeh's Last Days). Beirut: n. p., 1999: 74.

14 Said Taky ad-Din, "The Priest who confessed him" in Adel Beshara, *Syrian Nationalism: An Inquiry Into the Political Philosophy of Antun Sa'adeh*. Beirut: Dar Bissan, 1995: Appendix 5. Hereby referred to as "The Priest who confessed him."

15 Said Taky ad-Din, "The Priest who confessed him."

16 Ibid.

17 Najam al-Hashim, *op. cit.,* 75.

18 Ibid.

19 Ibid.

20 Ibid.

21 Ibid.

22 Antoine Butrus, *Qissat muhakamat Antun Sa'adeh was i'damehe* (An Account of Antun Sa'adeh's Trial and Execution). Beirut: Chemaly & Chemaly, 2002: 126.

23 Ibid.

24 Said Taky ad-Din, "The Priest who confessed him."

25 *An-Nahar*. Beirut, 10 July, 1949.

26 *Al-Sayyad*. Beirut, 14 July, 1949.

27 Said Taky ad-Din, "The Priest who confessed him."

28 *Az-Zaman*, 11 July, 1949.

29 Said Taky ad-Din, "The Priest who confessed him."

30 Ibid.

31 *Az-Zaman*, 11 July, 1949.

32 Gibran Jreige, *Ma' Antun Sa'adeh* (In the company of Antun Sa'adeh): 179–180.

33 Said Taky ad-Din, "The Priest who confessed him."

34 Ibid.

35 Ibid.

36 *Beirut*, 9 July, 1949.

37 Ibid.

38 Ibid.

39 Said Taky ad-Din, "The Priest who confessed him." The firing squad aimed at the chest, since this is easier to hit than the head. A firing squad aiming at the head produces the same type of wounds as those produced by a single bullet, but bullets fired at the chest rupture the heart, large blood vessels and lungs so that the condemned person dies of haemorrhage and shock. It is not unusual for the officer in charge of the firing squad to have to give the prisoner a "coup de grace" – a pistol shot to the head to finish them off after the initial volley has failed to kill them. A bullet produces a cavity which has a volume many times that of the bullet. Cavitation is probably due to the heat dissipated when the impact of the bullet boils the water and volatile fats in the tissue which it strikes. According to Dr Le Garde, in his book *Gunshot Injuries*, it is proved both in theory and by experimentation, that cavitation is caused by the transfer of the momentum from

the fast moving bullet to the tissue which is mostly comprised of incompressible liquid. Persons hit by bullets feel as if they have been punched – pain comes later if the victim survives long enough to feel it.

40 Ibid.
41 Ibid.
42 For an in-depth account on the fate of Sa'adeh's corpse see Antoine Butrus, *Qissat muhakamat Antun Sa'adeh was i'damehe* (An Account of Antun Sa'adeh's Trial and Execution). Beirut: Chemaly & Chemaly, 2002: 132–157.
43 *An-Nahar*, Beirut, 11 July, 1949.
44 Ibid.
45 *An-Nahar*, Beirut, 15 July, 1949.
46 *The Times*, 18 July, 1949.
47 *An-Nahar*, Beirut, 21 July, 1949.
48 *An-Nahar*, Beirut, 22 July, 1949.
49 *An-Nahar*, Beirut, 20 July, 1949.
50 Ibid.
51 Ibid.
52 *An-Nahar*, Beirut, 18 August, 1949.
53 Ibid.
54 Ibid.
55 Ibid.
56 Naim Mughabghab, who turned parliamentarian later on and was assassinated in 1960.
57 The Reichstag fire was a pivotal event in the establishment of Nazi Germany. At 21:15 on the night of 27 February, 1933, a Berlin fire station received an alarm call that the Reichstag building, the assembly location of the German Parliament, was ablaze. The fire was started in the Session Chamber, and by the time the police and firemen arrived, the main Chamber of Deputies was in flames. Inside the building, the police quickly found a shirtless Marinus van der Lubbe. Van der Lubbe was a Dutch Jewish insurrectionist communist and unemployed bricklayer who had recently arrived in Germany, ostensibly to carry out his political activities. The fire was used as evidence that the communists were beginning a plot against the German government. Van der Lubbe and 4000 Communist leaders were arrested. Then-chancellor Adolf Hitler urged President Hindenburg to pass an emergency decree in order to counter the "ruthless confrontation of the KPD". See Hans Mommsen, "The Reichstag Fire and Its Political Consequences" in Hajo Holborn, *Republic to Reich The Making of the Nazi Revolution*. New York: Pantheon Books, 1972: pp. 129–222.
58 *An-Nahar*, Beirut, 3 August, 1949.
59 Ibid.
60 *An-Nahar*, Beirut, 12 August, 1949.
61 *An-Nahar*, Beirut, 31 August, 1949.
62 Ibid.
63 *An-Nahar*, Beirut, 31 August, 1949.
64 Ibid.
65 See Ahmad Asfahani (ed.), *Antun Sa'adeh wa al-Hizb al-Suri al-Qawmi al-Ijtimae' fi Awarq al-Amir Farid Chehab, al-Mudir al-Ome lil al-Amn al-Ome al-Lubnani* (Antun Sa'adeh and the Syrian Social Nationalist Party in the Private Papers of

Emir Farid Chehab, the General Director of the Lebanese General Security).
Beirut: Dar Kutub, 2006: 68–70.

66 Hassan Hallaq, *Al-Tayyarrat al-Siyyassiyah fi Lubnan: 1943–1952* (Political Currents in Lebanon: 1943–1952). Beirut: Maahad al-Inma' al-Arabi, 1981: 180.

67 See Kirsten E. Schulze, *Israel's Covert Diplomacy in Lebanon*. London: Macmillan Press Ltd, 1998: 32–34.

68 Abdullah Sa'adeh, *Awraq Qawmiyyah* (Nationalist Memoirs). Beirut: n.p., 1987: 44–45.

69 See *An-Nahar*, Beirut, 1–2 September, 1949.

70 Ibid.

71 *An-Nahar*, Beirut, 14 August, 1949.

72 *The New York Times*, 18 July, 1949. A number of barracks had to be turned into prisons to hold the extra number.

73 *The Times*, 18 July, 1949.

74 The most important suspect on the loose was George Abdul Massih, who was able to elude the authorities despite the strict security measures and efforts of the regime to have him extradited from Syria first then Turkey where he was thought to be hiding. See *An-Nahar*, Beirut, 11 August, 1949.

75 *An-Nahar*, Beirut, 11 August, 1949.

76 *An-Nahar*, Beirut, 18 August, 1949.

77 The newspaper in question was *Al-Alam al-Arabi* (The Arab World). *An-Nahar*, Beirut, 29 August, 1949.

78 Ibid.

79 *An-Nahar*, Beirut, 20 August, 1949.

80 The Syrian government issued a formal statement on 22 September, 1949, denying official Lebanese claims that Sa'adeh's wife had been evicted from Syria at the behest of the Lebanese government. See *An-Nahar*, Beirut, 22 September, 1949.

81 Thurman Arnold, "Due process in trials," *Annals of the American Academy of Political and Social Science*, Vol. 300, July 1955: 123.

82 J. Dickson Phillips, Jr., "The Appellate Review Function: Scope of Review," *Law and Contemporary Problems*, vol. 47, no. 2, Spring 1984: 2–3. The clemency authority should permit an applicant, his supporters, the state authorities, and the public at large to comment upon a clemency petition. Because of the breadth of factors involved in a clemency application, participants could urge granting or denying clemency for any reason. To protect the accuracy of the process, any person should also be permitted to comment upon other submissions to the clemency authority, and all comments should be public, so that factual errors or distortions might be challenged.

83 Roscoe Pound, *Appellate Procedure in Civil Cases*. Boston: Little, Brown and Co., 1941: 3.

84 Benjamin B. Ferencz, "Nurnberg Trial Procedure and the Rights of the Accused," *Journal of Criminal Law and Criminology*, Vol. 39, No. 2 (July–Aug, 1948): 151.

85 "Brasillach's file was put together in the days following his trial by de Gaulle's immediate staff, with official documents from the Court of Justice of the Seine, the Ministry of Justice, the Bureau of Criminal Affairs, and from Brasillach's defense lawyer, along with whatever unofficial letters were received by de Gaulle

from the public at large. The file is thick, surprisingly thick, given that there were only eighteen days between Brasillach's trial and his execution." Alice Kaplan, *The Collaborator: The Trial and Execution of Robert Brasillach*. Chicago: The University of Chicago Press, 2000: 202.

86 See M. Walzer, *Regicide and Revolution: Speeches at the Trial of Louis XVI*. [London, New York]: Cambridge University Press, 1974.

87 See Nathan Olson, Cynthia Martin and Brent Schoonover, *Nathan Hale: Revolutionary Spy*. Mankato, Minn.: Capstone Press, 2006.

88 See C. V. Wedgwood, *A Coffin for King Charles: The Trial and Execution of Charles I*. New York: Macmillan, 1964.

89 See Evan Carton, *Patriotic Treason: John Brown and the Soul of America*. New York: Free Press, 2006.

90 He was charged and convicted for impiety (that of not acknowledging the same gods that the state believed in) and for corrupting minors. See Thomas C. Brickhouse and Nicholas D. Smith, *The Trial and Execution of Socrates: Sources and Controversie*. New York: Oxford University Press, 2002.

91 See James T. Brady, J. L. Boyle, John Beall, and Orville Hickman Browning, *Letters and Manuscripts Relating to the Case of Captain John Beall*. n.p., 1865.

92 See Richard Marius, *Thomas More: A Biography*. New York: Knopf, 1984.

93 Betty Burnett, *The Trial of Julius and Ethel Rosenberg: A Primary Source Account*. New York: Rosen Pub. Group, 2004.

94 Sidney B. Fay, "The Execution of the Duc d'Enghien II," *The American Historical Review*, Vol. 4, No. 1 (Oct., 1898): 32.

95 *An-Nahar*, Beirut, 9 June, 1949.

5

REACTION

It is a widely held view in law that, although administrative action may be imperative to a government where there is insufficient evidence that a political opponent has acted unlawfully, it is far better for the reputation of the government to leave the decision to the judiciary.[1] For the public is far more likely to accept the decision of the court if the trial is conducted in accordance with due process than if it is perceived to be a fraudulent instrument for achieving the political objectives of those possessed of power. Kirchheimer describes how neutrality and fairness, when observed, can work to the advantage of the government as follows:

> Judicial proceedings serve to authenticate and thus to limit political action. Power holders may have an infinite number of security interests. Some of them, though perhaps far-fetched, are arrived at rationally; others are the product of imagination. By agreeing to a yardstick, however nebulous or refined, to cut down the number of occasions for the elimination of actual or potential foes, those in power stand to gain as much as their subjects. Authentication removes the fear of reprisals or liquidation from multitudes of possible victims, and encourages a friendly and understanding disposition towards the security needs of the power holders on the part of their subjects.[2]

Likewise, Professor Laurence Tribe of Harvard Law School, in describing the need for justice and openness in criminal proceedings, has well noted that "The courthouse is a 'theatre of justice,' wherein a vital social drama is staged; if its doors are locked, the public can only wonder whether the solemn ritual of communal condemnation has been properly performed."[3] This legal percept is not merely a policing device to constrain government action. It rests on substantive grounds as well – the principle of equal respect for persons, a basic norm of morality as well as of legality.[4]

The trial and subsequent execution of Antun Sa'adeh affords an example of how the naked elimination of a political opponent can backfire on those in power. By depriving Sa'adeh of procedural rights, the government all but destroyed the value of the authentication process and what little that was left of its reputation and legitimacy. Its image was dealt a few telling blows from the press, its critics, the public, and even some of its own supporters. Moreover, by throwing all the weight of its power against a single person, the government stirred up public sympathy for the accused and turned him into a martyr pitted unfairly against a large, powerful institution. This is evident from the reactions that Sa'adeh's trial and execution evoked, both inside and outside Lebanon. If, however, it is necessary to recognize the logic of these reactions across time, as well as to situate them in their proper political and legal context, then it is equally important to understand how the government counter-reacted and whether it was successful in silencing its critics.

The Reaction in Syria

The Syrian people were deeply disturbed by the trial and the verdict. However, strict censorship of the press and fear of government reprisal meant that few dared to comment on the case. It was left to Archbishop Ignatius Hraikah of the Archdiocese of Hama to provide a sophistical response that took cognizance of not only the actual consequences of the act, but also the probable or logical consequences. Writing under the pseudonym "an important figure in Hama" to avoid official retribution, the Archbishop scolded the Lebanese government for the execution of Sa'adeh and rendered its action as a measure of real backwardness:

> I was once talking to Mr. Yusuf As-Sawdah, Lebanon's Minister to Brazil. He noted that Lebanon was the most superior of all Arab states and, to prove his point, cited a study by an American claiming that more than fifty percent of the people in Lebanon speak foreign languages, something not to be found in any other country in the world . . . I have no idea what Mr. As-Sawdah will have to say now about the 'progress' of Lebanon after he reads about the trial of . . . Antun Sa'adeh.[5]

Speaking foreign languages is not necessarily a sign of progress. The benchmark for that is human dignity and how society treats its gifted individuals and utilizes their talents and abilities: "Any conscientious person in Syria or Lebanon who has read what the press has published about the trial of Antun Sa'adeh and the speed with which he was executed . . . will not be able to hold back his tears not just out of grief for this outstanding hero, but also out of sorrow over a nation whose rulers are so careless about human lives."[6] Sa'adeh was the real hero because he did not hesitate to put his life at risk to fight against the political prejudices and corruption of the state. His execution was a clear aberration from the path of truth and justice.

To prove the point, the Archbishop drew comparisons with the Suleiman al-Murshid episode in Syria.[7] A man of origin humble, al-Murshid became the rallying point for thousands of Syrian Alawites during the 1930s and 1940s, acquiring within a short span of time "a fortune as well as a considerable political following."[8] He amassed that fortune by sending his followers to make the uneducated villagers (especially elderly women) sign away their properties to him under the guise of special taxes for him as holder of the virtual sword of Ali Ibn Abu Talib.[9] With that wealth and power al-Murshid succeeded in keeping Damascus' authority out of Alawi territories until 1946, when he was captured and executed on charges of subversion. With simple comparative analysis, Archbishop Hraikah used the al-Murshid episode to make an eloquent, vicious invective against the prosecutors of Sa'adeh:

> Antun Sa'adah . . . was a man of a patriotic mission and national call, whose political opinions and ideas of unification continued, for fifteen years, to occupy popular minds in Lebanon and Syria, at home and abroad. He was a man whose ideology was embraced by hundreds and thousands of intellectual Arab youth . . . [Yet, in his trial] the attorney Mr. Lahhoud, was not even given twenty four hours to examine the file and prepare his defense. Conversely, the trial of Suleiman al-Murshid, the thug, instigator and rebel against the country who conspired against it, lasted for several months, during which all information and evidence were registered and attorneys defended him in closed and public sessions for days and days.[10]

The article ended with an accelerated attack on the Lebanese regime for "offering Sa'adeh's head on a silver platter to the mobs of Al-Kataib . . . just as Herod offered the head of John the Baptist to his daughter Herodias."[11] *Al-Qubas* was banned for fifteen days for publishing the article![12]

Naturally, after Zaim's downfall and execution in August 1949, the mood in Syria changed. A stream of condemnatory writings, mostly memoirs, appeared in the Syrian press expressing local disgust at Sa'adeh's betrayal and killing. The most sensational piece, which probably did more than any other single act to arouse interest and passions, was Qubbani's reflections in *al-Dunia* newsmagazine in 1949. The opening paragraph would suffice:

> Sa'adah was not sentenced to death for staging a revolution. His execution or assassination was pre-determined before the infamous Al-Jummaizah incident. Contrary to reports published in the Lebanese magazine *Al-Jamhur*, there was no strong friendship between the two leaders [Zaim and Sa'adeh]. There is a world of difference between a man of morals and conviction and you know what.[13]

Another dramatic condemnation of Zaim came from his brother-in-law and private secretary at the Presidential Palace, Nadhir Fansah:

> I used to be very fond of Zaim and admire his simple nature, charm, piety and compassion, even when his personality took extremist turns due largely to his diabetes. In spite of all this, I consider the Antun Sa'adeh affair the biggest black mark against his short regime. Not a single drop of blood sullied his regime until the moment it was sullied by Antun Sa'adeh's blood, and then by his own blood and that of his prime minister, Husni al-Barrazi.[14]

Almost all biographies of this period depict a general revulsion of public feeling over the affair, and a bitter indignation against Zaim for his part in it. Some authors denounced the execution as cruel and degrading due to the nature of the death penalty; others termed Zaim's betrayal of Sa'adeh as a sad day for Syria and a blot on Arab honor.[15] The repulsion that exploded after Zaim's execution translated into popular sympathy for Sa'adeh and subsequently into significant political gains for his party in Syria. The SSNP went on to win several seats at the next elections. Its position in the Syrian Army gained in strength and it became a key player in Syrian politics until the Malki Affair in 1955.

The Reaction Abroad

Overseas reaction to the news of Sa'adeh's execution was mixed. In the Western hemisphere it was generally welcomed in the press as a positive step in the global fight against fascism. The *New York Times* expose of his execution is a case in point:

> Anton Saadeh, who tried from the little mountain land of Lebanon to become the Hitler of the Middle East and had maintained branches of his Syrian Popular Party in the United States and Latin America, died early this morning before a firing squad.[16]

Echoed throughout the American press, the report described Sa'adeh as the "fuehrer" of a "completely Fascist organization," who "may have been influenced by the Fascist movement in Brazil at that time."[17] For all the talk of individual rights and due process in law, one is struck not only by the paucity of the report but also by the lack of any reference to the unfairness of the trial or to the severity of the sentence. The fact that the verdict was made in advance for the purpose of obtaining a conviction was completely overlooked. Ironically, the flaw was picked up by the Reverand Joseph Awad, a Maronite priest who "favoured outright military alliance between Israel and Lebanon."[18] Awad offered the following qualified response: "Albion Ross' were the earliest full reports to reach this country of the suppression of Antun Saadeh's attempt to destroy the independence of Lebanon. Welcome as that news was to us here, to most of us – I must point out – the summary execution of Saadeh seemed a painful departure from Lebanon's tradition of regard for constitutional human rights."[19] Coming from a staunchly pro-Kataib (Sa'adeh's arch-rival) figure[20] this was truly an important concession and reflected the remarkable transformation that Sa'adeh's execution was causing in Lebanon and abroad.

British press reports about the saga were equally uneven. As elsewhere, the emphasis was on the transgression rather than justice and the event was stated too exactly to fit the minds of the war-weary British public:

> Antoun Saadeh, founder of the National Syrian Party in the Lebanese republic, has been executed after a secret trial by court-martial. The activities of the party culminated in terrorist acts and the formation of armed bands which attacked police stations. It has been vigorously

suppressed by the government, who arrested Saadeh and more than 500 adherents.[21]

Governmental reaction to the saga was muted. Despite its farcical nature, on the whole, Western governments remained tight-lipped relying on continued uncritical acceptance of the official Lebanese version of events, while routinely rejecting all arguments to the contrary. What role, if any, Sa'adeh's image as a relic of fascism played can only be speculated. Still, the question is interesting. At the very least, Sa'adeh symbolized everything the West opposed – a fact which prompted unfavorable coverage of his case in the foreign press – although he was regarded (and remained for many years after his death) as Britain's man in the Near East.

One other fact bears recording. Several days after Sa'adeh's execution, adherents of the Syrian National Party in the Ghanaian capital of Accra cabled Eleanor Roosevelt, Chairman of the Human Rights Commission at the United Nations and a draftee of the Universal Declaration of Human Rights, imploring her to act:

> In the name of Rights of Man for which you nobly struggled, Syrian Social Nationalists and hundreds of immigrants strongly protest against [the] cruel prosecution and arrest [of] party members and tyrannous execution of leader Antoun Saadeh by Lebanese Government which actions contradict Man's rights as ratified and accepted by UNO members. Please use your influence for immediate enquiry and stoppage of bloodshed.[22]

A crusader for social justice who became an advocate of the rights and needs of the poor and the disadvantaged,[23] Eleanor Roosevelt conveyed the telegram to the US Department of State. A month later, on 4 August, 1949, she received a tepid reply from the Assistant Secretary, George McGhee, expressing a cavalier attitude of noninvolvement:

> According to the information available to the Department, the members of Syrian Popular Party, beginning on July 2 and continuing for several days, staged an armed rebellion against the Lebanese Government. The leader of the party, Antoun Saadeh, was captured on July 7, tried by court martial and executed on the morning of July 8. Although the action taken may be considered of a summary nature, the Department feels that the Government of Lebanon was

acting within the sovereign rights in suppressing this revolutionary activity which aimed to overthrow the Government by force, as well as in punishing those who took part in it. It would not be appropriate for the Government of the United States to protest this action, which is a strictly internal matter within the jurisdiction of the Lebanese Government.[24]

Elsewhere, in the Lebanese diaspora, the mood was one of bewilderment and disbelief. A telegraphic memo signed by two hundred and sixty prominent Syro-Lebanese figures in Brazil – artists, writers, professors, students, journalists and industrialists – expressing regret at the conduct of the trial was cabled to and published in the Lebanese daily *an-Nahar*. The message deplored the execution as a blatant violation of Sa'adeh's basic human rights and international conventions "stipulated and declared by the United Nation."[25] *An-Nahar* deleted the condemnatory passage from the memo to avoid legal action. On another front, reports reached the Lebanese Foreign Ministry in July 1949 that the Lebanese Legation in Argentina was attacked by local Lebanese expatriates appalled by the government's execution of Sa'adeh: the minister plenipotentiary in Buenos Aires, however, denied the reports.[26]

The Reaction Inside Lebanon
In a bid to pre-empt public criticism of Sa'adeh's trial and execution, the Khoury regime issued on 9 July a public statement presenting its version of events. The statement sought to present the SSNP and Antun Sa'adeh at once as enemies of Lebanon and Arabism in order to placate various components of the Lebanese population, Christians as well as Muslims:

> Freedom of opinion and freedom of association were among the leading principles adopted by the Lebanese government in the era of independence and national rule. The government demonstrated its devotion to the spirit of these principles by authorizing political institutions, parties and organizations to hold their meetings and engage in their activities within the framework of the law. Although the Syrian National Party, headed by Antun Sa'adeh since its establishment, never embraced the Lebanese national creed, or Arabism, the government's tolerance, first in allowing the SSNP leader to come back to Lebanon from Argentina, and then in permitting

the party to resume its activities and issue a newspaper, stemmed from its desire to respect freedoms and political beliefs on the one hand, and also from the pledges made by the SNP leadership that their political activities would not contravene the existing Lebanese entity and correct Lebanese belief.[27]

The customary depiction of Sa'adeh as a traitor hell-bent on destroying the Lebanese State was regurgitated but in still vaguer terms: "The Social National Party had been steered by its leader to destroy the Lebanese entity as a preliminary step towards a coup . . ."[28] The statement's wildly chaotic presentation of the relevant material manages to conceal the circumstances that led to the insurrection. Instead, it concentrated on the government's own response to it, while scrupulously keeping more significant information under wraps. In terms of content, the statement signaled no substantive departure from the fragmentary reports published earlier in the press. It scrupulously avoided any mention of trial procedure. Judicial violations were cleverly concealed behind relevant articles of the military penal code to convey a sense of legitimacy and credibility to the government's action. Basic details about the appellate stage were also deliberately falsified to shield the government from criticism. The statement recounted familiar judicial procedures to give both finality and sanctity to procedures and an appearance of law and order to the regime. Its description is not supported by the evidence, however.

The statement gave rise to much criticism by segments of Lebanese public opinion as well as by the comparatively free domestic press. Virtually every important newspaper in Lebanon condemned the government and ridiculed the trial. The tone was set by Kamil Mruwi of the generally pro-Solh *al-Hayat* newspaper. Less than twenty-four hours after the publication of the government's statement, he deplored the circumstances of the affair and the legal facade that the Government was hiding behind with a fiery front-page article:

> *Al Hayat* yesterday published the first government communiqué concerning the execution of Antun Sa'adeh. With all due respect to the explanations mentioned therein, popular opinion about the case has not changed. A case that has resulted in the arrest of thousands of young men, death or injury to many, an intervention from the army, and finally death sentences, such a case calls for more than merely a hundred lines to be pronounced by the government after a whole month of silence.[29]

[144]

Ghassan Tueini, the distinguished editor and publisher of *an-Nahar*, delivered a stinging and eloquent riposte in which he described the execution of the SSNP leader as outright assassination: "The people are not sure whether Antun Sa'adeh was executed or killed, whether it was a trial or a conspiracy that took place."[30] He added:

> The authorities have succeeded in arresting Sa'adah, giving him a speedy trial, sentencing him, and executing him, in such a speed which left most people dumbfounded and bewildered. It was difficult to comprehend the reasons for this most unusual and un-called for action, especially that the rebellion was successfully and swiftly suppressed. Even Sa'adeh's arch-enemies were at a loss of words to justify the Government's action. Those same enemies are now saying, "What a great tragedy". Although the Government wanted to get rid of the man as speedily as possible, fearing he would bring terror to Lebanon, yet, by its rash action it has created a great giant, stronger than Sa'adeh ever was, and has made of him a martyr, not only to his followers but to those who never wished him better than death.[31]

In 2004, speaking to an audience of SSNP members who gathered at the Issam Fares Auditorium in Beirut to celebrate what would have been Sa'adeh's 100th birthday, Tueini reflected on the circumstances of his article: "On that horrible night, I was still at the *an-Nahar* offices with Gibran Hayek and other worried reporters like us, when a young officer came into the room . . . and described to us Sa'adeh's execution in detail. So I erased all that I had already written and I wrote with Gibran Narawi the story of the execution, minute by minute."[32]

As more details about Sa'adeh's killing emerged, other newspapers which had initially supported the government now joined the anti-regime campaign. On 20 July, the chief editor of *Al-Sayyad* newsmagazine published a moving and sympathetic article on Sa'adeh. Its author, Said Frayha, depicted Sa'adeh as brave and dignified as any man could hope to be in the last moment of his life: "He accepted the death sentence as though he was accepting an invitation to lunch."[33]

The criticism continued. On 30 September journalist Elias Abdallah Khoury savaged the government in an article entitled "Lebanon's incumbent government before public opinion."[34] Questioning both the wisdom and legality of the government, the author accused key members (Khoury, Solh and Majid Irslan, the then Minister of Defense) of a crime of international proportions: "Working in cahoots with one another, those tyrants killed Sa'adah, the mentor, in such a way that cannot be accepted by any sound-thinking mind, one that can only be undertaken by people who still follow the manners and behavior of the bygone Turkish era."[35] The author likened the Lebanese leadership to the Nazi Germans and melodramatically visualized them standing before an international tribunal to account for their "atrocious" crime:

> If those three "prominent" persons were brought before judges like those who sentenced the German criminals in Nuremberg to death by hanging, what would their sentence be after they have perpetrated the worst crime the world has ever witnessed? There is no doubt in my mind that these judges would pass a law with great speed, faster even than the time it took to execute Sa'adeh, to have them executed by more horrific methods than hanging, thus allowing justice to take its course with these exceptional criminals.[36]

An interesting sidelight in the article is the affirmation, probably for the first time after his execution, of Sa'adeh's loyalty to Lebanon: "Sa'adeh was never an enemy of the Lebanese State. The truth is that he loved Lebanon more than anything else, and never did put anything before it. He was a man of an honorable cause, but was conspired against and killed."[37] In comparison, the Lebanese leadership was "indeed barbaric, unfit to rule the cultured people of Lebanese."[38] The author added, "Yet, what is to be expected from people who snatched power through forged elections? Stifling people's freedom, dragging their pride through the mud and executing free people whenever they pleased and whichever way they pleased are the only things to be expected. They are tyrants akin to Jamal, the thug."[39]

Men of religion also added their voices – and names – to the chorus of condemnation. While continuing the attack on the fairness of the proceedings, the reverend Mikhael Dhaybah focused on the human tragedy in the Sa'adeh saga – the decision to deny the defendant "the right to see his daughters and wife under the pretext that they were not in Beirut."[40] Exposing the trial as a brazenly political exercise, he described the execution as a disgraceful act by a regime that now stands at the lowest end of human civilization. Justice and political tolerance of dissidents and rebels, he pointed out, were observed better under European occupation than they were under national government. "A few days ago," he confessed, "I expressed my displeasure at Father Awad's criticism of Lebanon's government and the publisher of *al-Huda*. Yet, it presently became clear to me that they were both right in their sharp criticism of that wayward government."[41]

As always, there was an exception to the rule. The Lebanese Phalange greeted the execution with all the fanfare of a grand public occasion. Hours before the execution, the editor of its daily *al-Amal* wrote, "The hanging ropes, the blindfolds, the columns, and the pits are all but for this moment . . . we must not delay it any further."[42] Not content, the Phalange proceeded to ask the Khoury regime to close down the American University of Beirut (AUB) because "it had been a center of agitation of Antun Sa'adeh."[43] At one point, *al-Amal* described the AUB as

> . . . a slum that stinks with intrigues against Lebanon and her existence . . . [where] all those who conspire against us from our neighbors have learned hatred of Lebanon and methods of working against her.[44]

The Lebanese press judged the remark as distasteful and furiously attacked the Lebanese Phalange over the matter. It was dismissed as a symptom of its narrow sectarian mentality and enduring Francophilia:

> The Falange is one of the principal representatives politically of the largest religious group in the country, the Maronite Catholics, who are strong supporters of the historic Roman Catholic French University of Saint Joseph . . . During the French mandate the American University's student body acquired a reputation of being the center of opposition to the mandate while Saint Joseph was not only a French institution but received a French Government subsidy and was a great center in this part of the world of Catholic French culture. The American University, representative of Anglo-Saxon culture, was originally founded by Protestants.[45]

A week later, the Lebanese Phalange recanted and its leader Pierre Gemayyel formally apologized to AUB President, Stephen Penrose, for the "misunderstanding."[46] Its newspaper, *al-Amal*, performed a somersault that same week saying, "We would be barbarians to ask the closing of the American University."[47]

Meanwhile, the line of disgruntled Lebanese was taken up in Parliament. Much of the campaign, though, was waged by vocal opposition leaders through the forum of *an-Nahar*, as well as in other, less frequently published periodicals. First up was the presidential aspirant Camille Chamoun.[48] More than any other Lebanese politician of the time, Chamoun ideally fitted the role of an arbiter on the Sa'adeh saga due to his even relationship with both the regime and the SNP. He was a liberal politician, an Establishment figure, and a fervent Lebanonist, which precluded the possibility of bias or compassion toward Sa'adeh. As part of a political serial published in *an-Nahar*, Chamoun blasted the regime (*ahd*) for its mismanagement of Sa'adeh's trial and even claimed that the military tribunal which condemned Sa'adeh had failed to prove the main charges against him, "his connection to a foreign state and contact with the Jews of Israel."[49] What is interesting about Chamoun's exposé is that it gave great prominence to Sa'adeh's dedication to Lebanon and to the constructive role that his party played during the independence fervor of 1943 and subsequent years:

> After the outbreak of the Second World War, the independence of Lebanon was proclaimed in 1941 and achieved in 1943. These two developments fostered the sentiment of Lebanese patriotism within the ranks of the Syrian National Party and, consequently, its leaders and members set out to serve Lebanon with courage and self-sacrifice alongside the most dedicated of the Lebanonist organizations.[50]

Encouraged by parliamentary immunity, Chamoun raised the banner against the regime higher still. Emphasizing an essentially pragmatic approach, he placed the responsibility for Sa'adeh's rebellion squarely at the government's feet. The regime's "policy of duplicity and favoritism," he argued, "is to blame for Sa'adeh's misfortune. The SNP leader was a mere victim of this policy."[51] While never directly absolving Sa'adeh of his transgressions, Chamoun's commentary seemed to offer a subdued repudiation of the charge of high treason on which Sa'adeh was tried. In a style reminiscent of the article which put Tueini behind bars, it concluded with the following admonition: "We must deduce from these tribulations a final and useful lesson, namely, that if the situation in Lebanon remains as it is, the deceased leader of the Syrian National Party will become a victim, or a martyr, or an immortal."[52]

Kamal Jumblatt's involvement in the Sa'adeh case was longer and more prolific. Like Chamoun, he was halfway between the regime and Sa'adeh, but sympathetic with some of Sa'adeh's progressive ideas and fond of his strength of character. Jumblatt took a keen personal interest in Sa'adeh's case from its outset and did not show the restraint that others did. He was rather outspoken about the case, daring, even reckless. Like Emile Zola in the Dreyfus Affair, Jumblatt published his *Interpellation*[53] destined to become one of the most important manifestos on the Sa'adeh case. Jumblatt pulled out all the stops. He accused the regime and prominent members of the government of having conspired to convict an innocent man through false evidence and an illegal trial, suppressing evidence that would have revealed his innocence. Jumblatt similarly charged the regime of having knowingly violated the law in order to convict a foe and of having followed orders from outside to ensure that he did not get anything less than the penalty of death. He made these charges without being able to prove them and on the basis of much guesswork. Still, he created a new excitement, and many have justified his recklessness in terms of that accomplishment.

Jumblatt knew that many of his charges were reckless and potentially libelous. He knew they could not be proved in a court of law. But it seems clear enough that his goal was to put life back into the case, and in that goal he certainly succeeded, well beyond what he intended. The national attention caused by his *Interpellation* arose more from the attempt to suppress it than from the impulsive charges it advanced. It started when the government barred the local press from publishing a short interpellation that Jumblatt had made to parliament on Sa'adeh's trial. During its session of 16 August, Jumblatt asked the Speaker of the House about the fate of his interpellation and why it had not been distributed to members of parliament. When told that it was due to technical problems, he burst out against the government and accused it of harboring a "personal grudge" against Sa'adeh and bowing to "foreign fingers." The Prime Minister, Riad as-Solh, who was attending the session that day, objected to a parliamentary discussion of the interpellation saying that the case "has been a glorious deed for Lebanon and the people of Lebanon."[54] He furthermore said that it was disgraceful for the Chamber to consider a discussion of Jumblatt's interpellation when, in fact, "we had come here expecting to be decorated for what we did . . . I implore this esteemed Chamber to reject [the interpellation]."[55] The Chamber voted in favor of the motion prompting a disappointed Jumblatt to walk out but not before he said to Solh, "You are a criminal. You should be put on trial."[56]

The next day *an-Nahar* published the interpellation, exposing the reason why the government had been tenaciously against it. Jumblatt called on the government "to conduct an inquiry into the mysterious circumstances that surrounded the elimination of Antun Sa'adeh, the leader of the [Syrian] National Social Party, after a procedure that was so fast that it resembled an administrative cleansing operation . . ."[57] Several days later, Jumblatt submitted a second interpellation outlining the areas in which the government had violated the law in Sa'adeh's case. He questioned the validity of the emergency law under which Sa'adeh was tried and the accuracy of the judicial process. For the investigation and trial of criminal cases before a military tribunal to be lawful, he said, certain procedures had to be observed:

1. The examining magistrate must first investigate the case and then, on the basis of the evidence, refer the matter to the military court of justice.

2. The prosecuting attorney must then draw up a bill of indictment against the accused.

3. The prosecuting attorney must issue a writ of habeas corpus to the accuser three days at least before the hearing is due to take place. The writ should include, in addition to the date of the trial, a full statement of the legal provisions and clauses and the names of all the witnesses who will be required by law to testify.

4. The state must ensure three days prior to the commencement of the trial that the accused has chosen a defending lawyer or appoint one for him if he has not done so.

5. The case file must be made available to the defense lawyer at least twenty four hours before the first session of the trial.

6. In case of capital punishment, the death sentence must not be carried out until after the Pardon Committee had been consulted and the President of the Republic had given his approval. It must also be preceded by a thorough re-examination of the case records and papers, which could run into the hundreds.[58]

That, in Jumblatt's view, precluded a dispassionate trial for Sa'adeh:

If we add all the minimum time delays allowed under the law, from when the accused is arrested to the first session of the trial, it would take seven days at least. If we then add to this period the time taken up by the sessions of the military court itself – it is impossible for judges to study and thoroughly investigate a case of such magnitude and gravity in one session – and also the time taken up by interrogation, subpoenaing of witnesses, listening to their testimonies, examining in detail the case files, proceedings, sentencing the accused, sending the case files to the Pardon Committee for a systematic examination of the case and then to the Honourable President for approval, the minimum period would be no less than fifteen days.[59]

Jumblatt tendered his interpellation for parliamentary discussion on 30 August, but was again blocked on technicalities. The person responsible for blocking it was Riad as-Solh again, who barred the interpellation on the flimsiest excuse that it was not on the parliamentary minute. "There is no need for the interpellation to be read out and I request it remains unread,"[60] he told parliament. Jumblatt was naturally unimpressed and again accused the Prime Minister of dodging the real issue. A war of words broke out between the two men, compelling the Speaker of the House to intercede to stop them. Jumblatt dropped the issue but only after telling Solh to his face, "What you did was criminal in the first degree."[61]

Unable to break through the cordon that as-Solh and his supporters had set up in the Chamber, Jumblatt turned to the local press. *An-Nahar* seized the moment and published the third of Jumblatt's interpellations in full. Its 9 September issue carried the front-page heading, "Parliamentarian Kamal Jumblatt clarifies with the pen what he could not clarify with the tongue." Compiled in secret and imbued with a tone of outrage, the third interpellation gave a detailed explanation of how Sa'adeh was convicted of a crime for purely political and personal motives; showed that the real culprit was the regime and blasted its conduct; revealed the immensity of the cover-up in the case; named countries involved in perpetrating the cover-up; and accused these countries of conspiring to eliminate Sa'adeh and everything he stood for. Jumblatt in writing the interpellation and *an-Nahar* in publishing it hoped to provide the public with a succinct overview of the facts of the Sa'adeh case and thereby mobilize public opinion against the regime.

The next day, the Lebanese press reported that the government would ask the Chamber to have Jumblatt's parliamentary immunity lifted in preparation for his prosecution. Jumblatt responded with a cynical challenge in an open letter to the Speaker of the Chamber:

> Since I have always taken and still take full responsibility for my words, and for every action of mine in all its requisites, as a self-respecting politician, and as a member of this new generation which channels its efforts to awaken and foster a sense of conscience and responsibility in the souls of individuals and masses, and at the behest of some friends and brothers, I would be honored to ask both you and the government to accept this proposal of mine to have my parliamentary immunity lifted. Should you fail to do so, I'll take an additional step compelled, of course, by the government's reluctance to carry out its threat.[62]

More than any time before, Jumblatt seemed to be attempting to duplicate Emile Zola's famous part in the Dreyfus affair. Zola came to prominence in that affair through his *J'Accuse!* article, which he published in the Paris literary newspaper, *L'Aurore* (The Dawn)[63] in the hope of provoking authorities into criminally prosecuting him for having written the article, so that at his trial new evidence could be produced and made public concerning Dreyfus's innocence. The *J'Accuse!* article was an instant sensation, electrifying France and stimulating a gradual but inexorable shift in public opinion in favor of Dreyfus. It also brought the Dreyfus case worldwide attention. From then on, the entire civilized world marveled at the French spectacle, with very few people outside France believing that Dreyfus was guilty.[64] Jumblatt probably had something similar in mind. He aspired to become the shining hero in the Sa'adeh case, as Zola did in the Dreyfus affair, but the government was more alert than the French government was during the Dreyfus affair and did not fall for the trick: Jumblatt did not get his wish and the subject was dropped.

The Government's Counter-reaction

Without expressing a single regret at the conduct of the trial, the Khoury government responded to the condemnatory avalanche that appeared in Lebanese newspapers by arresting leading editorialists and using them as a warning to any others who might be tempted to follow their example. Ghassan Tueini, editor and publisher of one of Lebanon's leading newspapers and son of the former Lebanese Minister to Argentina, was arrested for his article "Sa'adeh the Criminal Martyr," which criticized the speed and secrecy with which Sa'adeh was tried and executed. Tueini was charged with libeling the military court and his trial took place before the same military tribunal that had sentenced Sa'adeh. The prosecution drew attention to the title of the article and to specific phrases such as "trial or plot" and "Is it murder or execution?" and argued further that these were insinuations that offended the morale and the prestige of the army and the court-martial.[65] The accused pleaded not guilty, declaring that he meant no insult to the army, but legitimately criticized the legal procedure in Sa'adeh's trial:

> The target [of Tueini's article on Sa'adeh's execution] was not the military tribunal but the government, which interpreted the charges [against Sa'adeh] in a way that would guarantee an end to the leader of the Social Nationalists in the quickest possible time out of fear that hell might break loose before it could kill him.[66]

The tribunal did not agree with the defendant and sentenced him to three months' imprisonment. On hearing the judgment, Tueini derisively remarked: "I am proud of this verdict, and I harbor no resentment because I am young and the future is for the young not for those who want to startle the free people of this country."[67]

The government then swung the cleaver towards Muhammad Baalbaki, the chief editor of *Kul Shay*, and his partner Said Sarabiyeh. The pair was arrested for publishing a leading article considered to cast reflections on army morale and stature in connection with Sa'adeh's execution. Like Tueini, they were charged with vilifying the military tribunal.[68] At their trial, the pair was quizzed over the article and two other pieces: a colloquial song deriding Husni az-Zaim and a report entitled "Syria apologizes to the wife of Antun Sa'adeh."[69] Interestingly, as in Tueini's case, the prosecution tried to make a case for libel on the basis of out-of-context extracts drawing particularly on the expression, "Sa'adeh met his fate in the manner known to all," much to the bewilderment of the accused, who saw nothing libelous in it:

Q: Do you consider Antun Sa'adeh a criminal?
A: Surely the Military Tribunal has already determined that!

Q: What is your opinion on the verdict handed down by the Military Tribunal?

A: The judgments of the Military Tribunal have the respect of all and I, as Lebanese, respect the rulings of the judicial system.

Q: I am proud of the sound national ethos encapsulated in the answer.

A: Thank you.

Q: How do you reconcile between it and your remark in the article regarding the way that Sa'adeh died: "Sa'adeh met his fate in the fashion we all know"?

A: There is nothing about this expression that is quizzical or inquisitive. Rather, it is affirmative.

Q: But what did you mean exactly by it?

A: I meant that he died in a manner that everyone is now familiar with and as dictated by the Military Tribunal. The purpose of the expression was merely to save four or five columns on the reader describing Sa'adeh's trial and execution because the central issue in the article was strictly about how Zaim surrendered Sa'adeh.

Q: And the condemnatory mark at the end of the sentence? What is its purpose?

A: This is called exclamatory not condemnatory mark. There is nothing unusual about it and it has to be understood in the context of the whole sentence and not just the last word or two.

Q: But can we not infer from placing it after you say "in the fashion . . ." that you disapprove with the way that Sa'adeh died or that you are perplexed by it?

A: Nothing of the sort. It should be observed the term "fashion" had been left unglossed as to exact meaning. Just because somebody chooses silence need not mean that they have adopted a specific idea.

Q: So there is ambiguity as to what this "fashion" means? It could be something positive or something negative and, therefore, possible for the reader who does not know your intention to infer that it is being used in a negative sense?

A: There is no ambiguity but silence. In any case, I have already stated to the tribunal my opinion on its judgment.

Sometimes, in its eagerness to bring defendants to trial in a court of law, the government filed absurd or unrealistic charges and, consequently, laid itself open to charges of injustice and improper use of the courts.

The attempt of the Lebanese government to prosecute the dissident editors over a sarcastic song entitled "Oh eternal One, every other one has his day!" is a case in point:

> Q: What did you intend to achieve by the song "Oh eternal One, every other one has his day!"? The tribunal can, if it wants, interpret it as meaning that the tribunal is next in line, that the Nationalists will seize the reins of power and prosecute it like it did to Sa'adeh, whose conviction was made with clear conscience, and that had Sa'adeh succeeded he would have spared no one.
>
> A: This is a popular song all around. It was on everyone's lips in Damascus, especially during all last week, and its publication was not directed at anyone in particular.

Overall, the trial highlighted yet again how sensitive the Khoury regime had become to criticism. No one attempted to defend Sa'adeh's rebellion, but the proceedings occasionally displayed admiration for his good character against government wishes. "Sa'adeh," said one lawyer, "was deemed by the writer [Baalbaki] as a loyal and honest man. This is true. There is no record that he embezzled or falsified and the revolution he declared was not a notorious crime that bears on honor. If the accused had stated that Sa'adeh was a man of honor it is because he was indeed an honorable man . . ." Baalbaki was subsequently sentenced to one and a half months in prison and Sarabiyeh was let off. The case revealed starkly the regime's insecurity and contributed to a swing in sympathy towards the Sa'adeh camp.

In a country like Lebanon, in which the local press has a far greater grasp over opinion forming than any other institution, such intimidating actions do not always achieve their intended targets. By menacing local editors and publishers, the Khoury regime may have hoped to "take the heat off," but the exercise seemed to have badly backfired on it. The arrests provoked an unprecedented show of solidarity in the Lebanese press. It became more articulate and more conscious of its strength as a body. Lebanese newspapers rallied behind the *an-Nahar* editor, openly denouncing the government's action as a clear violation of freedom of political expression.[70] Politicians also announced their dissatisfaction in bold print. Camille Chamoun, former Lebanese Foreign Minister and leader of the opposition in Parliament, entered an interpellation on the arrest which stated:

In the communiqué of Saturday, July 9, justifying the execution of Antun Sa'adeh, the Government invoked the principle of liberty of opinion and assembly which, it stated, was the basis of its general policy. Nevertheless, this communiqué hardly had appeared in the newspapers when the Government turned over to military justice Ghassan Tueni and his brother Walid Tweni, respectively editor and publisher and managing editor of the newspaper *An-Nahar*, for an article appearing in this daily. Ghassan Tueni was arrested immediately while his brother is being sought by the police.

The Government would have been better inspired to answer this paper with evidence calculated to convince public opinion of the justice of its policy in the measures which it took to execute the leader of the Syrian Popular Party, under conditions which excluded the public from knowledge of the realities of the case and its accompanying circumstances. To persecute journalists and throw them into prison for the simple reason that they expressed their opinions is contrary to the pretension of the Government that its policy is to respect liberty of opinion.[71]

More damaging to the government was the bad publicity it subsequently received from *an-Nahar*. The morning following Tueini's imprisonment the editorial column in the popular Beirut daily carried a defiant article sardonically entitled "Freedom" that poured ridicule on the ruling clique:[72]

There is a faction in this country that is intoxicated with freedom and independence, but it knows not the meaning of either. This faction extols freedom, glorifies it, and idolizes Lebanon because Lebanon is the country of freedom. But this faction has done absolutely nothing for Lebanon's freedom. It has conspired with those who seek to subjugate the Lebanese people by drugging the people with resounding words and enthralling symbols and aphorisms that have almost pulled the people away from the real issues.

Any country whose rulers subjugate the people, whose rights are violated, and whose law is trampled on, is not a free country and its independence is hollow. Independence does not mean the evacuation of foreign armies, or the establishment of authorities that lurk behind the formalities of the Law, or the erection of a tower in one of the city's public squares under which people gather to discuss their power lusts.

Independence is not merely to say to the masses at every turn: we have ceased to be a passage or a landing-spot for colonialism. Neither is independence to hound the people that we have struggled for over a quarter of a century for its independence!

Those who struggle for independence and freedom know who the free-thinking men are, appreciate their demands, and listen to them with an open-mind.

Those who were persecuted in the cause of freedom do not persecute freemen!

Those who struggle in the cause of the people and homeland do not exploit the people and homeland, but remain devoted to the people. They share its tribulations and exert all effort to make the homeland a happier place.

Those who struggle in the cause of the people and freedom know exactly that popular anger cannot be treated through terror and that its challenge cannot be put down with force!

Those who rule by force do not rule the hearts of the people, but subtly intimidate them. If the people do not rise up right away they will eventually do so when the powerful have lost their strength.

Those who struggle in the cause of freedom rule the people with their free assent, building up their self-confidence and striving to set their minds at ease. They strive to budge the people out of any rejection they may voice by reassuring them that the country is being taken care of by an honest and dependable hand.

But those who use terror as their means to power renounce freedom, subjugate the people, and create a gulf between the people and its rulers. They end up with only the submissive by their side, those who have neither honor nor self-respect, and, eventually, are abandoned by everyone once their power has diminished.

Every power has its day save that of God and the people.[73]

An-Nahar continued to upbraid the government with witty remarks and aggressive editorials. On 18 July, the regime raided the offices of the Lebanese Phalange after two port workers were shot by armed guards of the party "for making undue noise in the street"[74] and found a cache of hand-grenades and other light weapons. An-Nahar remarked: "Will the government have the audacity to deal with the Kataib as it did with Sa'adeh's party during the al-Jumaizzaih incident, given the stark similarity between the two situations?"[75] Of course, it did not. All of an-Nahar's previously bottled-up political emotions then seemed to surge forth. Its incarcerated editor, Ghassan Tueini, spearheaded the crusade from his prison cell with short commentaries nicely blending exaggeration with understatement. At one point Tueini, using the kinder, gentler type of Horatian satire, derided the government as stupid and cruel and still maintained something that resembled a continuous plot. The following imaginary conversation between two characters, a youth and an imprisoned *qawmi* (nationalist), is a case in point:

> *The youth*: Why are you in prison and what are they accusing you of?
>
> *The qawmi*: They are accusing me of taking part in a conspiracy against the State and endeavoring to overthrow the government by force.
>
> *The youth* (smiles and looks at the *qawmi*, a slender university student, and derisively) says: You? Do you know how to use a weapon?
>
> *The qawmi* (smiling): I don't know how, but there are those among us who do know and they have staged an armed revolution and engaged government forces in battle, but were defeated and their weapons were confiscated. Six of them were executed on top of their leader [Sa'adeh] and many others had their death sentence commuted. And it is not over yet.
>
> *The youth*: How many rifles were confiscated from the group?
>
> *The qawmi* replying with a tone of pride: More than twenty rifles and about ten guns.
>
> *The youth* (with a loud burst of laughter): You really thought that you could topple the government with weapons like these? And is this the conspiracy you have been planning all these years? God forgives you. Why did you not come to me, for I could have sent you to a million families and clans that own hundreds of guns and rifles. In fact, I personally would have been able to organize a gang with fewer weapons than what you had and yet it would have been sufficient to chase the government away . . .[76]

Another commentary that deserves to be put on record deals satirically with the issue of human rights in Lebanon:

> Let it be known that Lebanese citizens fall into two categories, a category that exercises its rights to embezzle the state and to trample on the laws and systems of the country and a category that exercises its right to beg if impoverished, to be content if it is better off, and to take its own life if it is downcast and has grown weary with God's mercy. What's more, our citizen can enter jail anytime he wants. All he has to do is say or write down something critical of [a government] ministry and it is all the way to jail. Our citizen even has the right to choose the way he might like to die. Should he choose death before a firing squad all he has to do is refuse to submit to the ways of *al-qabadayyat* and henchmen of the ministry and his desire comes through . . .[77]

Critical editorials damaging to the incumbent administration also appeared in other Lebanese newspapers. *Al-Sharq* wrote: "It is often said journalism can lead to everything, by which it is meant that journalism can lead to the highest level of political and social glory . . . but here in Lebanon it leads only to jail."[78]

The publicity which swirled about the imprisoned editors, particularly about Tueini, severely damaged the regime's reputation. Consequently, it found itself on public trial and forced to answer a stream of criticism that would not go away. The regime's pretension as defender of democratic freedom was exposed as hypocritical and many Lebanese were upset by the imbalance that its actions were creating between their individual liberty and the state's right to protect itself. More importantly, the arrest of Tueini and others succeeded in breaking open the Sa'adeh issue again. It dragged some politicians into the fray, ensuring almost daily reports and comments on Sa'adeh. These politicians may have acted out of political self-interest to unsettle the regime, but their evaluations in the Lebanese press were most useful.

A Political Affair Averted

A political affair transpires when a trial develops into something more than a strictly legal issue of innocence or guilt. To become an affair, writes Albert Lindemann,

> . . . a trial must engage powerful and also conflicting emotions in large numbers of people over an extended period. It must attract important numbers of prominent individuals who are willing to devote their energies to winning 'justice', a concept that has diametrically opposed meanings for the opposing sides, since each side sees itself as motivated by selfless, high ideals. An affair must mobilize large numbers of ordinary citizens to the extent that they are willing to sign petitions, attend rallies, or engage in action in the streets. They must passionately believe in the guilt or innocence of the accused and also be persuaded that justice is not being served.[79]

A classic example of a political affair is the Dreyfus case. It underscored and intensified bitter divisions within French politics and society and threatened to destroy the young French Republic. The controversy involved critical institutions and issues, including monarchists and republicans, the political parties, the Catholic Church, the army, and strong anti-Semitic sentiment. Likewise, the Beilis Affair in Kiev in 1913 provided the occasion for open and sharp discussions among the various Jewish and Russian groups on profound societal issues transcending the original problem of ritual murder. Such discussions over small details often provoked sharp conflicts. In a nutshell, a political affair "occasions, legitimizes, and intensifies demands for major or minor corrective changes in the existing political formula."[80] In the process, society is apt to disagree over the nature and extent of the required change and, in some cases, over whether change is necessary at all. As the groups debate, fundamental issues pertaining to social and political life in general, and to state institutions in particular, come to the fore and legitimate political and bureaucratic leaders increasingly are dragged into the controversy.

As a drawn-out event, a political affair can be a cumbersome risk for any government. However, notes Nathan Yanai, if managed within the boundaries of the law it may serve as "an extraordinary, nonstatutory catalyst for irregular political change:"[81]

> The affair coalesces various cumulative tensions and brings them to a head, thereby creating an exceptional opportunity, or even a necessity, to redefine, confirm, or modify the existing political formula governing a democratic polity – the particular choice of leaders and political parties in power and their interaction with other political groups and social elites and the treatment of existing rules and institutions. Hence the affair.[82]

The Sa'adeh case contained at least four properties that were capable of turning it into a major political affair:

1. The transgressions relate to the condition of the political society as a whole: national identity, established authority, individual and democratic rights, sectarian politics, and social justice – all issues that struck deep roots in the soil of Lebanon.
2. There existed substantial evidence of serious misconduct committed for personal and political ends by, or at least with the tacit approval of, the legitimate political, bureaucratic, and military leaders.
3. The case included within its folds cumulative tensions and grievances that previously lacked either a common, legitimate focus or sufficient resiliency.

4. There was a clear obstruction of justice in the investigation and litigation of the initial offense including, as we shall see later, fabrication of evidence.

As well, the "interactive factors"[83] that go into the making of a political affair were readily obtainable in Lebanon: (1) an active press to "pursue and expose the properties of the incipient affair, to define sharply the issues involved, and to strive persistently to turn it into a full-fledged political affair."[84] (2) Sufficient opposition to the regime "to justify the exposure of the affair, to sustain public interest in it, and eventually to vindicate their own professional judgment and performance."[85] Another factor is the presence of a vocal intellectual stratum whose use of the case can, in one way or another, help to build and sustain it as a living issue. Intellectuals may be drawn in either to defend the Establishment or to fight its enemies. Some may even be dissenters against the Establishment. Certainly, in Lebanon, there was no shortage of intellectuals. Many of those who became involved in the Sa'adeh saga were, on the whole, professional intellectuals with some or strong political ambitions. In fact, the categories "intellectuals," "journalists," and "politician" overlapped so much that they were at times indistinguishable.

Yet, for all these factors, the political and journalistic commotion that followed Sa'adeh's execution failed to crack open the case as some Lebanese may have hoped. It did not have a drastic effect on the status of the Khoury regime or give birth to procedural reviews even when the press campaign seemed to pose a serious threat to the stability of the government. There were no public demonstrations, no disruption to political life, and no international outcry to speak of. Even more ironic was the silence of Lebanon's judicial and human rights bodies, which recognized the injustice that was done but did nothing. The only recorded exception was that of Emile Tian, the Attorney General, who resigned in protest against what he saw as government interference in the judicial system.[86] However, the controversy was diffused at the initial stage, without any larger impact on the political process.

To understand why the Sa'adeh case remained just that – a case – it is necessary to look more closely at the time and political context within which the saga unfolded. The press is an ideal starting point. Overall, most Lebanese dailies keenly followed the conflict between Sa'adeh and the regime to its final stages. Each newspaper actively promoted the case by writing continuously about it or by extensively repeating and commenting upon each other's material. Some newspapers, like *an-Nahar*, adopted a proactive stance and devoted their primary energies to exposing the regime's transgressions. Collectively, those newspapers that prioritized the goal of exposing government corruption and cover-ups fostered an awareness of a political scandal even when this was far from their intention. They may even have succeeded in making a political affair out of Sa'adeh's case if not for government harassment of editors and owners after the execution. As a result of this harassment, many newspapers abandoned their search for the truth.

Another issue is this: back then the Lebanese press was very different from the press today, anywhere. Most newspapers were short, only four pages, with eight pages just beginning to be adopted, slowly; most were creating, slowly but surely, the thought of an independent Lebanon and so were not predisposed to Sa'adeh; most had small readerships and a limited, select clientele, whose prejudices they addressed with similarly slanted journalism. Few of them circulated outside the metropolitan centres of Beirut or other main towns or reached the countryside and outlying areas. Public visibility, therefore, was poor and many Lebanese missed out on or only belatedly discovered the injustice that was done. Furthermore, most newspapers in that era were – and still are today – given over to what may best be described as propaganda efforts. They concentrated their journalism on invective rather than on substance and, on the whole, were reluctant to reveal the details correctly or to publish critical editorials contrary to their sponsor's financial and political interests. As a result, after Sa'adeh was executed, his story slowly slipped into obscurity and the whole notion of justice was crunched-up between abstract principle and immediate practical considerations. Its intrinsic meaning was lost to political rhetoric or used for partisan and personal political advantage, to the general detriment of justice. Eventually, as the press passed into abstention, interest in the case as a critical matter of criminal justice fizzled out.

Standing up for Sa'adeh was no easy matter. The conflict was too bitter and too often violent. The Lebanese press played a crucial role in keeping the issue alive, but it was not able to prolong the controversy or to produce a lasting sensation. Part of the reason for this was due to the weakness and pusillanimity shown by the Lebanese intellectuals during the saga. As stated earlier, a political affair needs strong embrace from society's intellectuals. It is the intellectuals who bestow political and cultural credibility on issues and bring forward a new tone of debate in the public sphere. This desire for a critical discussion is exemplified by what Edward Said called "speaking truth to power."[87] To do such a thing, intellectuals need to position themselves outside the masses and question in a radical way the very idea of the public sphere itself. As Noam Chomsky had once noted:

> Intellectuals are in a position to expose the lies of governments, to analyze actions according to their causes and motives and often hidden intentions. In the Western world, at least, they have the power that comes from political liberty, from access to information and freedom of expression. For a privileged minority, Western democracy provides the leisure, the facilities, and the training to seek the truth lying hidden behind the veil of distortion and misrepresentation, ideology and class interest, through which the events of current history are presented to us. The responsibilities of intellectuals, then, are much deeper than . . . the "responsibility of people," given the unique privileges that intellectuals enjoy.[88]

When we take a look at the birth of intellectuals in Europe (and more specifically after the Dreyfus affair), we see that intellectuals are the most important sociological actors of change. As a matter of fact, their struggle for critical rationality and civil liberties goes hand in hand with their critique and refusal of instrumental rationality and spirit of domination. The Dreyfus Affair itself would not have been if not for the French intellectuals and the active participation of exemplary figures like Georges Clemenceau, Joseph Reinach, Jean Jaures and Emile Zola, in particular.[89]

In contrast, the Sa'adeh saga suffered deeply from intellectual abstention. In those days, Lebanese intellectuals constituted a small but substantial force; though a minority, they were numerous enough to be weighty in the much fragmented political system, and they were a growing movement. Yet few are the intellectuals who adhered to the campaign against the regime or who were easily moved by the struggle waged at first mainly through the press. Even those who dared to clamor displayed only flickers of interest in the case. There was, on the whole, a reluctance to diagnose the facts or to "speak truth to power" – to use Edward Said's phrase again. This was a serious shortcoming in more ways than one. By distancing themselves from the deceit and distortion surrounding the saga, Lebanese intellectuals, especially the most able of them, dragged the general public down with them since the "power of the government's propaganda apparatus is such that the citizen who does not undertake a research project on the subject can hardly hope to confront government pronouncements with fact."[90] It was also important for allowing the government a sense of collective strength and giving it added force in national politics. When finally something did happen, it came chiefly from semi-intellectual journalists and politicians rather than from the cultivated men of words – or men of letters – whose opinions generally carry more weight than any others and, occasionally, determine outcomes.

One can refer briefly to the reasons for this intellectual abstention and lack of concern for the truth by saying that they were caused by utter fear – fear of depravation in a highly restricted job market; fear of retribution from the government; fear of being humiliated or retaliated against by those who wished Sa'adeh no other ending; fear of being branded as unpatriotic or *sans-patries* as Dreyfusards before them were labeled by their opponents in France. Fear everywhere acts as a brake on the freedom and creativity of the pen. That much is true. Nonetheless, intellectuals are expected to overcome such limitations, to put courage ahead of fear. As a credible sector of society, it is up to the intellectuals to expose government corruption and the misuse of power in high places. Doing justice or undoing justice to one person or more is and should be among their primary concerns. What meaning and what value would intellectuals otherwise have if they remained passive onlookers in the face of evil?

Other reasons for abstention come to mind: a lack of experience in intellectual activism; social indifference to human and political justice; the absence of a general sense of community or commonality even among intellectuals; and the predominance of a subservient mentality and a tradition of deference to authority. The saga's overtly political character was also obstructive. Comparatively few people paid attention to the underlying issue of justice, and most Lebanese either believed the government or cared little about what happened. Since the country was in the throes of newfound independence, they were too intoxicated by their recent success against the French to care about something that seemed anathema to them. Political continuity was thus put ahead of government accountability in the name of national interest.

The third factor in the unmaking of the Sa'adeh affair was the absence of sufficient opposition. At the beginning of the affair, the Lebanese state was severely divided. Although bound by a central government, it was nevertheless much fragmented by sectarian, regional, and ideological differences which made its supposed unity an illusion. People in many parts of the country felt more reason for attachment to their own sect than they did to the claims of Lebanese nationalism. They were not an integral nation-state but a composite bound together by necessity or convenience. In the six years that the Khoury regime had been in power a sense of commonality had slowly evolved based upon but by no means resting entirely on a gentleman's agreement dubbed the National Pact. By 1949 a national Lebanese identity had become better established but its conflict with sectarian and regional particularism had not disappeared. Old, familiar forms of state corruption aggravated the problem as politicians vied to enrich themselves individually without care for morality, law, or the interest of Lebanon as a whole. A vocal opposition did slowly form but it was scarcely distinguishable in political orientation from those holding the reins of power. Its antipathy to the regime involved a complex of reactions against current practice that coalesced in 1947 with rigged elections. After that, the opposition renewed itself and assumed a vigorous, reshaped form, on the basis of a definite program. The immediate focal point of that program was the apparent corruption and ineffectuality of the government: it did not concern itself with the organic defects associated with the mediocre National Pact and viewed widely as responsible for the country's slow political progress. In other words, the Lebanese opposition was part and parcel of the Establishment and belonged to the same ruling elite as the regime in power.[91]

This political compatibility between the regime and the opposition precluded the possibility of a political affair. It served as a corrective, defensive reaction to the saga in two ways. First, it reduced the receptivity of the political process to an affair since both sides stood at an identical distance from Sa'adeh. Reasonable persons neither from the government nor from the opposition, therefore, felt compelled to pursue the saga or to seek to have it placed on the political agenda. Some politicians, like Jumblatt and Chamoun, may have voiced disgust at the conduct of the trial but they were scarcely taken seriously by the general population. Most cared too little for discovering truth. Second, political compatibility between the regime and the opposition over the governing political formula insulated the public from the saga and helped to ensure a gradual return to normality. The process was aided by the passive reaction of the general population which, in the usual tumult of events, had more important problems to think about. Although ordinarily skeptical of politicians, most Lebanese had definite negative convictions about Sa'adeh and wanted desperately to sustain the governing political formula, although some variations were discernible. Moreover, for many, the ideas and values associated with the saga seemed very much strange to them. Making sense of the affair required knowing its underlying causes, the sequence of events, and why things turned out the way they did, all of which were beyond the reach of most ordinary Lebanese.

Naturally, the case was confounded by the secrecy and speed with which it happened. Both elements precluded the possibility of public involvement since the details were scant and unclear. It left critics with little time and space to deal with the fundamental legal and political principles which formed the fulcrum of the saga. Moreover, the government's refusal to publish the trial transcripts after the execution all but killed off the potential for political crisis and effectively isolated the process for participation and mobilization. In so doing, it deprived the Lebanese polity of an exceptional opportunity, or even a necessity, to re-evaluate itself and reap the potentially high benefits that flow from political affairs:

> The political affair [is] a form of democratic ritual highlighting questions of public sovereignty and trust in a representative government. It may create the notion that in one redeeming act of politics – doing justice or undoing injustice to one person or more – society can cleanse itself and regain a new measure of authority over its elected leaders.[92]

Moreover, by dodging a political affair the government did not seriously consider the potential for greater hazards. Instead of petering out as it widely anticipated, the Sa'adeh case became a lingering problem that kept leaping back and forth to haunt the regime at every turn. No sooner had Sa'adeh's followers regrouped and the political pendulum swung back in their favor, which happened quickly with Zaim's overthrow in Syria, than the case spun out of control and became a political nightmare for the Khoury regime. It refused to go away; it has not gone away to this day.

Conclusion

Reactions to Sa'adeh's trial and execution exceeded all expectations. No doubt, the action of the regime was made in the incredible belief that any hostile response, from the public or the polity, would scarcely matter since the main centres of power in the state, namely the army and the political institutions, were firmly under its control. The fact that Sa'adeh had the backing of none of the major sects that supported the political system was also important and precluded the possibility of a public backlash. There was also the real chance that the government was encouraged by its principal regional and international allies.

It was left primarily to the national press to expose the regime's transgressions. The press enabled ordinary Lebanese to gain a real idea of how the Sa'adeh case was actually conducted and to sense the injustice that was done. The regime tried to intimidate editors but to no avail. Every response provoked more criticism until local newspapers became glutted with negative news about the regime. This bred cynicism for and distrust in the government. More importantly, it emboldened other public figures to step forward and speak more openly about the case. An example is that of Lieutenant Colonel Zahran Yameen, who was jailed for two months on charges of aiding the rebellion and released without trial. Yameen published a four-part series on his role in the rebellion that cast additional doubt on the government's version of events.[93] He could not ignore the dishonesty and opportunism of some people. The publication of such personal recollections as those of Yameen, alongside regular reports on the subsequent trials of Sa'adeh's supporters and official harassment of local editors exercised a fundamental effect on public opinion and added powerfully to the drama and the ironies of the case.

Still, the question remained: why would a government, any government, execute a person who, in its own estimation, had lived on the margins of the political system and exercised no significant influence over the various sectarian communities that supported and helped to bring it into existence? The question is intriguing. It has given risen to several theories about Sa'adeh's execution, some believable and some fanciful.

NOTES

1 John Dugard, "The Political Trial: Some Special Considerations." *South African Law Journal*, 91 (1974): 60.
2 Otto Kirchheimer, *Political Justice: The Use of Legal Procedures for Political Ends.* Princeton, N.J.: Princeton University Press, 1961: 6.
3 Laurence H. Tribe, *American Constitutional Law.* 2nd ed. Mineola, N.Y.: Foundation Press, 1988.
4 Alan Donagan, *The Theory of Morality.* Chicago: University of Chicago Press, 1977: 65–74.
5 *Al Qabas*, Damascus, 12 July, 1949.
6 Ibid. Sa'adeh did once himself say that the nations that squander their talented individuals are like children who break their toys and then cry over them.
7 See Gitta Yaffe, "Suleiman al-Murshid: Beginnings of an Alawi Leader." *Middle Eastern Studies*, 29 (4):624–640.
8 Itamar Rabinovich, "The Compact Minorities and the Syrian State, 1918–45." *Journal of Contemporary History*, Vol. 14, No. 4 (Oct., 1979): 693.
9 See by Abd al-Aziz Karam, *Al-Rabb al-Buzayyaf Salman al-Murshid* (The False God Salman Al-Murshid). Damascus: Maktabat Dimashq, 1947.
10 Hashim Uthman, *al-Muhakamt al-Siyassiyah fi Suria* (Political Trials in Syria). Beirut: Riad El-Rayyes Books, 2004: 117–142.
11 Ibid. The Archbishop likened prosecutor Youssef Sharbel to Andry Vishinski, who gained worldwide notoriety as an aggressive and vengeful courtroom lawyer during the purges of the 1930s.
12 *An-Nahar*, Beirut, 19 July, 1949.
13 Reproduced in Abdul Ghani al-Atari, *Sa'adeh wa al-Hizb al-Qawmi* (Sa'adeh and the National Party). Damascus: Al-Dunia Printers, 1950: 158–205.
14 Nadhir Fansah, *Ayyam Husni Zaim: 137 Yawman Hazzat Suria* (Days of Husni Zaim: 137 Days that Shook Syria). Beirut: Dar al-Afaq al-Jadidah, 1983.
15 See Hani el-Kheir, *Adib al-Shishakli Sahib al-Inqlab al-Thalith fi Suria* (Adib al-Shishakli: Leader of the Third Coup in Syria). Damascus: Dar al-Sharq al-Jadid, 1995: 42–27; and Ali Rida, *Suria min al-Istiqlal hatta al-Wihda al-Mubaraka, 1946–1958* (Syria from Independence to the Sacred Union, 1946–1958). Aleppo: Dar al-Insha', 1983: 96–97.
16 *New York Times*, 9 July, 1949.
17 Ibid.
18 Kirsten E. Schulze, *Israel's Covert Diplomacy in Lebanon*. London: Macmillan Press Ltd, 1998: 32. Schulze writes: "In spring 1948 a meeting between a Lebanese-American Maronite priest, Joseph Awad, and Eliahu Ben-Horin and Sulamith Schwartz of the American Zionist Emergency Council resulted in direct Zionist funding of Father Awad's visit to Lebanon in April and May 1948. Father Awad from Waterville, Maine was militantly anti-Arab and anti-Muslim. He favoured outright military alliance between Israel and Lebanon. The purpose of his visit was to sound out Lebanese opinion in the war against Israel and the Maronites' opposition to the as-Sulh government. It was at this point in time that the Kataib or Phalange Libanaise entered into unofficial Israeli-Lebanese relations. The Kataib became the core of opposition to the Riad as-Sulh/Bishara

al-Khoury government. Awad, who was a cousin of the patriarch and nephew of Sheikh Tewfic Awad, met with Patriarch Arida, Lebanese President Bishara al-Khoury and Kataib leader Pierre Gemayel. On his return to the US, he reported to Gideon Ruffer (Rafael), counsellor in Israel's delegation to the United Nations."

19 *The New York Times*, 5 August, 1949.
20 In his letter to *The New York Times*, the reverend describes the Kataib as a "strong, progressive Christian youth movement." Ibid.
21 *The Times*, Saturday, 9 July, 1949.
22 US Department of State 89OE.88/7-1849 (Cable dated 12 July, 1949) According to Mansour Azar, the Arabic community in the Ghanian capital closed their commercial and trading premises in protest against Sa'adeh's execution. See *al-Bina'*, Beirut, 17 July, 1999.
23 See Joseph Lash, *Eleanor and Franklin*. New York: W.W. Norton, 1971.
24 US Department of State 89OE.88/7-1849.
25 *An-Nahar*, Beirut, 19 July, 1949.
26 *An-Nahar*, Beirut, 23 July, 1949.
27 *An-Nahar*, Beirut, 10 July, 1949.
28 Ibid.
29 *Al-Hayat*, Beirut, 9 July, 1949.
30 *An-Nahar*, Beirut, 9 July, 1949.
31 Ibid.
32 Nada Raad, "Tueini talks about his turbulent relationship with SSNP." *Daily Star*, Saturday, May 22, 2004.
33 *As-Sayyad*, Beirut, No. 267, 1949.
34 *Al-Haqeeqah*, Beirut, 30 July, 1949.
35 Ibid.
36 Ibid.
37 Ibid.
38 Ibid.
39 Ibid.
40 *Al-Huda*, Beirut, 22 July, 1949.
41 Ibid.
42 *Al-Amal*, Beirut, 7 July, 1949.
43 *The New York Times*, 11 July, 1949.
44 *Al-Amal*, Beirut, 13 July, 1949.
45 *The New York Times*, 11 July, 1949.
46 Ibid.
47 Ibid.
48 *An-Nahar*, Beirut, 17 July, 1949.
49 Ibid.
50 Ibid.
51 Ibid.
52 *An-Nahar*, Beirut, 17 July, 1949.
53 All three interpellations can be found in Antoine Butrus, *Qissat muhakamat Antun Sa'adeh was i'damehe* (An Account of Antun Sa'adeh's Trial and Execution). Beirut: Chemaly & Chemaly, 2002: 223–240.
54 *Lebanese Parliamentary Record*, 16 August, 1948: 613–614.
55 Ibid.

56 Ibid.
57 See Jumblatt's "First Interpellation".
58 See Jumblatt's "Second Interpellation".
59 Ibid.
60 Ibid.
61 *Lebanese Parliamentary Record,* 16 August, 1948: 613–614.
62 *An-Nahar,* Beirut, 17 September, 1949.
63 *L'Aurore,* Paris, Thursday, 13 January, 1898.
64 See Norman Podhoretz, "J'accuse!", *Commentary,* Vol. 74, No. 3 (Sept. 1982): 21–31.
65 *The Times,* 15 July, 1949.
66 *An-Nahar,* Beirut, 12 July, 1949.
67 *An-Nahar,* Beirut, 15 July, 1949.
68 *An-Nahar,* Beirut, 20 August, 1949.
69 *An-Nahar,* Beirut, 22 August, 1949.
70 Ibid., 2.
71 *New York Times,* 12 July, 1949.
72 *An-Nahar,* Beirut, 16 July, 1949.
73 *An-Nahar,* Beirut, 17 July, 1949
74 *The New York Times,* 19 July, 1949.
75 *An-Nahar,* Beirut, 20 July, 1949.
76 *An-Nahar,* Beirut, 11 August, 1949.
77 *An-Nahar,* Beirut, 23 July, 1949.
78 *Al-Sharq,* Beirut, 15 July, 1949.
79 Albert Lindemann, *The Jew Accused: Three Anti-Semitic Affairs (Dreyfus, Beilis, Frank) 1894–1915.* Cambridge: Cambridge University Press, 1991: 5.
80 Nathan Yanai, "The Political Affair: A Framework for Comparative Discussion." *Comparative Politics,* Vol. 22, No. 2 (Jan., 1990): 185.
81 Ibid.
82 Ibid.
83 Ibid., 187.
84 Ibid.
85 Ibid., 187–188.
86 *An-Nahar,* Beirut, 1 September, 1949.
87 See Rashid I. Khalidi, "Edward W. Said and the American Public Sphere: Speaking Truth to Power." *Boundary* 2, Vol. 25, No. 2 (Summer, 1998): 161–177.
88 Noam Chomsky, 'A Special Supplement: The Responsibility of Intellectuals.' *The New York Review of Books,* Vol. 8, No. 3 (23 February, 1967).
89 On the role of each of these figures in the Dreyfus Affair see Robert L. Hoffman, *More than a Trial: The Struggle over Captain Dreyfus.* London: Collier Macmillan Publishers, 1980: 96–116.
90 Ibid.
91 See Eyal Zisser, "The Downfall of the Khuri Administration: A Dubious Revolution." *Middle Eastern Studies,* Vol. 30, No. 3 (Jul., 1994): 486–511.
92 Yanai, *op. cit.,* 196.
93 See *an-Nahar's* August–September issues, 1949.

6

THE SCENARIOS

✧

S a'adeh's execution by the Lebanese State on 8 July, 1949, evoked a torrent of questions inside and outside Lebanon: What were the real reasons for the killing of Sa'adeh? Why did the Lebanese government opt for the death penalty rather than for the more conventional life imprisonment or exile? Was there a conspiracy against Sa'adeh? Was it a purely Lebanese domestic issue, the outcome of a political struggle that went very wrong, or was the regime simply a tool in a much larger plan? What did the regime hope to gain from executing Sa'adeh? Who were the principal beneficiaries from Sa'adeh's execution? The Sa'adeh trial provides no conclusive answers to these questions, but it does offer insight into all of them.

Initially, the question of just who may or may not have been involved with Sa'adeh's execution and why was discussed in the mainstream press. However, given the lack of detailed information available at the time, the precise content and actual arguments deployed by the Lebanese press were highly selective. It soon became clear that the affair was far more complex than had earlier been described. After the downfall of the Khoury regime in 1952, it diversified into other genres of literary and political writings, but after 1962 it petered out when any form of writing on Sa'adeh became an intolerable risk. In the early 1970s and more vigorously in the 1980s and 1990s a new push for the truth was enlivened by the publication of personal memoirs of key political figures from Sa'adeh's era. These memoirs, however, illuminated only part of the picture, and because of their restricted scope, did so in a necessarily subjective manner.

This chapter will attempt to outline the major theories (in no particular order) that have surfaced over the years on the Sa'adeh saga. An exploration of these theories is vitally important, as the existing literature is concerned mainly with what happened to Sa'adeh rather than why it happened. That, in turn, may encourage a much more detailed exploration of events still kept secret by a nearly total silence on the part of the Lebanese State and by the missing official transcripts of the trial.

1. The Official Line

Contrived by the Khoury regime in 1949 and replicated by successive Lebanese governments, the official discourse is based on a simple logic: Sa'adeh was a conspiratorial criminal who sabotaged the security of the state and betrayed the homeland, the penalty for which is death. The saga is depicted as a limited local battle between two irreconcilable forces, ending in the triumph of the righteous (the State) over the villain (Sa'adeh). It is an open-and-shut case that holds Sa'adeh entirely responsible for his fate.

The official version of the events surrounding the Sa'adeh trial thus makes it out to have been much less planned than was likely the case. Moreover, it is often presented in a prosecutorial way: Sa'adeh, ambitious and fanatical in his political belief, was full of traitorous designs to subvert the regime and ready to take the law into his own hands. The response of the regime, therefore, was that of a responsible government compelled to act decisively and swiftly to protect the country's independence. All the while a pretense is made of adhering to standard judicial procedure: indictment, judges, counsel, witnesses, and the accused's right to make a final statement:

> The trial took place all through the 7th of July. The accused was cross-examined meticulously and thoroughly. Witnesses were brought in. The General Prosecutor, Youssef Charbel, then delivered a long speech in which he gave a lucid and unequivocal inventory of the evidence [against the accused]. After that the Court went into a brief recess. When proceedings resumed the defense counsel gave a speech in which he pleaded for leniency on psychological and intellectual grounds. Next up was Sa'adeh who delivered a defense lasting more than an hour. He dealt in the first part of it with the principles of his party during which he gave a comprehensive explanation of them and claimed that he was not opposed to the Lebanese entity! And in the second part of the speech he talked about the rebellion absolving himself of any wrong-doings and placing the responsibility for what happened on other Syrian

nationalists. He cooked up an excuse for them that they did what they did in self-defense against government intimidation as though it is intimidation to the public for a government to invoke its right and duty to protect the security of the country!

After deliberating for an hour the court then announced its verdict of death to the accused and dissolution of the Syrian National Party. After that the file was sent to the Pardon Board, which returned it unanimously endorsed and a decree for the execution of the verdict was issued. At four in the morning of 8 July the sentence was carried out after a priest was brought in to help the accused complete his religious obligations.

After the publication of this tense explanation the Khoury regime made no further comments on the case. It expected the matter to peter away once the media frenzy had subsided. That did not happen. The case was a powerful propaganda weapon and government critics took full advantage of it. The publicity which swirled about the trial and subsequent disclosures of the regime's very substantial role in the affair served as a constant reminder of the case and kept these critics on tenterhooks. These disclosures strengthened the conviction that the government was dictated by feelings of pride and unwillingness to admit a mistake. It also confounded its ability to respond. Most Lebanese would have favored a detailed statement on the sordid affair. But, as a policy of constructive engagement, this approach required a factual response which the government clearly was in no position to produce. Its other option would be to trump up new allegations about Sa'adeh, but that had very little chance of getting through to the public after all the publicity. Even if it succeeded, the government would still have had to answer its critics over its quick and tawdry handling of the case.

It took almost two months for the Khoury regime to make up its mind. Towards the end of 1949, it finally issued a documented monograph entitled *Qadiyat al-Hizb al-Qawmi* (The Case of the National Party), a 303-page, three parts volume. The first seventy pages is an outline of the SNP's inception, organization, ideology and political history to 1949. The next sixty pages contain legal fragments from the case against the party (but not against Sa'adeh), including some thirty-three pages on the public prosecutor's trial speeches. The rest of the book, amounting to 170 pages, consists of fragments of documents seized during government raids on the party's offices in Lebanon after the Jummaizeh incident in June 1949. Only six pages of the book pertain directly to Sa'adeh, though there is nothing about his defense or address to the court or about actual trial procedures.

A close scrutiny of *The Case of the National Party* would reveal that it is among the most spectacular frauds ever published on Antun Sa'adeh and his party. In a field littered with crass propaganda, forgeries and fakes, this was no mean distinction. The fraud in the book is so pervasive and systematic that it is hard to pluck out a single thread without getting entangled in the whole unravelling fabric. The fraud falls into two basic categories:

1. The evidence that the Government adduces to document Sa'adeh's political life is almost entirely falsified.
2. The conclusions that the Government draws from its documentary study of Sa'adeh and his party are not borne out by the documents it presents.

The deception is apparent from the opening statement to the book: "From the dawn of our independence to this day, the incumbent regime has been, and continues, to respond to challenges, in the general sense, with the wisdom and forbearance that are expected of authorities whenever these challenges threatened the Lebanese entity and infringed on its independence. Did not those who built this independence pay the price for it from themselves and with their bodies?"[1] Yet, anyone familiar with Lebanon's history would surely realize that the only casualty in the 1943 independence campaign was a member of Sa'adeh's party.[2] As for "wisdom and forbearance," it was out of all bounds of the regime's corruption and duplicity, which reached unprecedented levels under Khoury.[3] The author's wildly chaotic presentation of the relevant material, though, manages to conceal this fact to some extent.

Another interesting comment in the introduction concerns the Jummaizeh incident: "The Jummaizeh incident was not the reason that precipitated legal prosecution on the part of the authorities (the authorities were preparing the grounds for this prosecution long before that) . . . Jummaizeh occurred in the spur of the moment and was a very ordinary incident from the point of view of the government and judiciary . . ."[4] This remark belies the regime's explanation of events since it contains a clear acknowledgement that plans to prosecute Sa'adeh and his party were laid down *before* and not *after* the Jummaizeh incident. It also begs the question that if Jummaizeh was an average incident, as alleged, why did the government blow it out of proportion and use to strike hard at Sa'adeh? Perhaps Jumblatt was right when he claimed that the government engineered the Jummaizeh incident for its own objectives.[5]

The thrust of the book is that Sa'adeh had been in touch with foreign powers during World War II, and had conspired against the interests of Lebanon and Syria. The Lebanese Government claimed that Sa'adeh, while he was in South America, tried to approach certain foreign powers in an effort to convince them to withdraw their support for an independent Lebanese state.[6] Among other things, the book refers to an entry in Sa'adeh's diary, dated 3 September, 1941, in which he was alleged to have written the following:

> Today, I have written to the Executive General of the Province of Minas (Brazil) and to Edward Sa'adeh, directing them to travel to Rio de Janeiro and submit the following requests to the German Ambassador: 1 – Germany's recognition of the geographic unity of Syria. 2 – Germany's recognition of the sovereignty of the Syrian National Party as the only spokesman for Syria. 3 – A frank declaration by Germany that the national independence of Syria is necessary and in line with the new order which Germany and her allies are attempting to enforce. 4 – Germany's agreement with the Syrian National Party alone on all these points and its admission that the Syrian National Party is the only party which is in a position to speak for the Syrian nation. 5 – Germany's abandonment of her support of the reactionary elements in Syria. 6 – That we are ready to listen to the demands of the Germans.[7]

The alleged report from Sa'adeh's diary then goes on to say:

> I have explained to the Executive General at length how to approach the Germans. At the same time, I have requested him to contact my brother Ernest Sa'adeh, who is employed by the American Embassy in Rio de Janeiro, and ask him to serve as a link between us and the Democratic camp.[8]

Sa'adeh's alleged entry elicited the following response from the Lebanese Khoury regime:

> Antun Sa'adeh demands from the Germans the recognition of the geographic unity of Syria without defining the boundaries on logical principles or, maybe he did not wish to define them for bargaining purposes. Anyhow, what is his Syria? Could it be the Syria which would have best suited the interest of the New Order in Germany?[9]

As for using his brother, Ernest, as an intermediary between the Syrian National Party and the Democratic camp, it proves that Sa'adeh lacked morality in negotiating simultaneously with the Axis and the Allies:

> What is noteworthy of observation is that in a report he wrote during the same day, Sa'adeh discloses that he tried to negotiate, at the same time, with two warring camps that possessed conflicting ideologies . . . This is the best proof of the man's lack of character. He is, without the least doubt, an opportunist who saw not difference between a democratic government and a Hitlerite regime.[10]

Then the Lebanese Government goes on in its tract on the Syrian National Party to show how Sa'adeh attempted to line up with whom he thought would end as victor of World War II. It said:

> When in 1943 it became increasingly apparent that Sa'adeh's Nazi friends were losing the war and that the Allies were winning it, he changed colors and switched over to the Democratic camp. On April 11, 1943, he wrote, "all what could be done now is to try to reach an agreement with the Anglo-Saxons, in as much as the principles of the Party permit." Sa'adeh must have forgotten, at that moment, that his Party was the fore-runner of Nazi principles in Syria and Lebanon.[11]

The obvious, if unstated, upshot of this argument is that Sa'adeh is to blame for the political (if not moral) tribulation that befell his party and himself. He is constantly presented in the tract in a Nazi outfit to help situate him in the anti-Nazi hysteria of the time. Yet, the method is flawed in three crucial respects: (1) During World War II public opinion in Syria and Lebanon was pro-Axis in general and pro-Nazi in particular on account of Germany's anti-Jewish, anti-Zionist, position. Antun Sa'adeh, however, placed the Third Reich on a par with Britain and France;[12] (2) the relation of Sa'adeh and his party with foreign powers was based on negotiation and bargaining power rather than submission.

Sa'adeh merely made suggestions to Germany and the United States and declared that he was ready to consider counter-suggestions from those two powers on Syria's future. He did not try to "sell" the country to the foreigners, as insinuated in the book, but merely attempted to gain foreign recognition of Syria's independence. As such, he did "not offer foreigners his services but made demands which were in line with his country's best interests;"[13] (3) even if Sa'adeh could be shown to have been a Nazi, it does not bear on the charge for which he was prosecuted, namely, seeking Lebanon's destruction.

As for Sa'adeh's trial and execution, *The Case of the National Party* merely built on the rendition touted in earlier press releases. Its main thrust is not the trial proceedings *per se* but the person of Sa'adeh. A roster of trumped-up charges dominates its pages ranging from nurturing aggressive elements among his followers, harboring fascist and Nazi tendencies, hostility to Lebanon, and contempt for the state. In so far as the tract had sought directly to counter the effects of the press blitz on the Khoury regime it did so predominantly by posing a negative counter-image of Sa'adeh, rather than by seeking to refute the negative image of the regime. The result is a shallow account that portrays Sa'adeh as a traitor who sold his comrades out in an attempt to save his own life.[14] Yet anyone even slightly acquainted with Sa'adeh's past will be struck by the absurdity of this narrative. It is difficult to know what to make of this report, particularly without knowing more about the source and the conditions under which the information was obtained. If the allegation is true why did the government keep the trial records under wraps from the general population? Why is it, also, that no part of the trial proceedings was appended to *The Case of the National Party* to verify the claim? In fact, there is no credible, direct evidence to support any of the tract's revelations. Even the document section is highly suspect: it does not allow us to draw any conclusions about the actual scale of collaboration or conspiracy alleged against Sa'adeh. Nor does it tell us anything about Sa'adeh's intentions and movements.

A naïvely self-serving account of the Sa'adeh saga, *The Case of the National Party* is a treatise in character assassination. Nearly all of it is directed specifically against the person of Sa'adeh, distorting and ridiculing his life and vocation, playing up dissensions, and depicting him as a debauched warmonger carrying on his "nefarious" activities against the true wishes of the Lebanese people. By contrast, the regime brazenly portrays itself as the true exponent of "peace" and "democracy," the only protector of the country. Such renditions may pass in countries where the law plays a negligible role over the political system and other areas of life but not in an open country like Lebanon, where the press is active and witty.

Indeed, the tract turned out to be a colossal and multifaceted hoax. It had to be withdrawn from circulation because the documents were pitiable and incoherent. The monograph incorporated many claims, none of which could sustain close scrutiny and which, overall, were common to the vast body of literary myth surrounding Sa'adeh. More importantly, the purposes that the author had set for himself produced confusion. One is never sure of the strand in Sa'adeh's conduct that is being challenged. When a strand does appear it is belied by the actual documents produced in the monograph. For example, allegations concerning Sa'adeh's "obstructions" of the military campaign in Palestine are contradicted in the supporting documents, which reveal a more sober picture of the SNP leader working earnestly to set up a commando unit in Jerusalem and to obtain weapons for the fighting. At the same time, those fragments in the book that paint Sa'adeh as a hostile enemy of Arabism are completely unwarranted. There is no evidence against Sa'adeh that could justly condemn him for national treachery, no definite proof of preparation of money or arms, no evidence of any regular organization of troops which could threaten the safety of the state, and no proof of complicity in a plot to overthrow the political system or the Constitution. Rather, the fragments of evidence that the monograph does offer the reader rely almost exclusively on mangled statements taken completely out of context and presented in a wildly chaotic fashion. The result is a book at war with itself.

The Lebanese public had the right to expect a detailed and thoroughly convincing account of the Sa'adeh case. Instead, all it got was a disoriented and an ambiguous explanation. *The Case of the National Party* contained none of the crucial information about the trial, except for a few regurgitated snippets from the Lebanese press. As a historical reference, the tract is ultimately disappointing and misleading. It is doctored history intended to justify a given version of events acceptable to those in power. Thus, "it may not be able to follow where the evidence leads. It may have to overlook or even suppress pertinent information. It cannot, consequently, meet the tests of objectivity, balance, and independence of judgment. At best a bland, cautious, diluted version of the truth . . ."[15] It reads and sounds like a propaganda tale out of the old Soviet Union.[16] Its tone is strikingly totalitarian, from both the legal and factual standpoints, and it blatantly bypasses the outrageous travesties of justice perpetrated against the defendant. Moreover, like totalitarian material, the focus is on the dispute, not on the reasons for it. Thus, while it is apparent what issues are in dispute, the precise content and actual arguments are not clear.

For those not fully within the local perspective, the questions that have been most insistently raised over the years are these: if the government believed that the evidence against Sa'adeh was compelling why did it resort to secrecy and speed? Why did the dispute so strongly stimulate the need for imposition of an official version, produced in a particular and problematic form? Why did the regime subsequently give an entirely distorted account of what actually took place? And why did it issue press statements that were the exact opposite of the truth? The inability of the Lebanese state to produce satisfactory answers to these questions or to release essential information that can be analyzed and empirically verified have furthermore eroded the credibility of the official line. Until some practical steps are taken to redress the situation, the official line is likely to remain where it has always been, in the ash heap of history.

2. A Clash of Personality

This thesis was first raised by Kamal Jumblatt in his 1949 interpellation to the Lebanese parliament.[17] It rests on two premises: (1) that responsibility for Sa'adeh's execution lies squarely with Riad Solh and (2) that the saga bears the imprint of a personal vendetta orchestrated by Solh to remove Sa'adeh out of his way. The role of individual personalities in politics will always be a contentious subject. There is good reason to suppose, however, that in this case personal differences served as an important source of friction between Solh and Sa'adeh.

According to Jumblatt, the first acrimony toward Sa'adeh appeared in 1946 when the SNP leader sought to recover his personal travel documents to return to Lebanon:

> I was the minister of economy then. It was therefore possible for
> me to keep tabs on this conflict as it passed from one stage to the

next. I may have missed out on some of the details, but I will try to link events as much as possible. When Sa'adah tried to come back home, the Foreign Ministry refused for a long time to grant him a visa on the orders of the then Prime Minister, Mr. Riad Solh, and that is clearly an arbitrary act sanctioned neither by international conventions nor by Lebanese law.[18]

Solh did, in fact, play a confused but stubbornly delaying action to deter Sa'adeh from returning. He exercised undeniable pressure on the Foreign Ministry and the Lebanese Legation in Argentina and utilized bureaucratic red tape to achieve his goal. In unison with this, in 1944, Solh cut a deal with the party's home-based leadership in which he agreed to grant the SNP a license to operate freely and legitimately in Lebanon in return for major concessions from the party, including changes to its name and political platform. The SNP had to re-orient itself to Lebanese realities, as defined in the National Pact, dump Syrian statehood as an objective, and abandon its confrontational style. Solh also demanded that Sa'adeh be excluded from the party's leadership:

> Contacts took place between the chairman of the Supreme Council in the National Social Party and the Prime Minister to settle the issue. This all took place in my presence and with my help. His Excellency, Prime Minister Solh, all the time insisted that Sa'adeh should be excluded from management of the party.[19]

Behind this assault on Sa'adeh stood complex emotions connected with Solh's self-image as leader *par excellence* of the unionist movement in Lebanon. Sa'adeh seemed to Solh little more than a poseur who represented a sentimental fiction of unity that stood in the way of his own union schemes. The Lebanese premier never quite rid himself of the dislike he felt for Sa'adeh after their first and probably last encounter in 1936 when the SNP leader, who "was not a man who would bend or ingratiate himself," refused to "pay tribute to Solh or pledge his loyalty to him" in keeping with the political ritual of the day. Nor, it seemed, was Solh able to forgive Sa'adeh for siding with Kheir Din Al-Ahdab in the 1937 parliamentary elections which, according to Abdullah Qubarsi, may have cost Solh the victory he required to claim the Lebanese premiership.[20]

Sa'adeh's judgmental attitude towards Lebanon's independence has also been advanced as a likely reason for Solh's aversion:

After 1943, His Excellency blamed Sa'adeh for saying that independence was gained with the aid of British spears. However, Solh wanted people to believe that he alone was the hero of independence. He thus regarded this [remark] as a personal insult aimed at him personally. His Excellency would constantly repeat before those who were prepared to listen, "Get rid of him for me, gosh!"[21]

Apparently, when the issue of Sa'adeh's return was broached, Solh exploded into a rage that "left everyone of us [in the cabinet] completely amazed and baffled."[22] His strident tone came out even more sharply after Sa'adeh delivered his inflammatory speech on 2 March, 1947. The Lebanese stalwart was offended by Sa'adeh's aloof and crude assault on Lebanon's nascent statehood and came to regard his remarks as an attack on his person. He was offended all the more by Sa'adeh's swift reinstatement as undisputed leader of the SNP and by the collective expulsion from the party of his (Solh's) sympathizers in one single blow. Solh counteracted this action of Sa'adeh by encouraging the expellees to form a separate political party, but the scheme backfired and the SNP reconsolidated firmly around Sa'adeh.

Even outside the party the impact of Sa'adeh's personality and political views was considerable. His tactical flair and lightning intelligence, his rousing personal appeal, his defiance of the government, and his success with the Lebanese press irritated Solh to the core. It brought into focus Solh's intellectual inadequacy and arrogance and exposed him as a caricature of the tragic reaction of the old school. Hence Jumblatt's characterization of the animosity as the outcome of an inferiority complex in Solh:

> Through his personal capabilities and knowledge, Sa'adeh had single-handedly managed to create a massive and highly organized party, a state within the state as was noted by [public prosecutor] Charbel, comprising many members from various countries and sects. Without help, he knew how to breathe in them the spirit of nationalism and the will to fight. In contrast, the pan-Arab leaders have had to resort to churches, priests, threadbare and decadent expressions, as well as sectarian partisanship to spread their ideas and control the masses.[23]

The situation was gravely aggravated by two other closely related issues. The first issue grew out of the 1948 Palestine war. The doubts that the war raised in the people's minds about the competence of the old leadership in Lebanon translated into gains for Sa'adeh. He was able subsequently to expand his party into urban centers that had up to that time been solid Solh territory and to lure to the party prominent Beiruti Sunnis, including Muhammad Baalbaki, editor of the Beirut daily *Kul Shay* and one of Solh's most trusted backers. As Yamak has observed:

> . . . the traditional political leaders and particularly Riyad al-Sulh and his followers were greatly concerned about its [i.e., the SSNP] relative success among those segments of the population whom they regarded as their natural supporters. It is thus believed that the idea to get rid of Sa'adeh and the SSNP began to take form about that time, i.e., toward the end of 1948.[24]

The second issue is what may be described as a guarded desire in Solh to prevent Sa'adeh from claiming the nationalist mantle. Historically, Sa'adeh and Solh shared certain general common characteristics: both men made their political debut as Syrian nationalists; both had a secular outlook; both initially had rejected Lebanon as a nation-state; and both had Arabist aspirations of one form or another. But whereas Sa'adeh remained ideologically committed to his national and secular ideals, Solh abandoned his unionist leadership role and assimilated into Lebanon's sectarian political system. Solh continued to regard himself as the foremost representative of Arab nationalism in Lebanon, but after becoming Lebanon's first premier when the little country became independent in 1943, his dedication to Lebanon overshadowed his faith in pan-Arabism. As *Time* magazine succinctly noted, "Solh stood for Lebanon's complete independence."[25] It is not entirely impossible, then, that Solh became indignant of Sa'adeh for undermining his popularity inside the Sunni community from which he drew substantial support and for overtaking him in the national leadership role that he, Solh, had once held but then gave up to become a leader in a small country.

Whatever the truth, in Lebanon at least, the "personality clash" hypothesis remains a talking point to this day. Many Lebanese accept it because personal feud is a dominant feature of their political life. Personal feuding in politics is of course common to almost all political systems. The British historian Correlli Barnett once said, "Any political rivalry, whether it is within a party or between parties, is almost always rooted in mutual personal dislike."[26] Personal rivalries have occurred throughout history even when they were dressed up as ideological differences. In Victorian Britain, for example, rival prime ministers, Benjamin Disraeli and William Gladstone, "loathed each other's guts."[27] Somebody once asked Disraeli if he knew the difference between a disaster and a catastrophe. Disraeli thought for a few minutes then explained that a disaster would occur if Mr Gladstone ever fell into the River Thames. A catastrophe would happen, he continued, if someone should pull him out. The Indian parliamentary system, which followed the British model, had its own famous political feuds, the most famous one being between Krishna Menon and Acharya Kripalani, both veteran parliamentarians. Kripalani, who hated Menon, contested against him in every election and lost. However he would win an election later and come to parliament and then would give Menon a harrowing time in the parliament during the question-answer sessions. In one of those verbal duels, Kripalani was harassing Menon (who was then the defense minister) for not sharing adequate information on a defense deal. Menon, who was well known for an acid tongue, retorted "I can give the respected member all the information he needs, but I am sorry, I cannot give him the intelligence to understand the issue."[28] They remained sworn enemies until their death.

Occasionally, personal rivalries have led to actual physical violence and death. Was Elizabeth I's sending Mary of Scotland to her death much different than the murder of Trotsky by Stalin, except for being dressed up as an official action of the state? Former Uruguayan president, founder of newspaper *El Dia* and Colorado Party leader José Batlle y Ordóñez and founder of *El Pais* newspaper and Blanco Party member Washington Beltran traded jabs through their respective editorials until Batlle accused Beltran of libel. Not willing to retract, Beltran accepted a duel. Batlle killed him with a bullet to the heart on 2 April, 1920. And who could pass over the political feuds between two of the founders of the United States, Alexander Hamilton and Aaron Burr? After Hamilton stymied Burr's attempts to become president in 1800 and governor of New York in 1804, their mutual animosity culminated in a duel that saw the Vice-President of the United States, Burr, shoot and kill the Secretary of the Treasury.[29] Strangely enough, Burr is not the only Vice-President to have shot somebody while in office.

In the Solh–Sa'adeh dispute opinions are divided over the importance of their personal rivalry. For Kamal Jumblatt it was the "principal factor that accelerated the plot to bring down the SNP, and

Sa'adeh in particular." Others have placed it alongside domestic and regional causes. The hypothesis is not altogether implausible if it can be shown that Solh was the key player behind Sa'adeh's demise. Here it is worth quoting Zisser at length:

> Such reactions, as well as various attempts made by PPS members to take revenge for the death of their leader, caused Khuri to deny any responsibility for Sa'ada's trial and disclaim any involvement in his execution. In his memoirs, he depicts his own role as altogether passive, saying that Sulh alone had conducted the whole affair, informing him only at the very last moment. He relates how Sulh woke him up at 2.30 a.m. on 7 July 1949, telling him over the phone that "Sa'ada has been seized and is being held at the base camp of the gendarmerie. I was greatly surprised . . . for as far as I knew Sa'ada was at Damascus enjoying Za'im's protection."
>
> As against this, people close to Sulh painted a very different picture. They asserted that Sulh had been against the death sentence; it was only under pressure from Khuri that he had given consent for the execution to be carried out. 'Azm noted in his memoirs that Sulh later admitted to his friends that this had been a mistake, made solely in order not to spite Khuri. It was, Sulh conceded, one of the three major mistakes of his career (the other two being his support for Khuri's re-election as president and his consent to the dissolution of the customs union with Syria). But 'Azm's convoluted relations with Sulh should caution us not to take his version too literally.
>
> Viewing the picture as a whole, there can be no doubt that Sulh was the prime mover in the series of events ending with Sa'ada's death. He had thought of him as an instrument in the hands of Za'im, the man he hated most. But then, if Za'im and Sa'ada posed a threat to anyone in Lebanon, it was to Khuri rather than to Sulh. Moreover, Khuri was in control of the army and the security services who in turn were in charge of Sa'ada's extradition, trial and execution. Therefore, he must have had at least as much of a say in the matter as Sulh. It is thus extremely difficult to accept Khoury's claim that Solh informed him only at such a late date of a matter so important to both their careers and to their country.[30]

Andrew Rathmell, in his terse study of the Sa'adeh affair, puts a different spin to the rivalry, but arrives at a comparable conclusion:

> At the time the Lebanese government was in the hands of President Bechara al-Khuri and President of the Council of Ministers (Prime Minister) Riyad al-Sulh. Khuri had been elected to the Presidency

in 1943 and was widely regarded as 'Britain's man' as the United Kingdom had backed him against his pro-French rival Emile Edde. Sa'adah clashed with Khuri soon after his return as he opposed Khuri's plans to amend the constitution to enable him to serve a second term as President when his mandate expired in 1949. The antagonism between Sulh and Sa'adah was more deep-rooted. In 1937 Sa'adah had backed Khayr al-Din al-Ahdab's government against Sulh's challenge. More fundamentally, the SSNP's ideology was in total contradiction to the terms of the National Pact which Sulh had been instrumental in negotiating in 1943. Under this informal arrangement, the Lebanese Sunni elite had agreed to accept the existence of a Greater Lebanon separate from Syria in return for Christian acceptance of the country's position in the Arab world.

During 1948 tensions between the SSNP and the government increased as Sa'adah intensified his criticism of Sulh's government for its failure to deal with Israel, the existence of which Sa'adah intransigently opposed. These tensions often spilled over into violence as gendarmes broke up SSNP rallies. By early 1949 Sa'adah was convinced that Sulh was out to destroy his party and had come to believe that co-existence between the SSNP and the government with its 'feudal allies' was impossible and that it was 'them or us'.[31]

Solh's supporters in Lebanon disagree. They argue that since the President was the person responsible for the ratification of the death penalty, the blame for Sa'adeh's death lay squarely with Khoury not Solh.

It is difficult with all these claims and counter-claims to determine the soundness of this hypothesis, but it is interesting. Of course, a fuller and more detailed study would have to take into account the attitudes and perspectives of both Solh and Khoury and other key politicians who had an innate interest in Sa'adeh's destruction. These were many but their role is still unclear. Moreover, given the lack of detailed information available, the effect of the complex characters is highly conjectural. Thus, while it has been apparent what issues were in dispute, the precise content and actual arguments deployed by either side have not been clear.

It is also wrong to dwell exclusively on the question of personalities. At stake were genuine political differences, particularly over the attitude towards the national question, which can be traced back to the opposing principles that existed for many years. These differences came into clear focus just as the Lebanese State was attempting to consolidate itself as an independent entity. The idea that Sa'adeh was the victim of an esoteric "personal vendetta" mounted by Solh must not be dismissed lightly, but it must not overshadow the ideological and political rift that Sa'adeh had with the Lebanese State.

The clash of personality hypothesis rests on the assumption that Solh and Sa'adeh were locked in a personal feud, that it was all about personalities rather than principle, that there was no ideological daylight between the two men, and that any tension arose solely from one's overriding ambition to destroy the other. This contains some truth, but it presupposes the existence of a feud between the two men and it doesn't explain Sa'adeh's part in the feud or whether he seriously thought of Solh as a nemesis. Besides, the ideological differences between the two men were in place long before the personality fissure evolved. In the ensuing struggle, Solh comes across as the hothead whose distaste for Sa'adeh was deeply personal and sometimes cruel, but the information about Sa'adeh's attitude toward Solh is so incomplete and dispersed that historians have had little to work with.

3. A Grand Conspiracy

The idea that Sa'adeh was killed as part of an international grand conspiracy arose almost immediately after the execution. Since then it has gotten stronger and more widely accepted. This increase in belief in a conspiracy has taken place even though the accumulation of evidence has lagged behind the list of theories. Moreover, in the absence of realistic evidence, such conspiracy thinking itself has ironically taken on the characteristics of a new "regime of truth" possessing its own discursive rules, diffusion networks and ideological struggles.

1. France

Various observers have raised the possibility that France was behind Sa'adeh's destruction. The basic premise for the allegation about France is that the French, for political and historical reasons, had always harbored the strongest desire to topple Sa'adeh. Examples of this kind of thinking range from the mundane to the truly plausible. One popular version of it has sought to explain the execution as the outcome of France's continuing interests in Lebanon and concern for the fate of its Christian Lebanese clients in the event of an SSNP ascendancy. The earliest exponent of this view was Adel Arslan, Zaim's Minister of Defense at the time.[32]

A slight variation of this theory was put forward by the pan-Arab man of letters Abdullah al-Alayili. He placed Sa'adeh's execution in the context of British-French rivalry in the Near East, arguing that it was the upshot of:

> A sinister French current that emerged from an Anglo-Latin – or British-French – rivalry. For as long as Sa'adeh was around the potential for a Greater Syria was always present. It was this factor which led to his death. The British formed the first post-independence government from Beshara el-Khoury and Riad as-Solh and snubbed anyone who dared to challenge this Anglo-Saxon strategy. But Beshara el-Khoury and the primary regime ideologue, Michel Shiha, and others soon deserted to the Latin-French position. They did all that they could possibly do in order to weaken the British position so that the Latin current would grow. This current then turned on the Syrian National Party taking its leader as a symbol of its strategy.[33]

Others stress the alleged role played by French financial and strategic interests in backing the Zaim coup, claiming that Sa'adeh's destruction was orchestrated or tacitly supported by the French for nefarious reasons relating to the stalled Bank al-Isdar deal and other financial agreements.[34] Another motive frequently attributed to France was its supposed objection to the formation of a Greater Syria under Sa'adeh's leadership and British sponsorship.[35] Although British governments reiterated the argument that they did not have any vested interest in a Greater Syria, they were never able to sway French opinion, which explains why the French, when they had the mandate over Lebanon and Syria, incessantly rebuked Sa'adeh as a British agent.

There were unquestionably many people in the government in Paris at the time who would have been delighted to see Sa'adeh disappear. Their hostility toward him had been reflected in a number of decisions during the Mandate era, which became a serious irritant in relations between the SNP leader and authorities. The idea of French complicity in Sa'adeh's execution is tempting also since France exercised considerable influence over Zaim: "All the Western powers, for different reasons, looked with favor on the new regime in Damascus. The French saw in it an opportunity to consolidate their influence in the Arab East and spared no effort in persuading other countries to recognize the new regime. One of Za'im's first acts as prime minister was to sign a currency agreement which ushered in a new era of improved understanding and close economic cooperation between Syria and France."[36] The argument flowing from this is that France persuaded Zaim to ditch Sa'adeh in order to retain the Syrian leader as a bulwark against a Greater Syria and, concomitantly, to protect its interests and influence in its former mandatories from the SSNP.

We will not know with any certainty if France was directly involved in the Sa'adeh affair until the French official records are open to researchers, and even then we may never know for sure. Many things are undoubtedly unrecorded and unknowable. At this point we are not even sure exactly what the French did. They have published no useful clarification to date, and Syrian accounts disclose no tangible details, as opposed to suppositions, about France's complicity. Certainly, the explanation is highly plausible in view of France's undeniable meddling in Syrian affairs, profound interest in Zaim's regime, and its animosity toward Sa'adeh. However, as with all other cases, we need to know more. At this point, we can neither prove nor disprove that the French were complicit in the plot against Sa'adeh and, if so, what exactly they did to influence Zaim.

2. Israel and the United States

The most popular candidates in the conspiracy theories surrounding Sa'adeh's downfall are Israel and the United States. This theory could be plausibly constructed as follows: Sa'adeh's vehement anti-Israeli rhetoric, particularly after the proclamation of the State of Israel in 1948, and his vociferous call for armed struggle against the nascent state brought him to the attention of the Israeli leadership, which then fomented the plot to kill him, by intrigue or force.[37] This was done, so the argument goes, either with the consent of the United States or its active cooperation.

There is no need here to elaborate on Sa'adeh's attitude towards Israel. This has been convincingly and amply done by other writers.[38] Suffice it to say that Sa'adeh rejected the Israeli entity and regarded its destruction as a national duty. He wrote extensively on the Palestine issue, with occasional bursts of theoretical creativity, and pursued the matter to the end. His commentaries bravely exposed worrying trends about the state of thinking amongst the local political leadership and provided inspiration in a time of gloom and darkness.[39] Sa'adeh also matched his words with deeds: he started a concerted campaign of awareness about Palestine; he sought without success to obtain arms and ammunition; he set up a local militia and instructed the military officers in his party to enlist volunteers to fight in Palestine; and he put forward creative ideas on how to conduct the battle against the Zionist state and its Western allies.[40] One such idea, for which he has not been given credit, concerns the value of oil as an international weapon:

> From the mere ratification of the American Tapline Agreement it has become clear that we have not used this oil weapon to put a limit to US support of the Jews in Lausanne, Palestine and the United Nations. We have allowed the United States to go on supporting the Jews and sanctioned its actions by ratifying an important sensitive agreement of vital importance to it in relation to future military operations.[41]

In'am Raad has sophisticatedly used these events to construct a plausible-sounding theory on the execution. Sa'adeh, he claims, was killed by an organized conspiracy involving the United States, Zionism and Arab reaction as part of a concerted campaign to remove anyone perceived to be remotely a danger to the status quo in the region and to Israel's existence in particular.[42] There is at least one piece of evidence to support this theory. It comes from Jam'a, a former officer in the Syrian Intelligence. Jam'a has claimed that the plot against Sa'adeh was hatched during a spate of secret meetings between US Assistant Military Attaché, Major Meade, President Zaim and the then Israeli foreign minister, Moshe Sharett. At the time Jam'a was the officer-in-charge of the guards around Hotel Bludan where the alleged meeting took place:

> My duties at Bludan were monotonous until that day at the beginning of June, which I will never forget as long as I live. As usual Zaim arrived at Hotel Bludan about ten o'clock in the morning accompanied by Captain Riad Kaylani. Shortly after this Amir Adel Irslan and Salah al-Tarazi turned up, followed by Major Mead and the Turkish General, Fouad Orbey, who left the hotel just before lunch. Towards midday, the guard at the entrance of the hotel announced the arrival of Captain Ibrahim al-Husseini. I rushed to the entrance where I saw a Ford Buex with al-Husseini in the back seat with an officer in a Syrian military uniform that I could not recognize. I noticed al-Husseini dealing very courteously with the officer, a Lieutenant Colonel by rank, walking few steps behind him as a gesture of respect. It looked rather odd because

al-Husseini was not known to fear military officers regardless of their rank because of his close camaraderie with Zaim.[43]

The mysterious officer turned out to be Moshe Sharett, the then foreign minister of Israel. He was in the Syrian capital seeking a permanent peace treaty with Syria. According to Jam'a, the groundwork for the undisclosed summit was laid in meetings held in al-Jaounah, on the Syrian-Palestinian borders, between Zaim's liaison officers and Israeli officials. Four days later another meeting took place in Bludan between Zaim and Sharett, "wearing the same uniform."[44]

With conspiratorial tone, Jam'a then offers a bitter and somewhat paranoid exposition of the plot against Sa'adeh:

> The reality is that there was an American plan to destroy the SSNP and its leader, Antun Sa'adeh. Only the first part of this plan was disclosed to Zaim and then only to placate his ambitions and pride. The plan consisted of three phases:
>
> 1. Enticing Sa'adeh to Syria.
> 2. Exhorting Zaim to persuade Sa'adeh to stir up an armed rebellion in Lebanon that would not succeed.
> 3. Delivering Sa'adeh to the Lebanese authorities for execution.
>
> Major Mead, who put this plan together, asked Zaim to implement the first clause without telling him about the other two clauses. The Syrian leader welcomed the idea because he thought it would gain him the support of a highly organized and politically influential organization. Zaim was true and unequivocal about his intentions. When it was time to put the two other clauses into action Major Mead told Zaim that the SSNP and its leader had to be dispensed with for regional security reasons and to protect American vital interests in the area. He then asked Zaim to implement the rest of the plan and Zaim acceded to his request with misgivings.[45]

The precautions set in place to ensure that the plot would proceed as planned were as follows. First, Zaim would entice Sa'adeh to Syria on the pretext of common enmity toward the Lebanese regime. Next, Zaim would encourage Sa'adeh to rebel against Lebanon by offering him unlimited military support: "Zaim . . . offered to send a large number of Syrian army troops in SSNP uniforms and military insignia (the Tempest) to fight alongside the Party in Lebanon. But Sa'adeh told him that he did not need men but weapons, to which Zaim replied: 'The weapon storehouses of the Syrian Army are at your disposal,' and then turned to Captain Ibrahim al-Husseini and instructed him to give the party anything it needs."[46] Finally, with al-Husseini's help, Zaim would ensure that the rebellion was defeated to pave the way for Sa'adeh's destruction. This was to be done in two tactful ways:

1. By supplying the SSNP with faulty weapons: "At the beginning of July al-Husseini began to put Zaim's instructions (or should we say, Major Meade's instructions) into action. He gave the SSNP a large cache of weapons taken from the confiscated weapons and ammunition dumps. Most of the weapons were obsolete or worthless."[47]

2. By stealthily notifying the Lebanese regime of the rebellion: "On July 3, al-Husseini called Sami Solh and Munib Solh and notified them of the exact border points from where the SSNP rebels would cross into Lebanon so that they would pass this information to their cousin, Riad Solh, the Prime Minister of Lebanon at the time. On the following day the Syrian Nationalists crossed into Lebanon expecting victory, only to find the Lebanese Army waiting for them. Several people were killed and many more were apprehended. The rebellion failed just as the Americans had planned."[48]

The Americans, we are told, went to all that trouble with the following reasons in mind:

1. because the concept of national sacrifice advocated by the SSNP "bothered them more than anything else."[49] It had the potential to affect the security and interests of Israel. The party was also difficult to control or infiltrate as long as Sa'adeh was alive and its secular platform clashed with US strategy in the region built, as it was, on the continuation and exploitation of sectarian differences;

2. to eliminate the SSNP in Lebanon or scale down its operation as far as possible in order to give the Kataib Party and Maronite and Sunni leaders with American or Western connections more political space. The idea was to keep Lebanon as a hub for the manufacture of intrigues and instability for the Arab States adjacent to or in the vicinity of Israel; and

3.   to facilitate Zaim's downfall "now that his role was over"[50] and, through that, to create long-term uncertainty and instability for Syria.

This theory is intriguing for the important revelations about Zaim's secret dealings with the Israelis. However, it offers an easy, automatic explanation of the Sa'adeh saga, one that grants unimaginable cleverness and resources to the parties involved. The theory starts with a conclusion and works backward to find evidence, and its story-line requires the cooperation of countless people over long periods of time and across many institutions. It rests on unspoken assumptions of superhuman prescience, monumental cynicism, and appalling recklessness on the part of the Americans, and the Israelis, and the Syrians. More difficult to accept, the plotters are thought able to foresee with incredible accuracy the reactions of other parties to their necessarily devious scheme.

Moreover, the theory exhibits several explanatory virtues but in ways that undermine their strength. For example, its theoretical approach is built on the assumption that Sa'adeh's fate was sealed during Zaim's secret meetings with Sharett. Yet these meetings, if we accept Jam'a's claims, took place before Sa'adeh's first and most crucial encounter with Zaim. What's more, even if we accept the account as factual, we would still need to know how the conspiracy was coordinated with the Lebanese authorities. Jam'a's silence on Lebanon's role confines the plot largely to Israel and Syria, with an almost nihilistic degree of scepticism about the behaviour and motivations of the parties and the social institutions they constituted.

3. Egypt and Saudi Arabia

One of the most plausible and widely accepted scenarios blames Egypt and Saudi Arabia. Both countries stand accused of being deliberately and culpably involved in Sa'adeh's death on three counts:

1.   their shared animosity towards any attempt to generate union in the Fertile Crescent;
2.   their common interest in preserving the status quo in the Arab world;
3.   and their categorical support of Zaim and the Lebanese State during the Sa'adeh saga.

One thing is certain: Sa'adeh's elimination served both Egyptian and Saudi long-standing hostility toward the Fertile Crescent: "Egypt, as the most populous, was determined to avoid the creation of a powerful new rival in the north – a governing principle in the endless struggle between the Nile Valley and Mesopotamia, of which this was merely another installment. For their part the Saudi dynasty flatly refused to admit any advantage to the family it had only recently chased out of the Arabian Peninsula."[51] The Saudi-Egyptian line was supported by both Syria and the Lebanon who "objected to the possibility of having to give up their republican oligarchies, and for the Christian Arab community in the Lebanon there was the additional fear of being swamped in a large Muslim state."[52]

Second, Egypt and Saudi Arabia were on good terms with both Syria and Lebanon and attuned to their politics both through the Arab League and at the elite political level. Both Egypt and Saudi Arabia were also a reference point for Lebanon and Syria on burning domestic and regional issues. Since 1943 they had actively provided financial and diplomatic support to the two states to keep them outside Hashimite spheres. Logically, then, the Sa'adeh saga could not possibly have occurred without the foreknowledge and blessing of Egypt and Saudi Arabia. Much was at stake for their interests in the Fertile Crescent. There are even grounds to believe that Sa'adeh's fate may have been sealed in a deal negotiated with Egyptian and Saudi help in the final days leading up to his betrayal and execution, whereby Zaim agreed to abandon Sa'adeh in return for a comprehensive resolution of all outstanding problems with Lebanon. The deal was capped off with an economic agreement signed between the two countries a few days after Sa'adeh's execution.

Thirdly, most narratives of the period implicate Saudi Arabia and Egypt on the grounds that they were kept up to date on Sa'adeh's activities. This was done largely through the good offices of Muhsin al-Barrazi, the Syrian Prime Minister at the time and former ambassador to Cairo, and Riad al-Solh, who had broad connections with the Egyptian and Saudi leaderships. Solh visited Egypt on more than one occasion during this period. Khoury's memoirs are revealing here:

> We took advantage of Fouad Hamzi's travel to the Kingdom of Saudi Arabia and sent with him a letter to King Abdul al-Aziz imploring him to advise our unpredictable and impulsive Syrian

neighbor to carry out his part of the friendship undertaking he promised to follow with Lebanon but failed to fulfill.[53]

Just as illuminating are Sabri Qubbani's recollections. A senior bureaucrat in Zaim's administration and a close confidant of the Syrian leader, Qubbani spoke explicitly about the pressure that Egypt and Saudi Arabia exercised on Zaim to get him to ditch the SSNP leader:

When his [i.e., Zaim's] patience wore out, he cried, "Listen to the Englishman (he meant Sa'adah); he works for King Abdullah. I have evidence from various reports. I saw with my own eyes the weapons that he received across the border from East Jordan; they were antitank guns. You know that I never equipped him with any weapons . . . That is why I was convinced that the English were arming him to fire sedition in this part of the Middle East (i.e., Syria and Lebanon), which would be a justification for him to interfere in our affairs. Syria has become well-established today, and I would hate to see any obstacle standing in my way."

I calmly responded, "Perhaps these excuses can convince someone else but not me. I am aware of the extent of our power. You can never be intimidated by Sa'adah's movement. You even told me before that he was a weapon in your hands. He could never have been used against you because you are aware that he was a noble man and that he pursued a noble goal. Besides, for the sake of argument, if you were really afraid of something, wouldn't it have been better to ask him to leave the country instead of handing him in like a criminal to be executed? I consider myself responsible for this man's life, who came to us seeking refuge. We flooded him with rosy promises and then turned him in to his enemies on a silver platter. Had Lebanon mobilized all of its security forces to get him, they would never have found any trace of him." The man listened to me with his head resting on his hand, as if he was wrestling with an idea or turning it over in his head. He then raised his head and said, "I had no choice but to hand him in. King Faruq sent me his private messenger, Brigadier General, Muhammad Yusuf, on a private plane, to inform me that the Egyptian intelligence bureau had abundant and corroborating information that Sa'adah's movement was British-inspired and intended to stir up trouble along this coast of the Middle East so that the two Hashemite governments would ostensibly interfere and from behind them, Britain. I became convinced after the Brigadier General showed me the personal letter sent by the Lebanese Prime Minister to His Majesty, King Faruq, in which he said that I was supporting Sa'adah and providing him with weapons in an attempt to destroy Lebanon. He also asked that Sa'adeh be handed in to them in order to be tried, or else he would be forced to seek military aid from the Jordanian government or any other government in the following three days, to nip the revolt in the bud.

"You know that the interference of the Jordanian army and their entrance into Lebanon would mean isolation for Syria, and restraining it within its borders. At that point, I realized I was forced to hand in Sa'adah and sacrifice him, or else the axis that we formed would disintegrate; the axis of Damascus – Cairo – Riyadh. It never occurred to me that they would execute him that fast." I replied, "This all makes sense, but it does not justify his handover to Lebanon. You could have asked Sa'adah to leave the country and then closed the borders between Lebanon and Syria to stamp out any suspicions of Syria and refute charges of stirring up a revolt in Lebanon. I swear, had Sa'adah resorted to Israel, they would not have done to him what we did. They would never have turned him in, even if America itself had asked for him."[54]

In view of this unanimity, it is hardly surprising that Egypt and Saudi Arabia have been incriminated in Sa'adeh's execution. This incrimination owes its existence not only to the powerful influence that the two countries exercised over the Levant, but to a common belief in Lebanon that Solh and Khoury could not possibly have acted on their own accord. Repeated references to Egypt and Saudi Arabia in autobiographies covering Sa'adeh, imperfect as they may be, have also helped to confirm and strengthen such feelings and contributed further to a sense that Egypt and Saudi Arabia were in daily communication with the Syrian-Lebanese authorities and thus gave their wholehearted endorsement to the execution. They are seen acting as silent partners in the saga.

Of course, there never had been any direct evidence of an Egyptian-Saudi complicity in the Sa'adeh affair or in the events that led inexorably to the tragic moment of execution. There are no supporting documents to prove or disprove the various allegations against them. Most of the information comes to us from personal accounts, although some of these accounts are fairly trustworthy and independent. Without official documents it is difficult to determine exactly the nature and extent of Saudi and Egyptian influence on the course of events. Did they want Sa'adeh out of the way enough to kill him? Moreover, there are some errors and inconsistencies between the various accounts that make it difficult to construct a coherent picture. For example, Qubbani's storyline is slightly different from that of Nadhir Fansah, Zaim's first secretary and brother-in-law. Fansah's account is also important, but it exonerates the Egyptians and their King, Faruq:

> The following morning, I was handed a copy of *Al-Ahram* newspaper with my breakfast. One of its main headlines read "Antun Sa'adeh has been handed over, tried and executed." I was stunned by this news. I immediately picked up the phone and rang Karim Thabet and told him that I refuse to go back to Damascus because I object to being deceived in such a ludicrous and underhanded way by senior government officials who make promises but then break them. When I saw King Farouk several hours later with Karim Thabet they appeared deeply disturbed by the whole thing.[55]

The crudity of Fansah's account, however, permits two positive conclusions: either King Faruq had put on an act to his Syrian guest in order to cover his tracks or that Fansah had twisted the facts to protect the King who had decorated him with an Egyptian state honor. There is much that is personal as well as political in his narrative. Fansah's recollection of the trip to Egypt is also factually inaccurate: he claimed that he was calculatedly sent to Cairo ahead of Sa'adeh's betrayal, yet his trip to the Egyptian capital occurred on 7 July, that is, after Sa'adeh's delivery to Lebanon.[56]

4. Freemasonry

For mysterious reasons, "Freemasonry" seems to pop up whenever conspiracy theory is spouted. Abraham Lincoln,[57] John F. Kennedy,[58] Jack the Ripper,[59] and the Princess of Wales are just some of the public names that have been linked to Freemasonry plots. There have also been occasional attempts to find causes of major historical events, such as the French Revolution,[60] in Masonic lodges. Even the September 9/11 terror attack has been woven into a masonry conspiracy theory.[61]

Predictably, after his death, Antun Sa'adeh was made to be the victim of a Freemasonry conspiracy undertaken jointly by local and regional masonries. This theory, which originated in the 1950s and flourished as the event became more distant, does not point to purported Masonic symbols as evidence of the conspiracy but emphasizes a series of coincidental factors: (1) Sa'adeh's public repudiation of Freemasonry;[62] (2) the active involvement in his saga of certain men widely suspected of being Freemasons, most of all Riad el-Solh and King Farouk of Egypt; (3) and the peculiar idea that Freemasonry, as a Jewish front for world domination, partook in Sa'adeh's downfall as a service to Israel and world Jewry. Fed by a growing literature, the theory takes as its starting point an internal party edict issued by Sa'adeh on 3 January, 1949 proscribing members from joining the Masonic movement:

> The internationalist circular and ambiguous objectives of Free-masonry are in direct conflict with the Social Nationalist objectives [of our movement] in such a way that render allegiance to the two at the same time irreconcilable. Therefore, in so far as doctrine and objectives are concerned, a person has either to be a social nationalist or a Freemason [but not both]. Anyone who is a Freemason and wishes to join the Social Nationalist order and become a member of the [Syrian] Social National Party must repudiate the principles of Freemasonry, dissociate himself from its associations, and sincerely declare that in the application form.[63]

An unflattering proclamation concerning Freemasonry made on 10 May, 1949,[64] purportedly "accelerated the conspiracy against Sa'adeh"[65] by uniting influential Masons against him. Apart from Solh and Farouk, the conspirators are thought to include the Lebanese President Beshara el-Khoury, the then Chairman of the Lebanese Chamber Habib Abi Chahla, "and other Masons holding top level positions in the State."[66] The proclamation re-affirms the position stated in the edict of 3 January, but makes three pointedly anti-Masonic points:

1. That Freemasonry is an international Jewish establishment, whose history, influence and symbols are Jewish.
2. That an essential element in the Masonic grandiose plan is to re-build the Temple of Solomon on the Temple Mount in Jerusalem as a "symbol of Jewish authority over Syrian land."
3. That Masonry conceals its secrets from all except the Adepts and Sages, and uses false explanations and misinterpretations of its symbols to achieve "destructive" objectives.[67]

Three crucial points are noteworthy: (1) Sa'adeh did not divulge the secret symbols of Freemasonry or criticize its rituals; (2) he did not call for a ban on Freemasonry; and (3) he did not attack public stonemasons. Sa'adeh merely accused Masonry of constituting a separate system of loyalty that was inconsistent with loyalty to the national cause. Hence his declaration "in so far as doctrine and objectives are concerned, a person has either to be a social nationalist or a Freemason [but not both]." The Masonic movement in Lebanon did not respond to the proclamation.

The charge against Freemasonry rests on the assumption that Freemasons pledge to come to each other's aid under circumstances of distress. Yet hypotheses based upon the notion that certain classes of people actively conspire together, though emotionally attractive, are essentially implausible. In his essay "On nationalism," George Orwell discussed the common habit of considering people as monolithic groups like "species of insect." His criticisms stemmed from the fact that such classification is crude and misleading.[68] It is probably true that at least some Masonry ideas circulated among Lebanon's politicians, even at the highest level of the State. But those ideas were not entirely accepted by the political establishment – so the existence of any sort of direct influence is difficult to argue. At the very least, it is highly unlikely that Lebanese Masonries could have overcome their own internal religious, personal and political differences in time to pull off something quite as dramatic as the Sa'adeh killing.

Even today, many Lebanese who are not otherwise given to thoughts of grand conspiracies and who don't identify themselves with Sa'adeh can harbor vague suspicions towards groups like the Freemasons. But proving the existence of a nefarious Masonry conspiracy against Sa'adeh is just as difficult as proving every other theory on Freemasonry wickedness.

Other than that, there is the problem of ascertaining if the conspirators in the Sa'adeh case (allegedly Solh, Khoury, Farouk and others) were Freemasons at the time of the event. There has been no published information about their Masonry membership. Nor has anyone addressed the question of to what extent Freemasonry influenced their way of thinking and interpersonal relations. Therefore, it is wholly conjectural. On most occasions, the 'conspirators' behaved contrary to the ethics and moral philosophy of Freemasonry, which requires its members to extend fraternal indulgence at all times. They fought to outbid each other in politics and often placed their personal political interests ahead of other interests, Freemasonry or not.

Another shortcoming is this: As it stands, the Freemasonry conspiracy theory against Sa'adeh provides a pattern of explanatory reasoning about events and situations of personal, social, and historical significance in which a "conspiracy" is the dominant or operative actor. On closer analysis, though, the theory is highly confusing. It leaves the investigator wondering who the guilty party in the conspiracy really was: Freemasonry for using its front men to conspire against Sa'adeh, or the front men for using Freemasonry to achieve their objectives. Such a misconstruction is not a mere mistake but rather the expression of a tendency to interpret the world in a particular way.

Overall, this theory reflects the predilection of many in the Arab-Iranian-Muslim Middle East to make sense of their worlds through frequent use of conspiracy notions.[69] It is not necessarily wrong but, as with the other cases, it needs many more details. At this point, we can neither prove nor disprove that Freemasonry fomented a plot, but there is little evidence, as opposed to supposition, that it did, and some of the arguments advanced are weak and highly hypothetical. Nevertheless, the theory can be analysed empirically to obtain some conclusions about the motives and reasons for its propagation in the first place.

4. A Conspiracy From Within

The various conspiracy theories concerning Sa'adeh were started by his closest associates and inner-circle comrades. *Why?* It is especially interesting to know whether they did it for genuine reasons or for ulterior motives they hoped will remain hidden.

If we accept that they believed what they said, then from a socio-psychoanalytical perspective, the reason for theorizing about conspiracy theories lies somewhere among the following possibilities:

1. Because the perpetrators needed an outlet from the social alienation and political disempowerment that followed Sa'adeh's execution.
2. Because they were desperate for "a tangible enemy"[70] on which to externalize their angry feelings. Ted Goertzel calls it anomia – a syndrome whereby insecure or discontented people look for an enemy to blame for problems which otherwise seem too abstract and impersonal.[71]

3.   Because the available evidence in the public record and the press did not correspond with the common or official version of events.

In recent years, however, an alternative theory based on self-interest has been advanced. Its adherents believe that those who fomented conspiracy theories about Sa'adeh may have done so to create a diversion away from their own responsibilities in Sa'adeh's downfall or to conceal evidence of misdeeds that may somehow be linked to the crisis. Sensing the existence of a cover-up, they suspect that Sa'adeh may have been the victim of a conspiracy from within the party. What they lack in hard evidence they make up for with empirical observations and rational scrutiny. The theory has two broad elements: it emphasises questions of personal conduct, character, and motives rather than the event itself and it attempts to look at Sa'adeh's tragic end from within to determine whether it could have been prevented and whether or not the party's senior leaders had the opportunity to stop it but did not.

Proponents of the theory utilize memoirs, narratives and accounts that are almost entirely concerned with Sa'adeh and written by his chief advisors and people at the highest level of party policy. Next, through content analysis and evaluation, they identify the properties that point to a potential cover-up. One is the existence of wide discrepancies between the various descriptions. Another is the manipulation of facts and circumstances for personal ends. A third property is the inability to unravel the past in a clear and unbiased fashion or to develop a larger or more useful picture of reality. Such equivocation, it is argued, makes it almost impossible to construct a coherent, unified account of what actually happened to Sa'adeh and serves to divert attention from the complex production of the truth. The underlying assumption is that, by twisting the facts, these narrators are either hiding something important or telling half-truths to camouflage their own shortcomings in Sa'adeh's downfall.

The theory draws heavily on individual conduct, or more specifically, on blatant transgressions committed by members of Sa'adeh's inner circle. Suffice it to recount four transgressions that stand out:

1.   During the cleanup operation triggered by the Jummaizeh incident government forces found a basket of hand grenades inside the printing press building where the clash occurred. Apparently, it

was brought into the building by George Abdul Massih, Sa'adeh's right-hand man, without anyone's knowledge. Although the small cache was not used during the ensuing clash, it gave the government a ready-made charge to make against the party. It also gave segments of the press physical evidence over which to condemn Sa'adeh. When quizzed, Abdul Massih retorted that it was done purely for precautionary reasons, but said nothing about why he kept the matter entirely to himself!

2. It is now commonly accepted that Sa'adeh's fate was sealed on 24 June at the Shtura meeting between President Zaim and his Lebanese counterparts, Solh and Khoury. One of the most startling revelations to emerge from this meeting is that Adib Shishakli, an SNP member and a close friend of Sa'adeh, was at the meeting and witnessed its entire proceedings. For mysterious reasons Shishakli did not inform Sa'adeh about the meeting, despite the gravity of the situation. What would have happened had he done so is now immaterial, but we can safely conjecture that Sa'adeh would have changed trajectory and the July uprising would not have taken place.

3. Any insurgency involving direct armed resistance against an established government demands leadership, openness, communication, and transparency as well as the absolute commitment of its members and leaders. Yet during the ill-fated rebellion in the early days of July, the attitude of some of Sa'adeh's top advisors was so apathetic and careless it harbored on total treachery. At one point, three of them took to Damascus' nightlife even as the rebellion was falling apart and defeat was staring Sa'adeh in the face. Others lied to Sa'adeh, virtually:

> Yes, it was I who uttered those words [that the uprising will go ahead with or without Sa'adeh] because the insurgency had been declared and there was no turning back after all the preparations we had made. I retorted "How dare you tell Sa'adeh that you are not prepared to cancel the uprising when it was you who told me that the insurgents were not ready for battle. What's more you confirmed to Sa'adeh that there will be more than seventy men under your command and yet it was hard for you to assemble seventeen of them. In fact, you managed to assemble only twelve. With such a flimsy number you encouraged Sa'adeh to go ahead [with the uprising] and to bear the responsibility for its failure?"[72]

Recklessness was widespread. No one even considered putting together an escape plan for Sa'adeh in the event of failure.[73] When the uprising was crushed it was every man for himself:

On the next day I returned to Damascus. The moment I entered the town I sensed something unusual in the atmosphere. I got out of the car and walked in the direction of Yahya's house. Before I entered Suq Sarouja I met George Salameh, Joseph's brother, who told me that he had managed to escape from Beirut. He was in a terrible state of anxiety. He said "You should go back to Amman. Everybody's being hunted in Syria."

I inquired about Sa'adeh. He said that he had disappeared from sight and nobody knew where he was.

Once again I was assailed by that sense of pervasive fear which I had experienced in Beirut. I felt the blood chilled in my veins. We had come to be pursued in Syria as we had been, and still were, in Lebanon. Thus in the twinkling of an eye Damascus turned from a friendly, safe haven into a terribly dangerous place like Beirut.

I hurried to Yahya's house, but he wasn't there. I went to the Oasis and found him sitting by himself reading a newspaper. As he caught sight of me he cried, "What are you doing here? Why did you come back? Haven't you heard the news?"

He gave me an account of the rumors that had been spreading in Damascus to the effect that Adib Shishakly had been discharged or removed from his post, that Husm ez-Zaim had handed Sa'adeh over to the Lebanese Government and that the Mazza Prison was brimful with prisoners. I sat down, feeling totally exhausted and awfully starved. I got up and went with Yahya to a small restaurant opposite Socrates Restaurant. We ate fatit maqadim which lifted my spirits somewhat. Over the coffee Yahya said, "The main thing is that we should arrange for your return to Amman. We should first get you an exit visa from the Security."[74]

There is an amusing passage in Abdullah Qubarsi's memoirs where the author describes how a band of SNP fighters heading to the front picked up a civilian officer of the party from his hotel room in Damascus and took him along for the ride even though he had no previous military experience.[75] The officer was conducting business in the Syrian capital even as the rebellion was taking place!

4. Following Sa'adeh's disappearance on the evening of 6 July, his followers had ample time to mount a rescue mission. Why it did

not cross anyone's mind to attempt to save him is anyone's guess and rests squarely with those in the party's hierarchy who were privy to his disappearance but failed to report it. After Sa'adeh's execution, the party was consumed with frustration and finger-pointing directed mainly, but not entirely, at Maaruf Saab, Sa'adeh's political advisor, and his wife Adele, whose residence was Sa'adeh's last pick up point. Quoting Juliet El-Mir Sa'adeh:

Party officials used to drop in at the house [where I was staying] and there would be heated debates between them and the members. At times the debates would take place among the officials themselves, and it was entirely about recent events – how this or that person proceeded and what action he should have taken and why he didn't take it. Among those who came under close scrutiny from the party members and trustees was Maaruf Saab. Some queried why the appointment with Husni al-Zaim was allowed to go ahead in the first place and why he didn't report it to the trustees. What's more, why did Maaruf Saab feign the meeting at the [Presidential] Palace to trustee Abduallah Muhsin, even though the latter told him that he had significant news concerning Sa'adeh and that it was vitally important that he got it before the meeting? Maaruf Saab's answer to Abdullah was that the meeting had been cancelled and that Sa'adeh's whereabouts were unknown or that he could not divulge it to anyone. Delighted by the news of the cancellation, trustee Abdullah then left.[76]

Adele Saab evidently aroused the suspicion of party members when details of her misconduct came to the fore:

Maaruf Saab and his wife were also given a tongue-lashing from Abla Khoury, who turned up at the Saab's residence and explicitly told Adele that she [i.e., Abla] had been sent by her uncle Faris el-Khoury to pass to Sa'adeh extremely sensitive information.

Adele: Sa'adeh is not here.
Abla: But I cannot emphasize enough the importance of the matter especially that it is from my uncle Faris. I must speak to him at once.
Adele: I can't help you. These are orders from Sa'adeh himself.
Abla: Then ask him yourself and come back to me. Tell him that it is important and potentially dangerous and comes from my uncle.

[203]

Adele: Don't waste your time. It is impossible to report to him.[77]

Abla left the Saabs fuming with anger and cursing them for their arrogance.

The effect of such reckless behaviour was to spawn an atmosphere of the deepest despair in party ranks. It raised doubts about the sincerity of Sa'adeh's field helpers during the uprising and about their contribution, consciously or unconsciously, to his downfall. The fact that party leaders failed to inquire into the nature of the transgressions and punish the perpetrators has provided an even greater cause for suspicion. Paradoxically, in the end, the main suspects, George Abdul Massih and Maaruf Saab, were promoted to the highest offices in the party after Sa'adeh's death, and a third, Adib Shishakli, later on became a Syrian president. For some, though, that makes the case for conspiracy even *stronger*.

This brings us to the other side of the theory: why did the perpetrators betray Sa'adeh and what exactly did they expect to achieve? For some it was for political expediency: the conspirators provided opportunities for Sa'adeh's demise in order to seize control of the party and pursue their own political agendas. Others place more emphasis on character motives: out of envy of Sa'adeh's charismatic leadership or out of resentment for his disciplinary ideological style. Whatever the reason, both sides back up their claims by drawing on the political and ideological deviation that surfaced inside the party after Sa'adeh's death. Such deviation, however, is typical of movements that lose their prophetic leaders unexpectedly: "In the case of prophetic leaders, lines and processes of succession are usually cloudier. Conflict may quickly engulf a movement's top echelons as secondary figures scramble for the mantle of leadership. Because prophetic leaders are less likely to routinize their authority than administrative leaders, the movement may falter in factional infighting."[78]

As so often the case, it is difficult to ascertain with exactitude the validity of this theory. While it tends to adhere to reasonable standards of critical thinking based on eye-witness accounts, the evidence on which it rests is patchy and open to various interpretations. The theory offers no factual evidence to condemn anyone and the allegations depend on unverifiable data. On the existing evidence we cannot lightly condemn the "perpetrators" for hypocrisy and spite; and even if our final verdict should be unfavourable, it is wrong to pass it without attempting to penetrate to some degree into the minds and motives of these men, to try to understand why they could, and thought they should, commit a crime so seemingly damnable.

In any subjective theory as this, it is often more than difficult to analyse precisely human motives and to distinguish the genuine from the specious: no man knows his own heart well enough for that. Within Sa'adeh's inner-circle there were many who, while they might feel the meaner motive, were nonetheless sincere when they joined themselves to the party, and who gave true life and meaning to its cause. It would be unfair to penalize these people for the selfish actions of a few and to do so while the confessions themselves contain inherent improbabilities. Yet it would be equally unfair to let the issue pass before we have all the facts needed to establish the truth.

The proportion of misconduct by Sa'adeh's confidants was high and inexcusable, especially where intrigue was common and always potentially dangerous. However, only time will tell whether it was part of a greater scheme aimed at Sa'adeh's destruction or if it was purely the result of individual incompetence and ineptitude. For now, the trail is not clear enough to substantiate or disprove either possibility.

5. A Victim of Circumstances

Detractors of conspiracy theories and some scholars discount the presence of a deliberate plot against Sa'adeh. Rather they see his execution largely as a domestic Lebanese issue, the culmination of a power play between competing interests in which Sa'adeh played his cards and lost. He was, in other words, a victim of circumstances over which he had no control nor adequate resources and experience to deal with. His death is thus explained as basically the result of false impressions and bad politics.

The most recent exposition of this theory can be found in Eyal Zisser's solid and illuminating study on Lebanon's independence era:

> Rather than being the villain of the piece, Sa'ada thus was to some extent a victim of circumstances. The weakness of the Lebanese regime, its irritability, the panic to which it was then becoming subject – all these had as much to do with Sa'ada's trial and execution as his own actions. Yet he was no innocent victim: he entered in the confrontation with open eyes and willingly allowed Khuri's rivals to exploit him. Moreover, he did not hesitate to challenge publicly the

Lebanese political system and to question the right of the Lebanese state to exist. In doing so, he hastened his own end.[79]

In Zisser's view, Sa'adeh advanced his own demise by positioning himself outside the political establishment and in the direct line of fire between the incumbent regime and its opponents. Internally, that included Chamoun and Jumblatt as leaders of a new alliance precipitated by the fraudulent election in 1947. Externally, the opponent was the Zaim regime in Syria: "The Lebanese regime soon came to think of itself as facing a common front formed by Za'im in Syria, its traditional rivals at home and its new adversary, Sa'ada."[80] Zisser goes on to paint a political picture depicting the Khoury regime in a state of panic exacerbated by "Za'im's overt support for Sa'ada, and his conjectured covert support for other opponents of the regime."[81] Another worry for the Lebanese establishment was Britain, thought to be backing both the Lebanese opposition to secure the Lebanese presidency for Chamoun, and Sa'adeh out of a shared interest in Greater Syria: "It was against this background that, in the summer of 1949 [sic], the government decided to take action against the PPS."[82] It was a decision taken "from an overall sense of being threatened"[83] by the aforesaid forces.

Next, Zisser purported to show that Sa'adeh "was no more than a pawn on a chessboard on which a larger game was being played."[84] Each player in this game had his own agenda but none really cared about Sa'adeh. The players on his side of the chessboard backed him against the Lebanese regime but purely out of self-regard rather than for the ideas he represented. Thus, they discarded him when he ceased to be of any service to them – all of which was made easier by Sa'adeh's trusting nature, political inexperience, and misapprehension of events:

> True, [Sa'adeh] had chosen the road of confrontation, but he may not have understood what course events were bound to take. He may have deluded himself that, as in the past, the Lebanese government would recoil from serious action; or else he may have believed in the promises given him by Za'im as well as by Chamoun and Junbalat.[85]

Before examining Zisser's thesis, some factual corrections are in order:

1. The contention that the PPS anthem opened with the words "Syria, Syria above all" is untrue.[86]

2. The assertion that the Lebanese public "unquestioningly" accepted the claim of the Khoury regime that Sa'adeh had planned to bring down the regime is questionable.[87] It is belied by Zisser's observation that Sa'adeh's death "elicited harsh reactions in Lebanon."[88]

3. True, the cabinet convened the evening of the Jummaizeh incident on 9 June, 1949 to proclaim the PPS an illegal organization,[89] but according to Farid Chehab the decision to ban the PPS was taken during a secret meeting held before the incident.[90]

4. There is no evidence to suggest that Sa'adeh entered into an alliance with Chamoun and Jumblatt. In fact, he didn't.

The main problem with Zisser's thesis is that it raises more questions than it answers. It doesn't really tell us, for example, why the Lebanese government persisted with the execution of Sa'adeh after he was extradited from Syria. If the matter was as simple as the picture painted by Zisser, why didn't the regime attempt to use Sa'adeh as a bargaining chip after it had resoundingly crushed his rebellion? Would the regime have responded differently had it been a person other than Sa'adeh? Given the alarming nature of the crisis, did any other external forces, apart from Syria, become involved? Zisser's thesis thus requires more elaboration. The thrust of his analysis seems to be on the confrontation between Sa'adeh and the Khoury regime rather than on its dramatic outcome. At one point Zisser states: "Altogether, it is more than doubtful whether Sa'ada posed an actual threat to Lebanon."[91] Yet he doesn't clearly explain how and why the Khoury regime came to regard him as a threat. Nor does he explain why the regime refused to accommodate Sa'adeh after the PPS leader openly accepted Lebanon's existence and allowed his supporters to participate in local elections. If the main issue at stake was "the wish of Khuri's opponents – whether domestic, or in Za'im's time, Syrian – to turn Sa'ada into an instrument to serve their own purposes,"[92] then it is necessary to explain why the regime did not attempt to lure Sa'adeh from its principal internal opponents (Chamoun and Jumblatt) or from President Zaim later on, by pacifying the PPS leader: both Khoury and Solh were master-players in this game. Finally, how could a regime that enjoyed wide international recognition and support, particularly from the United States, Britain and France, feel threatened by a quasi-militia?

The real threat to the Khoury regime during this time came from its principal domestic opponents, not Sa'adeh. The SNP leader did not command enough electoral support to topple the government. Like the communists, his support was cross-sectional, not sectarian. This placed them outside the confessional system of Lebanon. In contrast, Chamoun and Jumblatt were integral members of the system and true sectarian leaders in their own right, a pre-requisite for electoral success under the Lebanese confessional system. They were primed more than Sa'adeh to bring down the Khoury regime. By Zisser's own account, both men approached President Zaim and openly cooperated with his regime during the same period. Zisser notes that "that Za'im's promises to the Lebanese opposition had included the supply of arms and army personnel."[93] Why, then, did the Khoury regime take forcible action against Sa'adeh and not against them? As early as 1948, the Lebanese Phalange had contemplated an armed Maronite revolt against Khoury, with Israel's help. A year later, on 17 July, 1949, Lebanese security forces captured a large cache of "machine-guns, pistols, ammunition and hand grenades . . . secreted in the garden"[94] of their central headquarters. Likewise, in 1948, a disgruntled Druze chieftain called Nouhad Arslan staged an unsuccessful military coup against the Khoury regime that claimed as many fatalities as Sa'adeh's short uprising, a single Lebanese gendarmerie. It was apparently planned and executed with the knowledge and moral support of a senior Maronite clergy who was himself openly stirring sedition against the Khoury regime. Yet on every single one of these occasions the government dealt with matters in a conciliatory way as though nothing serious had happened. The main drawback in Zisser's explanation is the lack of attention to regime duplicity in dealing with potential threats.

Zisser's thesis that the Lebanese government had acted out of despair is also seriously flawed. On the eve of Sa'adeh's trial, the fear that stemmed from Zaim's tactical embracement of Sa'adeh was extraneous to the questions at issue. It was relevant up to a certain point during the early phases of the power struggle between Sa'adeh and the Khoury regime, but became virtually extinct prior to Sa'adeh's trial. At that juncture the regime in Lebanon was under no threat over Sa'adeh from either the Lebanese opposition or Syria: the Lebanese opposition had no real interest in Sa'adeh and Syria's relations with Lebanon were on the mend and getting better. In fact, with the international and regional order on its side, the Khoury regime was in a commanding position to conduct the trial without any "fear" or "panic" at all. It could not have acted out of "political despair" either because theoretically despair is a state of mind for someone who is the victim of circumstances rather than their master.

All in all, the "victim of circumstances" or "politics of despair" theory is useful as an historical framework. It provides an essential context by which to reconstruct and evaluate the chain of events prior to the trial, but it does not provide adequate explanations as to why the Lebanese State behaved the way it did at the trial. The theory is based on circumstantial evidence that does not always connect. It is also myopic in that it devotes little space to the various forces that influenced proceedings from outside. Thus, it has the effect of overemphasizing the power struggle in the affair and a concomitant failure to be critical of the role of peripheral players. Beyond these general themes, the material obviously leaves open many lingering questions. Anyone with little or no familiarity with the saga would be able to gain from it at least a cursory understanding of what happened but not answers to the questions that continue to intrigue scholars to this day.

Why Was Sa'adeh Really Executed?
Whether Antun Sa'adeh's drastic course of action was morally and ethically appropriate will remain a matter of opinion. But his intention, to fight back against a regime that had tried relentlessly to silence him and to cow his supporters into submission, has to be appreciated in order to understand why he was executed immediately. It is also crucial to the overall irony of his saga, namely this: why would a regime lay itself open to charges of injustice and improper use of the courts by seeking to eliminate a political adversary who, in its own estimation, was a mere social deviant? Until now, all attempts to answer this question have centred largely on Sa'adeh's threat to the regime's grip on power. Of course, there never had been any doubt about that. However, one cannot depend exclusively or even mainly on this explanation because it leaves far too many questions unanswered: Why did the Khoury regime expedite the execution rather than assure Sa'adeh a more dignified passage to his end? Why did it adopt a hands-off approach with respect to its other adversaries and not with respect to Sa'adeh? And why did it not attempt to negotiate with him after he was captured and handed over to the authorities?

As is true of similar occurrences, Sa'adeh's elimination cannot be understood without critical analysis, and critical analysis reveals that he was killed for reasons primarily related to state repression: why and how political authorities use coercive power when faced with potential or existing challenges and challengers. State repression may be defined as a set of intentional actions, brute or cunning, attempted by the power-holders to contain challenging and threatening claims by "unruly" groups or individuals. It involves

> the actual or threatened use of physical sanctions against an individual or organization, within the territorial jurisdiction of the state, for the purpose of imposing a cost on the target as well as deterring specific activities and/or beliefs perceived to be challenging to government personnel, practices or institutions.[95]

Three points are especially noteworthy: (1) not all state challengers are repressed at all times. Each state may have some threshold of tolerance to challenge depending on the issue, size, timing, persistence, and unity of the challenger; (2) while challengers perceive state repression as a barometer of political opportunities,[96] state repressive effort is dually an indicator of how threatening the challengers appear to the state power-holders;[97] and (3) variations in state repression are conditioned by challenger power as much as they are by existing resources. In other words, the kind of response that challengers will receive from the state has much to do with the breadth and depth of the challenger's influence on the larger society.[98]

In terms of the Sa'adeh killing, the most relevant model of repression is that which is commonly associated with state-sponsored killing of a movement's leader. According to this model, "All too frequently, governments kill social movement leaders in an attempt to halt challenges to state power."[99] Apparently, governments engage in the practice out of the conviction that repression can obviate a movement's recovery after its leader's murder:

> In broadest terms, repression reduces the political opportunities that facilitate movement development. It makes organizing difficult and dangerous, as those who seek to activate indigenous organizations or form new ones become easy targets for sanctions. Repression can therefore cause ordinary movement participants to drop out, fearing

the costs and risks involved. Additionally, repression can inhibit the formation of new resistance groups that seek similar goals. Less directly, it can create a sense of hopelessness and resignation, undermining the "cognitive liberation" often seen as crucial to mobilization. Finally, repression may also generate internal tensions and destroy unity, as activists suspect one another of being infiltrators or government collaborators.[100]

The proposition advanced here deals with a particular genre of social movement leaders: the prophetic type. These are leaders who have deep conviction about goals and are prepared to go against conventional wisdom.[101] Prophetic leaders are set apart from ordinary men by their exceptional personal qualities or extraordinary insight and accomplishment. On the whole, prophetic leaders share some or all of the following features: (1) espouse ideas that challenge fundamental aspects of the society; (2) possess great symbolic and mobilizing power over different segments of the population; (3) exercises significant effects on elements extending well beyond the organizations they titularly head; (4) display uncompromising behavior toward traditional authority or the power-holders; (5) occupy the centre-stage within their movements and (6) inspire loyalty and obedience from followers and have no significant backing from abroad. It is claimed that prophetic leaders are prone to physical elimination more than other genre of leaders because they are often irreplaceable and thus more rewarding for the purpose of a movement's destruction:

> Although the loss of an administrative leader will be a serious blow, recognized succession processes and designated deputies can limit disruptions after the killing. By contrast, in the case of prophetic leaders, lines and processes of succession are usually cloudier. Conflict may quickly engulf a movement's top echelons as secondary figures scramble for the mantle of leadership. Because prophetic leaders are less likely to routinize their authority than administrative leaders, the movement may falter in factional infighting.[102]

Looking at Sa'adeh's killing from this perspective gives meaning to his execution as a predictable but necessary step in the destruction or weakening of his political movement. Two factors support this perspective. The first is the breadth of Sa'adeh's challenge, which displayed features that have consistently been found to increase states' uses of repression against a movement's leader. Sa'adeh held a distinct leadership role in his political movement and was also its public voice and key administrator. In particular, he was instrumental in popularizing the movement and wrote prodigiously, often in visionary terms, and without concessions. In addition, Sa'adeh was central to the movement's key mobilizations, not only planning and orchestrating them but also providing their inspirational core through his speeches and courage. The fact that he was perceived by the regime as the most prominent figure in his political movement and its primary source of popularity and strength made his killing all the more necessary.

The second factor relates to the character of the Khoury regime. Scholars of state repression generally explain the use of coercive tactics in terms of the degree of democracy in a political system, with autocracies behaving more repressively and full democracies less so. In an extension of this point, a threshold has been placed on the relationship between democracy and repression with scholars now arguing that not all steps toward democracy exert an equal, negative impact on levels of state repression. In other words, the incentives for repression are likely to be strong as democracy is extended before it is fully institutionalized.[103] In that case, attributing Sa'adeh's killing to state repression makes a lot of sense because the Khoury regime was a transitional regime (or a mixed regime with elements of autocracy and democracy)[104] and transitional regimes, on the whole, appear to perpetrate the greatest violations against dissidents. Alyssa Prorok explains why:

> The logic of this argument is based on the convergence, in mixed regimes, of three factors. First, the partial opening of a political system provides previously excluded groups the ability to mobilize in an attempt to change the "political and distributive order". Because semi-democratic states open enough to allow the public expression of dissent, but not enough to alleviate sources of dissatisfaction, citizens of these regimes are likely to make a large number of demands, which, due to the lack of stable institutional infrastructure in mixed regimes, cannot be adequately channeled into the political arena. Finally, institutional fragility and incoherence, and the tenuous nature of legitimacy in mixed regimes, make dissident threats more dangerous to leaders of these states than to either democratic or autocratic governments. Fearing popular revolt and political overthrow, mixed regime leaders feel compelled to respond harshly to opposition threats. Proponents of this theory thus predict high levels of repression in mixed regimes as threats to the ruling elite

increase and alternative methods of social control are rendered ineffective or nonexistent.[105]

Thus, Sa'adeh's killing, like that of other prophetic leaders, was symptomatic of regime repression directed at prominent leaders who hold a great moral and symbolic authority within movements. What would the outcome have looked like if Sa'adeh had been a mere figurehead within his movement, or if he had had strong ties with a foreign state, or if the scope of his influence was negligible, or if he had been more conciliatory toward the power-holders and more accommodating of the state? The answer to this question is inevitably speculative, but if the Lebanese state's treatment of "unruly" individuals before and after Sa'adeh's execution in 1949 is any indication, the outcome is apt to be different: probably a political compromise with the SSNP without Sa'adeh being required to even put in an appearance before the court.

There exists two other closely related issues that must be stated. The first is that the idea of killing Sa'adeh as a way of destroying or weakening his vision and movement did not originate with the Khoury regime. As early as 1936 a senior officer of the French *Sûreté Générale* is reported to have said: "If we must eliminate the Syrian National Party we must then eliminate its leader Antun Sa'adeh, for Sa'adeh is the Syrian National Party and the Syrian National Party is Sa'adeh."[106] The French detected an automatic correlation between Sa'adeh and his party and tried to take it apart through soft repression, such as imprisonment and exile. The Lebanese regime that killed Sa'adeh in 1949 went one step further: when all else failed, it turned to physical extermination. As a barometer of its repressive behavior, the idea of eliminating Sa'adeh tempered the Khoury regime on at least three occasions before it succeeded in 1949.[107] The first time occurred in 1947 when it issued a warrant for his capture "dead or alive" after Sa'adeh refused to present himself for interrogation. As a rule, the appellation of "dead or alive" is invoked against dangerous political offenders and only under conditions of extreme necessity as a last resort. It is principally a de facto license to kill with the offer of prosecutorial immunity to the killer. In the present context, the main stimulus for the appellation was Sa'adeh's head – an actuality made even stronger by the fact that the Lebanese government issued the deadly warrant even though it knew where Sa'adeh was "hiding." The second time that the Khoury regime targeted Sa'adeh occurred at Jummaizeh in June 1949. Jummaizeh was a definite plot against Sa'adeh and not a mere an act of immediate danger. It occurred with the foreknowledge of the Khoury regime and possibly with its direct involvement.[108] What is not clear is the priority that Sa'adeh's killing occupied in the scheme of things. The incident was planned either to induce a grave slip-up for greater retribution against Sa'adeh or to secure the murder of Sa'adeh through the agency of a third party. The third and perhaps most conspicuous attempt on Sa'adeh's life by the Khoury regime occurred after he was taken into custody on 7 July, 1949. On this occasion, the security men who took delivery of Sa'adeh from the Syrians on 7 July were instructed to eliminate Sa'adeh along the way using the familiar pretext that he was shot while trying to escape: the ruse was aborted at the last minute.

The second issue is more complex but just as important. To execute a political figure of Sa'adeh's stature is not simple by any standard, even with the right pretexts. It is a risk that most governments would much rather avoid. Therefore for the Lebanese government to have taken this risk certain propitious factors had to be present or else it would not have attempted it.

As with other aspects of the Sa'adeh saga, it is difficult to determine accurately why the Khoury regime did not regard execution as a risk. The matter is less obvious than traditionally assumed and remains intensely debated and researched by historians. Nonetheless, at least four factors are clearly discernible. The first was the impression that since Sa'adeh had no powerful allies his execution would not pose a particular danger to regime power. Sa'adeh is mainly to blame for this. During his struggle with the Khoury regime, he purposely maintained a certain distance between himself and the political forces in the country out of the belief that both the government and the opposition were part of the same political establishment.[109] Such neutrality enabled Sa'adeh to retain ideological credibility, but deprived him of political allies to lean on in difficult times. Although the Lebanese opposition was just as determined as he was to get rid of the Khoury regime, it did not get directly involved with him and refused to come to his aid at the crucial moment. Like most Lebanese, it found his vision of radical change too extreme for its liking. The Khoury regime was thus able to proceed against him self-assured that its action would be likely to evoke no more than scant protest.

Second was the belief that execution precluded the possibility of sectarian disturbance against the regime. An Orthodox Christian at birth, Sa'adeh did not regard himself, nor was he regarded, as a sectarian leader. His antipathy towards the religious establishments placed him outside the support network that other Orthodox Christians were entitled to under the country's confessional structure. The Orthodox Church acknowledged no commitment toward him, nor did Sa'adeh acknowledge any commitment toward the Church. In fact, the Orthodox Patriarch showed no visible interest in Sa'adeh or in his row with the Khoury regime and adopted the same carefree attitude as that of other denominational Christians. From a practical point of view, that made Sa'adeh's execution a less risky undertaking than it might otherwise have been. It probably would not have happened had Sa'adeh had been a Maronite or a Druze or a Sunni Muslim leader. At any rate, that is the considered view in Lebanon at present.

Third was the anticipation that Sa'adeh's execution would not evoke condemnation in the "civilized" world. No Arab country was likely to object to his killing: Egypt and Saudi Arabia had strong aversions to Syrian nationalism; Syria had already made its feelings quite clear; and Jordan and Iraq had no apparent interest in Sa'adeh despite their common interest in the Fertile Crescent. Execution of a belligerent adversary was also in Israel's national interest. Condemnation from the international community was also improbable in view of Sa'adeh's revolting image abroad: the French considered him an agent of British interests; the British saw him as a threat to the regional status quo; the Soviet Union reviled his brand of nationalism; and the United States loathed his 'fascist' doctrines. This serene opposition to Sa'adeh conveyed an atmosphere of unmatched cordiality for his execution and allowed the Khoury regime to move quickly without worrying about the external fallouts.

Fourth was the repressive atmosphere of the post-war era and the drive to clean up the world of undesirable radicals – the "kooks," bigots, and Nazi sympathizers, even Communists.[110] Michal Belknap describes it as an era "of notable political trials, characterized by resort to vague conspiracy charges, prosecution of individuals more for what they represented than for what they had done, and lack of concern about due process."[111] The prosecution of the leaders and members of the American Communist Party during the Foley Square trials in 1949 is a case in point.[112] The Nuremberg trials, between October 1945 and November 1946, of twenty-two Germans selected as representatives of organizations and episodes from the Third Reich that the victorious powers found particularly reprehensible, are another feature of that era. Elsewhere, the crackdown on subversives reflected a policy of extermination of ideological enemies.[113] Antun Sa'adeh was executed in this climate of repressive hysteria, a fact alluded to by Kamal Jumblatt in his interpellation in 1949:

> Most of us would have noticed, not long ago, how a surge in political assassinations, trials, and intimidation of powerful leaders and political parties swept across the states of the Near East one after the other. It moved from Iran, where reputable progressive figures and parties, including the Communist parties, were harassed and battered, to Iraq and then to Egypt where unknown assailants killed the spiritual leader of the Muslim Brotherhood, to Damascus where all political parties were dissolved and their leaders persecuted. It was only a matter of time for Lebanon's turn to come and, naturally, after everyone else because, thanks God, we always come last.[114]

Sa'adeh's reputation abroad as a fascist made it easier for the Khoury regime to prosecute and sentence him to death knowing in advance that it would not be condemned for its action. Its constant reference to fascism and Nazism at his trial and in its tardy explanations has to be seen and understood within this psychological context. The same principle applies to the deliberate omission of any reference to Sa'adeh's anti-Communist tendencies, which might have caught the attention of Western governments.

Conclusion

The scenarios discussed in this chapter succeed in the task of illuminating an aspect of a political event that clearly has been ignored for too long. They offer different perspectives and different conceptual insights into why it happened and who may have been involved at one point or another. Judgmental scenarios that attempt to explain the saga in strictly political or personality terms may appeal to people who prefer cognitive simplicity over complexity. Conspiracy theories, on the other hand, suggest something much bigger and much more sinister, and are attractive. The reason is silence, and "silence implies mystery":[115] it is the most damning piece of evidence for a conspiracy. The fact that someone has gone to such pains to create a false impression points to a conscious effort to deceive.

Overall, the scenarios discussed in this chapter are both inconclusive and highly speculative. The complexities presented by each scenario confirm, above all, the need for deep political analysis, as opposed to conventional "conspiratorial" analysis, and thus for a framework that incorporates "all those political practices and arrangements, deliberate or not, which are usually repressed rather than acknowledged."[116] From that vantage point, understanding the Sa'adeh execution at a deeper level requires a crisp, clean, clear, insightful, and penetrating map that encompasses the roles of the key players and their motives, as well as analysis of the events surrounding Sa'adeh's death, and of the structural defects within the Lebanese system that allowed such a crime to occur and to go unpunished.

If the Lebanese State had been more forthcoming with the information, much of the mystery around Sa'adeh's execution would have been dispelled. By refusing to open its files the Lebanese State has not only perpetuated the cycle of suspicion but has also denied the public the opportunity to know the truth. Until new flows of information are obtained many questions are likely to remain forever unanswered and we may never know for certain what really happened.

NOTES

1 Lebanese Government, *Qadiyat al-Hizb al-Qawmi* (The Case of the National Party). Beirut: Ministry of Propaganda and Information, 1947: 5–6.
2 Said Fakhr ad-Din was killed during a French-led attack on the Lebanese government temporary headquarters in Bshamoun on 15 November, 1943. He was subsequently decorated with the medal of National Struggle (al-Jihad al-Watani) by President Khoury! See Gibran Jreige, "Ma'rakat al-Istiqlal" (The Battle of Independence), *Sabah el-Kheir*, 11 June, 1983: 42–43.
3 See relevant sections on the Khoury regime in by Michael C. Hudson, *The Precarious Republic: Political Modernization in Lebanon*. New York: Random House, 1968.
4 Lebanese Government, *Qadiyat al-Hizb al-Qawmi*: 8.
5 See *Istijwab Jumblatt al-tarikhi lil-hukuma hawla istishhad Sa'adeh ome 1949* (Jumblatt's Historic Interpellation to the [Lebanese] Government over Sa'adeh's Martyrdom in 1949). Beirut: SSNP, 1987.
6 *Qadiyat al-Hizb al-Qawmi*. Beirut: The Lebanese Ministry of Information, 1949: 32.

7 Ibid., 35–56.

8 Ibid.

9 Ibid., 38–39.

10 *Qadiyat al-Hizb al-Qawmi*: 38–39.

11 Ibid.

12 See Urfan Salloum in "Defense of the Social Nationalist before the Military Tribunal in Damascus" (in Arabic). Damascus: n.p., 1955: 22–28.

13 Ibid.

14 *Qadiyat al-Hizb al-Qawmi*: 27.

15 Martin Blumenson, "Can Official History be Honest History?", *Military Affairs*, Vol. 26, No. 4 (Winter, 1962): 153.

16 A classic example in this respect is Dudley Collard, *Soviet Justice and the Trial of Radek and Others*. London: Victor Gollancz Ltd, 1937.

17 See Kamal Jumblatt, *Istijwab Jumblatt al tarikhi lil hukuma hawla istishhad Sa'adeh ome 1949.*

18 Ibid.

19 Ibid.

20 See Abdullah Qubarsi, *Memoirs*. Vol. 4. Beirut: Dar al-Furat, 2004.

21 Kamal Jumblatt, *Istijwab Jumblatt al tarikhi lil hukuma hawla istishhad Sa'adeh ome 1949.*

22 Ibid.

23 Ibid.

24 Yamak Z. Labib, *The Syrian Social Nationalist Party: An Ideological Analysis*. Harvard: Center for Middle Eastern Studies, 1969: 65.

25 *Time*, Monday, 30 July, 1951.

26 Correlli Barnett, *The Human Factor and British Industrial Decline: An Historical Perspective*. London: Working Together Campaign, 1977: 21.

27 Ibid.

28 See M. V. Pylee, "Free Speech and Parliamentary Privileges in India." *Pacific Affairs*, Vol. 35, No. 1 (Spring, 1962): 11–23.

29 See Gordon S. Wood, "The Real Treason of Aaron Burr." *Proceedings of the American Philosophical Society*, Vol. 143, No. 2 (June 1999): 280–295.

30 Eyal Zisser, *Lebanon: The Challenge of Independence*. London: I. B. Tauris, 2000: 179.

31 Andrew Rathmell, *Secret War in the Middle East: The Covert Struggle for Syria, 1949–1961*. London: I. B. Tauris & Co., 1995.

32 See Adel Arslan, *Mudhakkirat* (Memoirs). Beirut: Dar al-Taqaddumiyyah, 1994.

33 *An-Nahar*, Beirut, 4 July, 1992.

34 See, for example, Robert G. Rabil, *Embattled Neighbors: Syria, Israel and Lebanon*. Boulder, Colorado: Lynne Rienner Publishers, 2003.

35 For an elaboration of this point see Adel Beshara, "Sa'adeh and the Greater Syria Scheme," in *Antun Sa'adeh: The Man, His Thought*, ed. Adel Beshara. Reading: Ithaca Press, 2007: 121–162.

36 Avi Shlaim, "Husni Za'im and the Plan to Resettle Palestinian Refugees in Syria." *Journal of Palestine Studies*, Vol. 15, No. 4 (Summer, 1986): 71.

37 For a chronological breakdown of this theory see Naji Jurji Zaydan, "Man Qatala Antun Sa'adeh? Al-Dawr al-Israeli" (Who Killed Antun Sa'adeh? The Israeli Role). *Fikr*, No. 73 (July 2000): 69–74.

38 The most elaborate is In'am Raad, *Harb wu-Jud la Harb Hudoud* (A War of Existence, not a War of Borders). Beirut: Dar Bissan, 1999; *Al-Sahyuniah was al-Sharq al-Awsatiyyah min Herzel ila Peres* (Zionism and the Greater Middle East From Herzel to Peres). Beirut: Sharikat al-Matbu'at, 1998.

39 See Vols. 14, 15 and 16 of Sa'adeh's *Complete Works*.

40 See Haytham Kader, *The Syrian Social Nationalist Party: Its Ideology and Early History*. Beirut: n.p., 1990.

41 See Vol. 16 of Sa'adeh's *Complete Works*: 123.

42 This theory can be found in In'am Raad's various books particularly his *Harb wu-Jud la Harb Hudoud* (A War of Existence, not a War of Borders). Beirut: Dar Bissan, 1999.

43 Sami Jam'a, *Awraq min Daftar al-Watan, 1946–1961* (Pages from Homeland Records, 1946–1961). Damascus: Dar Tlas, 2000: 65–82.

44 Ibid.

45 Ibid.

46 Ibid.

47 Ibid.

48 Ibid.

49 Ibid.

50 Ibid.

51 John Major, "The Search for Arab Unity." *International Affairs* (Royal Institute of International Affairs 1944), Vol. 39, No. 4 (Oct., 1963): 551–563.

52 Ibid.

53 Beshara Khoury, *Haqa'iq Lubnaniyyah* (Lebanese Truths). Vol. 3. Beirut: Awraq Lubnaniyah, 1961: 238.

54 See The Social Nationalist Reform Committee, *al-Thamin min Tammouz: Wathaiq al-Thawra wa al-Istishhad* (The Eighth of July: Documents on the Revolution and the Martyrdom [of Sa'adeh]). USA: n.p., 1992.

55 Nadhir Fansah, *Ayyam Husni Zaim: 137 Yawman Hazzat Suria* (Days of Husni Zaim: 137 Days that Shook Syria). Beirut: Dar al-Afaq al-Jadidah, 1983: 82.

56 *Al-Bina'*, nos. 981–982 (17 July, 1990): 94–95.

57 See George Johnson, *Architects of Fear: Conspiracy Theories and Paranoia in American Politics*. Los Angeles: Tarcher/Houghton Mifflin, 1983.

58 James Shelby Downard and Michael A. Hoffman II. "King-Kill/33°: Masonic Symbolism in the Assassination of John F. Kennedy," 1987. Website excerpt, 1998. Retrieved 16 July, 2007.

59 See Stephen Knight, *Jack the Ripper: The Final Solution*. London: George G. Harrap Co. Ltd., 1976.

60 John M. Robison (1739–1805), *Proofs of a Conspiracy Against all the Governments of Europe, carried on in the secret meetings of Free Masons, Illuminati, and Reading Societies*. Edinburgh: Printed for William Creech; and T. Cadell, Junior, and W. Davies, London, 1797.

61 http://www.enterprisemission.com/tower2.htm

62 Sa'adeh joined a local Masonic lodge founded by the Syrian diaspora of Brazil in the mid-1920s but it was for only a short period of time. See Nawaf Hardan, *Sa'adeh fi al-Mahjar: 1921–1930* (Sa'adeh Abroad: 1921–1930). From about the mid-1800s, Freemasonry attracted some of the leading thinkers in Syria like Maroun Aboud, Ya'qub Sarrouf, Jirgi Zaydan, Amin Rihani, and Sa'adeh's father,

Dr. Khalil Sa'adeh. The movement was perceived as an embodiment of the new-age principles of the French Revolution and, by some, as a temporary refuge for political and national agitation. See Souhail Suleiman, *Athar al-Banna'een al-Ahrar fi al-Adab al-lubnani* (The Impact of the Freemasonry on Lebanese Literature: 1860–1950). Beirut: Noufal Press, 1993.

63 Sa'adeh, *al-Athar al-Kamilah* (Complete Works). Vol. 16. Beirut: SSNP Cultural Bureau, n.d.: 185.

64 Reproduced in *al-Bina'*, Beirut, 11 July, 1992: 9–10.

65 Ibid.

66 Ibid.

67 Ibid.

68 George Orwell, *Notes on Nationalism*. London: Polemic, 1945.

69 See in this regard Daniel Pipes, *The Hidden Hand: Middle Eastern Fears of Conspiracy*. New York: St. Martin's Press, 1998.

70 Vamik D. Volkan, "The Need to Have Enemies and Allies: A Developmental Approach." *Political Psychology*, Vol. 6, No. 2, Special Issue: A Notebook on the Psychology of the U.S.-Soviet Relationship (Jun., 1985): 219–247. Also, *The Need to have Enemies and Allies*. Northvale, NJ: Jason Aronson, 1988.

71 Ted Goertzel, "Belief in Conspiracy Theories." *Political Psychology* 15 (1994): 733–744.

72 Juliet al-Mir Sa'adeh, *Mudhakkirat al-Amina la-Ula* (Memoirs). Beirut: Dar Kutub, 2004: 110.

73 Ibid.

74 Hisham Sharabi, *al-Jamr wa al-Rimad* (Embers and Ashes). Beirut: Dar Tali'a: 1978.

75 Abdullah Qubarsi, *op. cit.,* 53.

76 Juliet al-Mir Sa'adeh, *Mudhakkirat al-Amina la-Ula* (Memoirs): 124–5.

77 Ibid., 125.

78 Clifford Bob and Sharon Erickson Nepstad, "Kill a Leader, Murder a Movement? Leadership and Assassination in Social Movements." *American Behavioral Scientist,* 50 (2007): 1380.

79 Eyal Zisser, *Lebanon: The Challenge of Independence*. London: I. B. Tauris, 2000: 177.

80 Ibid., 183–3.

81 Ibid., 185.

82 Ibid., 183.

83 Ibid.

84 Ibid.

85 Ibid.

86 Ibid., 177.

87 Ibid., 176.

88 Ibid., 188.

89 Ibid., 183–4.

90 See Youmna Asseily and Ahmad Asfahani, *A Face in the Crowd: The Secret Papers of Emir Farid Chehab, 1942–1972*. London: Stacey International, 2001.

91 Ibid., 186.

92 Ibid., 177.

93 Eyal Zisser, *Lebanon: The Challenge of Independence*. London: I. B. Tauris, 2000: 167.

94 *The New York Times*, July 19, 1949.

95 Christian Davenport, "State Repression and Political Order." *The Annual Review of Political Science,* Vol. 10 (2007): 1–23.

96 See Donatella Della Porta and Mario Diani, *Social Movements: An Introduction.* Malden, MA: Blackwell, 1999.

97 See Charles Tilly, *From Mobilization to Revolution.* Reading, MA: Addison-Wesley 1978.

98 See Vincent Boudreau, *Resisting Dictatorship: Repression and Protest in Southeast Asia.* Cambridge: Cambridge University Press, 2004.

99 Clifford Bob and Sharon Erickson Nepstad, "Kill a Leader, Murder a Movement? Leadership and Assassination in Social Movements." *American Behavioral Scientist,* 50 (2007): 1370.

100 Clifford Bob and Sharon Erickson Nepstad, "Kill a Leader, Murder a Movement? Leadership and Assassination in Social Movements." *American Behavioral Scientist,* 50 (2007): 1375.

101 See Len Oakes, *Prophetic Charisma: The Psychology of Revolutionary Religious Personalities.* Syracuse: Syracuse University Press, 1997.

102 Bob and Nepstad, *op. cit.*, 1379.

103 See Helen Fein, "Life-Integrity Violations and Democracy in the World." *Human Rights Quarterly*, Vol. 17, No. 1 (1995): 170–191.

104 Thus, Davenport and Armstrong assert that only when democratic institutions exist in combination do they mutually reinforce one another to prevent states from engaging in repression: "Until there is a particular combination of institutions and behavioral factors in place, authorities will not be compelled to respect human rights. Below the critical point, the constraints are not comprehensive or severe enough to deter repressive action nor are the social control mechanisms well enough situated to provide viable alternatives for state repression." Davenport and Armstrong, "Democracy and the Violation of Human Rights: A Statistical Analysis from 1976–1996." *American Journal of Political Science*, Vol. 48, No. 3 (2004): 538–54.

105 Alyssa Prorok, "Still More Murder in the Middle? A Reassessment of Repression in Mixed Regimes." Paper presented at the annual meeting of the APSA 2008 Annual Meeting, Hynes Convention Center, Boston, Massachusetts, 28 Aug., 2008.

106 *Al-Massa'*, Beirut, 18 November, 1935.

107 Anis Sayigh argues that the plan to get rid of Sa'adeh was conceived the moment his plane touched the tarmac at Beirut Airport on 2 March, 1947. See his *Anis Sayegh a'n Anis Sayegh* (Autobiography). London: Riad El-Rayyes Books, 2006.

108 Yet doubters remain: "But it must be remembered that the Phalanges, though generally cooperating with Khouri, were opponents of Sulh." Eyal Zisser, *Lebanon the Challenge of Independence.* London: I. B. Tauris Publishers, 2000: 184. True, but in the days leading up to the Jummaizeh incident Premier Sulh and the Kataib were on good terms and had actually struck a deal for unity and cooperation.

109 In 1948 Sa'adeh told his followers: "Our objective is not to get rid of the government or those in power, but rather to establish a new system for national life in its totality. And in this clear endeavor it was difficult for us to find a single group among the opposition forces willing to understand this conception and to join us in our pursuit of it." Antun Sa'adeh, *al-Muhadarat al-Ashr* (The Ten Lectures). Beirut: SSNP Publications, 1978: 147.

110 See U.S. Congress, Senate, Select Committee to Study Governmental Operations with Respect to Intelligence Activities, *Alleged Assassination Plots Involving Foreign Leaders*, with an introduction by Frank Church (New York, 1976).

111 Michal Belknap (ed.), *American Political Trials*. Westport: Greenwood Press, 1994: 179.

112 See Michal Belknap, *Cold War Political Justice: The Smith Act, the Communist Party and American Civil Liberties*. Westport: Greenwood Press, 1977.

113 See Julius Ruiz, *Franco's Justice: Repression in Madrid After the Spanish Civil War*. London: Oxford University Press, 2005: 9.

114 In *Istijwab Jumblatt al-tarikhi lil-hukuma hawla istishhad Sa'adeh ome 1949* (Jumblatt's Historic Interpellation to the [Lebanese] Government over Sa'adeh's Martyrdom in 1949). Beirut: SSNP, 1987.

115 William Hanchett, *The Lincoln Murder Conspiracies*. Urbana: University of Illinois Press, 1992: 242.

116 Peter Dale Scott, *Deep Politics and the Death of JFK*. Berkeley: University of California, 1996: 6–7.

7

REPERCUSSIONS

It is probable that the authors of the plan to eliminate Sa'adeh did not visualize all the potential implications of such an undertaking. Two scenarios have emerged about their state of thinking: (1) that the potential for retribution and political unrest was likely to be negligible once Sa'adeh had been exterminated; and (2) that execution would create a break point from which his followers would be unlikely to recover quickly. "All too frequently," wrote Bob and Nepastad, "governments kill social movement leaders in an attempt to halt challenges to state power. Sometimes, such repression yields its intended effect; other times, it produces a powerful backlash, strengthening mass commitment and bolstering protest."[1] In the case of Antun Sa'adeh, elimination produced divergent outcomes. On the one hand, it deprived his followers of a strong leader and disrupted the function and administrative unity of the party; on the other, it let loose a torrent of anger against the regime that proved difficult to contain and cost lives.

From a strictly Lebanese perspective, the saga fostered two major tendencies: a disposition towards authoritarianism aimed at critics of the regime, and another towards piecemeal reforms to deflect attention away from the real issues and to placate an emerging public agenda. Both aspects were the function of a concerted drive by the Khoury regime to re-assert its central authority over the country and frighten the opposition into submission. It succeeded only tentatively with the first and failed miserably with the second, quite the opposites of what it had intended to achieve.

This chapter explores the repercussions of the Sa'adeh saga in its effects on individuals as well as on the wider polity. Though political consequences are sometimes difficult to identify with any certainty because of the complexity of Lebanese politics, other outcomes were more tangible, particularly at the military institutional level, which witnessed a decisive change in its scale of activity, and at the national press level, which gained in importance and identity despite strict censorship and physical intimidation of journalists and editors.

It is important to note that the event, the trauma and tremors, the shocks and the solitude, the criminality of the act and the callousness of the authorities continue to haunt the Lebanese State to this day. At times, as in 1958,[2] the wounds showed signs of recovery, but it was always ephemeral dictated by political interest rather than genuine forgiveness.

The Impact on Lebanon

Sa'adeh's execution produced no discernable changes in Lebanon's political system. There is little indication that the saga had any salutary effect on the political administration of the country or on the thinking of the Lebanese people, as evidenced by their general apathy. The Khoury regime, though shaken, remained intact, daily life returned to normality and, apart from a vociferous press, most Lebanese seemed eager to put the matter behind them and get on with life. It does not mean that the saga passed quickly and unnoticeably. Press revelations about the government kept the affair politically alive and helped to expand its outcome. The press intensified the crisis of the regime not only by what it did or said, but also by provoking more blunders from the government.

1. Regime Austerity

In the first place, the saga introduced a dynamic and unpredictable element into the country's dominant political culture. It led to changes in the governing style of the Khoury regime and gave the government fresh justification for draconian laws along the whole range of the political spectrum. Any person known to have shown sympathy for the rebels was dismissed from positions of public influence. Suspect soldiers and army officers were degraded or repatriated. The repression even entered schools where teachers were subjected to a new code of conduct penalizing them for infractions of state orders. Worst hit was the Lebanese press, which became an instant target of various intimidating and censorship rules designed to silence it into submission. Intimidation was carried out against newspaper owners or key editors deemed by the authorities as hostile to 'national security' or 'neighborly Arab relations.' At the same time, Lebanese authorities revived older censorship rules and threatened to shut down newspapers if they failed to adhere to censor's instructions.[3] These instructions included foremost a strict ban on Sa'adeh's ideology and his saga. News about the SNP was also among the forbidden topics. Certain words and complete paragraphs were systematically censored to render targeted articles totally incomprehensible or to stifle criticism of the regime. Any subtle expressions of sympathy to Sa'adeh were strictly controlled or banned.[4]

Strict control over printed material was also exercised by invoking a particular clause in the Press Law dealing with the licensing and distribution of newspapers in the country. Through this clause, the Lebanese government could prohibit publications from entering the country or confiscate any material sent from overseas if it determined that the publication contravened censorship rules. Thus, on 28 August, a decree was issued proscribing the overseas weekly newspaper *al-Alam al-Arabi* (The Arab World) from entering Lebanese territory "because it publishes news about the Syrian Social National Party."[5] Another casualty of the decree was the Paris-based *al-Arab* newspaper, but there were other casualties as well.[6] The main targets of these bannings were Lebanese expatriate journalists who had the freedom to condemn the regime more openly than their counterparts back home. South American Syro-Lebanese diaspora journalists were particularly active in this regard owing to their personal acquaintance with Sa'adeh during his expatriate years among them. Officials also kept a close watch for signs of agitation and subversion in the publishing and printing presses of Beirut. They revived an earlier practice of forcing bookstores to hand over banned material. A short book about Sa'adeh's life entitled "from al-Mahd to Glory" was apparently seized just as it was leaving the printing building and the author, Naim al-Zublu', as well as the printer's owners were detained and interrogated.[7]

Lebanese newspapers, on the whole, had no qualms about censorship of material dealing with sensitive military secrets or matters affecting security. But when censors became excessively touchy and capricious in their application of the law it turned the government into a laughing stock and drew cynical polemics from the press. In one polemic an author, using the penname of 'shahid' (martyr), addresses a hypothetical Human Rights Council of the United Nation saying: "You ask about human rights in Lebanon. Well, let me assure you that human rights in this country are protected – in fact, sanctified . . . A citizen has only to say something or to dot down anything and it is all the way to a prison. More than that, he has the right to choose how he wants to die."[8]

The Khoury regime also implemented specific measures to bring the state bureaucracy to heel. Public servants, especially in the military and security departments, were directly affected, even career men who had nothing to do with recent events. Conducted under an established law that made it unlawful for a government employee to have membership in any political organization, it aimed to eliminate public servants with markedly SNP records without permitting the entry of those with the slightest SNP or Communist leanings. All sorts of standards were applied. The procedure often deteriorated into political witch-hunting and flagrant denials of justice. There were no appeal boards to review cases and no avenues of relief for sufferers, which created enormous hardship for the dismissed persons and their families. In some cases, suspects were indicted and tried and sent to prison or degraded to lower-paid jobs on flimsy evidence. Naturally, members of the armed forces were the worst hit.

The Government then swung the cleaver in the direction of political parties. In a move designed to undercut a growing threat from militant groups, it declared that all political parties in the country would be disbanded until further notice. Brought to a crisis "by the armed rebellion of the Syrian Popular Party,"[9] the matter quickly developed into a public debate over the authority of the state and the continued existence of paramilitary groups. Naturally, political parties were all up in arms about the proposition, especially the militant Lebanese Phalange which expressed its opposition to it in a philosophical way:

> Rumors have increased that the Government is going to dissolve all parties, including the Phalange. That is easier said than done. It is as if dissolving the parties which are working against Lebanon were the same thing as dissolving parties which are working for Lebanon. In this age of independence in which we are living, this report about dissolving all parties has a bad effect on the nation.[10]

In reply, the press friendly to the Government argued no republic can hope to live in which political organizations, no matter how loyal, maintain private armed forces.[11] The issue exploded again when authorities clashed with the militant Phalange organization in response to the wounding of two port workers for making "undue noise" in front of the

Phalange headquarters.[12] The pro-government press seized the moment to renew its call for the dissolution of political parties and the concentration of authority in the Lebanese Government as the only legitimate policing entity in the country. However, the government stifled the debate by watering-down the proposition. It now said that what it was really proposing was that paramilitary organizations should in the immediate future change their operations to become normal political parties. The move was justified on the ground that "such a change would present as a competitor to the Communist menace an active example of democratic procedure."[13] Both the Lebanese Phalange and the Najjade, the country's largest paramilitary organizations at the time, acquiesced in the new law and promised to became regular political parties. Other parties were not so lucky, particularly the Communist Party. It was brutally suppressed after authorities learned that Communists, organized on a secret cell basis, were operating a regular program among Palestinians both inside and outside the refugee camps. Though it did not reach the intensity of the anti-SNP campaign, the drive against the Communists deprived the Lebanese body politic of the only two clearly identifiable secular organizations in the country (the SNP and the Communist Party), and left the political field wide open to sectarian forces.

2. The Military Establishment

Another important and largely unstudied aspect is the extra new attention that the Khoury regime began to give to the armed forces and other agencies of the military establishment. Up until the Sa'adeh saga, the Lebanese state appeared content with comparatively small armed forces and was one of the least active buyers in the arms market. The Lebanese army, numbering less than 5000 officers and men, was widely seen as a relic of the French Mandate, a toy army that scarcely sufficed for the maintenance of domestic law and order, let alone defense against external aggression.[14] In the face of inter-communal quarrels, its function was almost wholly domestic either to umpire elections or help the gendarmerie. After the July uprising and Sa'adeh's execution, the Khoury regime instituted policies which emphasized the modernization and expansion of the armed forces and the acquisition of new military hardware. In a radical departure from traditional Lebanese policies on military matters, based as it was on little government and minimal spending on public services, including the armed forces and security apparatus, the government decided to increase the annual military budget and to mechanize the army with new weaponry:

> In view [of] local disturbances caused by attacks on isolated gendarmerie posts by well armed bands of Socialist Popular Party [sic], Lebanese Government considers its army must be strengthened to prevent possible widespread rebellion. Government has approached Legation requesting it ascertain whether Lebanese application for purchase communications equipment for army might be favorably received. It also desires purchase [of] turret assemble complete with primary and secondary armament and ammunition and certain turning gear components to condition and complete 20 Sherman medium tanks now being reconditioned in Lebanon.[15]

At the same time, the regime realized that without a devoted, modern army it could not impose its will on a disunited population. To insure the loyalty of the army, on 10 July it announced an additional US$4,000,000 for national defense and, for the first time, the introduction of universal compulsory military service.[16] A government communiqué reported that "the army will be reinforced with new units, as will the gendarmerie. Both also will be provided with new weapons." It also said that military training would be introduced in all Lebanese schools for all able-bodied men. According to a *New York Times* report, the "Government decided after the brief armed rebellion of the Syrian Popular Party and the execution of its leader, Antone Saadeh, that the time had come to do away with paramilitary political groups as a potential menace to the state."[17]

The Sa'adeh saga, thus, brought the national army and other security agencies to the forefront of Lebanese politics. It helped to establish them as an important pillar of the state and led to the veneration of the army as the symbolic incarnation of the country. It was the first open and decisive incident in which the army took on a role outside its nominal domestic duties. Moreover, the Lebanese army's success against the uprising, in spite of its size and the relative paucity of its means, bolstered its image as a truly national institution deeply committed to the existing order. It demonstrated that the military was as critical to conflict termination and nation building in Lebanon as any other institution.

3. Retribution

There is doubt whether the Khoury regime grasped the full implications of using police-state tactics in a liberal environment such as that of

Lebanon. Any persecution is a heavy drain on the social energy of a people, the resources of the national economy, and upon the ability of a government to perform what may be called more ordinary functions.[18] Moreover, a government is seldom completely effective in trying to suppress certain types of behavior over a short period of time. It "frequently results in consequences that were little dreamed of when a given policy was adopted."[19] It may even elicit a hazardous reaction:

> The very psychic will to suppress, even if it does not reach the stage of using political power to attain the end, tends to give the ideas under fire and the emotional reaction surrounding them an importance that they otherwise would not have. Emotional reaction produces an alternating fungus-like growth of further depth of feeling.[20]

The hard-line policy of the Khoury regime quickly ran its course and, by the end of 1949, it was largely over. Changing public sentiments undoubtedly had a lot to do with this: there were many critics of the strategy, including many figures not generally noted for their liberalism. Many ordinary Lebanese became fed up with the restrictions imposed on them and simply wanted to attend to daily cares. At the first sign of resistance, the regime became less decisive in pursuing its goals and its policy of austerity slowly gave way to compromise and concessions. This was a critical mistake. It tarnished the image of the Khoury regime as a serious government. Concessions and indecisiveness in such circumstances can be easily construed merely as a sign of weakness: "It should be clear that indecisiveness is one of the greatest faults of those who embark on strong political policies."[21] Indeed, as soon as the Khoury regime began to waver from its hard-line policy a new situation set in, providing Sa'adeh's supporters with the long-needed excuse to retaliate.

Even before the start of this second phase, Sa'adeh's execution had already fostered an atmosphere of fear in the Lebanese state. Following Zaim's cold-blooded execution in Syria (see below) reports quickly spread that the SNP had regrouped under the leadership of the elusive George Abd al-Massih,[22] Lebanon's most wanted person at the time, and that it had made Solh and Khoury their next targets of revenge for Sa'adeh's death. To add to government woes, Lebanese newspapers started to cover Syrian Nationalist activities in Syria and elsewhere even at the risk of prosecution under the new censorship restrictions.[23] Worried by the "subversive" reports, the Khoury regime intervened to halt the publishing of information related to Sa'adeh and the SNP by expanding the screening process, but to no avail. The press in Lebanon reported on.

On 10 August, a report about Zaim's betrayal of Sa'adeh appeared in *The New York Times* claiming that the SNP "had made the assassination of Marshal Zayim their priority No. 1."[24] It added: "Marshal Zayim now never moves without a whole phalanx of guards and the President and Premier in Lebanon are guarded very heavily day and night."[25] Ten days later *an-Nahar* disobeyed the censorship rules and republished the report in its entirety in Arabic. It did not say in as many words what it hoped to achieve from that, but the message was loud and clear: the SNP was far from being a spent force and was making a comeback. A subtle reference in the report about how the "present Lebanese regime was heartily abhorred by a large part of the Lebanese population because of its corruption and incompetence"[26] was yet another impetus. The report demonstrated the limitations of the Khoury regime and aroused the instincts of the SNP for reprisal.

Early in March, 1950, the party struck back with an assassination attempt on Solh. The attack happened while the Premier was attending a banquet in his honor given by a prominent Lebanese citizen, but missed its mark. Two bystanders were killed and three others were wounded, not including the assailant, who was injured in the shootout and arrested. He was later tried and sentenced to death, but this was commuted to life imprisonment after the Premier withdrew all personal charges against him in an attempt to placate the SNP.[27] The party did not reciprocate. After the incident Solh would rarely venture outside even as the force of guards around him was increased for extra protection. He remained a man marked for murder.[28]

Unbeknownst to Solh was that another SNP member was staking him with the same deadly intent. Michel el-Dik had vowed to Sa'adeh's wife to assassinate the Lebanese Premier at the first opportunity, but the security cordon set up around Solh had proved too strong to make any attempt feasible. In early July 1951, he followed Solh to Amman, the Jordanian capital, accompanied by one Mohammed Adib as-Salah, a Palestinian ex-sergeant in the Arab Legion. The pair was soon joined by Aspiro Wadiah, a sympathetic Jordanian citizen who acted as their chauffeur. As Solh drove out to Amman airport in Abdullah's limousine under heavy security, at a lonely stretch of the road, a car with the three men in it drew ahead of the limousine and opened fire immediately, with one assailant calling out "take this from Sa'adeh." Solh was shot through the jaw and heart and died instantly. The assassins Mohammed as-Salah and Michel el-Dik then turned the guns on themselves while Aspiro escaped on foot with the Jordanian police in hot pursuit. Mohammed as-Salah died instantly and Michel el-Dik, who was taken to a military hospital unconscious, committed suicide soon after at the same hospital by ripping open his wounds and falling off his bed. When news of the assassination reached Beirut, heavy rioting broke out in the city:

> The toll of rioting here was believed to be two dead and fifteen injured. Hundreds of shop windows were broken; cars, streetcars and buses were partially wrecked. Eyewitnesses said the rioters had broken windows in 300 stores on the principal business street of the city and a great deal of damage was done in other sections. Damaged automobiles stood empty throughout the central portion of the city. Heavy police forces then took over the center, but the situation remained tense. The rioting was brought under control when the military intervened with armored cars and armed patrols. A heavy guard was placed around certain sensitive points, including the Jordanian Legation. Six heavy tanks took up position in the central Square of the Martyrs, together with two armored cars. Other armored cars patrolled the streets.[29]

As the coffin bearing Solh's body made its way through the crowded silent streets of Beirut, demonstrators shouted "Abdullah, where is Riad?" A week later, on a visit to the Dome of the Rock in Jerusalem, King Abdullah was reported saying: "If Riad had come to Jerusalem, as I asked him, he would not be dead." Ironically, they were Abdullah's last words before his own murderer's bullets found him.[30]

The third casualty of the Sa'adeh saga was Youssef Charbel, the Public Prosecutor at Sa'adeh's trial. He was shot on 16 February, 1954 by two SNP partisans under strict instructions to inflict maximum bodily harm rather than kill him. Charbel was paralyzed by the shooting and resigned his post as Chief of State Council. The man charged with the investigation, Colonel Nour ad-Din al-Rufaee', became delusional after the incident. Fearing for his life over his part in Sa'adeh's killing, he gave the SNP a written undertaking to drop all charges against the perpetrators of the Charbel shooting in return for a vow to spare his life.[31]

The SNP policy of targeted killing had strategic effects on Lebanese politics. It increased the feeling among most Lebanese that the long arm of the SNP was capable of reaching their most intimate surroundings. It touched the highest ranks of the political leadership and provided retribution and revenge for a group under siege. Although the campaign was limited it played havoc with the authorities and forced open the possibility for political compromise. A senior SNP officer who lived through this period conveyed the atmosphere of fear and confusion it created:

> One day Solh was attending a major banquet on the banks of al-Qassimiyyah held by some of his acquaintances and among the invited was Archbishop Bulus Khoury, an uncle of my wife . . . No sooner had they sat down Solh called out to the Archbishop: "My Grace. Put in a good word for me with your brother-in-law, Abdullah". The Archbishop gave him a disapproving look. Yet Solh returned: "The Party wants to kill me and Abdullah can save me."

Although the SNP publicly distanced itself from the reprisals and maintained throughout that they were entirely the work of embittered individuals, most Lebanese remained unconvinced. Yet, their reaction to the killings was rather subdued. Apart from the riots that broke out upon Solh's assassination, which were directed largely against the Jordanian and Lebanese authorities,[32] people did not turn out on the streets to protest the party's reprisals. Neither the government nor the immediate victims of the reprisals attempted to retaliate, but some Lebanese expressed their discontent with the practice. This would seem to have been due as much to the dwindling support of the Khoury regime as to the empathy that Sa'adeh's execution was beginning to generate. Perceptions of the killings as isolated incidents aimed at specific individuals rather than the State was also a contributing factor. On a different level, the reprisal campaign helped to refocus the attention of press and politics on Sa'adeh and encouraged wider interest in his case. The SNP achieved notoriety and became a feared organization. Its morale lifted and its Lebanese branch rejuvenated despite the legal ban imposed on it by the Khoury regime.

4. The Downfall of the Khoury Regime

A final issue that must be addressed is to what extent did the Sa'adeh controversy directly contribute to the Khoury regime's downfall? Although the Sa'adeh saga could not be directly linked to the 'revolution' that overthrew Khoury in September 1951, the atmosphere of discontent and instability it fostered in Lebanon help weaken his regime politically ahead of its demise. This happened in a number of ways. First, the fiasco of the trial and execution process resulted in a loss of faith in the administration and helped to revive and expand the disgruntlement with the regime. It provided an essential public forum and refuge for criticism of the government against a background of eroding legitimacy and growing popular frustration. The government's response to the saga of trying to restrain the press by authoritarian means, such as suspending the publication of newspapers which had published articles offensive to the administration and arresting their editors, "were counterproductive as they were interpreted by the public as reflecting loss of control on the part of the administration, and ultimately served not to curb but only to increase the wave of public criticism against it."[33]

Second, the saga contributed to the administration's downfall by driving to the opposition a substantial number of influential Lebanese. Under Sa'adeh the SNP stood outside the power-struggle between the opposition and the government. Although the party and the government never could get along and were separated by deep-seated ideological and political issues, the Lebanese opposition was hardly able to benefit from the SNP. The tenor of its opposition to the Khoury regime rose and fell during this period but never lapsed into open support for the opposition. After Sa'adeh's execution, however, the SNP placed its full political weight behind the opposition. Although battered by the loss of its leader and government persecution, its defection at such a critical moment consolidated the public agenda for change and gave added momentum to the crisis facing the Khoury regime. Viewed in broader perspective, the SNP's new discourse contributed to the president's downfall both in the sense that it had discredited the President's authority amongst a sizeable number of Lebanese in 1947,[34] and also because it contributed themes that were later revived, not always with acknowledgement,[35] by Jumblatt and others in 1952.[36] The SNP was also probably the first political party in Lebanon to raise the idea of a united front against Khoury.[37] It was tendered during the parliamentary elections of 1947, but received no more than a lukewarm response because politicians "were motivated by personal gains and not by nationalist or collective principles of any kind."[38]

The assassination of Riad Solh is another factor worthy of consideration. Solh's death in that year has been judged as the single biggest blow to Khoury and the factor that precipitated the downfall of his regime.[39] As Wade R. Goria has succinctly put it, "While Solh lived, and continued to maintain tolerable relations with Khouri, the President's position vis-a-vis the opposition remained tenable. Solh's death undermined Khouri's position completely."[40] Michael Hudson presents a similar view:

> . . . the President might well have served out his second term – in spite of the domestic corruption, the Palestine problem, and the radicalization of politics – had he been able to maintain his alliance with Riad Sulh. Their separation and then Sulh's assassination in July 1951 eroded Khoury's support among the Sunnite masses.[41]

Solh's assassination deprived the administration of the only leader to whom most Lebanese Muslims – especially Sunnis – could gravitate. His death also robbed Khoury of a powerful statesman whose enormous influence in the Chamber of Deputies and political skills had been an important pillar of strength and a source of stability for the regime.

Finally, the SSNP contributed to Khoury's downfall through its participation in the National Socialist Front (NSF). Formed after the general election of 1951, the NSF was a loose coalition of various groups and politicians disillusioned by Khoury's presidency. In the summer of 1952, after a series of cabinet crisis which culminated in the resignation of the Prime Minister, Sami Sulh,[42] the Front organized a country-wide two-day general strike against the President after he refused to step down despite the growing opposition to his presidency. It was at the height of this strike that Khoury finally tendered his resignation.

The SSNP was represented in the NSF by Ghassan Tueini, a long-time member of the party and editor-in-chief of the well-known daily newspaper, *an-Nahar*.[43] He was elected to the Chamber of Deputies in the parliamentary elections of 1951 along with Pierre Emile Edde,[44] who also won his seat in the district of al-Matn with the support of the SSNP.[45] Through Tueini, the SSNP was able to participate in the regular meetings of the National Socialist Front and contribute to its program.[46] The heavy turnout of supporters that the party achieved at a mass rally organized by the NSF at Dayr al-Qamar in 1952 highlighted its influence still further. Mustafa Abd al-Satir describes in his *Ayyam wa Qadiyya* the atmosphere at the rally as follows:[47]

> The government and public opinion were stunned by the rebirth of the party which they thought had ended with Sa'adeh. This revival revealed itself in a huge party gathering at the western entrance of Dayr al-Qamar which then marched in serried ranks that totalled thousands like an irresistible flood until it submerged the festival square after filling the streets and the other squares of the town. This demonstration of strength gave considerable impetus to the organizers of the rally and in fact dealt the final blow to President Khoury's will to fight on . . .[48]

Even if the actions of the SSNP did not decisively precipitate the downfall of the Khoury regime, they clearly contributed to it and accelerated it. When the president finally bowed out, the party greeted the end of his rule with a sense of relief and renewed optimism. The SSNP never gave up hope of returning to Lebanon, but its chances were slender as long as Khoury and Solh were in charge.[49] During the parliamentary election of 1951, the President tried to win its favour, but failed.[50] Its assassination of Riad Solh six months later, despite his rift with the President, ruled out any further contact between them.

The Impact on Syria

Sa'adeh's betrayal and subsequent execution at the hands of the Khoury regime is generally considered to be among the contributing factors to Zaim's blood-spattered downfall in August 1949. Planned well and convincingly executed, the handover dangerously weakened Zaim's standing with many of his supporters and with other Arab governments and gave his opponents a powerful new reason to oust him. He was disparaged as a sell-out, a betrayer of the nation, not only for the crudeness of his treachery but also for the callousness with which he excused and justified his action.

Zaim attempted to dodge the treachery charge by claiming that Sa'adeh was arrested on Lebanese soil during the rebellion. A public statement issued by the press office of the Syrian government on 11 July stated that Sa'adeh was not handed over to Lebanon, but was arrested by the Lebanese authorities while circulating along the border between the two countries, and was apprehended in Lebanese territory. As an extra precaution, Zaim ordered the local Syrian press to publish only the official version of events and pressured the Lebanese government into backing his account. The Lebanese leadership acquiesced because it was part of the deal for Sa'adeh's surrender. But the Lebanese press got wind of the deal and published the story as it really happened:

> True to their agreement, the Lebanese authorities announced that Sa'adeh had been arrested on the Lebanese side of the Syrian frontier, indicating that he had been caught escaping from Lebanon. But the censorship in Damascus fumbled and some papers there published the news that he had been arrested inside Syria, and one or two Lebanese papers, ignoring censorship, published the news of his arrest in Damascus.[51]

Diplomatic fumbling from the Lebanese side may have also inadvertently contributed to the embarrassment, probably to humiliate Zaim:

> A few hours too late the Lebanese reacted with an inspired report that the Damascus arrest stories were mistaken. By that time, however, the chief of police had talked personally to foreign correspondents – off the record – and boasted of his exploit. Riad es-Solh had also told his intimates, who told everybody, and even Marshal Zayim does not seem to have realized how important it was to keep the matter secret.[52]

News of Sa'adeh's betrayal quickly damaged Zaim's reputation and intensified the feeling on all sides that he could not be trusted. It shattered every Arab idea of honor: "Even among those who had no use for Saadeh, Zaim was considered to have violated the traditions of Arab hospitality by betraying his guest who had sought the safety of his house – something not taken lightly by a people who are immensely proud of their record in that respect."[53] As disgust mounted, his closest confidants began to desert him, including his brother-in-law and first secretary, Nadhir Fansa: "From the moment Zaim surrendered Sa'adeh I began to distance myself from him, and his regime began to live out its final weeks."[54]

Sa'adeh's betrayal also precipitated Zaim's downfall by alienating a group of army officers who might have supported him in a counteraction against an attempted coup. The SNP commanded strong support in the

Syrian officer corps, including well-known figures like Salah Jadid, Fadhlallah Abu Mansour, and Captain Adib Shishakli, who became a President of Syria in 1953. These officers joined the growing rank of disgruntled military men offended by Zaim's extravagance and arbitrary promotion of officers loyal to him personally.[55] Once a safety valve for the regime, they became a heavy and dangerous burden on it. And so, when the moment to depose Zaim finally came in a pre-dawn coup, they became its spearhead with one purpose in mind: to avenge Sa'adeh's betrayal.

The main core of conspirators that would overthrow Zaim consisted of Colonel Sami al-Hinnawi; Captain Khalid Jada, Hinnawi's aide and bodyguard; Captain Islam Mraywad, an Iraqi who had become a pilot in the Syrian Air Force; Captain Muhammad Ma'ruf; Captain Muhammed Diyab; As'ad Talas, Hinnawi's brother-in-law and the liaison between the army officers and politicians during the preparation and execution of the coup, and First Lieutenant Fadhlallah Abu Mansour, who was an active member of the SNP and commander-in-charge of the armored car company in the First Brigade which was to furnish the troops to be used in the coup. Angry at the betrayal of Saadeh, and believing that he and Amin Abu Assaf were on the list for dismissal from the army, Abu Mansour decided to assassinate Husni az-Zaim even before the idea of a coup was raised. The occasion he selected for that was a tour of the front by Zaim with some Tunisian guests. He placed his weapon, ammunition, and several days' supply of fuel and provisions into his jeep, and followed Zaim's party from Ayn Ziwan, where they had reviewed the army, to Jisr Banat Yakoub, where al-Hinnawi's command post was located. When Zaim went forward to inspect the front line position, Abu Mansour stopped his jeep by the side of the road and waited for Zaim's return to the command post where he could kill him and have a good chance of escaping afterwards. But Alam ad-Din Qawwas, al-Hinnawi's second-in-command, spotted the lurking officer and foiled the operation by impounding him long enough for Zaim to depart for Damascus with his guests.

Shortly after that incident, the First Armored Battalion was ordered to move to Suwayda, capital city of Jebel ad-Duruz. Amin Abu Assaf and Fadhlallah Abu Mansour construed this to be the first step in their liquidation. They believed that Major Husni Jarras, the commanding officer of the Jebel ad-Duruz military area and a loyal supporter of Zaim, would take command of the battalion from them once they reached the mountain; and that they would then be issued orders to report to Damascus. When the battalion reached Sheikh Miskin, Abu Mansour halted the armored car company and ordered it to rest. After consulting with Abu Assaf, he decided to delay their march until they could determine whether conditions in the capital were reasonably favorable for the immediate execution of a military coup. The key factor for them, and for the other conspirators, was that Zaim would be at home, for then he could be quickly located and taken into custody before mobilizing his loyal forces.

In order to further delay the movement of the armored unit to Jebel ad-Duruz, Hinnawi issued orders for it to move to Antara under a concocted military pretext. Pursuant to those orders, the move was made the following day, placing the battalion in the same town which had served as the staging area and headquarters for Zaim's coup. A week later, at 11 o'clock at night on 13 August, the conspirators decided on the final details of the coup d'etat which had been set for that very night. Specific missions were assigned at one o'clock in the morning. The key mission – that of the arrest of the President of the Republic, Husni az-Zaim – was entrusted to his would-be assassin of a short time before, Lieutenant Fadlallah Abu Mansour. For the accomplishment of his task, he was given the command of a force of six armored cars and sixty truck-mounted infantry. All other missions were to be held back until it was seen whether Abu Mansour had succeeded.

The column reached the outskirts of Damascus at 01.45 hours on the morning of 14 August when it stopped for last minute coordination. Sami al-Hinnawi gave Abu Mansour his final pep talk and informed him that the headquarters would wait there until his mission had been completed and the remainder of the operation was thus assured success. Abu Mansour led his force through the streets of Damascus until he reached Abu Rammaneh Street, in which Zaim's residence was located. In order to not alert the guards, the march was then slowed and noise was reduced to a minimum. When the palace was reached, after its guards were arrested and disarmed, the soldiers and armored cars were positioned at the main entrances and around the palace wall. Abu Mansour then pounded on the door of the palace. No response. He pounded again and again until lights finally appeared in the second floor living quarters of Husni az-Zaim, and the President appeared on his balcony. "What is this?"; "Who's there?"; "What's going on?", he screamed. "Surrender immediately," Abu Mansour ordered him, "or I'll destroy this castle on your head."

Zaim retreated into the palace, hastened by a burst from Abu Mansour's submachine gun. Abu Mansour then demolished the lock of the door with another burst from his submachine gun and entered the palace. Zaim was descending the stairs. He had had time only to pull on his military trousers and shoes. When Zaim reached ground-level, Abu Mansour approached him and slapped him viciously with a blow that echoed through the palace. "Don't hit me, mister," protested Zaim. "It's not proper. Have some respect for my military dignity!" Abu Mansour answered him rudely, his trembling voice betraying the nervousness which had prompted the blow; "I am the first to respect military dignity. I believe in it, I sanctify it and I would spill my blood for its sake; but there is no dignity nor honor to one such as you. Didn't you swear on an oath of loyalty to the Leader Saadeh, present your pistol to him as a pledge of your loyalty and then betray him, sending him to his death in violation of your oath?"

"I tell you I'm innocent, son. I was accused of that, but I'm innocent."

"Come on, let's go. There's no time for talk."

Abu Mansour then shoved Zaim in an armored vehicle and raced toward the rendezvous point, where Hinnawi was supposedly waiting, flanked by an armed jeep and a motorcycle. On the way, Zaim tried to weasel himself out of his predicament.

"Fahlallah," he said, "I'm in your hands. I have 80,000 Syrian pounds. Take 60,000 of them for yourself, distribute the other 20,000 among your soldiers, and let me go. Let me get out of the country."

"From where did you get all this wealth?" asked Abu Mansour. "Didn't you say that you entered the government poor and would leave it poor?[56] How did your poverty turn into wealth?"

"I tell you, son" said Zaim, "that I'm innocent. This is a British plot against me and aims at the undermining of the independence of the country."

"Don't worry about the independence of the country," he was told. "We covet it eagerly and know how to preserve it from any harm."

Turning his attention to the four soldiers who were in the armored car in an attempt to enlist their aid, Zaim said: "I swear that I'm innocent. I love you all. I'm a soldier like you."

He was answered by Sergeant Faiz Udwan; "If you loved us, why did you order our discharge without cause while we were at the front fighting the enemy of the country? You don't fear God or love anyone."

"I swear, my brothers, that I'm being abused. The one who discharged you was Abdullah Atfeh, Chief of the General Staff. I issued orders that you be given employment with Tapline."

Abu Mansour ordered him to keep quiet, and a heavy silence fell over the armored car. Zaim looked at Abu Mansour's pistol with its muzzle pointed at his face, then at the submachine guns in the hands of the soldiers, and fear glistened in his eyes.

An hour later, Captain Mraywad and two other officers arrived in an armored car, followed by a large car filled with soldiers. The new arrivals brought two additional prisoners with them: Prime Minister Muhsin al-Barazzi and his son.

The son stayed in the armored car while Muhsin al-Barazzi, dressed in pajamas and shivering from fear and the early morning chill, was led forward. In a trembling voice, he pleaded for his life: "Have mercy on me! I didn't have anything to do with what went on; Have mercy on me! Have mercy on my child! I throw myself on your mercy!"

Captain Mraywad delivered his orders to Abu Mansour: "The High Command sentenced Husni az-Zaim and Muhsin al-Barazzi to death. You must execute the sentence immediately. That is the order of the Council of War."

Abu Mansour seized Husni az-Zaim with his left hand, Muhsin al-Barazzi with his right, and led them to a low area occupied by a cemetery. He stood them side by side, facing toward the east, and placed the soldiers who had accompanied him in the armored car in position to act as a firing squad. Then he stepped back out of the line of fire.

A desperate Muhsin al-Barazzi suddenly screamed: "I beg of you . . . Have mercy on me . . . My child . . . I am innocent." In an attempt to bolster his companion's courage, Husni az-Zaim addressed him in French, "Don't be afraid, they won't kill us. It's impossible." The rearing chatter of the submachine guns sending their bullets into the two condemned men shattered the stillness of the night even as Zaim finished his sentence. Abu Mansour then ordered the corpses loaded into the armored car and took them to the military hospital where they were turned over to a thunderstruck officer of the day. After the bodies were placed in the morgue, Abu Mansour locked the door and pocketed the key. He proceeded to arrest Husni az-Zaim's brother, Bashir, who was in the hospital awaiting an operation. Bashir was subsequently impounded in the infamous Mezze prison and watched SNP members held there following the revolt of the previous June being released later during the same morning.

The Impact on the SNP

Sa'adeh's execution was bound to have an adverse impact on the SNP. A leader's killing creates an obvious break point in any movement's development, and if the leader is of the prophetic kind (in a Weberian sense), as Sa'adeh was, the break can be irreparable. Sa'adeh was acknowledged by the movement itself as undisputed leader and widely considered to be its key visionary and primary strategist. His persuasive visions of social change and advancement, clarity of purpose, and courage in challenging powerful opponents gave him great moral and symbolic authority within the movement and enabled him to galvanize and inspire mass mobilization even in the face of profound adversity. Because of all that, his replacement was bound to be difficult.

There is no question that the Lebanese State killed Sa'adeh with this factor on its mind. Sa'adeh's execution created a dangerous vacuum for the party not only because he was irreplaceable, at least in the eyes of its members, but also because he died before designating a successor. Although the party's leadership eventually overcame this problem by hastily electing George Abdul Massih as its next "President," it never was able to find anyone able to fill Sa'adeh's shoes or to be remotely as popular as him. Abdul Massih was an administrative leader with an aptitude at organizational tasks, but he lacked the flair and intellectual dynamism of Sa'adeh. Moreover, the scope of his authority and profile among the population, and even the movement itself, was much narrower than that of Sa'adeh. As a result, the tight, personalistic bond between leader and follower, so common to the dynamic of Sa'adeh's leadership, deteriorated under the new leader.[57]

Sa'adeh's killing also exercised significant effects on the movement's development. Initially, the event produced a new sense of solidarity among its members and a desire to reunite and resist state repression. The new leader skillfully used Sa'adeh's killing as a catalyst to generate greater mobilization and to establish new organizational bases on which to maintain or expand the party. However, no sooner had the situation calmed down, major problems quickly set in and the deleterious effects of Sa'adeh's loss became more apparent: conflict quickly engulfed the movement's top echelons as secondary figures scrambled for the mantle of leadership and members faltered in factional infighting. Moreover, the party developed new ideological trajectories and drifted waywardly into political currents with which it had few common grounds. As a result, its identity as an independent ideological movement suffered irreparable damage and its development as a whole slowed down.

In Lebanon at least, state repression reduced the political opportunities that facilitated the movement's earlier developments. It made organizing difficult and dangerous, as those who sought to re-activate its organizations or form new ones became easy targets for sanctions. Moreover, it caused ordinary movement participants to drop out to avoid the high costs and risks involved, and created a sense of hopelessness and resignation among those who were stunned by Sa'adeh's execution. But all was not lost. Despite the devastating loss of Sa'adeh, the party rebounded and could be seen back in action in Lebanon as early as 1950. Incensed by Sa'adeh's killing and eager to avenge it through any means, the movement gained unity and strength, even while the state suffered defections. Of course, the movement's strength still paled by comparison to the Lebanese state, and this prolonged the conflict for several more years.

Contrary to the State's expectations, Sa'adeh's killing played an important role in sustaining the party. The reason lies in the nature of repression. Sometimes the killing of a movement's leader may yield the anticipated results for the killers; other times it may produce a powerful backlash:

> At times . . . repression can backfire, leading to broader protest, augmenting movement resources, and ultimately tipping the balance of power against a state. In the wake of harsh repression, such as a leader's killing, mobilization by two broad populations is possible. Most important are actual or potential movement constituents, people from the aggrieved group itself, who usually have the greatest chance of achieving real change within their societies. In addition, third parties sympathetic to but not part of the aggrieved population may also be activated by repression, providing resources, personnel, and moral support that can strengthen a movement.[58]

In this case, state repression worked to the advantage of the SNP in four ways:

(1) By encapsulating the movement's broad grievances in a single dramatic event, repression inadvertently increased awareness of the SNP and created a basis for mobilization by potential but previously un-politicized constituents.
(2) It generated strong emotions around the SNP and created a "moral shock" among both the aggrieved group and the general population.
(3) It strengthened members' militancy as they sought to vindicate their "sunk costs" in a movement and as they perceived fewer options for working within the existing system.
(4) It increased the sense of efficacy and empowerment in the Party by fostering the impression that the authorities felt their power slipping away or considered the party to be a viable threat.

The Lebanese government's ambition to decapitate the SNP by killing its leader may have succeeded were it not for certain fortuitous circumstances. One of those was the overthrow of Husni Zaim in Syria, which re-opened that country up to the Party and provided new resources against the Khoury regime. Had Zaim remained in power, it would have taken the SNP much longer to recover and it may possibly have disintegrated under the strain of Lebanese repression. One of the first acts of the new Syrian regime was to lift all bans on Sa'adeh's wife and release party members from captivity, which gave the SNP a new breathing space to re-consolidate.

Another factor was the Lebanese government's inability to match the execution of the SNP leader with repression of its sub-leaders or to sustain the terror against its mass base. True, the government did crackdown hard on the party after the uprising, but it was low-level repression constrained by scanty resources and inadequate social support. It quickly ran out of steam to the party's advantage. Where even small opportunities remain, as in this case, movements stand a chance of rebirth.[59]

In another respect, Sa'adeh's perception of martyrdom as sometimes necessary in realizing important goals gave meaning to his killing as a tragic but predictable step in the realization of his vision.[60] It enabled the movement to convert him into a martyr after death and to instigate broader attention to its cause among the aggrieved population:

The concept of martyrdom is probably present to some degree in all cultures and can therefore be appropriated by many movements. But some movements may be better prepared than others to incorporate a martyred leader into the movement's story line. Probably the most important factor is the leader's own publicly expressed views of martyrdom. When leaders openly anticipate the possibility of their own murders and frame this as a sacrifice that will strengthen the struggle, they may help the movement transform tragedy into opportunity.[61]

Sa'adeh's regular uses of political imagery associated with martyrdom, encapsulated in clear idioms,[62] enabled the movement to garner its resources to re-galvanize itself. It meant that the party could continue to mobilize even after Sa'adeh's killing, ensuring that his death was not in vain. Moreover, because the martyr concept had broad resonance with Sa'adeh, the SNP was able to portray the execution as a meaningful martyrdom. With help from the Lebanese press, it quickly succeeded in validating Sa'adeh's sacrifice as an act precipitated by his courageous and outspoken views. This translated into solid support for the party, particularly in Syria where support and sympathy for its cause swelled. The party gained political recognition with the election of one of its leaders, Issam Muhairy, to the Chamber, and its strength inside the Syrian military grew further. Such results, reciprocally, gave its crusade inside Lebanon, where it had continued to work secretly and obtrusively under enormous risks,[63] a belated but much-needed boost.

By 1952, the situation had reversed to the evident advantage of the SNP: Riad Solh was there no longer, the Khoury regime had fallen, the Lebanese press had regained its freedom, and the party was back in action. After Chamoun's accession to power, the SNP and the Lebanese state began a new era of cooperation. The party was granted a permit to operate legally and its members who had been in prison were pardoned en masse and released. The party was also allowed to openly take part in parliamentary elections and even succeeded in getting its President, Asad al-Ashqar, elected to the Chamber. So great was the transformation in the relationship between the two sides that by 1958, when law and order broke down in Lebanon, the SNP, aside from Pierre Gemayel's Phalange party, would emerge as the primary backer of the State.[64]

The Impact on the Sa'adeh Family

At the time of his execution, Sa'adeh was married to Juliet al-Mir, a nurse he met during his exile in Argentina in 1941. They had three daughters: Sofia, Alissar and Raghida. Juliet al-Mir was an exceptionally gifted woman and a devoted wife. Unpretentious and modest in her conduct and lifestyle, firm but sympathetic and understanding toward others, she became an extremely dedicated and well-liked individual. She was gracious, even-tempered and of strong character, a person of cheerful disposition, totally devoted to her family and to the upbringing and education of her children. She ran an exemplary household, was industrious and efficient, and had a penchant for neatness and orderliness. There is no doubt that the Sa'adehs were, in many respects, an exceptionally closely knit family.

Sa'adeh always preserved a very close and special relationship with his wife. She was supportive and always there by his side. His cause was also hers. She performed her duties alongside him without grumble and encouraged discipline, industry and diligence, especially in party-work. Even during periods of grief and adversity she placed her husband above herself, providing for him material comfort, care and security. After Sa'adeh's execution, she was elected to the Supreme Council of the Party and remained an active member until her death in 1968. No wonder Sa'adeh insisted on seeing her and the children before execution.

After the Jummaizeh incident, Juliet al-Mir followed her husband to Syria to be by his side. In her recently-published memoirs, she gives a moving account of the hardship she confronted in Damascus trying to link up with Sa'adeh during the uprising:

> I went to the hotel at three in the morning. Yet, I was disturbed. I wanted to be near Sa'adeh. Why shouldn't I? If I went to one of the nationalists' houses to keep my daughters there with the house maid who takes care of them, I could then stay with Sa'adeh. The next day, Sunday, July 3rd, I was paid a visit by several comrades, including Adele Sa'ab. I said to her, "I need to be near Sa'adeh. He will never need me more than he does now." I asked her to give me a room at her place wherein my daughters and their maid could stay for a few days, so I could be with him. I also told her that I could not leave the hotel except with the security officers following me to the hotel door. When I go to the restaurant, they follow me and surround my table. Therefore, I cannot possibly head for

the residence where Sa'adeh is staying. However, she replied, "I am sorry I have rented one of the rooms in the house." "They could stay in the dining room", I returned. "This is an emergency." But, she repeated, "Impossible, sorry."[65]

On 6 July, as the revolution collapsed, Sa'adeh's safety came back to haunt her. Her solitary desire in those singular moments was to be by Sa'adeh's side:

> On Tuesday, news of the failure of the revolution was all across newspapers. I had the same feeling that I sensed the last time I met with Sa'adeh; that his life was in danger, and that no one was aware of that or took any precautions. It was foggy and I felt I was suffocating. No sooner had I seen a comrade, whom I think was Ajaj Al-Muhtar, who came to visit me at the hotel, than I burst in a voice screaming with pain and desperation, "Take me to Sa'adeh. I want to see him; I want to be with him. Place me anywhere, but take me out of here. I can go out alone, but where do I go and what do I know about the house I will step into?"[66]

The thought of suicide crossed her mind as she struggled to come to terms with her new circumstances: "When it was Friday, I decided to do something which may be against my conscience, since I no longer believed that there were people around Sa'adeh, who were quite near the hotel, and who kept coming and going, but who were unable to take me temporarily to any house anywhere! I felt that no one cared about my concerns."[67]

The following morning she heard that President Zaim had agreed to a meeting with Sa'adeh. Anticipating the worse, she went ballistic:

> I was horrified by this news, since I had, for the past days, been contemplating the heavy price we paid as a result of getting in touch with this fickle man. The moment I heard that, I screamed, "What understanding to reach with a man who broke his promise over and over again? How can we trust him? I only see that he is changeable; how can we trust him, given everything that has happened in this revolution?" I cried in pain, and begged Bashir saying, "I can't stay here another minute. I want to go to Sa'adeh; I want to talk to him. I do not feel good about this Hosni Az-Za'im. I want to say that to Sa'adeh. How come you all keep seeing Sa'adeh, while I, his wife, cannot see him for a second?"[68]

Eventually, she was whisked away to another location, but to no avail. The Syrian Security quickly discovered her new hideout and impounded her in the Saydnayya Monastery – "I had no idea that Sa'adeh had been handed over [to the Lebanese authorities] or that he was in their custody."[69] On her way to the Monastery, she told her liaison officer: "Tell Sa'adeh to leave the country at once, and not to stay for a single moment. Tell him to let them [ie., the Syrian authorities] be distracted by me, and not to take any action for my sake, whatever happens. I was under the impression that the leader was in hiding and that they were holding me back till he came. However, the situation was quite the opposite. The plot against Sa'adeh's life had already taken place while I was away."[70]

Juliet spent several days in Saydnayya Monastery uninformed of Sa'adeh's fate: "We headed for Saydnayya, and were received by the head of the monastery. She gave us a room to stay in: it had only an old bed and a wooden bench. We stayed there for two days, contemplating the situation. The maid asked for another bed to place on the ground. There were two beds, on which we and the children would spend the night. I used to see a security officer sitting on a chair outside the room. I hence grasped that we were technically under arrest."[71] Two days after Sa'adeh's execution, on 10 July, she discovered the truth:

On Sunday, July 10th, the personal maid of the Monastery's abbess came to me while I was washing my hands and bluntly and directly said to me, "You are a sensible woman. If I tell you that they killed your husband, you will not do anything rash." I could no longer tell whether I heard this while awake or asleep. I no longer knew what to say or what to do. Had this piece of news been true, my entire world had thus crumbled down, and everything was ruined in my eyes. I guess I started running from the first to the ground floor screaming for help, hoping to find any of my comrades. However, I could only see the sisters, each saying a word, or mumbling a phrase. Everything they said was nonsense, because they had no idea how tremendous the calamity was. I completely broke down, and found myself surrounded by the sisters, as if the whole world was dressed in grim black, as if the whole world was mourning a stranger.[72]

Sa'adeh's family remained in the Saydnayya Monastery contemplating its next move. With Lebanon closed to her and Syria wanting the family no more, Juliet was subjected to irresistible pressure from the Orthodox Patriarch to return to Argentina. "I have conditions," she replied. "They must first allow me back in Lebanon to pack my house and personal possessions. The government must also be prepared to handover Sa'adeh's corpse. Only then will I consider leaving."[73] Three days later the Patriarch returned with an answer: "Riad Solh will not allow you back in Lebanon, but is willing to pay for all your expenses provided you leave the country. The Government will be happy to send your entire possessions to Argentina, but readmittance to Lebanon is out of the question. You know too many of your husband's secrets." She retorted: "Well, in that case, leaving the country is also out of the question. If Riad Solh thinks he can buy Sa'adeh's blood with money, well I am not one who will sell it."[74] Several days later, the Argentinean Consul General in Lebanon showed up at the Monastery, allegedly at the request of the Lebanese Government, to persuade her to go back to Argentina, but to no avail.

Juliet al-Mir lost her husband but not her fighting spirit. She remained in Damascus, coping with life after Sa'adeh, and attending to family and party matters with renewed willpower. She was elected to the party's Supreme Council and became even more determined to carry on Sa'adeh's work. But her life was interrupted again in 1955, in an equally dramatic fashion, with the assassination of Adnan Malki by an alleged SNP member. Although she had nothing to do with the assassination, she was placed under house arrest and imprisoned for over a decade. She died in 1969 from cancer.

Conclusion

The impact of the Sa'adeh killing was far greater than the literature has allowed. Although it did not cause a massive haemorrhage on the national political system of Lebanon, it exercised considerable effect on the incumbent regimes in Lebanon and Syria. In Lebanon, it helped broaden the anti-government front and gave the opposition forces greater depth and scope than before. As a result, the Khoury regime found itself in a virtual state of suspended animation. It threatened and cajoled, and even used violence in an effort to defuse the explosive situation, but to no avail. Once the SNP caught its breath it struck back with vengeance, ensuring that Sa'adeh's killing would not pass unnoticed.

As with most political killings, it took some time for the full impact of Sa'adeh's tragic loss to surface. In Lebanon, apart from the violent reprisals it produced, the event weakened the nascent secular movement by robbing it of one of its most outspoken figures. It also reduced possibilities of dialogue, either deliberately or inadvertently, and thus, kept the country in a draining sectarian stand-off for decades. In Syria, the killing speeded up the movement to depose Zaim and, by extension, affected the fate of the Khoury regime in Lebanon. From another point of view, the killing robbed the SNP of its leader and threatened to destroy everything that Sa'adeh built. These outcomes suggest that the true impact of Sa'adeh's killing cannot be measured purely in short-run political terms. A broader longer-term perspective is essential to grasp its meaning.

Of course we cannot know just how different history could have been with Sa'adeh. The game of 'what if?' yields different answers for different people and for different political persuasions. And there will be many who ask: do individuals really matter so much in history, compared with mass social movements? Yet, we can say with certainty that had Sa'adeh lived, the trajectory of Lebanese politics would have been different. For one thing, the sectarian politicians, both the individuals who held the reigns of power and those who wanted to take it away from them, would not have had it as easy as they did. In Syria, Zaim may have remained in power, at least for longer than he did, and his regime may not have collapsed with the SNP by his side. The SNP would have profited more from Sa'adeh and probably become a political force in its own right. Assessing the event from this perspective brings Sa'adeh's killing into clearer focus and allows for systematic exploration of whether it produced its intended effects.

NOTES

1 Clifford Bob and Sharon Erickson Nepstad, "Kill a Leader, Murder a Movement? Leadership and Assassination in Social Movements," *American Behavioral Scientist*, Vol. 50, No. 10 (June 2007), 1370–1394.
2 See Adel Beshara, *The Politics of Frustration: The Failed Coup of 1961*. London: Routledge, 2005: 37–47.
3 Most of these censorship rules dated back to the Ottoman era of the late nineteenth century. See Donald J. Cioeta, "Ottoman Censorship in Lebanon

and Syria, 1876–1908," International Journal of Middle East Studies, Vol. 10, No. 2 (May, 1979), pp. 167–186.

4   The most notorious case in this respect was the truncated publication of a condemnatory note cabled by the Syro-Lebanese community in Brazil: censors deleted the condemnation in the cable and left only the names and signatories for *an-Nahar* to publish!

5   *An-Nahar*, Beirut, 29 August, 1949.

6   *An-Nahar*, Beirut, 31 August, 1949.

7   *An-Nahar*, Beirut, 27 July, 1949.

8   *An-Nahar*, Beirut, 23 July, 1949.

9   Ibid.

10   *The New York Times*, 18 July, 1949.

11   *The New York Times*, 19 July, 1949.

12   On 17 July, police raided and sealed the building and other Beirut offices of that organization. Twenty-five members of the organization were arrested, and Pierre Gemayel, chief of the Phalange, was summoned by the public prosecutor for questioning. *The New York Times*, 19 July, 1949.

13   Ibid.

14   See N. E. Bou Nacklie, "Les Troupes Speciales: Religious and Ethnic Recruitment 1916–1946," *International Journal of Middle Eastern Studies*, Vol. 25, No. 4 (Nov. 1993): 645–660.

15   US Department of State Incoming Telegram, 890E.00/7-749.

16   *The New York Times*, 21 July, 1949.

17   Ibid.

18   Francis G. Wilson, "Political Suppression in the Modern State," *The Journal of Politics*, Vol. 1, No. 3 (Aug., 1939): 245.

19   Ibid., 237.

20   Vilfredo Pareto, *The Mind and Society*, tr. from the Italian, 4 vols., Sec. 1757. New York: Harcourt, Brace and Company, 1935: 12.

21   Ibid.

22   Many rumours about Abd Al-Massih's whereabouts were reported in the local press. One report had him hiding in Turkey; another that he had sought political asylum in Israel. He turned up in Syria. See *an-Nahar*, 28 July, 1949.

23   In its issue of 4 September, 1949, *an-Nahar* carried a report on the election of Sa'adeh's successor. On another occasion, it published an interview with the Party's new Dean of Propaganda, Issam al-Muhairy.

24   *The New York Times*, 10 August, 1949.

25   Ibid.

26   Ibid.

27   See an interview with the assailant Tewfic Hamdan in *Sabah el-Kheir*, 7 July, 1984: 49–51.

28   See Abdullah Qubarsi, *Qubarsi Ya Tazakar* (Recollections), Vol. 4. Beirut: al-Furat 2004: 122.

29   *The New York Times*, 17 July, 1951.

30   *The New York Times*, 30 July, 1951.

31   Ghassan al-Khalidi, *Sa'adeh wa al-thawrah al-Ula* (Sa'adeh and the First Revolution). Beirut: Dar wa Maktabat al-Turath al-Adabi, 1997: 242.

32   Eyal Zisser, for example, writes: "Indeed, news of Sulh's death precipitated a wave of violence in Lebanese cities. The Sulh family implicitly accused Khuri of

being responsible for the murder." E. Zisser, "The Downfall of the Khuri Administration: A Dubious Revolution." *Middle East Studies*, 30 (1994): 286–311.

33 Eyal Zisser, "The Downfall of the Khuri Administration: A Dubious Revolution." *Middle East Studies*, 30 (1994): 286–311.

34 In its 1947 discourse, the SSNP publically questioned the integrity of the Khoury regime and spoke openly about its incompetence. In it, the party warned of "corruption in the administration, a never-ending clawing for power, economic stagnation, deterioration in ethics" and of "a danger that foreign interests might impose their will with the help, of course, of their veteran local allies." For more details see Antun Sa'adeh, *al-Athar al-Kamilah* (Complete Works), Vol. 14. Beirut: Syrian Social National Party Information Bureau, n.d.: 93.

35 Historical scholars do not make more than a passing reference to the SSNP's part in the 1952 events. Instead, they tend to focus on four other principal groups: 1. The Maronite leadership which abandoned the Khoury administration because of personal disputes or ambition. The two outstanding figures in this respect were Camille Chamoun and Hamid Franjiyyeh. 2. The National Progressive Socialist Party of Kamal Jumblatt. 3. The Nationalist Bloc of Emile Edde under his son's leadership. 4. Non-Maronite politicians like Majid Arslan, Sabri Hammada, Gabriel al-Murr and Adel Asairan, who were angry because they had lost their positions in the government.

36 For example, in 1947, the leader of the SSNP wrote: "The first measures by [the Khoury] government leave little doubt that it has almost modelled its tactics on some by-gone feudal principality out to extinguish every concept in the state that may go against the whims or interests of its leaders, and to abort all autonomous strength in our people lest they pose problems for their designs." (Ibid., 103.) Echoing Sa'adeh, Kamal Jumblatt of the PSP declared during the general election of 1951 that, under Khoury, "the state has become the property of a few parasites with an insatiable appetite . . . Those who call themselves heroes of the independence regime . . . who were raised to power by General Spears should be ejected by the people." (Quoted in Wade R. Goria, *Sovereignty and Leadership in Lebanon: 1943–1976*. London: Ithaca Press, 1985: 34–35.) Jumblatt's remark, just like Sa'adeh's, led to a series of prosecutions and to the suspension of those newspapers which reprinted it.

37 Ibid., 93.

38 Ibid.

39 For a description of the assassination plot see Adib Kaddoura, *Haqa'iq wa mawaqif* (Facts and Stances). Beirut: Fikr, 1989: 133–136.

40 Wade R. Goria, *Sovereignty and Leadership in Lebanon 1943–1976*. London: Ithaca Press, 1985: 34.

41 Michael C. Hudson, ibid., 273.

42 Sulh's resignation was preceded by a personal scathing attack on the President and his brother before parliament. He described both of them "as men of authority who rule without being responsible [and] intefere in every aspect of the state." See Sami Solh, *Memoirs*, 224–27, cited in F. I. Qubain, *Crisis in Lebanon*. Washington D.C.: The Middle East Institute, 1961: 23.

43 *An-Nahar* played a key role in criticizing and showing the corruption of the Khoury administration. Louis el-Hage relates in his book *Min makhzoun al-zakirah* (Old Memories; Beirut: Dar an-Nahar, 1993: 11–27) that President Khoury was incensed by the sarcastic reporting and editorials published in the paper. He

recalls how Khoury was infuriated by two article headings ("God's mercy upon [Sultan] Abdul Hamid and upon his era" – which appeared after one of the Sultan's descendants died and was buried in Beirut, and "It seems that even in Latin America the idea of a second presidential term is unpopular" – a reference to the turmoil which occurred in one of the Latin American countries after the parliament amended the constitution to allow the president to stay on for a second term) which appeared at the height of his presidential crisis.

44 Pierre Emile Edde was a Maronite candidate representing *al-Kutla al-Wataniyyah* (the National Bloc of his deceased father, Emile Edde). The SSNP supported him against Pierre Jumayyel, leader of the Kataib Party, who had the backing of *al-Kutlah al-Dasturiyyah* (the Constitutional Bloc of President Khoury).

45 Although still outlawed, the SSNP ran the election in the Matn openly under the banner "the battle of Jummaizeh." Jummaizeh, it will be remembered, was the place where the attack on the SSNP printing headquarters took place in 1949 by members of the Kataib Party. See Chapter 5 for more details about this incident.

46 For example, the ninth article in the program of the Front demanded the restoration of freedom of thought and the right for "all political parties" to operate freely and openly in Lebanon. For an outline of the program of the National Socialist Front and its minutes and regular meetings leading up to the general strike in 1952, see *The Progressive Socialist Party: A Quarter of a Century in Struggle*, Vol. 1. Beirut: Markaz al-Bouhouth al-Istiraqiyya, 1974: 56–7 and 65–76.

47 The rally was estimated at 30,000. See George M. Haddad, *Revolutions and Military Rule in the Middle East: the Arab States*, Vol. II. New York: Robert Speller and Sons, Publishers, 1971): 404.

48 Mustafa Abd al-Satir, *Ayyam wa Qadiyya* (The Cause We Lived For). Beirut: Fikr Research Centre, 1982: 112.

49 The party's relationship with the Lebanese regime after 1949 did not improve, despite the public outcry caused by Sa'adeh's tragic death in July of that year. For example, less than two weeks after its leader was put down, six of its members were executed in the same manner. Moreover, the ban that was imposed on the party after the infamous incident at Jummaizeh was never lifted and the army, in conjunction with the internal security forces, kept a tight control on its activities across the Syrian-Lebanese borders.

50 Eyal Zisser, Ibid., 504.

51 *The New York Times*, 10 August, 1949.

52 Ibid.

53 Ibid.

54 Nadhir Fansah, *Ayyam Husni Zaim: 137 Yawman Hazzat Suria* (Days of Husni Zaim: 137 Days that Shook Syria). Beirut: Dar al-Afaq al-Jadidah, 1983: 85.

55 See *Al-Ayyam*, Damascus, 23 August, 1949.

56 Referring to a remark which Zaim made during an address before a group of officers at the Damascus officers club where a party was given to celebrate Evacuation Day (17 April, marking the evacuation of Syria by the French Army), he said: "I am a son of the people. I was born poor, grew up poor, and now I assume the administration while I am poor. I promise to leave it, also while I am poor . . ." *An-Nasr,* 18 April, 1949.

57 See Ibrahim Yammut, *Al-Hisad al-Mur* (The Bitter Harvest). Beirut: Dar al-Rukin, 1993.

58 Clifford Bob and Sharon Erickson Nepstad, "Kill a Leader, Murder a Movement? Leadership and Assassination in Social Movements," *American Behavioral Scientist*, 50 (2007): 1375.

59 Ibid.

60 See Centre for Asian Studies, *Martyrdom and Political Resistance: Essays from Asia and Europe* (Comparative Asian Studies, 18) Amsterdam: Vu University Press, 1997.

61 Clifford Bob and Sharon Erickson Nepstad, "Kill a Leader, Murder a Movement? Leadership and Assassination in Social Movements," *American Behavioral Scientist*, 50 (2007): 1379.

62 Examples: "Life is but an honourable stand"; "the noblest sacrifice is the sacrifice of blood"; and "I don't care how I die but what I die for."

63 The SNP's survival lends further empirical evidence to the hypothesis that killing a movement's leader doesn't always yield its intended results.

64 See Margaret Bodran, "Violence in the Syrian Social Nationalist Party," MA, American University of Beirut, 1970.

65 Jukliet al-Mir Sa'adeh, *Mudhakarat al-Amina al-Oula* (Memoirs). Beirut: Kutb Publications, 2004: 111.

66 Ibid.

67 Ibid., 112.

68 Ibid.

69 Ibid., 112–113.

70 Ibid., 113.

71 Ibid.

72 Ibid., 114.

73 Ibid., 116.

74 Ibid.

8

VENERATION

Execution transformed Antun Sa'adeh from a controversial figure into a sacred emblem. The esteem suddenly shown Antun Sa'adeh after his demise re-affirmed the continuing power of his ideas and turned him into an object of reverence at a time when some people still held him in mixed or low regard. His reputation rose more dramatically than any other public figure not only in Lebanon but in the Arab world as well. Patrick Seale did not err when he said "Sa'ada inspired devotion as probably no other leader in Arab politics has done."[1]

For enemies of Sa'adeh, his death did little to alter their opinions. But for contemporary critics and supporters his death was an act of martyrdom that gave greater substance to his image as a heroic, self-sacrificing figure. He was declared a martyr because he chose to suffer and die rather than give up his convictions, and that made him a hero. Two things are important here. The first was Sa'adeh's willingness to place his cause above the value of his own life; the other, and most impressive, is the serenity and inner peace that he felt at the moment of his execution. His moral courage was there to the end:

> We believe that it would be a great honor for anyone able to place his life and destiny in one pan of a scale that would face the cause for which he strives in the other and that he could completely sacrifice himself to win either a martyrdom that will light up the path for others or overwhelming victory.[2]

Sa'adeh has been commemorated in all sorts of ways – prose, drama, paintings, plays, music, poetry, and even opera. The vision of Sa'adeh, based on these forms, was that of the patriot hero, the courageous individual who had fought the Western imperialists and their domestic cronies and thus redeemed the national honor. This vision was not constructed in a cultural-political void, and has to be placed in context and explained in relation to Lebanese society and politics. A number of developments, therefore, have to be kept in mind, particularly Sa'adeh's execution and how it was cultivated and received. Many aspects of his complex political ideology are also relevant. They provide a framework for understanding public perceptions of his image and how they have shifted over the years.

Ultimately, the heroic mystique that grew around Sa'adeh was used not only to sanction certain political ends but also to ensure that Sa'adeh would remain a revered figure in death as much as he was in life.

Creating the Myth

The explosion of affection for the murdered Sa'adeh was initially displayed in dailies. The public was blitzed by a wave of critical editorials revealing details of his execution and of the miscarriage of justice that had preceded it. Among the people who wrote publicly about Sa'adeh were political figures, newspaper editors and commentators, clergymen, poets, and essayists addressing a narrow audience of educated readers. All the writers provided useful information not only on his execution but also on general beliefs about Sa'adeh, although some articulated them better than others. Most writers typically included brief remarks about Sa'adeh's moral character, his service to the country in a troubled time, and his heinous execution. Statements issued by friendly newspaper editors followed no traditional design, but they covered the same ground as the politicians. Unfriendly editors paid their respects, too. They acknowledged their differences with Sa'adeh but dwelled on the merit of his ideas. Almost all condemned his execution.

An illustration of this would be the following extract from a long commentary by Said Freyha, a traditional critic of Sa'adeh:

> Sa'adeh's arrest took him by surprise. He never expected that six men would get into his car and arrest him. Nevertheless, he did not protest or shriek. He only turned around to one of the men and said "thank you".
>
> He remained silent and calm throughout the journey. At the border-crossing he was received by Amir Farid Chehab and several officers of the Lebanese army. Sa'adeh was first taken to a Lebanese police station and then to the interrogation room at the military tribunal.

The man retained his composure and calm not only when he was arrested but throughout his ordeal from the interrogation to the trial to the pronouncement of the death sentence, to the execution.

He remained cool, calm and collected from beginning to end. He stood for eight hours in the dock without bending a knee or leaning forward.

He improvised a defense for an hour and a half without stuttering or uttering one offensive word. He received the death sentence as if he was receiving an invitation for lunch.

After hearing the sentence, he went back to prison where he slept the sleep of the just . . . as if he had been sentenced to sleep not to death.

When awakened, they asked him: "What would you like to have before execution?" He requested a cup of coffee!

He drank the coffee with the same calm, nerve, and temperament as he always did. Then he walked to the post to which he was tied. And when they were about to cover his eyes, he said: "There's no need". They said, "It's the law". He replied: "So let it be".

He was forced to kneel down and his hands were tied. He asked his executioner to slacken the tight rope a bit and to remove the pebbles under his knees as they were hurting him.

Then, the bullets blasted and Antun Sa'adeh was finished.

He fell after he had proved in the most critical moments that he was a man of genuine decency and composure. Indeed, these attributes were an integral part of the man, who was a genius.

Yet, even genius and manhood are subject to eccentricity.

If it was not for his eccentricity and for breaching the law, Sa'adeh would not have ended up where he did. The man played his card and lost. Had he won, many Lebanese would have lost their fathers, sons, brothers and friends!

It was an adventure that ended with his death, to the safety of Lebanon and many heads of its citizens!

To Sa'adeh's soul, we send our salutation of respect and admiration.

To his adventurous and revolutionary soul, we send our deep sorrow and God's blessings and a cry of warning![3]

Another account worth quoting from is Kamel Mruwa's "A New Precedent: An Ideology Stated in Blood," published in *al-Hayat* on 9 July, 1949. Its closing section reads,

Thus the government decided that, to the very end, its conflict with the National Party should remain a private matter. It kept the public at bay from it until the very last moment. It leveled charges, arrested, prosecuted and killed without issuing, up to now, one statement to simplify abstract facts. The hopes were high that the impending trials would clarify all the points of contention and provide concrete material evidence to enlighten the people. However, the initial trial, that is the trial of Mr. Antun Sa'adeh, was carried out with 'reflexive' speed and its reality was not disclosed to the public until a few hours after the execution. We, therefore, do not understand if what happened was a trial of a defendant, or of an individual, or of a party, or of a doctrine.

After that, how do you expect the people to judge what happened? There are two premises for judgments in such cases: factual and emotional. As for the factual, we know very little about what happened because the government, to this point, has not disclosed the facts. Therefore, we are left with the emotional. But when emotions explode, the Lebanese usually split into two parts, and the cancerous symptoms from which we suffer, as citizens and as a state, quickly resurface.

All in all, Mr. Sa'adeh's case is a new precedence in our political life. And now that the door has opened far and wide, I feel that it may not be the last. It may even become one day a vehicle for other violations. It is now up to the new generation to judge it because time was too short for the present generation to pass its judgment.

Antun Sa'adeh has died for the sake of a political ideology with which his personality was born and into which it completely dissolved to the last breath of life. This is the basic truth behind his execution regardless of what has already been said about its causes and about his ideology. He was without a doubt the first Lebanese to be executed for political reasons since the Great War. It has happened in a country which has not for a generation known what it means to shed blood for the sake of one's beliefs, a country in which sectarianism, politics and social rank have clearly submerged the national virtues and precluded them from firmly resting in the hearts of its citizens.

It was with his own blood that Antun Sa'adeh had wanted to state his beliefs. For its part, the government likewise wished to state its judgment on Sa'adeh and his ideology in blood. In the perspective of long term history, nature, and the struggle for survival between ideologies we are individuals who amount to very little indeed and will fade with the passage of the years, as fate decrees whatever our desires be.[4]

The press campaign was not entirely successful; as a result, in the early 1950s, the SSNP sponsored publication of various periodicals dedicated entirely to Sa'adeh's discourses. Published in Syria, the periodicals ran many reports, articles, leaders, features and obituaries discussing Sa'adeh's life, the circumstances of his death, and his political agenda for the country. The facts associated with the circumstances of death, the poignant aspects of each event, and individuals' names were often recalled in surprising detail, and sometimes reported and reacted to with visible emotion. A four-part work entitled "Sa'adeh is alive in our midst" by the Palestinian scholar Hisham Sharabi[5] may be taken as an illustration of the vision developing around Sa'adeh:

> Throughout the Syrian homeland there are thousands of youth who believe in the discourse of Social Nationalism and sanctify its founder, leader, and martyr in a way that borders on deification. That is not surprising because from the day that Sa'adeh founded the Syrian Social National Party on 16 November 1932, a tremor struck this nation penetrating its spiritual-intellectual-social being to the core.[6]

Poetic statements were equally informative. These sought to portray in compelling language the emotional reaction to Sa'adeh and his death. "The Land Said" was the title of an epic poem by the renowned Syrian poet Adonis, with Sa'adeh again the heroic character. Its last stanza reads,

> *Syria, Syria rejoice!*
> *For it is you that has given the ages*
> *Pride and all that sustain this.*
> *You bestowed on history a glorious epic,*
> *Conferring a splendid panoply of gifts.*
> *– Time awake to inquire of this land*
> *And with pounding arteries*
> *Enrich us with unending duration.*
> *Have you known the virgin dough*
> *– The creation and the day that created*
> *Our being, still smouldering from fire?*
> *That is March . . . The first of March*
> *And this is your Great Son – Sa'adeh*[7]

Numerous eulogies also appeared during this period, evoking a variety of meanings and responses. They centered around two main themes: the character of the Lebanese regime and the character of Sa'adeh. Some eulogies were replete in their praise of Sa'adeh; some regretted his death at such an early age. Most eulogies portrayed Sa'adeh sympathetically and reflected the broadest range of opinion. They provide no infallible key to the people's attitude toward Sa'adeh, but they do give preliminary insight into both the general conception of Sa'adeh during the days and weeks following his death and the way ideological and political ideals informed that conception.

By far the most interesting and most moving piece of literature to appear about Sa'adeh was "The Priest who Confessed Him" by the prominent Lebanese literati and playwright Said Takyideen.[8] A dead simple but beautifully composed masterpiece, "The Priest who Confessed Him" recreates Sa'adeh's final hours on earth from the point of view of the clergyman who witnessed his departing moments. Takyideen introduced the narrative in an exquisite but soft tone, as if there was an aura surrounding the characters and settings:

> I was a bit upset that this man of religion did not at first assume a solemn demeanor but rather talked in a detached manner. Yet as he narrated the events that he observed [on that night], his voice, his tone, and his humility became tinted with emotions and real grief. He became like a master musician playing a moving piece on a piano, his fingertips lightly cherishing the ivory keys, until his discourse soared to an elevated music not of this world. We felt that the walls of the room had opened up and that it was lighting up those within it. We became there with Sa'adeh in his prison, in the church, in the cemetery addressing the world, among his people in the diaspora, in palaces, in court, in diplomatic missions, in the hearts of all who knew him and grieved for him, in the pride of struggles standing in the presence of the arrogant or in the face of executioners, in the calmness of the faithful, in the cave of treachery as bayonets that pursue criminals, flags that urge armies on, as the tempest that crushes and the cry that makes history pause in its forward march. The priest brought out a paper from the folds of his voluminous black cassock taken out of an exercise book, and was about to read it when I said: "Talk to me instead, don't read your papers even if they are memoirs."

Another important tribute came from South America, where Sa'adeh once lived, from the outstanding diasporian writer Gibran Massouh:[9]

> Antun Sa'adah has fallen in the field of honor while carrying the fate of his nation in his hand. By his example he taught it how to face death after he taught it how to approach life.

His murderers pierced the noblest chest with the most ignoble of bullets which though will bear their names for eternity just as his breast will carry his name for eternity.

It was Antun Sa'adeh who lifted from the life of his nation the slavery of two thousand years and then proceeded to reconnect it anew with its glorious history.

It was a people who used to hang on what others would decide in its destiny but thanks to Sa'adeh it became a people that took part alongside all the reminder of dignified nations in deciding the destiny of the world.

Antun Sa'adah awakened the gifts and capabilities long latent in the nation but paralyzed in a slumber very like death.

He restored to it its self-confidence. I am saying that he restored its self-confidence but it is rather the case that he lifted it up from the grave.

Antun Sa'adah was ahead of his age one hundred years at least. Had he been spared to live he would have directed the march of this nation in its entirety over that vast area.

Antun Sa'adah developed a national cause that stemmed from the depth of the people not some relationship with outside actors.

He brought together under its banner the Moslem and the Christian so that they would be ready in its cause in a joint choice. This is a miracle that no one before him had been able to achieve.

The wombs of the women of the East will have to take rest for one thousand years for them ever to be able thereafter to bear anyone like Antun Sa'adeh.

But the man has not died. Rather, today his real life begins.

Sa'adeh has engraved his image in the soul of every individual in his nation. If this image is still unclear that is because it is still in its formative phase. But one day it will be completely clear and sharp.

Sa'adeh knew all the sickness of our society and gave each its proper name with no fear or hesitation. In that he is among the greatest of the reformers who have appeared on earth in all eras.

As for the remedies that Sa'adeh devised for these illnesses and of what those medicines will be made up, this is a matter that is still being addressed by the great thinkers of the world and, indeed, is a war in which a sword and a pen cooperate for the first time in the life of the human race.

To this date, there has not yet taken place the decisive battle that will determine who will emerge victorious. But the source of our pride in this global victory is that Sa'adeh was one of its greatest leaders until he fell on the battlefield as the greatest of its martyrs.

The published material of this period attests to an unconscious effort to preserve Sa'adeh in living memory. An idealized image of a hero gradually formed, which further enlarged the cultural power of Sa'adeh's martyrdom and brought it closer to the life of the people. It also added to its prominence as a symbol of society's consensus and divisions. As a result, most people gained new insights and they came to appreciate achievements and character traits in Sa'adeh they had not appreciated before and to forget faults they had previously criticized. Also, many critics discovered admirable qualities in the same Sa'adeh they had once maligned, and they were sincere when they publicly conceded the discovery. However, none of the things said about Sa'adeh in oratory or print revealed any virtues that were not known by his supporters before he died. Nor did friendly commentaries ignore faults for which his opponents previously held him to account. Criticisms were certainly stated more gently and with more qualification after his death than before it, but they were stated nonetheless.

Execution also put Sa'adeh in a glorifying light. A cult was built around his person and a new national day was born: that which commemorated his death by execution on 8 July. Mohamad Maatouk described this development as follows:

> Sa'ada's death happened to be in Tammuz (July), which is the name of Adonis in Syrian mythology. This coincidence was shrouded in mystery in the Party's literature and led to the revival of the myth of Adonis, only now with modern connotations. The eighth of July of each year is celebrated by the Party in Syria and all over the world, with a new vote of confidence in Sa'ada. The ceremonies that commemorate the occasion bear a great resemblance to religious rituals, with the very important exception that Sa'ada, though described in official literature as 'immortal', is never referred to as being divine. Leading figures in the Party themselves, however, took part in a bizarre ritual that took place in 1949 only days after Sa'ada's execution where part of a little finger of his and a lock of hair cut from his corpse were wrapped in a handkerchief and touched collectively in a pledge of loyalty to his doctrines.[10]

For others, the myth evoked another meaning through the association of death with life:

> Another date which is celebrated and is performed as yet another vote of confidence in Sa'adeh's leadership is the first of March, his

birthday. As the date falls close to the beginning of spring, Sa'adeh's birthday is associated with the return of life, as his death is considered a day of martyrdom. So, as is the case with Tammuz of the old myth, Sa'adeh dies in July and is brought back to life in March and is thus *Khalid* (immortal).[11]

Perhaps the most politicized and systematic exposition of the Sa'adeh myth[12] was made by the highly celebrated *Tammuzi* movement, a group of free-thinking poets who drew their initial inspiration from Sa'adeh's masterwork *Al-Sira' al-Fikri fi al-Adab al-Suri* (Intellectual Struggle in Syrian Literature).[13] Known also as "the Shi'r Group" and consisting of distinguished modern poets of widely varying talents,[14] the movement attempted to relate the ancient gods to the modern Arab World through *al-shi'r hurr*, or what they called *al-shi'r al-hadith*. They rejected all the conventions of Arabic poetry and all the accepted values of form and use of language. They contended "it was possible to remain an Arab poet without using the conventional form, style and themes of classical literature."[15] In other words, they were against the unchanged values and predetermined rules of the Arabic literary heritage and in favour of moulding the language, its grammar and style, to the new demands of the modern era. Moreover, in their poetry they concentrated on the idea of the change of the seasons, giving hope to the winter of Arab discontent after the Palestinian disaster of 1948 and to the possibility of rebirth. This idea meant that winter will give birth to spring, and death will ultimately produce life and resurrection. The adoption of myths in poetry served, according to Salma Khadra Jayyusi, as "interpretation of present Arab history in positive and concrete terms."[16] Moreover, as poets of the Arabic language, the Tammuzis not only proclaimed a relation to a deep tradition (an ancient order newly rediscovered) but spelled out a further struggle (a second liberation from within the culture and the language) to create "a poetry that establishes another concept of identity – one that is pluralist, open, agnostic, and secular."[17]

Although Tammuzis were not men of action, through their poetry and writings they fostered an idealized conception of Sa'adeh. The mythological aura they created around him translated into specific modes of veneration for the slain leader and transformed his execution into a silently straightforward symbol of national sacrifice. The result was a verification of Sa'adeh's credentials as a loyal nationalist and an appreciation of, but by no means total agreement with, his work as a strong nationalist. Tammuzis also conferred an apolitical dimension on Sa'adeh's execution by creating a passionate interest in and a lively historical debate around his thought.[18] The cultural emphasis that was subsequently placed on Sa'adeh's execution further enhanced Sa'adeh's image as a mystical figure standing at the apex of martyrdom. The elevation of his mind too is evident; his heroic action is so apparent that one thinks of nothing else. "Sa'adeh's literary views," wrote Muhammad al-Abed Hammoud, "rendered him, in my opinion, the most important among the founders of the Modernization Movement, which has reached its dead end by deviating from its right way and its deep [true] identity as designed and affirmed by Sa'adeh."[19] Tammuzis kept Sa'adeh's posthumous reputation alive and fostered a sentimental fondness for Sa'adeh across Lebanon's intellectual community. Artists, novelists and writers became involved subtly, if not directly. Some paid a high tribute in their dedication and preface, as well as in the title of the book, and in the selection and arrangement of the material included they were to a large extent guided by his judgment. George Masru'ah, the celebrated Lebanese novelist, is very much a case in point. The dedication of the second edition of his novel *Ibn Zikar* speaks volumes: "To the one who said, 'This is one of the best works that the SSNP has produced during my long compulsory absence,' to my teacher and leader, Antun Sa'adeh."[20]

The De-emphasization of Sa'adeh after 1955

The literary frenzy that followed his execution elevated Sa'adeh to a new and higher plane, but it was not extensive enough to make dramatic a shift in public opinion. One reason for that was the regime's ability to maintain tight control over factual information, which precluded the possibility of public discussion beyond literary circles. As a consequence, the Sa'adeh saga failed to strike a relevant chord with the lay people and significant numbers of Lebanese either remained oblivious of the saga or unable to understand its complexities. Another reason was intellectual powerlessness. It is especially noteworthy that, generally speaking, professional thinkers in Lebanon were and still are, to a very large extent, salaried employees of the state and its confessional institutions. They are not endowed with the kind of autonomy and status that intellectuals elsewhere enjoy under liberal systems. Hence, most Lebanese intellectuals remained uninterested in the larger issues revealed by the Sa'adeh saga or unwilling to take risks even when moral issues appeared to be at stake. At its simplest, their inaction kept the matter beyond the grasp of the general public. It undermined the difficult task of those intellectuals and artists who took up the mantle of Sa'adeh's cause and discouraged others from stating their views.

More significantly, the intellectual antipathy shown towards the saga provided a favorable terrain for cynicism. To be sure, Sa'adeh was subjected to criticism even as his commemoration in the press and in the work of sympathetic artists and intellectuals was taking place, although the grumblings at that time were not effective enough to seriously challenge his hero status. Instances of that can be found in the negative press reports that appeared intermittently in hostile newspapers, and in pamphlets published by political critics. Two in particular are worth paying some attention to: *al-Uruba baina Du 'atiha was Mu'aridhiha*[21] by the "spiritual father of Arab nationalism,"[22] Sati' al-Husri; and *Adwa' ala Haqiqat al-Qadiyya al-Qawmiyya al-Ijtima'iyya as-Suriyya: al-Fikra al-Qawmiyyah*[23] by Kamal Jumblatt. Al-Husri, who met Sa'adeh only once, in 1948, published an extensive critique of Sa'adeh's political doctrine in 1952 in the hope that this would "help Sa'adeh's followers to develop and advance in the service of the Arab countries and the renaissance of the Arab nation."[24] Jumblatt launched into Sa'adeh from a similar perspective, which was basically to gain control of his supporters. At any rate, both critiques drew strong responses from Sa'adeh's pupils and produced a lively debate which, in some respect, helped to remove some of the glaring misrepresentations of the man.[25] Neither Jumblatt nor al-Husri, though, attempted to malign Sa'adeh's reputation or the memory of his execution. Occasionally they criticized his style of leadership, but that didn't matter much because it was not exclusively leadership which made Sa'adeh a martyr. As the historian Gwyn Williams has so succinctly put it in the instance of the Dic Penderyn legend in Welsh working class history, "What makes a man a martyr? Death of course – but *unjust* death. It is his innocence, his representative character; it is the sense of injustice."[26]

From about 1955, an eerie silence fell on the formerly venerated Sa'adeh due to a sudden upswell of opinion hostile to his party. A host of officially and unofficially inspired articles appeared castigating his legacy and ideas. Their objective was more than a personal attack and reflected a crusade to uproot the merits of his school and to eradicate his influence completely. Some intellectuals responded with shock and rage, but most, knowing that they would face illegal harassment, intimidation, censorship and even physical threats, dropped out quietly. Within a very short period of time Sa'adeh's views became anathema to the prevailing outlook and his political philosophy was declared valueless.

While the beginning of Sa'adeh's de-emphasization cannot be ascertained with certainty, some fruitful speculation is possible. De-emphasization appears to parallel the emergence of militant pan-Arabism after 1954, first in Syria, and then in Egypt after Nasser's power surge. It was most likely sparked by the assassination of Colonel Adnan Malki, who was slated to become Syria's Chief of Staff, allegedly for his support of Syria's alignment with Egypt. A sergeant in the SSNP was blamed for the assassination and the Party inevitably was accused of plotting to overthrow the government with US covert support. The investigation into the Malki affair then took an anti-Western turn, with "leftists exploiting [the] belief of some Syrians that there is [a] USG-SSNP connection."[27] The core of these leftists was the young radical nationalists of the Baath party,[28] who had been intriguing for all-out control. In the ensuing treason trials, these Baathists lionized their fallen comrade as a victim of American imperialism and unleashed a wave of anti-SSNP feelings that eventually drove the SSNP out of Syria. Events took a turn for the worse when the Syrian authorities discovered 'fresh evidence' implicating the SSNP with the US (the so-called Sharabi letters) and again, in 1956, when Abdul Hamid al-Sarraj, the Baathist colonel who served as Syria's chief of counterintelligence, snuffed out a CIA plot to trigger a pro-Western coup by "indigenous anticommunist elements within Syria" including the SSNP.[29]

The climactic and decisive moment that brought this about was Gamal Abdel Nasser's spectacular rise after 1956. Up until then, Arab nationalism as an idea had been essentially an elite endeavor of publicists, intellectuals and a few officers. Nasser took the theories and the emotions that lay behind the idea and transformed them into living images among the masses.[30] The result was nothing short of spectacular. Nasser's popularity among the people in Egypt and abroad exploded: massive rallies were organized in Cairo, where the crowds gathered to hear him speak, and for the first time the common people were mobilized in favor of the pan-Arab cause. Especially after the nationalization of the

Suez Canal in 1956 and the victorious (mainly because of the help of the United States) confrontation with Britain, France and Israel that followed, Nasser became the undisputed leader of the Arabs.[31] His nationalistic speeches gave pride to the Arab masses and a new strength to pan-Arabism.

> In that moment and in the high tide of his rule, Gamal Abdel Nasser was to millions of Arabs a classic example of Thomas Carlyle's 'hero': 'the man with savage sincerity', 'who comes into historical being to lead his people', 'who represents the aspirations of generations before and beyond him', 'the man whose valour is value', and 'whose work is achievements and calamities'.[32]

Nasser's ascendancy fueled a vehement rejection of Sa'adeh and gave rise to a negative evaluation of his life that would last until 1967. The young militant Arab nationalists in Syria, overwhelmed by Nasser's charisma and hero stature, turned on the SSNP and then on Sa'adeh himself. Their anti-Sa'adeh crusade approached the stage of demonization, a "process in which ambiguities of moral character are erased, so that the commemorated figure is seen as fully, intensely, and quintessentially evil."[33] It is a form of negative commemoration of an individual through a degradation process during which a person's past is scrutinized for indications of evil intent or ability and underlying motives are sought, assessed, and ascribed to confirm a deviant identity. With Sa'adeh, demonization was accomplished through a degradation process of massive proportions. It is almost impossible to describe the flood of abuse, contempt, execration and hatred that poured upon the name and reputation of Sa'adeh once the process started. The SSNP leader was pronounced fit only for Western imperialism, a sworn enemy of the Arabs and the "Arab Nation." Seizing on perceived affinities between his work and that of groups that faulted Arab nationalism or rejected it, they turned him into a trailblazer for *Shu'ubism*.[34] Others sought to make him wholly odious by linking his position on one issue with a range of other allegedly related issues. In contrast, Nasser was depicted as a man true to his cause, who embodied all those elements central to public virtue.

Sa'adeh's degradation in Syria transformed him into a nonperson, literally and figuratively erased from the social and physical landscape. All that could remain of him was his "treachery," the symbol of his perfect depravity. The rest of his existence was expunged. His legacy was encased and stashed away; his very name vanished from Syrian periodicals; and his works were not to be found in bookstores or in libraries. The Baathists pulled no punches. They revised the history books in such a way as to foster an extremely negative and unappealing perception of Sa'adeh, and deliberately exaggerated and manipulated facts when reference to him was unavoidable. Quite often Sa'adeh was linked to the Greater Syria Scheme and placed along King Abdullah as a stooge of the British.[35] If not that, he was depicted as a petit-bourgeois and an enemy of the toiling classes. At one point, Sa'adeh was identified with Western imperialism, fascism, Nazism, sectarianism (as a Christian Orthodox thinker),[36] bourgeoisism, and *Shu'ubism*[37] at one fell swoop. The irony was not lost on Syria's leading intellectuals and lay thinkers, but in the end they too toed the line and joined the Nasser hysteria.

Throughout the remainder of the 1960s, Sa'adeh and his views remained taboo in Syrian historiography and uniformly negative. Even after the break-up of the UAR in September 1961, the endeavor to efface the memory of Sa'adeh went on unabated. Baathist leaders, citizens, and publications maintained the thrust against his legacy using his party's dismal performances as alleged reasons. It was dramatically recounted on the annual anniversary of Malki's assassination, which Baathists celebrated as a national day of mourning from 1956 onwards. Many Syrians may have been internally critical of the political uses to which Malki's assassination and its memories were put, especially as they had been portrayed in military processions and posters, but it aptly served the doctrinal and political verbiage of Baathism (in recent years, the emotional and political significance of the Malki anniversary has waned). By 1970, a new generation that barely remembered Sa'adeh came of age in Syria. A dwindling number of party stalwarts kept the faith but were not allowed to speak openly about Sa'adeh or about the controversy around his execution.

In 1962, politics again impinged directly upon Sa'adeh's reputation and brought it to a new stage. This time it was Lebanon's turn, occasioned by an SSNP abortive coup against the Chehab regime.[38] As in Syria, annual commemorations of Sa'adeh's execution ceased completely. A blackout was imposed on his writings, and his books were confiscated and banned. The denunciation pitch was maintained at a high level for the remainder of Chehab's regime in 1964. The main new thing about the offensive on Sa'adeh was that, for the first time in over a decade, it was backed up by a state and could therefore be systematically organized and forced upon a whole citizenry. Furthermore, the offensive was undertaken while the mechanism for self-defense by Sa'adeh's supporters was in complete disarray both in Lebanon and Syria, just as it was back in 1949. Worse still, this time the secret apparatus of the State, the *Deuxième Bureau*, was more vigorously employed to ensure that the press completely conformed to the de-emphasization process. Tactics that had withered under the previous regime of Camille Chamoun were revived, anti-Syrianism was pushed to the forefront of propaganda operations, and official involvement in propaganda was stepped up. Seizing the occasion, Sa'adeh's detractors, in different branches and at various levels, cultivated and exploited the anti-SSNP mood to paint images of Sa'adeh of the most uncharitable kind. The obligatory expressions of sympathy that appeared after his execution suddenly counted for nothing and Sa'adeh was again elevated to the status of a public villain. As in Syria, the detractors reduced Sa'adeh in stature to a minor but troublesome character: a recidivist rebel.

There was hardly anything new in what these detractors published and, in most cases, the diatribe was nothing more than a rehashing of old clichés. Yet, it was enough to have Sa'adeh systematically consigned to the archives of Lebanon's universities for access mainly by scholars with special research purposes. What was left in household books, by him or about him, disappeared or was destroyed by their owners to avoid retribution: one of his pupils placed his entire collection on Sa'adeh in a large public bin and then informed the Jafet Library at the American University of Beirut of their whereabouts. The ban on Sa'adeh was total, but the irony was not lost on everyone. Under normal circumstances, states utilize legends and heroes to promote social unity or a sense of national belongingness,[39] a fact demonstrated by the proliferation of historical works produced by nationalists in many countries. It may also be argued that in any situation of political stress, as in Lebanon's case, there is a socio-psychological craving for heroes. In this case, the hero was cast aside and the villain in Sa'adeh, embodied and continued by his party, was utilized to promote national consensus around the official discourse. Paradoxically, the main elements of that discourse, or *al-nahj al-shihabi*, as it was commonly known, were intrinsically Sa'adian, molded and adapted within a strictly Lebanese context. A case in point is the question of citizenship, which the propagators of *al-nahj* defined in firmly societal rather than sectarian terms, as Sa'adeh had earlier done.[40]

Viewed from a broader historical perspective, the de-emphasization of Sa'adeh during this period, both in Lebanon and in Syria, paralleled that of other great men of history who were denigrated, even demonized, for the wickedness of others. Karl Marx is a clear example:

> For the West, during the Cold War, he was the demonic begetter of all evil, the founder of an awesomely sinister cult, the man whose baleful influence must be suppressed. In the Soviet Union of the 1950s he assumed the status of a secular God, with Lenin as John the Baptist and, of course, Comrade Stalin himself as the redeeming Messiah. This alone has been quite enough to convict Marx as an accomplice in the massacres and purges: had he lived a few years longer, by now some enterprising journalist would probably have fingered him as a prime suspect in the Jack the Ripper murders too. But why? Marx himself certainly never asked to be included in the Holy Trinity, and would have been appalled by the crimes committed in his name. The bastard creeds espoused by Stalin, Mao or Kim Il Sung treated his work rather as modern Christians use the Old Testament: much of it simply ignored or discarded, while a few resonant slogans ('opium of the people', 'dictatorship of the proletariat') are wrenched out of context, turned upside down and then cited as apparently divine justification for the most brutal inhumanities.[41]

Ultimately, Sa'adeh's image and representation in popular memory were inextricably bound up with socio-economic and political conditions. In particular, his shifting image was a result of political fluctuations, the mutable needs of the establishment, and various inputs from individuals, for reasons that were not always nationalist or even political. His followers, to be sure, devoted considerable resources and effort to develop a cult around their leader, but the campaign was a qualified success. Of course, such a qualification cannot be attributed solely to external factors: the rigid and unpopular policies of the SSNP hierarchy and its protracted use of the Sa'adeh legacy for political ends contributed to the negativity as much as any other factor. The SSNP hierarchy not only fully exploited the hero cult of its former leader: its political opportunism drew charges of manipulation and betrayal of the Sa'adeh legacy.[42] Such charges, however, must be seen in the political context of the day.

The Resurrection of Sa'adeh

After 1970, there was a renewed effort to put Sa'adeh back in an idealized picture. A gradual publication of narratives, personal recollections, and portrayals sought to highlight his accomplishments and character. The one critical theme that cut through most of those publications is that Sa'adeh lived and died for a cause in which he truly believed and practiced. In another respect, the strongest Sa'adeh supporters reflected in their eulogies lingering doubts about him. Sa'adeh really did not wish to become a dictator, they said. He really was not an atheist. He was not a teller of utopian ideas. He did not harbor ambitions beyond what he proclaimed. Openly defensive statements like these reveal that many were still unsure what kind of man Sa'adeh was: they answered some doubts about him and inspired new questions.[43]

Also, after 1970, commemoration of Sa'adeh's martyrdom was revived. His life and revolutionary career were embellished and refined[44] and new documents revealing a side of Sa'adeh that few people had seen before were published and circulated on a wide scale. In addition to published material, posters displaying Sa'adeh superimposed on a variety of images and a medley of nationalist symbols and references were another striking, elaborate image of memorialization to appear after 1970. Those posters, along with other paraphernalia such as calendars, created a public sphere in which participants and observers could discuss Sa'adeh from various perspectives, while simultaneously generating a forum in which public political debate occurred. The Lebanese press reflected this development by publishing celebratory articles on the occasion of his death. Special supplemental sections, lavishly illustrated and adorned with illustrations of Sa'adeh, appeared in various newspapers. Numerous intellectuals within and outside the party contributed flowery poetry in his honor and a selection of eye-catching photographs of Sa'adeh was released to the public to capitalize on the new interest in him.[45]

It was in the party's press that the hero cult of Sa'adeh shone. Leading luminaries went to great lengths to make the hero cult the focus of renewed devotion. The qualities attributed to Sa'adeh were excessive, but because they were complementary among themselves an impression of balance was created. The first qualities of his leadership were his strength of character and his powerful intellect. Sa'adeh was an irreconcilable man, hard as stone. His greatest merit was his selfless service to the homeland. He was a fearless battler, a victim of internal as well as external enemies, who was prepared to sacrifice his life on the national altar. Next to this Sa'adeh was known for his wisdom, his huge theoretical powers, the crystal clarity of his mind, and the crushing force of his logic. His thinking was scientific and creatively original. His writings were known for their clarity and extraordinary depth. The two aspects of Sa'adeh's leadership, his genius and his heroism, were reflected in the double title of "founder and teacher." Evidently, political receptivity to these images was by no means straightforward and encountered some opposition, especially in the Lebanonist press. Moreover, the image of the good citizen, warrior-hero was shunned by the traditional detractors like the Phalange, who continued to cast Sa'adeh as a national oddity.

The Sa'adeh myth was also captured in the form of objects such as sculptures and paintings that were used and displayed in everyday life. Such objects extended the mission of the mythified flesh-and-blood Sa'adeh into the private domain of the family home, serving as a constant reminder of his heroic status to onlookers. Sa'adeh's execution inspired commemoration in other ways too – music, poems, etiquette manuals, films, and opera recordings – but the interesting thing is that most of the participants did so of their own accord. They also contributed to the semination of the Sa'adeh myth by writing newspaper articles and creative artistic works that mirrored the message behind his martyrdom, and by organizing or taking part in literary competitions in memory of Sa'adeh.

Metaphors in praise of Antun Sa'adeh also proliferated during this period, and sometimes lurched out of control. These metaphors often lamented the deplorable state of affairs in the nation before Sa'adeh came on the scene, so as to increase the aura of power around his myth. Recited at public functions and party meetings, they were developed in a carefully thought out way so as to distance Sa'adeh from the common politicians. Metaphors also served the need to promote Sa'adeh somehow as an ongoing phenomenon and to illustrate the force and depth of his local cult. Coupled with the right images, they enabled trusted followers to project Sa'adeh through rose-tinted glasses – as a profound thinker, as a courageous fighter, as a statesman, as a man of principle, and as a leader of unquestionable integrity – and, thus, to enshrine his ideals in popular memory.

To cap off their work, the myth crafters created a series of ceremonies and rituals around Sa'adeh. The annual "8 July Ceremony" became the most revered of these ceremonies. It begins on the evening of 7 July with a visit to Sa'adeh's burial place during which a wreath is placed on his grave and pledges of all sorts are made. His supporters then gather in small lots, usually at party offices or members' homes, to remember his martyrdom.[46] At the precise time of Sa'adeh's execution they recite "The Priest who Confessed Him" and then stand in silence for three minutes in observance of their fallen leader. Formal commemorations are held the next day in the form of mass rallies attended by the general public, leading dignitaries, and all those who couldn't make it the previous night. Occasionally, Sa'adeh's execution is re-enacted at these rallies and children of different ages may participate in military-style parades. The commemorations usually end with a major public gathering during which organizers trot out speakers from a stable of poets and orators, generally professional men of letters and political speakers, for florid speeches. Antun Sa'adeh's heroic status could be called on by speakers to press for change within the system, or by the party to make an ideological statement. Or it could be invoked by his trusted followers to demand respect for his legacy and a share of the power.[47]

Sa'adeh's post-1970 hero myth represented the posthumous comeback of a reputation that was at its lowest ebb. Why did this comeback occur? And how did Sa'adeh regain his heroic stature if his impact on popular imagination was not great?

Here, a number of factors have to be kept in mind. Obviously, Nasser's fall from grace after the Six-Day War is crucial in that it inspired a new search in the Arab world for individuals or leaders who might qualify as popular heroes. The problem was complicated by the absence of anyone remotely as reputable as Nasser and by the explosion of revolutionary sentiments among the Palestinians and their Arab supporters. Nasser himself remained after the War an object of popular fascination, but there was concomitantly a radical shift towards prevalent icons of revolutionary struggle. Here, some found the hero in Marx or in Marxist revolutionary and public figures such as Lenin, or Mao Tse Tung, or Che Guevara; others turned for answers to the religious heroes in the Islamic past;[48] and others still rediscovered the hero in Sa'adeh, although the turn in his direction was somewhat slow and contingent on a deeper and more somber clarification of his ideas. Sa'adeh's stature received another boost in 1970 when Nasser died and Arab nationalism subsequently found itself demoralized and leaderless. Nasser's death provided a far different context for the Arab nationalists to operate in and to act and think more independently.[49] Their attitude towards Sa'adeh, as a result, softened considerably and many of them began to see positive aspects in him they had stubbornly refused to entertain while Nasser was alive. Some pan-Arab leaders even paid homage to Sa'adeh's legacy and began to fashion a new appreciation of his ideas, a trend evident in the increasing observance of the anniversary of his death. A measure of the transformation can be gauged from various pan-Arab testimonials of this period. Abdullah al-Mashnouq, the radical pan-Arab activist and editorialist who once reviled Sa'adeh, is a clear case in point. In 1979 he was quoted as saying, "When we speak about the Syrian Social National Party and its founder Antun Sa'adeh we should pause for in-depth reflection before the greatness of this party and the outstanding personality of its leader."[50] His colleague and government minister many times over, Bahij Taki al-Din, was even more flattering of Sa'adeh: "Antun Sa'adeh's crime in the eyes of those who committed outrages against him is that he opened our eyes at a time when we were oblivious to what imperialism was hatching for us . . . His greatest crime is that he alerted us to the imminent danger of Zionism while other leaders crawled around for a throne or a high position or status. As a result, Zionism managed to carve a place for itself in the heart of the Arab World, just as Antun Sa'adeh had predicted."[51]

It is also about this time that a number of biographies began to appear linking Sa'adeh to revolutionary thought and describing him as a humble hero. These biographies of individuals now in the twilight of life provided fundamental new insights into the atmosphere of Sa'adeh's execution as well as concrete details about his final days.[52] Some exaggerated his virtues in their intense reaction to his death; others were uniformly positive but nonetheless objective in their assessment. Biographical works also played an important role in transmitting the memory of Sa'adeh to the new generation. Thus, new generations of Lebanese had ready access to his saga and, by reading between the lines, could form their own opinions about him. More importantly, the derogatory opinions of Sa'adeh that many of the biographers themselves had valued gave way to occasional praises or kindheartedness. As a way of illustration: in the 1950s, the Syrian interrogator Sami Jama' flanked Abdul Hamid al-Sarraj in defaming Sa'adeh's name and legacy and persecuting his followers. Many years later, the image of Sa'adeh that he projected to both the nation and the world in his autobiography is one of a David defying the Goliath. Sa'adeh was now generally portrayed no longer as a villain but as a victim "of a long ordeal carefully planned by the Americans" and executed by local cronies.[53] This was similar to the image projected by other biographers, but there is no evidence that the sympathy displayed after 1970 was part of a conscious strategy.

Another major category of explanation is the collapse of the Lebanese confessional system in 1975. On the local level, consequently, Sa'adeh's fortunes shot up and his execution once again served as a reminder of what was wrong with the system: on the one hand, it highlighted how cruel and inadequate the system had been; on the other, it underscored Sa'adeh's veracity in challenging the system.[54] The memory of Sa'adeh was again called upon by erudite Lebanese and secular organizations as political ferment increased. The sense of urgency was significant and reflected the perceived desire for radical solutions. It provided the ingredients to exalt and to revitalize the perception of Sa'adeh as a revolutionary as well as a patriot and martyr. Some resurrected the national transformational aspect of Sa'adeh. Others set about writing new tracts in accordance with his canons and in a manner calculated to accentuate his role and merits in challenging the system.[55] Equally important was the way his followers performed during the long years of the war. Their aversion to confessional blood orgies and sturdy secular response to the conflict changed Lebanese perceptions of Sa'adeh and created renewed interest in his ideas. The party then was able to capitalize on popular memory to recast Sa'adeh as a victim of an unforgiving system.

However, Sa'adeh's legacy did not resonate with most Lebanese until after the June 1982 Israeli invasion and subsequent occupation of Lebanon south of Beirut. In the ensuing struggle between the occupiers and the fledging Lebanese resistance, Sa'adeh was invoked by his followers to cause a dramatic shift in the character of the struggle. Using his execution as a symbol of resistance, they instigated the elusive phenomenon of suicide bombings as an alternative form of guerilla warfare and as a secular rather than religious experiment. One after the other, young men and, for the first time, young women,[56] appeared on pre-recorded video footages recalling Sa'adeh's martyrdom and life struggle and urging others to follow in his footsteps. This placed Sa'adeh at the centre of attention not only in Lebanon but all over the Arab World and both at the governmental[57] and intellectual levels. His legend, as a result, again became politically operative in memory and a new, heroic mystique developed around him which recognized more fully his revolutionary stature.

More than any other factor, the "martyrdom operations" of the 1980s played a crucial part in sharpening local awareness of Sa'adeh as an active, self-conscious and enduring historical legacy.[58] It provided another opportunity for some to begin to rethink how he should be remembered. A flood of new articles projected Sa'adeh as the precursor of wars of national liberation and accentuated an earlier trend that identified him with seminal names in the field of national struggle. Apologist authors were more strongly outspoken about this than others. According to these writers, the fierce attacks that had been directed against Sa'adeh have come from those whose political or economic interests he had unrelentingly assailed. It is true that he was uncompromising towards them, they admitted, but this was only to further the cause of justice, not for his own gain. If Sa'adeh had fought the system, it was because it had failed to live up to its promises and obligations to the people. Occasionally, however, Sa'adeh's admirers helped tarnish his true image almost as much as his enemies. This is mainly because many who wrote favorably of him were former followers or belonged to groups which believe that, by lauding Sa'adeh, they are advancing their own cause, and the reader is therefore inclined to discount what they say as exaggeration. Many writers on Sa'adeh did nothing but repeat uncritically what others have said without investigating the facts for themselves.

But this was not the only way that the Sa'adeh cult changed. The tone of his commemorations picked up, his myth was emphasized as a valuable component of the resistance, and ideas about his political significance were elaborated and put into new theoretical framework. Sa'adeh was presented in books, journals and newspapers, in prose and poetry, in song, painting and sculpture, as a heroic figure on a par with similar extraordinary historical personalities. The Sa'adeh myth now was at a close look paradoxical. Next to being a leader and a teacher, he was also a heroic instrument of the people, of the renaissance, and of the nation. What is more, the virtues extolled in the refashioned myth – honor, fidelity, justice, earnestness, perseverance, temperance, chastity – and above all, courage and rugged simplicity, were vividly portrayed to keep Sa'adeh constantly in spiritual presence.

Martyr or Traitor: The Official Viewpoint

The martyr is common to every culture, and all societies are proud to acclaim the sacrifices of their heroes. However martyrdom as a concept is difficult to define, let alone distinguish from simple heroism or idiotic folly, because the awarding of the martyr's crown lies as much in the eyes of the beholder as in the logic of a precise definition.[59] As Lois G. Schwoerer has succinctly observed, "the line between martyr and traitor is very fine indeed, depending entirely on the viewpoint of the observer."[60] Schwoerer then sets down three interactive factors that go into the making of a martyr: (1) dying or enduring suffering with great courage on behalf of some cause or principle; (2) challenging a government that is powerful enough to execute or impose great hardship on its critics; and (3) the existence of individuals who survive the one who has died and who admire or love him, identify with his views, and strive, for personal, political, or altruistic reasons, to preserve his memory.[61]

The one common denominator in all martyrdoms (the word stems from the Greek *martur*, meaning "to witness" or "to attest") is that the martyr, in attesting to his or her faith, dies for a noble cause. Its antithesis says Klapp is treachery:

> Heroic deaths have two common themes: voluntary sacrifice for a cause and defeat by treachery. Frequently these two themes are combined, as when Roland, or Joan of Arc, is both betrayed and martyred. The martyrs are, of course, innumerable among the heroes, not only in the case of the Christian martyrs but in the familiar stories of Beowulf, Antigone, Njal, Cuchulain, Hereward the Wake, Benkei, Davy Crockett, and others. The martyred heroes usually die fighting for a cause against superior enemies or persecuted by a powerful tyrant.[62]

Technically, Sa'adeh is a martyr by the standard definition of the term: he died nobly, fighting for a cause, betrayed by his friends and overwhelmed by his enemies. Moreover, Sa'adeh's personality and character, his political role up to 1949, and his adherence to certain political and ideological principles were essential ingredients in making him a martyr. The term is also legitimately applicable to him since he did not escape when he easily could have, instead welcoming the chance to display his faith and fortitude.

Yet in the eyes of the Lebanese establishment Sa'adeh was neither a patriot nor a hero but a traitor. The choice of the word traitor to describe Sa'adeh was made for clear political reasons. By using this word, successive Lebanese governments were able to deny the political and social nature of his rebellion in 1949 or that there was any legitimacy to Sa'adeh's cause, making him a criminal instead. The tempo was set by the Khoury regime, which sought to project Sa'adeh as a politically insignificant figure and dismissed his uprising as a social deviance. Successor regimes, though more prudent in their judgment of Sa'adeh, never varied much from this initial official characterization. There have been occasions on which Lebanese politicians have partaken in public commemorations of Sa'adeh, but the Lebanese establishment has, on the whole, resisted any move to recognize him as a martyr.

In one respect this is quite an understandable position. Sa'adeh's elevation to the status of official martyr requires a whole new trial or a state decree overturning the original verdict. This is neither novel nor impossible. History offers many examples whereby individuals have been rehabilitated and then elevated to national stature: Augusto Sandino in Nicaragua is one example;[63] Emiliano Zapata in Mexico is another.[64] Figures who dared to challenge the institution of colonialism have also been recognized for their struggle. So in that respect, the scope is ample. The problem, however, is that Sa'adeh's rehabilitation, let alone his elevation to hero status, requires a major policy reversal on the part of the Lebanese State and condemnation of the political apparatus that killed him. Exploration of such an option would need to be sensitive to the diversities of local communities and their forms of political representation. Moreover, the invocation of Sa'adeh requires the projection of an alternative identity which the Lebanese state is neither prepared for, nor has the desire to adopt.

Whether Sa'adeh has or has not the right to the martyr's aureole is not all that is at stake. It is chiefly because of the broader historical implications that the subject is tricky; for this question bears upon the historical memory of the social groups in Lebanon and their own hero perceptions and myth-making. Venerating Sa'adeh under the present system has the potential to trigger a number of problems for which the Lebanese state is clearly unprepared: (1) it may open the floodgates for the veneration of numerous individuals who are perceived as heroes within their own constituencies or confessional milieus but not by society at large; (2) it could, by extension, create deep schisms among the groups and between the groups and the State; and (3) it would place the State at the receiving end of powerful groups who might feel offended by Sa'adeh's veneration. Moreover, turning Sa'adeh into a martyr of the state is politically explosive. It attests to an unconscious admission of guilt as well as an acknowledgement that Sa'adeh died for ideals and convictions and not as a common criminal. It is an act of self-condemnation, a direct attack against the state's legitimacy. Nothing would give greater credence to the truth of Sa'adeh's message than the spectacle of commemoration. In any event, recognizing Sa'adeh as a martyr demands a spectacular demonstration of national unity which is almost impossible in as divided a state as Lebanon.

Another cause for Lebanese State reluctance to embrace Sa'adeh is discomfiture. Consider the task facing the creators of an official textbook about Sa'adeh. The facts of Sa'adeh's career must be strung together in a narrative that is politically acceptable, coherent, and consistent with the larger textbook narrative of Lebanese history presented by the text. The facts (as they might have appeared to an official historian) include the following: Sa'adeh was the charismatic leader of a disciplined party. He and his followers sought the reunification of Lebanon with the rest of Syria because he felt that unification was healthier than division. Sa'adeh rose against the sectarian Khoury regime in support of a secular regime and fought to overturn the political system because it was corrupt and dysfunctional. He issued a complete national plan calling for sweeping reform. He gave his life in the struggle. From the point of view of a political system that bases its claim to legitimacy on a delicate formula of sectarian co-existence rather than real national unity, these are potentially inconvenient facts. They negate a compelling historical narrative that has persisted for decades. The creators of Lebanese history texts face an especially problematic task in interpreting the 1949 uprising and Sa'adeh's role in the struggle.

In recent years, official attitudes towards Sa'adeh have mellowed considerably, due in part to the integration of the SSNP into the Lebanese political system. Constant civil and political instability since 1950 have also played a crucial role in reshaping state perceptions of Sa'adeh. While right-wing detractors have continued to spin narratives of a power-drunk Sa'adeh, the changing political realities of regional and national politics fostered a grudgingly amiable view of Sa'adeh inside the Lebanese State, especially from critics frustrated with the system. Moreover, the moral resilience of his followers during the civil war and in the post-1982 national resistance endowed Sa'adeh's image with unusual vitality even at the top echelons of the state. One of the main ways in which that vitality was honored was by the participation of state officials in the ceremonies of commemoration held on the anniversary of Sa'adeh's execution. Year after year the ceremonies were attended by representatives of national, local (*qada'*) and municipal governments from around the country, as well as the Lebanese military and other branches of the armed forces. In keeping with tradition, the President and Prime Minister of the republic do not attend but send delegates, often cabinet members, to represent them or to speak on their behalf.

On the fiftieth anniversary of Sa'adeh's execution in 1999, the party staged a large public memorial in the Lebanese capital. The memorial was attended by dignitaries from across Lebanon's political spectrum including the then Prime Minister Salim al-Hoss and the Speaker of the House Nabih Berri. The speakers venerated Sa'adeh in typical local polemics but stopped short of demanding a retrial or his exoneration. Another significant commemoration was that held in 2004, on the centenary of Sa'adeh's birthday. The anniversary was celebrated with a variety of cultural and political events held through the year. The highlight of the celebrations was the unveiling of the "Antun Sa'adeh commemorative monument and cultural complex" at Dhur Shweir, Sa'adeh's hometown. The unveiling was attended by high-key officials from both the Lebanese and Syrian states. The Lebanese President was represented by Issam Fares, deputy-chairman of the Cabinet, and his Syrian counterpart by the Minister-in-charge of Presidential Affairs, Ghassan Lahham. Senior officers of the Lebanese army were also in attendance. So too were cabinet members; members of the national chamber; representatives of various local governments; heads of political parties, state functionaries, municipal authorities, and members of the Lebanese Press Syndicate and Labour Union. At the ceremony, Fares gave a resounding speech which remembered Sa'adeh in an orderly way and elevated him to national genius: "I would first like to convey to you the salutation of His Excellency the President of the Republic, General Emile Lahoud, who bestowed on me the honor of representing him at this celebration, and to express to you the sincerest sentiment of His Excellency on the occasion of the unveiling of this commemorative monument for one of the most extraordinary and most ingenious of men, namely, Antun Sa'adeh." The accolades kept coming:

> A century after his birth, do we not all feel his absence stronger than his presence? He is present in the party he established, in the ground-breaking writing he composed about life, mankind, the universe and society, in the ideals which continue to preoccupy researchers, thinkers and analysts, in the intellectual revolution he launched against the Mandate and imperialism and against iniquity, despotism, ignorance and backwardness. He is present in his spiritio-material philosophy which combines between the spiritual and material philosophies and calls for modernization and separation between religion and politics. He is also present in the call for one life on the basis of which national interests and the nation's freedom of will, sovereignty and wealth are determined. Finally, he is present in the Social National renaissance he initiated.

The Chairman of the Lebanese Press Syndicate, Muhammad Baalbaki, a veteran admirer of Sa'adeh, recreated the widespread adulation of the heroic Sa'adeh in his own skillful way: "We have journeyed to the National Resistance Square in Dhur Shweir to take part in the unveiling of a commemorative monument for the Great Leader Antun Sa'adeh. This is an act of unveiling to a man who unveiled with his penetrating thought the veneer that obstructed visions; the man who liberated minds and hearts with his own mind and heart; the man who gave up his life for the nation . . ." Such sobriquets boosted Sa'adeh's stature among a much wider audience, but did not gain him official recognition. The national government in Lebanon, wary of political and sectarian sensitivities, refrained from awarding him lasting honors. Despite its strong representation at the unveiling, it did not recognize him as a martyr or as a heroic figure of the state.

In their book *Heroes and Hero Cults in Latin America*, Samuel Brunk and Ben Fallaw argue that national states embrace departed heroes because "heroes help large numbers of people identify with a nation and internalize and accept as natural its basic principles and laws, thus producing greater unity in a population."[65] This unity, they add:

> . . . is often cultivated and exploited by officials seeking to extend state power into people's daily lives, where a state is defined as the civil and military bureaucracies of a territory and the officials those

who, in different branches and at various levels, control those bureaucracies. States presumably benefit from the national identity that heroes can help produce because people who feel themselves to be part of a single community may be less fractious and thus more easily governable than people who do not. But more than that, political leaders often invoke heroes in an effort to bolster their legitimacy through association with admired predecessors, or in the hope of making citizens more virtuous and productive by giving them models of behavior to follow.[66]

Sa'adeh was an energetic visionary and a charismatic leader, but the concepts of identity and nationality that he embodied precluded him from becoming a prominent member of Lebanon's national pantheon. If he had died fighting the system as a Lebanese rather than a Syrian national crusader his induction into the national pantheon might have taken place long ago. He may even have transcended the national setting to become an international icon. But his claim was for a national identity that was purer, deeper, and more legitimate than the existing identities and the fate they connote for Lebanon. As a result, Sa'adeh has remained an enduring enigma for the Lebanese State: it cannot adopt him because his vision is inimical with its existence; it cannot fully and liberally engage his legacy because the social and political situation in the country is impenetrable; and it cannot discard him because his myth and legacy are too deeply rooted in popular memory to ignore. In retrospect, Sa'adeh's enigma brings into focus the defectiveness of the confessional system in Lebanon: it shows that the system cannot spawn heroes or recognize them for the qualities and contribution they represent even if it is politically sensible to do so.

As a symbol of rebellion and intransigence Sa'adeh is highly admired in Lebanon, but it seems unlikely that he will ever be accepted as a national hero such as Churchill in Britain or Georgy Zhukov in Russia.[67] Indeed the extensiveness of his outlook is more reminiscent of great revolutionaries: those who place generalities ahead of specificities and sacrifice the all for one. His commemoration has thus been a partial one, confined mainly to his admirers, albeit with the sort of fervor that he once adopted himself, along with his like-minded followers.

Official and Unofficial Histories

Antun Sa'adeh died defeated and, in some quarters, despised. To this day, in the recycled histories of post-1943 Lebanon, he is ignored or belittled. Within a few brief sentences, his exploits are depicted as destabilizing though pointless. Their purpose is not, in any event, revealed. At no point is Sa'adeh connected to main issues, despite the gravity of his actions, and his role as a national crusader against French colonial rule is not acknowledged. Narratives that record Sa'adeh's participation in the fight against the Khoury regime and in the rebellion that subsequently exploded in its face, never explain exactly who Sa'adeh was or why he rebelled. Hence, the motivations of Sa'adeh and his followers are largely obscure. Other accounts allude to Sa'adeh's execution and note that his men fought on after his death, but they fail to explain who killed Sa'adeh or why.

In the decade after Sa'adeh's death, the history texts that the newly independent education ministry in Lebanon approved for use in public schools were, by and large, lightly revised and updated versions of histories produced under the French mandate. The textbooks were marked by extravagant praise for the independence era and critical assessments of Sa'adeh under an aversion to disorder and upheaval. In contrast, Solh and Khoury are celebrated as heroes of independence who presided over an era of economic and national progress. There is no recognition in these texts that their own policies may have contributed to the violence that exploded in 1949 and led to Sa'adeh's execution.

In the same books, Sa'adeh's posthumous career takes one step forward and two steps back. His identity is glossed over to ensure that only one cluster of accounts is honored. Transformed into that of a deviant and outcast, Sa'adeh's reputation is relegated to an area outside society's moral boundaries. The approved texts of later periods, particularly during the Chehab era, are hardly better. The narrative backdrop created by the versions of the independence era was recycled to provide an even more unsympathetic treatment of Sa'adeh. His physical invisibility and modest narrative stature in these books embody an implicit notion of historical agency, an answer to the question of who or what moves history. Those who make history, these books seem to suggest, are the men who struggle to bring the country to order. In contrast, Sa'adeh leads a premature uprising, which undermines official attempts to build the nation. Such men are interlopers, who get in the way of the real historical actors. At best, the books provide the most striking example of the phenomenon of willful disregard. This refers to "the conscious or unconscious rejection of the history of the other, and the refusal to agree to acquaint oneself with his personality, his role and his value. This neglect of the other may be more cutting than hostility or denigration."[68]

Whatever their long-term effect on Sa'adeh's image, these early versions reflected the immediate need of the political regimes to retain the loyalty of their partisans. They were composed basically to please sectarian sentiments and to reinforce sectarian identity at the expense of a national identity. In one respect, such histories reflect the way that every country teaches its national history:

> We have also had to bear in mind that history textbooks are no more than an academic product, composed, reviewed and revised according to specific criteria by the current political authority in a particular country in the light of current attitudes towards the country whose history is being formulated. It is also necessary to mention that the history that is taught in schools is totally different from the history which is related in the home. Family memory is different from the official history and the family often seeks to confront the official formulation of history which is taught to its children.[69]

In another respect, the pre-evaluative, obstinate prejudice against Sa'adeh, and the degree of partiality in Lebanese histories, is symptomatic of the wider problem of history writing in Lebanon. As in almost every facet of Lebanese life, historical objectivity is constrained by the sectarian spirit which pervades the country. The problem simply will not go away:

> Private schools, which educate about half the country's one million or so students, teach history based on books of their choosing, but approved by the Ministry of Education; public schools teach about two hours of history a week, based on textbooks virtually unchanged since they were written in the 1960s and 1970s. In one textbook, the students get to know the Ottomans as occupiers; in another, they read about them as administrators. In some, they study the French as colonialists; in others, they study them as examples to emulate. In some Christian schools, history starts with the ancient Phoenicians, who many Christians believe are their original ancestors, and the dawn of Christianity. In many Muslim schools,

the Phoenicians are glossed over and emphasis is placed on Arab history and the arrival of Islam. Whether Lebanon was occupied by the Ottomans, was subjugated by the Ottomans or was simply a principality of the Ottoman Empire depends on the sect and region, much like whether the French, who oversaw the country until the 1950s, are depicted as colonialists, administrators or models of emulation.[70]

Unofficial Lebanese histories have been problematical in a different way. Although they are not nearly as disrespectful or impartial in their treatment of Sa'adeh, the discourse they followed had depended ultimately on the extent of the franchise, latitude of freedom of speech, and political maturity and outlook of individual authors: Lebanonist authors have generally tended to follow the official line with perhaps a hint of criticism of the regime, although some authors have darkened the villainy of Sa'adeh more than official histories, thereby preserving the role of traitor as his master status; Pan-Arab authors of the 1950s and 1960s were merciless and often depicted Sa'adeh as the kind of person who might commit treason, having the requisite character traits, absence of virtue, and personal motivation. Thus, both unofficial Lebanonist and unofficial pan-Arab historians engaged in demonization, though some more than others.

After 1970, Sa'adeh fared better in Pan-Arab histories. An interactive process developed during which his reputation was re-formulated, debated, crystallized and commemorated to reflect the new reconciliation between Arab and Syrian nationalism. On the whole, Pan-Arab histories continued to propagate a grudgingly hostile view of Sa'adeh's nationalist ideals but refrained from attacking his person and, in some cases, displayed an astonishing sympathy for his execution and to the cause for which he stood. Students now encountered a richer, more candid portrayal of the execution and a fuller account of Sa'adeh's life.

At the other extreme, sympathetic histories depicted Sa'adeh as a colorful and enduring figure in the nation's remembered past. Taking his execution as a reference point, they saw him as a man of heroic virtues, a defender of national rights against powerful enemies, the father of secular reforms, and a martyr whose influence lives beyond his worldly deeds. However, since Sa'adeh cannot be a hero unless the regime which killed him is a villain, sympathetic accounts invariably presaged indifferent or hostile portraits of the Khoury regime. Recasting Solh and Khoury as the villains, they emphasized their thoroughly loathsome, despicable, corrupt nature and portrayed their regime as an example of the kind of regimes that need to be excised or guarded against.

Conclusion

The construction of the myth and indeed of the legend of Sa'adeh which developed after his execution was, quite naturally, much more complex than the images that have been analyzed here. What is evident from this examination of a few of the more notable themes in this construction is that his followers fully understood, even if only intuitively, the power of representing him in a particular light. In the process, they not only constructed an idealized image of Sa'adeh, but also laid the foundations of a legend around his person. Since then, the attempt to understand Sa'adeh from a wider ideological and philosophical perspective has continued incessantly.

While the manner of Sa'adeh's moral and physical resistance to authorities and the manner of his death certainly have that heroic quality which is almost synonymous with past heroes, in other ways he has remained a relatively obscure hero. Sa'adeh exerted on the mind an influence that we cannot properly appraise. He has swept aside all in his path and his hero-martyr myth, created in large part by his followers, has guaranteed him a lasting space in the popular memory of his people. Whether this space grows or shrinks will ultimately depend on political realities. The degree to which Sa'adeh as hero-martyr finds an echo in Lebanese society will also depend on whether his followers and admirers can finally learn to think *with* Sa'adeh rather than *about* him.

Skepticism and even opposition to the Sa'adeh myth will probably persist for many years to come. But to exercise an aversion for the myth purely because of the dangers inherent in myth-making is all too often merely an excuse for sparing ourselves the effort to appreciate human excellence and mortal spirits. The best antidote to this cynicism is to recognize that martyrs and heroes and the exemplary heroism and achievements of great individuals are an essential part of a developed society. As the Roman Stoic philosopher, statesman and dramatist Lucius Annaeus Seneca once said: "Cherish some man of high character, and keep him ever before your eyes, living as if he were watching you, and ordering all your actions as if he beheld them."[71]

NOTES

1 Patrick Seale, *The Struggle for Syria: A Study of Post-War Diplomacy 1945–1958*. Oxford: Oxford University Press, 1965: 69.

2 *Istijwab Jumblatt al tarikhi lil hukuma hawla istishhad Sa'adeh ome 1949* (Jumblatt's historical interpolation to the [Lebanese] Government In Regard to Sa'adeh's Martyrdom in 1949). Beirut: SSNP Information Bureau, 1987.

3 *As-Sayyad*, Beirut, 9 July, 1949.

4 *Al-Hayat*, Beirut: 14 July, 1949.

5 On Hisham Sharabi's association with Sa'adeh see Jan Daye, *Sa'adeh wa Hisham Sharabi* (Sa'adeh and Hisham Sharabi). Stockholm: Dar Nelson, 2004.

6 *Al-Jil al-Jadid*, 27 September, 1950.

7 See *al-Mashriq*. Melbourne: Vol. 5, No. 25, 2008: 57–65.

8 Said Taky ad-Din, "The Priest who confessed him".

9 Reproduced in Ghassan Al-Khalidi, *Sa'adeh wa al-Thawrah al-Ula* (Sa'adeh and the First Revolution). Beirut: Dar wa Maktabat al-Turath al-Adabi, 1997: 375–376.

10 Mohammad Maatouk, "A Critical Study of Antun Sa'ada and his Impact on Politics: The History of Ideas and Literature in the Middle East." PhD, University of London, 1992: 328.

11 Ibid., 329.

12 Myth can be defined as "a usually traditional story of ostensibly historical events that serves to unfold part of the world view of a people or explain a practice, belief, or natural phenomenon." This definition does not exclude the possibility that elements of a myth might be historically accurate. See *Merriam-Webster's Collegiate Dictionary*, 10th ed. Springfield, Mass.: Merriam-Webster, 1993: 770.

13 See M. G. Barout, "Tajroubat al-Hadetha fi Majallat Shi'r" (The Modernist Experiment in Shi'r), *Fikr*, Vol. 64 (Spring 1985): 44.

14 Such as: Khalil Hawi (1925–1982), Ali Ahmad Sa'id [known as Adonis] (b. 1929), Badr Shakir al-Sayyab (1926–1964), Unsi al-Hajj (b. 1937), Nazeer El-Azama (b. 1930), Fu'ad Rifqa (b. 1930), Isam Mahfuz (b. 1939), Taufiq Sayigh (1923–1971), Jabra Ibrahim Jabra (b. 1919) and Yusuf al-Khal (1917–1987). See Nazeer El-Azama, "The Tammuzi Movement and the influence of T.S. Eliot on Badr Shakir Al-Sayya," in *Critical Perspectives on Modern Arabic Literature*. Edited by Issa J. Boullata, 1st edition. Washington: Three Continents Press, inc., 1980: 215.

15 S. Moreh. *Modern Arabic Poetry 1800–1970*. Leiden, The Netherlands: E.J. Brill, 1976: 279.

16 Salma Khadra Jayyusi. "Contemporary Arabic Poetry: Vision and Attitudes." In R. C. Ostle (ed), *Studies in Modern Arabic Literature*. London: Aris & Phillips Ltd, 1975: 48.

17 http://wings.buffalo.edu/epc/authors/rothenberg/50s.html (6 June, 2008).

18 Nazeer El-Azama, "Sa'adeh, al-Ustura wa al-Shi'r." *Fikr*, Vols. 43–46, Dec. 1980–April 1981: 119.

19 Muhammad Al-'Abed Hammud, "Sa'adeh: A Scholar," *al-Bina'*, issue 880, 12/7/1997.

20 George Masru'ah, *Ibn Zikar*, 2nd. ed. Beirut: Dar al-Makshufah, 1954.

21 Sati Husri, *al-Uruba baina Du 'atiha was Mu'aridhiha* (Arabism between its Supporters and its Opponents). Beirut: Dar al-Makshufah, 1952.

22 Bassam Tibi, *Arab Nationalism: A Critical Enquiry* (trans. by M. and P. Sluglett). New York: St. Martin's Press, 1981: xi.

23 Kamal Jumblatt, *Adwa' ala Haqiqat al-Qadiyya al-Qawmiyya al-Ijtima'iyya as-Suriyya: al-Fikra al-Qawmiyyah* (Lights on the Truth Concerning the Syrian Social Nationalist Cause: The National Idea). Beirut: Progressive Press, 1987.

24 Sati al-Husri, *op. cit.*

25 See Sami Khoury, *Radd ala Sati' al-Husri* (A Response to Sati al-Husri). Beirut: n.p., 1956.

26 G. A. Williams, *The Merthyr Rising*. London: Croom Helm, 1978: 204.

27 Moose to DOS, tel. 27 April 1955, 783.00/4-2755, Decimal File NARG59. On the Malki affair, see Seale, *Struggle for Syria*: 238–46.

28 George Kirk, "The Syrian Crisis of 1957 – Facts and Fiction," *International Affairs*, 36 (1960): 59.

29 Douglas Little, "Cold War and Covert Action: The United States and Syria 1945–1958," *Middle East Journal*, 44 (Winter 1990): 66. See also Wilbur Crane Eveland, *Ropes of Sand: America's Failure in the Middle East*. New York: W. W. Norton, 1980: 191–192.

30 See Faysal Mikdadi, *Gamal Abdel Nasser: A Bibliography* (Bibliographies of World Leaders). London: Greenwood Press, 1991: 93–105.

31 See Anthony Gorst, *The Suez Crisis*. London: Routledge, 1997: 147–164.

32 Tarek Osman, "Nasser's complex legacy," on Open Democracy, www.opendemocracy.net, 29 May, 2008.

33 Lori J. Ducharme and Gary Alan Fine, "The Construction of Nonpersonhood and Demonization: Commemorating the Traitorous Reputation of Benedict Arnold." *Social Forces*, Vol. 73, No. 4 (Jun., 1995): 1316. The authors note: "Two important sets of evidence are produced by those involved in the degradation process: biography and motive. First, the process of applying and solidifying the pivotal identity of "traitor" is enhanced by the reconstruction of the offender's biography, such that events once seen as either virtuous, unremarkable, or irrelevant are reinterpreted and reclassified as confirmation of the deviant identity . . . Second, the underlying motives for the actor's offense are sought, assessed, and ascribed. These include the offender's accounts of his actions, as well as others' imputations of motive." See also J. Lofland, *Deviance and Identity*. Englewood Cliffs, NJ: Prentice – Hall., 1969.

34 For a detailed study of *Shu'ubism*, see Sami A. Hanna and George H. Gardner, "Al-Shu'ubiyyah Up-Dated: A Study of the 20th Century Revival of an Eighth Century Concept." *The Middle East Journal*, Vol. XX (1966): 335–355.

35 See Adel Beshara (ed.), *Antun Sa'adeh: The Man, His Thought*. Reading: Ithaca Press, 2007: 121–162.

36 A recent reproduction of this theory can be found in Hadhim Saghiyyah, *Qawmiyyu al-Mashriq al-Arabi* (The Nationalists of the Arab East). London: Riyad al-Rayyes Books, 2000.

37 See section on Sa'adeh in Muhammad Jamil Bayhum, *Al-Urubah wa-Al-shu'ubiyat al-Hadithah: Niqash ma'a Antun Sa'adah, Kamal Junbulat, Salamah Musa, Amir Baqtar wa-Ta'liqat ala' al-Shubuhat fi Muqaddimat Ibn Khaldun* (Arabism and Contemporary Shu'ubism). Beirut: Matabi' Da'r al-Kashshaf, al-Muqaddimah, 1957.

38 See Adel Beshara, *The Politics of Frustration – the Failed Coup of 1961*. London: Routledge Curzon, 2004.

39 Orrin E. Klapp, *Collective Search for Identity*. London: Holt, R. & W., 1969; Thomas Carlyle, *On Heroes, Hero-Worship, and The Heroic in History*. London: The Echo Library, 2007; Fitzroy Richard Somerset Raglan, *The Hero: A Study in Tradition, Myth and Drama*. Mineola, N.Y.: Dover Publications Inc., 2003.

40 Kamal Salibi, "Lebanon under Fuad Chehab 1958–1964." *Middle East Studies*, 2 (1966): 211–226; Bassim al-Jisr, *Fouad Chehab: Dhalika al-Majhoul* (Fouad Chehab: The Unknown). Beirut: The Corporation for Publications and Distribution, 1988; Tawfiq Kfoury, *al-Shihabiyyah wa Siyassit al-Mawqif* (The Basic Principles of Chehabism). Beirut: n.p., 1980.

41 Francis Wheen, *Karl Marx*. London: Fourth Estate Limited, 1999: 2.

42 Commemorations of Sa'adeh's execution, for example, were frequently used by the party leadership as a platform for fiery political speeches against opponents rather than as an occasion for celebration and contemplation. The time spent on Sa'adeh during these commemorations dwindled as the years passed, reflecting a growing preoccupation with immediate political needs and personal desires.

43 In 1970, the SSNP was re-issued a permit to operate legally in Lebanon, its hierarchy was released from prison, and the party was allowed to publish a periodical called *al-Bina'*.

44 See, in particular, In'am Raad, *Harb al-Tahrir al-Qawmiyya* (National Liberation War). Beirut, 1970. Raad noted: "Social nationalism and Marxist-Leninism converge in analyzing the capitalist economic side of imperialism. But social nationalism does not stop at this point in comprehending and rejecting the modern phenomenon of imperialism. For if imperialism is an extension of capitalism, this analysis applies to capitalist imperialism only. But there are various kinds of domination and aggression which take place on other bases and out of other motives."

45 Some of these photographs were reproduced in Gibran Jreige, *Ma' Antun Sa'adeh* (In the Company of Antun Sa'adeh), Beirut: n.p., n.d.

46 In recent years it has become fashionable to light up candles in public squares, where permissible, or small fires on mountain tops as part of the commemorations. Except when political risks are probable, the government hardly interferes in such activities and generally turns a blind eye to municipal participation in them.

47 See *Sabah el-Kheir* and *al-Bina'* for yearly coverage of the celebrations. Every year, both journals publish a commemorative issue on 8 July.

48 See Stephen J. Roth, *The Impact of the Six-Day War: a Twenty-Year Assessment*. Basingstoke: Palgrave Macmillan, 1988. Also, Jeremy Bowen, "How 1967 defined the Middle East" (http://news.bbc.co.uk).

49 Raghid Sulh, *Lebanon and Arabism: National Identity and State Formation*. London: Centre for Lebanese Studies, 2004: 307.

50 *Sabah el-Kheir*, Beirut, 7 July, 1949. Al-Mashnouq was a noted opponent of Sa'adeh in the late 1940s and entered into a fierce ideological debate with him in 1948–9 in the pages of *Beirut al-Masa'*. He was its editor-in-charge.

51 http://ssnp.net/content/view/5489/160/

52 See Sami Solh, *Ahtakimu ila al-Tarikh* (I Leave It to History to Judge Me). Beirut: Dar an-Nahar, 1970.

53 Sami Jam'a, *Awraq min Daftar al-Watan, 1946–1961* (Pages from Homeland Records). Damascus: Dar Tlas, 2000: 65–82.

54 The Chief of Lebanese General Security, Amir Farid Chehab, who took delivery of Sa'adeh on 6 July and handed him to the Military Tribunal the following day, stated in 1980: "I am Lebanese before all else. However, if I had known that Lebanon would end up where it is today I would have fought alongside Antun Sa'adeh." *Sabah el-Kheir*, Beirut, 12 July, 1980.

55 See Inam Raad, *Antun Sa'adeh wa al-In'izaliyun* (Antun Sa'adeh and the Isolationists). Beirut: Dar Fikr, 1980.

56 In contemporary times, the first suicide operation was carried out by Sana Mhaidli, a Lebanese female of Shiite origin and member of the Syrian Social Nationalist Party, and therefore secular. She died after driving into an Israeli outpost in 1985. This clearly shows that the secular connection to suicide missions predates the religious one.

57 Streets, squares, schools and other landmarks were named after the suicide bombers, particularly in Syria. As far away as Libya, a street was named after Sana Mhaidli, the first female bomber.

58 It seems the general Western view is that the suicide attackers are marginalised individuals, left with no place in their own societies, perhaps feeling the need to atone for some "deviant" behaviour. Yet, the evidence hardly supports this view, especially in relation to Lebanese bombers. See Natalie Bennett's review of *Female Suicide Bombers* by Rosemarie Skaine on Blogcritics Magazine (http://blogcritics.org/archives/2006/06/18/092605.php). Debra D. Zedalis, however, gives a more qualified view: "The reasons for women's participation in deadly attacks vary greatly and it is hard to generalize, for this phenomenon is too recent and the attacks have been too few. Either not enough research has been conducted yet or the sample size is too small to make effective generalizations." Although the data are limited, female suicide bombers, just like male suicide bombers, have one characteristic which typifies all – they are young. The average age varies from 21.5 (Turkey) to 23 (Lebanon), a small differential. Other characteristics do not hold. Some are widows and others have never been married; some are unemployed and others are professionals; some are poor and others are middle class. Most analysts can easily compare the Black Widows in Russia with the Palestinian suicide bombers, since both appear to be serving "struggles of national identity" with religious overtones. Additionally, as is true of the male counterparts, several female suicide bombers have experienced the loss of a close friend or family member." In Debra D. Zedalis, *Female Suicide Bombers*. Strategic Studies Institute, U.S. Army War College, 2004: 14.

59 Norbert J. Gossman, *The Martyrs: Joan of Arc to Yitzhak Rabin*. Lanham: University Press of America, Inc., 1997: 1–7.

60 Lois G. Schwoerer, "William, Lord Russell: The Making of a Martyr, 1683–1983." *The Journal of British Studies*, Vol. 24, No. 1 (Jan., 1985): 41–71.

61 Ibid.

62 Orrin E. Klapp, "The Folk Hero." *The Journal of American Folklore*, Vol. 62, No. 243 (Jan–Mar., 1949): 22.

63 See Donald C. Hodges, *Intellectual Foundations of the Nicaragua Revolution*. Austin: University of Texas Press, 1986.

64 Samuel Brunk, "The Mortal Remains of Emiliano Zapata." In Lyman Johnson (ed.), *Death, Dismemberment, and Memory*. Albuquerque: University of New Mexico Press, 2004.

65 Samuel Brunk and Ben Fallaw, *Heroes and Hero Cults in Latin America*. Austin: University of Texas Press, 2006: 3.

66 Ibid.

67 William J. Spahr, *Zhukov: The Rise and Fall of a Great Captain*. Novato, CA: Presidio Press, 1993.

68 Fauziya Al-Ashmawi, "The Image of the Other in History Textbooks in some Mediterranean Countries (Spain, France, Greece, Egypt, Jordan, Lebanon, Tunisia)". http://www.isesco.org.ma/english/publications/Islamtoday/13/P6.php (4 June, 2008).

69 Ibid.

70 Hassan M. Fattah, "Lebanon's history textbooks are politicized." http://yalibnan.com/site/archives/2007/01/lebanons_histor.php (Thursday, 11 January, 2007).

71 Quoted in John W. Spaeth. Jr., "Roman Hero Worship." *The Classical Journal*, Vol. 20, No. 6 (Mar., 1925): 354.

CONCLUSION

No trial in the legal history of Lebanon, and indeed the Arab world, has ever been held as rapidly and secretly as the Antun Sa'adeh trial. In all, it lasted from five in the morning of 7 July to eight in the evening on the same day. The entire procedure, including the pre-trial stage and execution, happened within the following tight schedule:

1. Investigation	5.00 a.m. – 12.00 noon
1. Trial start	12.00 noon
2. Cross-examination	12.00 noon – 1.30 p.m.
3. Prosecutor's speech	1.30 p.m. – 3.30 p.m.
4. Adjournment	5 minutes
5. Defense speech	3.35 p.m. – 3.40 p.m.
6. Sa'adeh's address	3.40 p.m. – 5.10 p.m.
7. Deliberation	5.15 p.m. – 7.30 p.m.
8. Sentencing	7.30 p.m. – 8.30 p.m.
9. Execution	2.50 a.m.

The case is without precedent not only because the authorities violated every elementary law in organizing the trial but because it was, to put it mildly, a compound of stupidity and hypocrisy. It was a trial that much more closely resembled a juridical play with the verdict largely resolved in the individual minds of the participating actors. Every aspect of the trial gives a clear sense of a predetermined rush to execute rather than of a commitment to achieve justice. The regime engaged in an unseemly and evidently politically motivated effort to expedite the execution by denying time for a meaningful appeal and by closing off every avenue to review the punishment.

As in all good dramas, it is difficult to weigh precisely all the pluses and minuses of the Sa'adeh affair. It could be argued, however, that so many minuses occurred that any semblance of judicial impartiality ended before the start of the trial. It was a classic example of "power reigns without rule or law."[1]

I

In sentencing Sa'adeh to death, the Khoury regime was influenced by three principal allegations. The first was Sa'adeh's "enmity" toward Lebanon. As a general rule, judgemental allegations of this nature would not hold up ten minutes in a normal courtroom. It is true that Sa'adeh did not regard Lebanon as a nation in its own right but that didn't necessarily make him an enemy of the country by any stretch of the imagination. He always maintained that the final national status of Lebanon would depend entirely on the Lebanese provided they were allowed to choose freely where they prefered to be. He did not believe in force or in arbitrary political mergers. In any event, the Khoury regime lacked both the right and the moral integrity to pass sweeping judgments on individual loyalty. Its efforts to assign social and personal identity in neotraditional terms and its tendency to equate its particular status interests with the general interests of the state through blatant corruption, embezzlement, rigging, nepotism, and sectarianism are scarcely exemplar. In any other country where accountability is a real constituent of the state, it would fail the first principles of democracy and loyalty.

The second allegation relates to treason. Here as well the case against Sa'adeh was completely mishandled through trumped-up charges based on falsified documents. If it had been judged in calmer times before a learned court, the great bulk of the evidence would have been excluded either on the ground of incompetence or irrelevance, and the verdict would certainly have been different. The fact that the regime manufactured the evidence against the defendant not only annihilates the charge of treason, but also is a terrible piece of evidence against the accusers themselves. Sa'adeh's whole life, everything he had said, written or done, is overwhelming proof of the falsity of this charge. Virtually all the evidence now shows that the real saboteurs during the 1948 Palestine War were those who hauled the charge of treason against Sa'adeh and that the Khoury regime was privy to their treasonous activities but did nothing.[2] Such inaction points to a degree of complicity with the alleged saboteurs on the part of the regime.

There was one allegation against Sa'adeh that the government considered serious enough to justify his execution if proven: the insurrection. However, the political nature of the offense precluded the death penalty and that, it seemed, compelled the government to turn to underhand methods. Instead of allowing the law to run its regular course it rudely interrupted the process to affirm the conditions that would render a death conviction almost inescapable: Distortion + Speed + Secrecy + Court-martial + Capital criminology. All five conditions were crucial to the success of the strategy: *Distortion* to compensate for the paucity of the evidence; *Speed* to avoid a public trial; *Secrecy* to circumvent a political trial; *Court-martial* to obtain the death penalty; *Capital criminology* to secure a court-martial. The plan put the final judgement beyond question. It did not seek the death sentence for Sa'adeh: it pre-determined it. The rules of procedure and principle of evidence, which we have already sufficiently commented on, were amended to the defendant's disadvantage; and there were inexplicable mysteries and suspicions, and less assistance than usual was rendered to the defense counsel. Moreover, much of the evidence came from individuals who were themselves on trial for their lives. The testimony of these witnesses may, of course, have been truthful, but their own self-interest in avoiding punishment and their positions in the insurrection must lead to questions about their veracity, questions that the court itself never asked.

The trial was objectionable in other respects. The speed of the proceedings, the nature of the evidence, and the identity of the judges all combined to preclude judicious decision-making and to guarantee an unjust outcome. It is inconceivable that the judges could have come to their task with open minds. But the biggest problem of military courts is what today is known as "command influence." Instead of an independent judge and a jury of citizens, the court has a panel of officers. These officers are part of the military command structure, reporting to the same commanders who decided to prosecute, and hand-picked by them (picked, perhaps, for readiness to convict). The defense lawyer is also an officer, part of the same command structure. If the commanders want a conviction, these officers know their careers are on the line, so they usually comply with the demand. No wonder it is common for military trials to yield absurd results.

Under Lebanese law, military judges have two main duties to perform: to decide whether the facts set out in the indictment have been proved; and also, if they decide that these facts have been proved, whether there are aggravating or extenuating circumstances in the case, to mitigate the crime. Yet, on the available evidence, the judges that sat on the Sa'adeh case were neither sufficiently versed in law nor acquainted with all the facts to carry out their duties in a satisfactory way. Worse still, they were staunch adherents to the regime and personal friends of the President and Premier Solh.

To say, as many have, that the trial was unfair because it was conducted too quickly only skims the surface of the imperfections. A detailed look at the trial proceedings produces a more precise understanding of the nature of the unfairness, especially in relation to secrecy. As far back as 1827, the English Utilitarian and leader of the Philosophical Radicals, Jeremy Bentham[3] outlined the perils of secrecy as follows:

> In the darkness of secrecy, sinister interest, and evil in every shape have full swing. Only in proportion as publicity has place can any of the checks applicable to judicial injustice operate. Where there is no publicity there is no justice. Publicity is the very soul of justice. It is the keenest spur to exertion and the surest guard against improbity. It keeps the judge himself while trying under trial.[4]

Openness as a vehicle of judicial accountability may apply even where a degree of secrecy is acknowledged to be necessary. What, then, if the reasons for secrecy are not compelling, as in the trial of Antun Sa'adeh?

In 1949, the Lebanese regime was less than six years old. As the first regime after independence, much was riding on its political performance. The irony is that Sa'adeh presented the Khoury regime with an opportunity to demonstrate its commitment to the rule of law and to provide a shared sense that the courts operate with integrity, and it didn't. It chose, instead, to place its own power and interest above the power and interest of the law. Law, says Carol Chomsky, "must be more than the routine exercise of power. It must 'guide and educate' those subject to it and validate itself ethically in the eyes of the governed as well as in the eyes of the ruling class."[5] She adds:

> Groups that form the policy must either share the norms of behavior reflected in the law or accept that the system that produces those standards represents the best interests of the community of which

they are a part, even if some individual rule is not consistent with their own self-interest. Law is justified – and effective – only insofar as it reflects the community's shared values or is the product of a process viewed as legitimate by the governed.[6]

Every consideration of government policy must give way to the principle of due process because the ideal of a fair public trial is the cornerstone of civilized government. It is the measure between good and bad governments:

> For most people it is the criminal trial that overshadows all other symbols as the dramatization that this is a government of law and not of men. It represents the dignity of the state as the enforcer of law and at the same time the dignity of the individual even though he be an avowed opponent of the state, a dissenter or radical, or even a hardened criminal. So important is the public trial to the whole ideological structure of any government that the adoption of more efficient and speedy ways of punishing individuals is a sure sign of instability and insecurity.[7]

In its determination to get rid of Sa'adeh the Khoury regime willingly abandoned its liberal façade and reverted to fabrication. It carefully drafted and revised the charges to compound the allegations against Sa'adeh and deliberately distorted the facts to cover up its misdeeds. Many years later insiders exposed the process of constructing false charges with cynical candor and revealed gross legal violations perpetrated by the regime. Apparently, the evidence against Sa'adeh was so weak and vulnerable that distortion became the only practical avenue for conviction. The desire to avoid a political trial and thus a potential verbal confrontation with Sa'adeh is another possible clue and may have had a lot to do with it.

On the surface, this desire seemed logical and reasonable given the potentially political nature of the evidence and, thus, the danger of the trial turning into a platform for political mockery.[8] However, it is ominous and downright treacherous when a government attempts to avoid a political trial through deliberate falsification of the facts and blatant disregard for the precepts of law. By depriving Sa'adeh of his right to a political trial, despite the overtly political character of his case, the Khoury regime cannot really be said to have acted fairly. For those who initiate a revolution, or make a futile attempt to do so, or even single-handedly hope to destroy what they consider despotism, by making it unsafe for the incumbent regime, are just as much political offenders as those who succeed.

Even more profound was the decision of the Khoury regime to consider the accused in the same breath as an ordinary criminal rather than as a political offender. This manner of looking at political criminality had ceased a long time ago and governments, notably in France, whose legal code forms the basis of the Lebanese Code, have since separated the political from the ordinary crimes and established for the former a scale of special penalties milder than the ordinary penalties. Moreover, unlike the older unenlightened practice, where all criminals were classified according to the physical facts of their conduct, the newer criminology considers the physical facts of the crime as merely some of the indications of the quality of the psychologic imperative conditioning the characteristics of the criminal conduct.[9] This means that, as a political offender, Sa'adeh should have been judged, not by the physical quality and physical circumstances of his acts, but by the psychological qualities and circumstances of his inner compulsion, "only in so far as that was a conscious part of his criminal act."[10]

So, was the trial simply an instance of miscarriage of justice?[11] Yes, to the extent that state institutions were used to bring about results, which appear, on the face of it to represent justice, when in reality they only represent a perversion of justice. However, it is not normal to assign the phrase "miscarriage of justice" to a case where the verdict springs from a deliberate human fault rather than from fortuitous circumstances infringing on the legal rules.[12] We cannot, for example, classify the trials of the Great Purge under Stalin as a "miscarriage of justice" because the entire procedure was stage-framed and carried out according to the general and direct orders of the regime. Likewise, we cannot speak of a "miscarriage of justice" in the Sa'adeh case because the trial was completely a frame-up: the "sentence" passed on Sa'adeh was almost assuredly drawn up and its wording decided upon before the trial had even started. The term is inapplicable because the trial was not in the slightest degree a juridical procedure designed to determine the truth or falsity of the charges brought against the defendant. History, facts, dates and evidence were as of little moment in the trial as human life and human dignity. The objective was to send the defendant to death by any manner of means possible.

II

The trial and execution of Antun Sa'adeh, then, were about revenge, not justice. The manner in which they were carried out – hurriedly, secretively, in the dark of night, in a mockery of any semblance of legal process – was incomprehensible. The trial was never designed to prove the truth or falsity of anything whatever, certainly not of the guilt of the defendant. To the extent that its intention was to defeat and destroy Sa'adeh, the Khoury regime achieved its goal with sublime complacency. However, from the point of view of truth and law, the trial goes down in history as the greatest disgrace to Lebanese justice.

Can the Lebanese redress this historic injustice and, if so, how? It would not be right to insist today that someone should be answerable for an unjustifiable act done many years ago. Redressing a historical wrong for venal reasons or to teach the perpetrators and their heirs a lesson is pointless and counterproductive. A sincere recognition that an injustice had been committed is all that would be required to ensure that it would not happen again. It would be a true measure of political maturity and an uncompromising expression of solidarity with the future if the Lebanese state could rise to the occasion. The moral and ethical obligations of the case demand it.

Redressing the injustice done to Sa'adeh requires, first and foremost, an acknowledgement from the Lebanese state that what happened was unwarranted and unjust. The Lebanese people too can do its bit for justice. They cannot change history but they can bring pressure to bear on the authorities to re-open the case. This is not to suggest that justice is prescriptive or that the lessons of the past lead inevitably to a higher and nobler consciousness. Far from it. The value of a new trial would simply be that it would alert those faced with moral choices to the myriad of possibilities that history presents and that actions and decisions that affect individual destinies must be weighed carefully.

The legalistic reasons for granting a new trial for Sa'adeh are numerous and may be classed as follows:

1. The flavor of misconduct sufficiently permeated the entire pro-ceeding to provide conviction that the tribunal was influenced by passion and prejudice in reaching its verdict.
2. The evidence was tampered with to prejudice the tribunal.

3. Tricks were disingenuously practiced to stifle the proceedings or to obtain an unconscientious advantage.
4. The verdict was improper either because it was against the law or excessive, and appear to have been given in consequence of prejudice rather than as an act of deliberate judgment.
5. New material evidence has been discovered since the trial which would probably produce a different result.
6. The death sentence was disproportional with the charges.

Today, most Lebanese speak affectionately of Sa'adeh. They no longer believe the fanciful stories weaved about him by his adversaries and believe that he was unjustly treated. The former Chief of Lebanese General Security, Farid Chehab, encapsulated the sympathetic upsurge toward Sa'adeh in a single statement when he said: "Some people applauded Sa'adeh's killing, others danced in joy, and others kept silent. I am a Lebanese above all else. However, if I knew that Lebanon would finish up where it is today I would have fought alongside Antun Sa'adeh."[13] Despite the affection, successive Lebanese governments have consistently ignored demands for a retrial.[14] Some say it is because the Lebanese system simply cannot cope with the political repercussions of a new trial, let alone of an official exoneration. Others cite technical problems arising from a lack of credible record of what took place at the trial or from the unavailability of key witnesses. Moreover, the Lebanese Criminal Code does not allow retrials for criminal cases with irrevocable sentences. This restriction applies more specifically to martial cases, which is probably another reason why the Khoury regime decided to court-martial Sa'adeh rather than send him to a normal criminal court.

It is true that retrials in some criminal cases are permissible under Lebanese Law but they do not apply to Sa'adeh.[15] The problem, though, is not irredeemable. One way to deal with it would be to amend the criminal code in relation to the relevant articles. That would remove an impenetrable legal barrier and pave the way for a posthumous retrial, but it would not entirely solve the problem. Without the original trial records a retrial would still be technically difficult. "Does this mean that whoever hid the file or destroyed it has closed all doors on the possibility of a retrial for Sa'adeh and for restitution of justice? It appears so."[16] At any rate, amending the Lebanese criminal code would be in the interests of justice whatever the public may feel about this tragic case.

An alternative course of action would be to set up an independent commission. This method has many historical precedents, but they are too varied and complex to be examined in detail here.[17] In Sa'adeh's case, an independent commission would have to meet very stringent conditions if it were to succeed. It would have to be created in a calm and rational manner to minimize political and personal prejudices and external interference from those with a direct stake in the case. Its members would need to have the competence to grapple with a case of such great sensitivity, which means that their grasp of both legal and political exigencies would have to be rock solid. At the end of the day, an independent commission into the poignant tragedy of Antun Sa'adeh would in great measure depend on Lebanese readiness to shrug off their somewhat blinkered view of justice and to acknowledge that truth and fairness are imperative for the challenges of tomorrow and the moral choices of today. At this juncture, Sa'adeh's case should serve as a "reminder of the risk of departing from due process and of blindly accepting that the interests of the state and those of justice necessarily coincide."[18]

It is true that no amount of compensation can serve as adequate restitution for a historical injustice, especially when a tragic death is involved. Nonetheless, a symbolic redress of such an unspeakable wrong would make of the Lebanese something other than what they might become:

> The utility in recognizing a historical wrong is in the meaning it shares with other potentially unjust events. That we condemn a historical injustice is to express a value which conditions our response to choices that we currently face. It also reinforces a tradition which allows us to avoid actions that would otherwise imperil our sense of identity and moral worth. We as a nation must pass moral judgement on historical injustices because it is in this particular way of understanding the past that we become open to it and accept those very ideas and values we as a democratic people profess and use in shaping the justness of our own actions.[19]

History provides the lessons by which the mistakes of the past would less likely be repeated. The importance of this should not be lost on those who understand the larger meaning of truth and justice.

III

The Antun Sa'adeh trial has long been held by his supporters as the act of a corrupt regime assisted by a contaminated judiciary prepared to frame and put to death a noble challenger as a means of diverting public attention from its reactionary policies. As we have seen, the conduct of the Khoury regime and the military tribunal fell well short of the standards expected of them. But this does not mean that Sa'adeh was killed for a crime. The events and plots preceding his trial point to a vehement behind-the-scene desire for liquidation as a principal reason for his execution. In that case, the July Uprising has to be seen as a pretext for the execution rather than as the reason for it.

Likewise, to regard Sa'adeh's execution as part of a sinister cabal chips away at the aberrant political behavior of those who sanctioned or encouraged it. The central reality of Sa'adeh's execution is that it was planned and carried out with a high degree of rationality and deliberation. It was consciously organized in order to undermine his influence and to shut down any accessible space for oppositional or contentious politics outside the standard limits. Its purpose, too, was loud and clear: to put a halt to the spirit of revolutionary optimism and independent thinking that Sa'adeh was fostering and spreading. States and regimes, we are told, are likely to resort to covert repression and physical elimination of adversaries if they cannot come up with the adequate skills and resources to deal with them:[20] the Khoury regime that killed Sa'adeh in 1949 belonged to this category.

In retrospect, then, Sa'adeh was killed because there was both a necessity and a will to kill him. His unifying vision and authentic new nationalist ascent, clarity of purpose, and courage in challenging powerful opponents gave him great moral and symbolic authority and made him unsuited to the established order of things. A man who carried such vision as this, thought many, ought not to be left at large if it could be helped. The Khoury regime may have from the first formed the irrevocable decision to put Sa'adeh to death, but it was not a decision made on the spur of the moment. An unerring belief that death was a necessary evil to rid the country of Sa'adeh and, by extension, of his political vision and movement was at the basis of that decision.

Long ago, J. Bowyer Bell wrote: "Some men are killed clearly as symbols; others are destroyed to eliminate the power vested in them."[21] The power that Sa'adeh commanded was neither political nor military but rather that of an "idea and movement" fired with an intense national consciousness and a thirst for independence and political freedom. Ironically, the "idea and movement" that were to become Sa'adeh's trademark in life would also become the *raison d'etre* for both his rise and fall.

In his death Sa'adeh may have achieved more for his cause than he could ever have hoped to achieve in life. But this should not detract from the great injustice that was done to him. Until complete clarity and the full truth are established, the description of his trial and execution as *un assassinat pur et simple* remains valid.[22]

NOTES

1 Robert B. Patridge, *'O Horrable Murder'*. London: Rubicon Press, 1998: 53.
2 See Antoine Butrus, "Matame' Sahyun fi Lubnan" (Zionist ambitions in Lebanon). In his *Qissat muhakamat Antun Sa'adeh was i'damehe* (An Account of Antun Sa'adeh's Trial and Execution). Beirut: Chemaly & Chemaly, 2002: 285–304.
3 Charles Milner Atkinson, *Jeremy Bentham: His Life and Work*. New York: A. M. Kelley, 1969.
4 J. Bentham, *Rationale of Judicial Evidence*, Vol. 1 (London: Hunt & Clarke, 1827) c. 10, cited by J. Dickson in Nova Scotia (A.G.) v. MacIntyre, [1982] 1 S.C.R. 175: 183–84.
5 Carol Chomsky, "The United States-Dakota War Trials: A Study in Military Injustice." *Stanford Law Review*, Vol. 43, No. 1 (Nov., 1990): 94.
6 Ibid.
7 Thurman Arnold, "Due Process in Trials." *Annals of the American Academy of Political and Social Science*, Vol. 300, Internal Security and Civil Rights, (Jul., 1955): 124.
8 The tactics of confrontation and antics employed at the Chicago Eight trial are illustrative of how this can happen. See A. H. Weiler, "Great Chicago Conspiracy Circus," *New York Times*, 31 May, 1971. Also, Clavir, Judy, and John Spitzer (eds.), *The Conspiracy Trial*. Indianapolis: Bobbs Merrill, 1970.
9 Theodore Schroeder, 'Political Crimes Defined'. *Michigan Law Review*, Vol. 18, No. 1 (Nov., 1919): 34.
10 Ibid., 35.
11 John Rawls describes miscarriage of justice as follows: "Imperfect procedural justice is exemplified by a criminal trial. The desired outcome is that the defendant should be declared guilty if and only if he has committed the offense with which he is charged. The trial procedure is framed to search for and to establish the truth in this regard. But it seems impossible to design the legal rules so that they always lead to the correct result. The theory of trials examines which procedures and rules of evidence, and the like, are best calculated to advance this

purpose consistent with the other ends of the law. Different arrangements for hearing cases may reasonably be expected in different circumstances to yield the right results, not always but at least most of the time. A trial, then, is an instance of imperfect procedural justice. Even though the law is carefully followed, and the proceedings fairly and properly conducted, it may reach the wrong outcome. An innocent man may be found guilty, a guilty man may be set free. In such cases we speak of a miscarriage of justice." See his *A Theory of Justice*. Cambridge: Harvard University Press, 1971: 85–86.

12 Ibid.

13 *Sabah el-Kheir*, Beirut, 7 July, 1980.

14 See Antoine Butrus, *Qissat muhakamat Antun Sa'adeh was i'damehe* (An Account of Antun Sa'adeh's Trial and Execution). Beirut: Chemaly & Chemaly, 2002: 178–181.

15 See articles 349–362 of the Lebanese Criminal Code.

16 Antoine Butrus, *Qissat muhakamat Antun Sa'adeh was i'damehe* (An Account of Antun Sa'adeh's Trial and Execution. Beirut: Chemaly & Chemaly, 2002: 178.

17 Three examples would suffice: In January of 1623, Antonio Foscarini was posthumously exonerated by the Council of Ten several months after it had unanimously found him guilty of treason and had him executed (see Murray Brown, "The Myth of Antonio Foscarini's Exoneration." *Renaissance and Reformation/Renaissance et Reforme; Societe Canadienne d'Etudes de la Renaissance*, Vol. XXV, No. 3: 25); In 1980, 347 years after he was condemned by the Roman Inquisition for teaching as fact the Copernican hypothesis that the sun is the center of the planetary system, Galileo was given a retrial and exonerated (See "Galileo Retrial: Now the World Turns." In *Science News*, Vol. 118, No. 18 (Nov. 1, 1980): 277); In the post-Stalin era, over a dozen leading figures of the 1930s, as well as those purged in the 1940s, especially those involved in the so-called 'Leningrad Affair,' were fully rehabilitated (See Samuel A. Oppenheim, "Rehabilitation in the Post-Stalinist Soviet Union." *The Western Political Quarterly*, Vol. 20, No. 1 (Mar., 1967): 97–115).

18 Brian Harris, *Injustice: State Trials from Socrates to Nuremberg*. London: Sutton Publishing, 2006: xii.

19 Bohdan Kordan, "Righting Historical Wrongs." *Canadian Speeches: Issues of the Day*, September 1993. http://www.infoukes.com/history/internment/booklet02/doc-095.html

20 See Jennifer Earl, "Tanks, Tear Gas, and Taxes: Toward a Theory of Movement Repression." *Sociological Theory*, Vol. 21 (2003): 44–68.

21 J. Bowyer Bell, "Assassination in International Politics." *International Studies Quarterly*, Vol. 16, No. 1 (Mar., 1972): 82.

22 *Fikr*, Beirut, No. 73, 1 July, 2000: 76.

BIBLIOGRAPHY

Archival Documents

Constitutional Rights Project (in respect of Zamani Lakwot and six others) v. Nigeria, (87/93), 8th Annual Activity Report of the African Commission on Human and Peoples' Rights, 1994–1995, ACHPR/RPT/8th/Rev.I

Istijwab Jumblatt al tarikhi lil hukuma hawla istishhad Sa'adeh ome 1949 (Jumblatt's Historical Interpellation to the [Lebanese] Government in Regard to Sa'adeh's Martyrdom in 1949). Beirut: SSNP Information Bureau, 1987.

Lebanese Parliamentary Record, 1948.

Merriam-Webster's Collegiate Dictionary, 10th ed. Springfield, Mass.: Merriam-Webster, 1993.

Ministry of Information, Lebanon. *Qadiyat al-Hizb al-Qawmi* (The Case of the [Syrian] National Party). Beirut: 1949.

Moose to DOS, tel. 27 April 1955, 783.00/4-2755, Decimal File NARG59.

Phalanges Libanaise, *Statutes*, 1 July, 1938.

Rababi, O., "The Phalanges Libanaise: Its Aim and Organization," a speech delivered on 5 February, 1939.

The Progressive Socialist Party: A Quarter of a Century in Struggle, Vol. 1. Beirut: Markaz al-Bouhouth al-Istiraqiyya, 1974.

The Social Nationalist Reform Committee, *al-Thamin min Tammouz: Wathaiq al-Thawra wa al-Istishhad* (The Eighth of July: Documents on the Revolution and the Martyrdom [of Sa'adeh]). USA: n.p., 1992.

UN Doc. CCPR/C/79/Add.77, April 1997.

US Congress, Senate, Select Committee to Study Governmental Operations with Respect to Intelligence Activities, Alleged Assassination Plots Involving Foreign Leaders, with an introduction by Frank Church (New York: 1976).

US Department of State 89OE.88/7-1849.
US Department of State 89OE.88/7-1849 (Cable dated 12 July, 1949).
US Department of State Incoming Telegram, 890E.00/7-749.
Wigmore. John H., *Evidence in Trials at Common Law*, vol. 5, sec. 1367, Chadbourn rev. Boston: Little, Brown & Co, 1974.

Dissertations

Bodran, Margaret, *Violence in the Syrian Social Nationalist Party*. MA, American University of Beirut, 1970.

Maatouk, Mohammad, *A Critical Study of Antun Sa'ada and his Impact on Politics: The History of Ideas and Literature in the Middle East*. PhD, University of London, 1992.

Makdisi, Nadim, *The Syrian National Party: A Case Study of the First Inroads of National Socialism in the Arab World*, unpub. PhD Dissertation, American University of Beirut, 1959.

Moghaddas, Ladan Madeleine, *Civil Society and Political Democracy in Lebanon*, MA Thesis, Jönköping (January 2006).

Internet Sites

http://www.cggl.org/scripts/index.asp
http://www.enterprisemission.com/tower2.htm
http://islamonline.net
http://www.opendemocracy.net
http://wings.buffalo.edu/epc/authors/rothenberg/50s.html
http://news.bbc.co.uk
http://ssnp.net
http://blogcritics.org/archives/2006/06/18/092605.php
http://www.isesco.org
http://www.ohlj.ca/archive/articles/34_1_leigh.pdf
http://www.physics.harvard.edu/~wilson/Fadhel.html
http://yalibnan.com/site/archives/2007/01/lebanons_histor.php
http://polisci.annualreviews.org
http://www.infoukes.com/history/internment/booklet02/doc-095.html

Periodicals

Al-Alam al-Arabi (Damascus)
Al-Amal (Beirut)
Al-Ayyam, (Damascus)
Beirut (Beirut)
Daily Star (Beirut)
al-Dayar (Beirut)
Al-Dunia (Damascus)
Al Haqeeqah (Beirut)
Al Haqeeqah (Rio De Janeiro)
Al-Hayat (Beirut)
Al-Huda (Beirut)
The Independent (London)
Al-Jil al-Jadid (Beirut)
L'Aurore (Paris)
al-Mashriq (Melbourne)

Al-Massa' (Beirut)
An-Nahar (Beirut)
An-Nasr (Damascus)
New York Herald Tribune (New York)
The New York Times (NY)
Oriente Moderno (Beirut)
Al Qabas (Damascus)
Al-Qubs (Beirut)
Sabah el-Kheir (Beirut)
Al-Sayyad (Beirut)
As-Sayyad (Beirut)
Al-Sharq (Beirut)
The Syrian Bulletin (NY)
The Times (London)
Az-Zaman (Damascus)

Arabic Sources (Articles)

Barout, G. M., "Tajroubat al-Hadetha fi Majallat Shi'r" (The Modernist Experiment in Shi'r). *Fikr*, vol. 64, Spring 1985: 44–57.

Butrus, Antoine, "Matame' Sahyun fi Lubnan" (Zionist ambitions in Lebanon). In *Qissat muhakamat Antun Sa'adeh was i'idamehe* (An Account of Antun Sa'adeh's Trial and Execution). Beirut: Chemaly & Chemaly, 2002: 285–304.

El-Azama, Nazeer, "Sa'adeh, al-Ustura wa al-Shi'r." *Fikr*, vol. 43–46, Dec. 1980–April 1981: 119–125.

Jreige, Gibran, "Ma'rakat al-Istiqlal". *Sabah el-Kheir*, 11 June, 1983: 42–43.

Muhammad, Al-'Abed Hammud. "Sa'adeh: A Scholar." *al-Bina'*, issue 880, 12/7/1997.

Zaydan, J. Naji, "Man Qatala Antun Sa'adeh? Al-Dawr al-Israeli" (Who Killed Antun Sa'adeh? The Israeli Role). *Fikr*, No. 73 (July 2000): 69–74.

Foreign Sources (Articles)

Arnold, Thurman, "Due Process in Trials." *Annals of the American Academy of Political and Social Science*, Vol. 300 (July 1955): 123–130.

Blumenson, Martin, "Can Official History be Honest History?" *Military Affairs*, Vol. 26, No. 4 (Winter 1962): 153–161.

Bob, Clifford and Sharon Erickson Nepstad, "Kill a Leader, Murder a Movement? Leadership and Assassination in Social Movements." *American Behavioral Scientist* (2007; 50): 1370–1395.

Bou Nacklie, N. E., "Les Troupes Speciales: Religious and Ethnic Recruitment 1916–1946." *International Journal of Middle Eastern Studies*, Vol. 25, No. 4 (Nov. 1993): 645–660.

Bowyer Bell, J, "Assassination in International Politics." *International Studies Quarterly*, Vol. 16, No. 1 (Mar., 1972): 59–82.

Britt, George, "Lebanon's Popular Revolution." *Middle East Journal* 7 (1953): 1–17.

Brown, Murray, "The Myth of Antonio Foscarini's Exoneration." *Renaissance and Reformation/Renaissance et Reforme; Societe Canadienne d'Etudes de la Renaissance*, Vol. XXV, No. 3: 25–42.

Brunk, Samuel, "The Mortal Remains of Emiliano Zapata." In *Death, Dismemberment, and Memory*, ed. Lyman Johnson. Albuquerque: University of New Mexico Press, 2004.

Carleton, Alford, "The Syrian Coups D'etat of 1949." *Middle East Journal*, Vol. 4 (1950): 1–11.

Chomsky, Carol, "The United States-Dakota War Trials: A Study in Military Injustice." *Stanford Law Review*, Vol. 43, No. 1 (Nov., 1990): 13–98.

Chomsky, Noam, 'A Special Supplement: The Responsibility of Intellectuals.' *The New York Review of Books*, Vol. 8, No. 3 (23 February, 1967).

Christenson, Ronald, "A Political Theory of Political Trials." *The Journal of Criminal Law and Criminology*, Vol. 74, No. 2 (Summer, 1983): 547–577.

Cioeta, J. Donald, "Ottoman Censorship in Lebanon and Syria, 1876–1908." *International Journal of Middle East Studies*, Vol. 10, No. 2 (May, 1979): 167–186.

Columbia Law Review Association, "The Accused's Right to a Public Trial." *Columbia Law Review*, Vol. 49, No. 1 (Jan., 1949): 110–118.

Davenport, Christian, "State Repression and Political Order." *The Annual Review of Political Science,* Vol. 10 (2007): 1–23.

Davenport, C., and D. Armstrong, "Democracy and the Violation of Human rights: A Statistical Analysis from 1976–1996." *American Journal of Political Science,* Vol. 48, No. 3 (2004): 538–54.

Dorraj, Manochehr, "The Political Sociology of Sect and Sectarianism in Iranian Politics: 1960–1979." *Journal of Third World Studies* Vol. 23, No. 2 (Fall 2006): 95–117.

Douwes, Dick and Norman N. Lewis, "The Trials of Syrian Ismailis in the First Decade of the 20th Century." *International Journal of Middle East Studies,* Vol. 21, No. 2 (May, 1989): 215–232.

Ducharme, Lori J. and Gary Alan Fine, "The Construction of Nonpersonhood and Demonization: Commemorating the Traitorous Reputation of Benedict Arnold." *Social Forces,* Vol. 73, No. 4 (Jun., 1995): 1309–1331.

Dugard, John, "The Political Trial: Some Special Considerations." *South African Law Journal,* 91 (1974): 59–72.

Earl, Jennifer, "Tanks, Tear Gas, and Taxes: Toward a Theory of Movement Repression." *Sociological Theory,* vol. 21 (2003): 44–68.

El-Azama, Nazeer, "The Tammuzi Movement and the Influence of T.S. Eliot on Badr Shakir Al-Sayyab." In *Critical Perspectives on Modern Arabic Literature,* edited by Issa J. Boullata, 1st edition. Washington: Three Continents Press, inc., 1980.

Fay, Sidney B., "The Execution of the Duc d'Enghien II." *The American Historical Review,* Vol. 4, No. 1 (Oct., 1898): 21–37.

Fein, Helen, "Life-Integrity Violations and Democracy in the World." *Human Rights Quarterly,* Vol. 17, No.1 (1995): 170–191.

Ferencz, Benjamin B., "Nurnberg Trial Procedure and the Rights of the Accused." *Journal of Criminal Law and Criminology,* Vol. 39, No. 2 (July–Aug, 1948): 144–151.

Ferrari, Robert, "Political Crime." *Columbia Law Review,* Vol. 20, No. 3 (Mar., 1920): 308–316.

Friedman, Leon, "Political Power and Legal Legitimacy: A Short History of Political Trials." *Antioch Review* 30 (Summer 1970).

Galbraith, John Semple, "The Trial of Arabi Pasha." *Journal of Imperial and Commonwealth History,* 7:3 (1979): 274–292.

Goertzel, Ted, "Belief in Conspiracy Theories." *Political Psychology,* Vol. 15, No. 4 (Dec., 1994): 731–742.

Goldberg, F. Jerome, "Right of the Prosecution to Attack the Character of the Defendant (A Limited Recognition of a New Exception)." *Journal of Criminal Law and Criminology*, Vol. 41, No. 4 (Nov.–Dec., 1950): 456–462.

Haddad, Simon, "Christian-Muslim Relations and Attitudes towards the Lebanese State." *Journal of Muslim Minority Affairs*, Vol. 21, No. 1 (April 2001): 131–148.

Hanna, Sami A. and George H. Gardner, "*Al-Shu'ubiyyah* Up-Dated: A Study of the 20th Century Revival of an Eighth Century Concept." *The Middle East Journal*, Vol. XX (1966): 335–355.

Hans, Mommsen, "The Reichstag Fire and its Political Consequences." In Hajo Holborn (ed.), *Republic to Reich The Making of the Nazi Revolution*. New York: Pantheon Books, 1972.

Hottinger, Arnold, "Zu'ama and Parties in the Lebanese Crisis of 1958." *Middle East Journal* (1961): 85–103.

Hughes, Matthew, "Collusion across the Litani? Lebanon and the 1948 War." In Eugene L. Rogan and Avi Shlaim (ed.), *The War for Palestine: Rewriting the History of 1948*, 2nd Edition. Cambridge: Cambridge University Press, 2001.

Jayyusi, Salma Khadra, "Contemporary Arabic Poetry: Vision and Attitudes." In R. C. Ostle (ed.), *Studies in Modern Arabic Literature*. London: Aris & Phillips Ltd, 1975.

Khalaf, Samir, "Changing forms of political patronage in Lebanon." In Gellner, E. and J. Waterbury, (eds.), *Patrons and Clients in Mediterranean Societies*. London: Gerard Duckworth and Co. Ltd., 1977: 185–205.

Khalidi, Rashid I., "Edward W. Said and the American Public Sphere: Speaking Truth to Power." *Boundary* 2, Vol. 25, No. 2 (Summer, 1998): 161–177.

Kilani, Hala, "National Pact: Myth or Reality?" *Daily Star*, Beirut, 21 November, 2002.

Kirk, George, "The Syrian Crisis of 1957 – Facts and Fiction." *International Affairs*, Vol. 36, No. 1 (1960): 58–61.

Klapp, Orrin E., "The Folk Hero." *The Journal of American Folklore*, Vol. 62, No. 243 (Jan–Mar., 1949): 17–25.

Krueger, S. Carl, "Constitutional Law: Public Trial in Criminal Cases." *Michigan Law Review*, Vol. 52, No. 1 (Nov., 1952): 128–138.

Landau, J. M., "Peaceful Change in the Lebanon: The 'Rose-water' Revolution." *World Today* IX, 1953: 162–173.

Little, Douglas, "Cold War and Covert Action: The United States and Syria 1945–1958." *Middle East Journal* 44 (Winter 1990): 51–76.

Major, John, "The Search for Arab Unity." *International Affairs*, Vol. 39, No. 4 (Oct., 1963): 551–563.

Ofeish, Sami A., "Lebanon's Second Republic: Secular Talk, Sectarian Application." *Arab Studies Quarterly*, Vol. 21 (Winter, 1999): 97–117.

Oppenheim, Samuel A., "Rehabilitation in the Post-Stalinist Soviet Union." *The Western Political Quarterly*, Vol. 20, No. 1 (Mar., 1967): 97–115.

Phillips, J. Dickson, Jr. "The Appellate Review Function: Scope of Review." *Law and Contemporary Problems*, Vol. 47, No. 2 (Spring 1984): 1–12.

Podhoretz, Norman, "J'accuse," *Commentary*, Vol. 74, No. 3 (Sept. 1982).

Prorok, Alyssa, "Still More Murder in the Middle? A Reassessment of Repression in Mixed Regimes." Paper presented at the annual meeting of the APSA 2008 Annual Meeting, Hynes Convention Center, Boston, Massachusetts, 28 Aug, 2008.

Pylee, M. V., "Free Speech and Parliamentary Privileges in India." *Pacific Affairs*, Vol. 35, No. 1 (Spring, 1962): 11–23.

Raad, Nada, "Tueini Talks About his Turbulent Relationship with SSNP." *Daily Star*, Saturday, 22 May, 2004.

Rabinovich, Itamar, "The Compact Minorities and the Syrian State, 1918–45." *Journal of Contemporary History*, Vol. 14, No. 4 (Oct., 1979): 693–712.

Reasons, Charles E., "The Politicizing of Crime, the Criminal and the Criminologist." *The Journal of Criminal Law and Criminology*, Vol. 64, No. 4 (Dec., 1973): 471–477.

Said, Taky ad-Din, "The Priest who Confessed Him" in Adel Beshara, *Syrian Nationalism: An Inquiry into the Political Philosophy of Antun Sa'adeh*. Beirut: Dar Bissan, 1995, appendix 5.

Salibi, Kamal, "Lebanon under Fuad Chehab 1958-1964." *Middle East Studies* 2 (1966): 211–226.

Schroeder, Theodore, "Political Crimes Defined." *Michigan Law Review*, Vol. 18, No. 1 (Nov., 1919): 30–44.

Schwoerer, Lois G., "William, Lord Russell: The Making of a Martyr, 1683–1983." *The Journal of British Studies*, Vol. 24, No. 1 (Jan., 1985): 41–71.

Science News, "Galileo Retrial: Now the World Turns." In *Science News*, Vol. 118, No. 18 (1 Nov., 1980): 277.

Shlaim, Avi, "Husni Za'im and the Plan to Resettle Palestinian Refugees in Syria." *Journal of Palestine Studies*, Vol. 15, No. 4 (Summer, 1986): 68–80.

Sokol, Ronal O., "The Political Trial: Courtroom as Stage, History as Critic." *New Literary History*, Vol. 2, No. 3 (Spring 1971): 495–516.

Solh, Raghid, "The Attitude of the Arab Nationalists towards Greater Lebanon during the 1930s." In *Lebanon: A History of Conflict and Consensus,* edited by Nadim Shehadi and Dana Haffar Mills (London: I. B. Tauris and Co Ltd, 1988).

Spaeth, John W. Jr., "Roman Hero Worship." *The Classical Journal*, Vol. 20, No. 6 (Mar., 1925): 352–355.

Volkan, D. Vamik, "The Need to Have Enemies and Allies: A Developmental Approach." *Political Psychology*, Vol. 6, No. 2, Special Issue: A Notebook on the Psychology of the U.S.-Soviet Relationship. Jun., 1985: 219–247.

Weiler, A. H., "Great Chicago Conspiracy Circus." *New York Times*, 31 May, 1971.

Wilson, G. Francis, "Political Suppression in the Modern State." *The Journal of Politics*, Vol. 1, No. 3 (Aug., 1939): 237–257.

Withington, Ann Fairfax and Jack Schwartz, "The Political Trial of Anne Hutchinson." *The New England Quarterly*, Vol. 51, No. 2 (June 1978): 226–240.

Wood, S. Gordon, "The Real Treason of Aaron Burr." *Proceedings of the American Philosophical Society*, Vol. 143, No. 2 (June, 1999): 280–295.

Yaffe, Gitta, "Suleiman al-Murshid: Beginnings of an Alawi Leader." *Middle Eastern Studies* 29(4): 624–640.

Yanai, Nathan, "The Political Affair A Framework for Comparative Discussion." *Comparative Politics*, Vol. 22, No. 2 (Jan., 1990): 185–198.

Zamir, Meir, "From Hegemony to Marginalism: The Maronites of Lebanon." In *Minorities and the State in the Arab World* edited by Ofra Bengio and Gabriel Ben-Dor, Lynne Rienner Publishers, Inc., 1999.

Zisser, E., "The Downfall of the Khuri Administration: A Dubious Revolution." *Middle East Studies* 30 (1994): 486–511.

Arabic Sources (Books)

Abdul Massih, George, *Muhadarat al-Mukhayyam al-Sayfi* (Summer Camps Lecture Series). Beirut: n.p., 1971.

Abdul Satir, Mustafa, *Ayyam wa Qadiyya* (The Cause We Lived For). Beirut: Dar Fikr, 1982.

Abdul Satir, Mustafa, *Shu'un Qawmiyyah* (National Issues). Beirut: Dar Fikr, 1990.

Al-Atari, Abdul Ghani, *Sa'adeh wa al-Hizb al-Qawmi* (Sa'adeh and the National Party). Damascus: Al-Dunia Printers, 1950.

Al-Hashim, Najam, *A'khir Ayyam Sa'adeh* (Sa'adeh's Last Days). Beirut: n.p., 1999.

Al-Hashimi, Taha, *Mudhakkirat* (Memoirs). Beirut: Dar al-Tali'a, 1967.

Al-Hindi, Hani, *Jaysh al Inqadh* (The Salvation Army). Beirut: Dar al-Quds, 1974.

Al-Jisr, Bassim, *Fouad Chehab: Dhalika al-Majhoul* (Fouad Chehab: The Unknown). Beirut: The Corporation for Publication and Distribution, 1988.

Al-Khalidi, Ghassan, *Sa'adeh wa al-Thawrah al-Ula* (Sa'adeh and the First Revolution). Beirut: Dar wa Maktabat al-Turath al-Adabi, 1997.

Al-Mouallim, Walid, *Souria 1918–1958: al-Tahhadi wa al-Muwajaha* (Syria 1918–1958: The Challenge and the Confrontation). Damascus: Babel Publications, 1985.

Arslan, Adel, *Mudhakkirat* (Memoirs). Beirut: Dar al-Taqaddumiyyah, 1994.

Asfahani, Ahmad (ed.), *Antun Sa'adeh wa al-Hizb al-Suri al-Qawmi al-Ijtimae' fi Awarq al-Amir Farid Chehab, al-Mudir al-Ome lil al-Amn al-Ome al-Lubnani* (Antun Sa'adeh and the Syrian Social Nationalist Party in the Private Papers of Emir Farid Chehab, the General Director of the Lebanese General Security). Beirut: Kutub Publishing, 2006.

As-Samman, Muti'e, *Watan wa Askar* (Homeland and Soldiers). Beirut: Dar Bissan, 1995.

Asseily, Youmna and Ahmad Asfahani, *A Face in the Crowd: The Secret Papers of Emir Farid Chehab, 1942–1972* (In Arabic). London: Stacey International, 2001.

Bashur, Hanna Toufiq, *Min Dhakirat Abi, Major Toufiq Bashour* (From My Father's Recollections). Damascus: Maktabat al-Sharq al-Jadid, 1998.

Bayhum, Muhammad Jamil, *Al-Urubah wa-Al-shu'ubiyat al-Hadithah: Niqash ma'a Antun Sa'adah, Kamal Junbulat Salamah Musa, Amir Baqtar wa-Ta'liqat ala' al-Shubuhat fi Muqaddimat Ibn Khaldun* (Arabism and Contemporary Shu'ubism). Beirut: Matabi' Da'r al-Kashshaf, al-Muqaddimah, 1957.

Butrus, Antoine, *Qissat muhakamat Antun Sa'adeh was i'idamehe* (An Account of Antun Sa'adeh's Trial and Execution). Beirut: Chemaly & Chemaly, 2002.

Daye, John, *Muhakamat Antun Sa'adeh* (The Trial of Antun Sa'adeh). Beirut: Fajr an-Nahda, 2002.

—*Sa'adeh wa Hisham Sharabi* (Sa'adeh and Hisham Sharabi). Stockholm: Dar Nelson, 2004.

El-Hage, Louis, *Min Makhzoun al-Zakirah* (Old Memories). Beirut: Dar an-Nahar, 1993.

El-Kheir, Hani, *Adib al-Shishakli Sahib al-Inqlab al-Thalith fi Suria* (Adib al-Shishakli: Leader of the Third Coup in Syria). Damascus: Dar al-Sharq al-Jadid, 1995.

Fansah, Nadhir, *Ayyam Husni Zaim: 137 Yawman Hazzat Suria* (Days of Husni Zaim: 137 Days that Shook Syria). Beirut: Dar al-Afaq al-Jadidah, 1983.

Hallaq, Hassan, *Al-Tayyarrat al-Siyyassiyah fi Lubnan: 1943–1952* (Political Currents in Lebanon: 1943–1952). Beirut: Ma'had al-Inma'·al-Arabi, 1981.

Hardan, Nawaf, *Ala Durub an-Nahda* (On the Pathways of the Renaissance). Beirut: Dar Bissan, 1997.

—*Sa'adeh fi al-Mahjar: 1921–1930* (Sa'adeh Abroad: 1921–1930). Beirut: Dar Fikr lil-Abhath wa-al-Nashr, 1989.

Husri, Sati, *al-Uruba baina Du 'atiha was Mu'aridhiha* (Arabism between its Supporters and its Opponents). Beirut: Dar al-Ilm lil-Malayin, 1952.

Ibrahim, Abu al-Fadl (ed.), *Diwan Imru' al-Qays* (The Treasures of Imru' al-Qays). Cairo: Dar al-Ma'arif, 1984.

Jam'a, Sami, *Awraq min Daftar al-Watan, 1946–1961* (Pages from Homeland Records). Damascus: Dar Tlas, 2000.

Jreige, Gibran, *Haqa'iq Ain al-Istiqlal: Ayyam Rashayya* (Truths About the Independence: The Rashayya Days), 4th edition. Beirut: Dar Amwaj, 2000.

—*Ma' Antun Sa'adeh* (In the Company of Antun Sa'adeh). Beirut: n.p., n.d.

Jumblatt, Kamal, *Adwa' ala Haqiqat al-Qadiyya al-Qawmiyya al-Ijtima'iyya as-Suriyya: al-Fikra al-Qawmiyyah* (Lights on the Truth Concerning the Syrian Social Nationalist Cause: The National Idea). Beirut: Progressive Press, 1987.

Kaddoura, Adib. *Haqa'iq wa Mawaqif* (Facts and Stances). Beirut: Dar Fikr, 1989.

Karam, Abd al-Aziz, *Al-Rabb al-Muzayyaf Salman al-Murshid* (The False God Salman Al-Murshid). Damascus: Maktabat Dimashq, 1947.

Kfoury, Tawfiq, *al-Shihabiyyah wa Siyassit al-Mawqif* (The Basic Principles of Chehabism). Beirut: n.p., 1980.

Khoury, Beshara Haykal, *al-Mahkmah al-Askriah wa khususyatuha* (The Military Court and its Particularities). Beirut: Sadr Publishing, 2005.

Khoury, Beshara, *Haqa'iq Lubnaniyyah* (Lebanese Truths), Vol. 3. Beirut: Awraq Lubnaniyah, 1961.

Khoury, Sami, *Radd ala Sati' al-Husri* (A Response to Sati al-Husri). Beirut: n.p., 1956.

Masru'ah, George, *Ibn Zikar*, 2nd. ed. Beirut: Dar al-Makshufah, 1954.

Qneizeh, Elias Jurgi, *Ma'ather min Sa'adeh* (Anecdotes from Sa'adeh). Beirut: Bissan Publishing, 1989.

Qubarsi, Abdullah, *Abdullah Qubarsi ya Tazakar* (*Recollections*), vol. 4. Beirut: Al-Furat Publishing, 2004.

—*Nahnu wa Lubnan* (Lebanon and Us). Beirut: al-Turath al-Arabi, 1988.

Raad, In'am, *Harb al-Tahrir al-Qawmiyya* (National Liberation War). Beirut, n.p., 1970.

—*Antun Sa'adeh wa al-In'izaliyun* (Antun Sa'adeh and the Isolationists). Beirut: Dar Fikr, 1980.

—*Al-Sahyuniah was al-Sharq al-Awsatiyyah min Herzel ila Peres* (Zionism and the Greater Middle East From Herzel to Peres). Beirut: Sharikat al-Matbu'at, 1998.

—*Harb wu-Jud la Harb Hudoud* (A War of Existence, not a War of Borders). Beirut: Dar Bissan, 1999.

Rida, Ali, *Suria min al-Istiqlal hatta al-Wihda al-Mubaraka, 1946–1958* (Syria from Independence to the Sacred Union, 1946–1958). Aleppo: Dar al-Insha', 1983.

Sa'adeh, Abdullah, *Awraq Qawmiyyah* (Nationalist Memoirs). Beirut: n.p., 1987.

Sa'adeh, Antun, *al-Athar al-Kamilah* (Complete Works). Beirut: SSNP Cultural Bureau, n.d.

Sa'adeh, Antun, *al-Muhadarat al-Ashr* (The Ten Lectures). Beirut: SSNP Publications, 1978.

—*Mukhtarat fi al-Mas'allah al-Lubnaniyyah* (Selected Works on the Lebanese Question). Beirut: Dar Fikr, 1978.

Sa'adeh, Juliet al-Mir, *Mudhakkirat al-Amina la-Ula* (Memoirs) Beirut: Dar Kutub, 2004.

Saghiyyah, Hadhim, *Qawmiyyu al-Mashriq al-Arabi* (The Nationalists of the Arab East). London: Riyad al-Rayyes Books, 2000.

Salamah, Yusuf, *Haddathani Y. S. Qala* (Memoirs). Beirut: Dar Nelson, 1988.

Salloum, Urfan, *Defence of the Social Nationalist before the Military Tribunal in Damascus* (in Arabic). Damascus: n.p., 1955.

Sayegh, Anis, *Anis Sayigh a'n Anis Sayigh* (Autobiography). London: Riad El-Rayyes Books, 2006.

Sayegh, Fayez, *Mashru' Suria al-Kubra* (The Greater Syria Scheme). Beirut: The Syrian National Party Information Bureau, 1946.

Sharabi, Hisham, *al-Jamr wa al-Rimad* (Embers and Ashes). Beirut: Tali'a Publications, 1978.

—*Images from the Past: An Autobiography* (In Arabic), Beirut: Dar Nelson, 1989.

Solh, Sami, *Ahtakim ila al-Tarikh* (I Leave it to History to Judge Me). Beirut: Dar an-Nahar, 1970.

Suleiman, Souhail, *Athar al-Banna'een al-Ahrar fi al-Adab al-lubnani* (The Impact of the Freemasonry on Lebanese Literature: 1860–1950). Beirut: Noufal Press, 1993.

Taki Deen, Suleiman, *Sirat al-Adib Saeed Taki Deen* (The life of the Literati Saeed Taki Deen). Beirut: Druze Heritage Foundation, 2004.

Uthman, Hashim, *al-Muhakamt al-Siyassiyah fi Suria* (Political Trials in Syria). Beirut: Riad El-Rayyes Books, 2004.

Yammut, Ibrahim, *Al-Hisad al-Mur* (The Bitter Harvest). Beirut: Dar al-Rukin, 1993.

Foreign Sources (Books)

Abel, Charles F. & Frank H. Marsh, *In Defense of Political Trials.* Westport: Greenwood Press, 1994.

Abouchdid, Eugenie Elie, *Thirty Years of Lebanon and Syria: 1917–1947.* Beirut: The Sader-Rihani Printing Co., 1948.

Aboud, Aboud, *The S.N.S.P.* Sydney: An-Nahda, 1982.

Abrahamian, Ervand, *Khomeinism: Essays on the Islamic Republic.* Berkeley: University of California Press, 1993.

Akl, George, Abdo Ouadat and Edouard Hunein, (eds.). *The Black Book of the Lebanese Elections of May 25, 1947.* New York: Phoenicia Press, 1947.

Akl, George, Abdo Ouadat, and Idwār Ḥunayn, *The Black Book of the Lebanese Elections of May 25, 1947.* New York: Phoenicia Press, 1947.

Allen, Francis A., *The Crimes of Politics: Political Dimensions of Criminal Justice.* Cambridge: Harvard University Press, 1974.

Aronson, Jason, *The Need to have Enemies and Allies.* NJ: Northvale 1988.

Atiyah, Edward S., *An Arab Tells his Story: A Study in Loyalties.* London, J. Murray, 1946.

Atkinson, M. Charles, *Jeremy Bentham: His Life and Work.* New York: A. M. Kelley, 1969.

Barnett, Correlli, *Human Factor and British Industrial Decline: An Historical Perspective.* London: Working Together Campaign, 1977.

Baron, Fitzroy Richard Somerset Raglan, *The Hero: A Study in Tradition, Myth and Drama.* New York: Vintage Books, 1956.

Becker. L. Theodore (ed.), *Political Trials.* Indianapolis: Bobbs-Merrill, 1971.

Belknap, Michal R. (ed.), *American Political Trials.* Westport: Greenwood Press, 1994.

—*Cold War Political Justice: The Smith Act, the Communist Party and American Civil Liberties.* Westport: Greenwood Press, 1977.

Bentham, J., *Rationale of Judicial Evidence*, Vol. 1. London: Hunt & Clarke, 1827.

Berrigan, Philip, *Prison Journals of a Priest Revolutionary.* New York: Holt, Rinehart and Winston, 1970.

Beshara, Adel (ed.), *Antun Sa'adeh: The Man, His Thought.* Reading, Ithaca Press, 2007.

—*Lebanon, The Politics of Frustration: The Failed Coup of 1961* (History and Society in the Islamic World). London and New York: Routledge and Curzon, 2005.

—*Syrian Nationalism: An Inquiry into the Political Philosophy of Antun Sa'adeh*. Beirut: Dar Bissan, 1995.

Boudreau, Vincent, *Resisting Dictatorship: Repression and Protest in Southeast Asia*. Cambridge: Cambridge University Press, 2004.

Brady, James T., J. L. Boyle, John Beall, and O. H. Browning, *Letters and Manuscripts Relating to the Case of Captain John Beall*. New York: n.p., 1865.

Brickhouse, Thomas C. and Nicholas D. Smith, *The Trial and Execution of Socrates: Sources and Controversies*. New York: Oxford University Press, 2002.

Brown, Walter L. (ed.), *Lebanon's Struggle for Independence, Part II, 1944–1947*. North Carolina: Documentary Publications, 1980.

Brunk, Samuel and Ben Fallaw, *Heroes and Hero Cults in Latin America*. Austin: University of Texas Press, 2006.

Bucknill, J. and H. Utidjian, *The Imperial Ottoman Penal Code*. London: Oxford University Press, 1913.

Burnett, Betty, *The Trial of Julius and Ethel Rosenberg: A Primary Source Account*. New York: Rosen Pub. Group, 2004.

Burns, Robert, *A Theory of the Trial*. Princeton: Princeton University Press, 1999.

Carlyle, Thomas, *On Heroes, Hero-Worship, and The Heroic in History*. London: The Echo Library, 2007.

Carton, Evan, *Patriotic Treason: John Brown and the Soul of America*. New York: Free Press, 2006.

Christenson, Ron, *Political Trials: Gordian Knots in the Law*. 2nd ed. New Brunswick, N.J.: Transaction Press, 1999.

Clavir, Judy and John Spitzer (eds.), *The Conspiracy Trial*. Indianapolis: Bobbs Merrill, 1970.

Collard, Dudley, *Soviet Justice and the Trial of Radek and Others*. London: Victor Gollancz Ltd, 1937.

Della Porta, Donatella and Mario Diani, *Social Movements: An Introduction*. Malden, MA: Blackwell, 1999.

Donagan, Alan, *The Theory of Morality*. Chicago: University of Chicago Press, 1977.

El-Gemayel, Antoine Elias, *The Lebanese Legal System*. Washington, DC: International Law Institute, 1985.

El-Khazen, Farid. *The Communal Pact of National Identities: The Making and Politics of the 1943 National Pact*. Oxford: Centre for Lebanese Studies, 1991.

Eveland, Wilbur C., *Ropes of Sand: America's Failure in the Middle East*. New York: W. W. Norton, 1980.

Ferri, E., *Criminal Sociology*. New York: D. Appleton and Company, 1916.

Goria, Wade R., *Sovereignty and Leadership in Lebanon: 1943–1976*. London: Ithaca Press, 1985.

Gorst, Anthony, *The Suez Crisis*. London: Routledge, 1997.

Gossman, Norbert J., *The Martyrs: Joan of Arc to Yitzhak Rabin*. Lanham: University Press of America, Inc., 1997.

Grafton, David, *The Christians of Lebanon: Political Rights in Islamic Law*. London: I. B. Tauris, 2004.

Haddad, George M., *Revolution and Military Rule in the Middle East*. 3 Vols. New York: Robert Speller and Sons, Publishers, 1971.

Hain, Peter, *Political Trials in Britain*. London: A. Lane, 1984.

Hanchett, William, *The Lincoln Murder Conspiracies*. Urbana: University of Illinois Press, 1992.

Hargrave, William, *A Treatise on the Court of Star Chamber*. London: Legal Classics Library, 1986.

Harris, Brian, *Injustice: State Trials from Socrates to Nuremberg*. London: Sutton Publishing, 2006.

Hensen, Marc, *A Show Trial Under Lenin: The Trial of the Socialist Revolutionaries*. London: Maetinus Nijhoff Publishers, 1982.

Hodges, Donald C., *Intellectual Foundations of the Nicaragua Revolution*. Austin: University of Texas Press, 1986.

Hoffman, Robert L., *More than a Trial: The Struggle over Captain Dreyfus*. London: Collier Macmillan Publishers, 1980.

Hourani, Albert, *Syria and Lebanon: A Political Essay*. Beirut: Librairie Du Liban, 1968.

Hudson, Michael C., *The Precarious Republic: Political Modernization in Lebanon*. New York, Random House, 1968.

Jamali, Mohammad F., *Experiences in Arab Affairs: 1943–1958*. (Located in Widener Library, Harvard University under the title: *Arab Struggle; Experiences of Mohammed Fadhel Jamali*, 1974).

Johnson, George, *Architects of Fear: Conspiracy Theories and Paranoia in American Politics*. Los Angeles: Tarcher/Houghton Mifflin, 1983.

Kader, Haytham, *The Syrian Social Nationalist Party: Its Ideology and Early History*. Beirut: n.p., 1990.

Kaplan, Alice, *The Collaborator: The Trial and Execution of Robert Brasillach*. Chicago: The University of Chicago Press, 2000.

Khoury, Philip, *Syria and the French Mandate: The Politics of Arab Nationalism 1920–1945*. New Jersey: Princeton University Press, 1987.

Kirchheimer, Otto, *Political Justice: The Use of Legal Procedures for Political Ends*. Princeton, NJ: Princeton University Press. 1961.

Klapp, Orrin E., *Collective Search for Identity*. London: Holt, R. & W. 1969.

Knight, Stephen, *Jack the Ripper: The Final Solution*. London: George G. Harrap Co. Ltd., 1976.

Lash, Joseph, *Eleanor and Franklin*. New York: W.W. Norton, 1971.

Lindemann, Albert, *The Jew Accused: Three Anti-Semitic Affairs (Dreyfus, Beilis, Frank): 1894–1915*. Cambridge: Cambridge University Press, 1991.

Lofland, J., *Deviance and Iidentity*. Englewood Cliffs, NJ: Prentice – Hall, 1969.

Major, Reginald, *Justice in the Round: The Trial of Angela Davis*. New York: The Third Press, 1973.

Marius, Richard, *Thomas More: A Biography*. New York: Knopf, 1984.

Mikdadi, Faysal, *Gamal Abdel Nasser: A Bibliography*. London: Greenwood Press, 1991.

Moreh, S., *Modern Arabic Poetry 1800–1970*. Leiden, The Netherlands: E.J. Brill, 1976.

Oakes, Len, *Prophetic Charisma: The Psychology of Revolutionary Religious Personalities*. Syracuse: Syracuse University Press, 1997.

Olson, Nathan, Cynthia Martin and Brent Schoonover, *Nathan Hale: Revolutionary Spy*. Mankato: Capstone Press, 2006.

Orwell, George, *Notes on Nationalism*. London: Polemic, 1945.

Pareto, Vilfredo, *The Mind and Society: A Treatise on General Sociology*. New York: Dover, 1935.

Patridge, Robert B., *'O Horrable Murder'*. London: Rubicon Press, 1998.

Pettigrew, Joyce J. M. & Ladislav Holy, *Martyrdom and Political Resistance: Essays from Asia and Europe.* Amsterdam: Centre for Asian Studies Amsterdam, Vu University Press, 1997.

Pipes, Daniel, *The Hidden Hand: Middle East Fears of Conspiracy.* New York: St. Martin's Griffin, 1998.

Ponlantzas, Nicos, *State, Power, Socialism.* London: New Left Books, 1978.

Pound, Roscoe, *Appellate Procedure in Civil Cases.* Boston: Little, Brown and Co., 1941.

Qubain, F. I., *Crisis in Lebanon.* Washington D.C.: The Middle East Institute, 1961.

Quinney, R., *The Social Reality of Crime.* Boston: Little, Brown, 1970.

Rabil, Robert G., *Embattled Neighbors: Syria, Israel and Lebanon.* Boulder, Colorado: Lynne Rienner Publishers, 2003.

Rathmell, Andrew, *Secret War in the Middle East: The Covert Struggle for Syria, 1949–1961.* London: I. B. Tauris & Co. 1995.

Rawls, John, *A Theory of Justice.* Cambridge: Harvard University Press, 1971.

Rawson, Samuel, *Reports of Cases in the Courts of Star Chamber and High Commission.* London: Camden Society, 1886.

Robison, John M., *Proofs of a Conspiracy Against all the Governments of Europe, carried on in the secret meetings of Free Masons, Illuminati, and Reading Societies.* New York: Printed and sold by George Forman, 1798.

Roth, Stephen J., *The Impact of the Six-Day War: a Twenty-Year Assessment.* Basingstoke: Palgrave Macmillan, 1988.

Ruiz, Julius, *Franco's Justice: Repression in Madrid After the Spanish Civil War.* London: Oxford University Press, 2005.

Sa'adeh, Sofia Antun, *The Social Structure of Lebanon: Democracy or Servitude?* Beirut: Dar An-Nahar, 1993.

Schulze, Kirsten E., *Israel's Covert Diplomacy in Lebanon.* London: Macmillan Press Ltd, 1998.

Scott, Peter Dale, *Deep Politics and the Death of JFK.* Berkeley: University of California, 1996.

Seale, Patrick, *The Struggle for Syria: A Study of Post-War Diplomacy 1945–1958.* Oxford: Oxford University Press, 1965.

Spahr, William J., *Zhukov: The Rise and Fall of a Great Captain.* Novato, CA: Presidio Press, 1993.

Sulh, Raghid, *Lebanon and Arabism: National Identity and State Formation.* London: Centre for Lebanese Studies, 2004.

Tibi, Bassam, *Arab Nationalism: A Critical Enquiry.* New York: St. Martin's Press, 1981.

Tilly, Charles, *From Mobilization to Revolution.* Reading, MA: Addison-Wesley, 1978.

Torrey, Gordon H., *Syrian Politics and the Military: 1945–1958.* Columbus: Ohio State University Press, 1964.

Tribe, Laurence H., *American Constitutional Law.* Mineola, N.Y.: Foundation Press, 2nd ed. 1988.

Vidal, G., *Cours de droit criminel et de science penitentiare.* (Cinquieme edition). Paris, 1916.

Vouin, Robert and Jacques Léauté, *Droit penal et procedure pénale.* Paris: Presses Universitaires, 1969.

Walzer, M., *Regicide and Revolution: Speeches at the Trial of Louis XVI.* London: Cambridge University Press: 1974.

Wedgwood, C. V., *A Coffin for King Charles: The Trial and Execution of Charles I.* New York: Macmillan, 1964.

Wheen, Francis, *Karl Marx.* London: Fourth Estate Limited, 1999.

Williams, G. A., *The Merthyr Rising.* London: Croom Helm, 1978.

Yamak, Labib Z., *The Syrian Social Nationalist Party: An Ideological Analysis.* Harvard: Center for Middle Eastern Studies, 1969.

Zedalis, Debra D., *Female Suicide Bombers.* Carlisle, PA: Strategic Studies Institute, U.S. Army War College, 2004.

Zisser, Eyal, *Lebanon: The Challenge of Independence.* London: I. B. Tauris, 2000.

INDEX

French-Lebanese political leadership, 17
French Mandate, 9, 10, 18
French News Agency, 29
French penal code, 92
French Republic, 159
French rule, 8
French treatise, 92
Freyha, Said, 256
Friedman, Leon, 94

G
Galilee Battalion, 124
El-Gemayel, Antoine, 95
Gemayel family, 86
Gemayyel, Pierre, 147
Gendarme Barracks, 64
Gendarmerie, 68
Gendarmerie posts, 51
General Assembly, 66
General pardon, 109
General Staff Office, 40
German criminals, 146
Germany, 176, 177
Gladstone, William, 183
Goertzel, Ted, 199
Goria, Wade R., 234
Gouraud, Henri, 3
government-appointed Trial Commissioner,
    82, 112
government's legal strategy, 68
Grand Liban, 3, 7
Grand Mufti, 7
Great Syrian Revolt, 17
Great War, 258
Greater Lebanon, xviii, 3, 4, 5, 7, 185
Greater Syria, 5, 45, 187, 188, 206
Greater Syria project, 21, 45
Greek Catholics, 2
Greek Orthodox, 2
Guevara, Che, 273

H
al-Hadath, 39
el-Hage, Badr, xi
Haifa, 43
Hale, Nathan, 129
Hamilton, Alexander, 183
Hammoud, Muhammad al-Abed, 264
Hananu, Ibrahim, 130

Hannawi regime, 126
Harvard Law School, 137
Hashemite, 52
Hashimi, Taha, 32
Al-Hayat, 77, 144
Hayek, Gibran, 145
Hayek, Michel, xi
Heikal, Muhammad, 46
Helou, Charles, 56, 107
High Arab Committee, 124
High Commissioner, 19
High Court, 128
Hitlerite regime, 176
Hollywood, xiii
al-Hoss, Salim, 280
Hotel Lebanon, 73
Hourani, Akram, 32
Hraikah, Archbishop Ignatius, 138, 139
al-Hreiki, 73
al-Huda, 147
Hudson, Michael, 234
Human Rights Council, 225
al-Husri, Sati', 265
Hussein, Kamal, 33
al-Husseini, Ibrahim, xiii, 41, 45, 52, 53–55,
    191

I
Ibn Abu Talib, Ali, 139
Independence Era, 7
Indian parliamentary system, 183
Irslan, Majid, 110, 145
Islamic, 11
Isorni, Jacques, 128
Israel, 32, 33, 43, 65, 95, 124, 125, 141, 148,
    188, 197, 267
Israeli collaborator, 43
Israeli-Maronite contacts, 125
Israeli passport, 125
Israeli payroll, 64

J
Jacobites, 2
Jadid, Salah, 237
Jafet Library, xi, 269
Jamali, Mohammad Fadhel, 45
Al-Jamhur, 140
Jarras, Major Husni, 237
Jaures, Jean, 163

Jawwad, Mohammad, 112
Jayyusi, Salma Khadra, 263
al-Jazairi, Abdul Kadir, 130
Jerusalem, 231
Jewish home, 21
Jewish State, 82, 122
Jewish support, 43
Jews, 2, 21, 32, 33, 41, 76, 123, 148, 160, 189
al-Jil al-Jadid, 31, 32, 33, 36
Jordan, 30, 54, 65
Jordanian government, 195
Jordanian Legation, 231
Jumblatt, Kamal, 85, 107, 109, 110, 148–52,
    165, 179, 206, 207, 265
Jummaizeh incident, 36, 37, 38, 41, 42, 49,
    121, 140, 157, 174, 175, 214
Jummayel, Pierre, 36
June incident, 38
Justice of the Peace, 112

K
Kaddoura, Adib, xix
Karam, Lieutenant Assaf, 51
Karam, Lieutenant Colonel Anwar, 68
Kayyas, Amal, xi
Khneisser, Riad, xi
Khoury, Archbishop Bulus, 232
Khoury, Beshara, 6, 7, 8, 10, 20, 27, 37, 46,
    49, 56, 67, 70, 107, 109, 110, 120, 128,
    131, 145, 174, 184, 185, 187, 195, 197,
    201, 229, 233, 235
Khoury era, xv, xvii, xviii
Khoury, Khalil, 68, 110
Khoury, Michel, 68
Khoury regime, xvi, xvii, 11, 32, 40, 42,
    63–65, 84, 88, 91, 125, 131, 152, 155,
    165, 166, 171–3, 175, 177, 206–8,
    212–4, 223, 224, 226, 227–30, 232, 233,
    235, 243, 249, 278, 279, 283, 285, 294,
    297, 298, 299, 302
Kirchheimer, Otto, xvii, 94, 97, 137
Kripalani, Acharya, 183
Kul Shay, 31, 52, 153, 182

L
Lahhoud, Emil, 69, 80, 139
Lahhoud, Lieutenant Jamil, 112
Latakia, 47, 48
Latin America, 141

Latin-French position, 187
Latins (Roman Catholics), 2
Law of Summary Trials, 114
Lawyers Syndicate, 69
Lebanese Administration, 28
Lebanese Army, 40, 55, 56, 68, 83, 227, 256
Lebanese capital, 38
Lebanese Chamber, 85
Lebanese Christian nationalism, 15
Lebanese Christians, 3, 11
Lebanese Code, 298
Lebanese confessional (or consensual) politics,
    28
Lebanese confessional system, 275
Lebanese Constitution, 4
Lebanese Criminal Code, 91, 92, 300
Lebanese criminal system, 95
Lebanese economy, 7
Lebanese electoral politics, 20
Lebanese emissaries, 55
Lebanese entity, 15, 17, 27, 30, 80, 123, 144,
    172, 174
Lebanese Establishment, 32
Lebanese Foreign Ministry, 143
Lebanese Gendarmerie, 37, 38
Lebanese General Security Forces, 119
Lebanese government, ix, x, 7, 11, 20, 27, 31,
    32, 35, 36, 41, 42, 46, 51, 52, 55, 84, 85,
    97, 115, 142, 143, 155, 171, 175, 176,
    184, 208, 213, 225, 227, 228, 236, 248,
    278
Lebanese history, xv, xviii
Lebanese homeland, 14
Lebanese independence, 4, 50
Lebanese issue, 205
Lebanese judicatories, 91
Lebanese judicial history, 129
Lebanese judiciary, 64
Lebanese justice, 299
Lebanese law, 84, 91, 92, 95, 106, 121, 295
Lebanese law and political system, xv
Lebanese leadership, 20, 146
Lebanese Legation, 143, 180
Lebanese literati, 110
Lebanese military law, 121
Lebanese Minister of Justice, xiv
Lebanese national quest, 8
Lebanese nationalism, 165
Lebanese nationalists, 6, 13, 17, 28
Lebanese Parliament, 85, 107
Lebanese particularism, 5, 15